Robert Browning
A life within life

Robert Browning
A life within life

Donald Thomas

Weidenfeld and Nicolson
London

First published in Great Britain by
George Weidenfeld and Nicolson Ltd
91 Clapham High St, London sw4

Designed by Myles Dacre

ISBN 0 297 78092 1

Printed in Great Britain by
Butler & Tanner Ltd, Frome and London

Whoever takes this goal of godliness seriously or literally, will soon be compelled to flee from real life and compromise, by seeking a life within life; if fortunate in art, but more generally in pietism, neurosis or crime.

Alfred Adler, *Individual Psychology, its Assumptions and its Results* (1914)

Went in to dinner with Burne-Jones ... he told me lots of things worth remembering. Called Browning's outside 'moss', and said the works of a man were his real self.

Mary Gladstone, *Diaries and Letters* (1930)

> Our interest's on the dangerous edge of things.
> The honest thief, the tender murderer,
> The superstitious atheist, demireps
> That love and save their souls in new French books –
> We watch while these in equilibrium keep
> The giddy line midway: one step aside,
> They're classed and done with.

Robert Browning, 'Bishop Blougram's Apology', *Men and Women* (1855)

For David and Hazel

Contents

Preface

It seems an irony of Browning's posthumous reputation that he, so jealous of his privacy, should acquire a type of fame unmatched by his great contemporaries. In the mass of critical and biographical attention, Tennyson or Dickens outweighed him. Yet neither they nor any comparable figure stood revealed to a mass audience in the manner of Browning. The success of *The Barretts of Wimpole Street* in the London West End and on Broadway, and the subsequent Hollywood portrayals of Browning by Fredric March in 1934 and Bill Travers in 1957, stamped his image upon the popular consciousness of the twentieth century.

Because he loved and saved Elizabeth Barrett he was recast as the great romantic hero. Millions who cared little about his poetry would recognize him at once in this role. For them his poems survived as snatches of motto-length wisdom or nostalgia. What these partial revelations of work and personality obscured was that Browning indeed partook of romanticism. Yet it was the romanticism of the mid-nineteenth century which still reflected the cruelty and darkness of human conduct as well as its passionate idealism and love undaunted.

There was also in Browning a strong vein of post-romantic modernism which exploited the minutiae of reality with such powerful effect. Like a handful of other great Victorians, he left his voice upon record, a wax cylinder made in the summer of 1889. Tennyson and Gladstone recorded their self-confident oratorical performances. Browning reads – or rather misreads – 'How they brought the good news from Ghent to Aix'. He falters in the middle and apologizes: 'I'm most terribly sorry that I can't remember my own verses.' In the manner of his own writing, his is the only voice which holds a conversation with posterity.

A man who guards his inner life as closely as Browning is the more likely to attract posterity towards it. To his contemporaries that life seemed an enigma, to his successors an object of legitimate fascination. To that fascination, the studies of Browning responded, with affection and discretion by Alexandra Orr in 1891, with wit and aphorism by G. K. Chesterton in 1903, with insight and concision by Betty Miller in 1953, with discursive enthusiasm by Maisie Ward in 1968-9, and with spacious scholarship by William Irvine and Park Honan in 1974.

Whether or not Browning was the greatest poet of his age, he was clearly the most intriguing personality among the great poets, in the view of his contemporaries. He resisted more vigorously than any of his rivals a definitive view of his life and poetry. The approaches towards the truth of his personality, repeated more freely after his death, had already begun during his lifetime. Most famous among these was the thesis of Henry James who – as it were – threw up his hands in despair and imagined the existence of two Brownings. One was the loud, self-confident figure of London society, the other the private poet who lived, locked from the world, in a domain of his own disturbing creations. James was later to take this view of Browning to the limits of fictional conjecture in his story 'The Private Life'.

To a degree seldom true of other literary figures, each biography of Browning has traced a different path to the secret creative world, as if to the dark tower which is Childe Roland's destination in his own poem. There is no mystery in Browning's public life, except that it should have existed at all in such hearty philistinism. Yet the dark tower of thought, where he undertook his microscopy of the human heart, remains obscure. Within it he dwelt upon the aberrations of love and holiness, of cruelty and moral cynicism, 'the dangerous edge of things'. The approach to it in the present biography relies rather more upon the poetry and rather less upon the correspondence than is usually the case. He did not, indeed, 'unlock his heart' fully in the poetry; yet he described far more of his inner life there than even in the letters to Elizabeth Barrett.

Browning suffered, like Tennyson, from the looting of his poetry after his death to provide mottoes in thread or poker-work which proclaimed that God was in His heaven and all was right with the world or that a man's reach should exceed his grasp. The characteristic irony of the first case was that the lines came from a poem whose major preoccupations were adultery, murder, and prostitution – voluntary and enforced. Yet there is much in Browning's poetry, more indeed than in Tennyson's, that ought to be rescued from the academic game-reserve and made available as general reading. By a happy coincidence, as this biography goes to press, Penguin Books have printed the complete poems of Browning in two paperback volumes, making available such neglected achievements as *Red Cotton Night-Cap Country* and the haunting felicities of description in poems like *Fifine at the Fair*. If this present account of his life persuades readers of biography to become readers of his poetry, and readers of his better-known poetry to move on from *Men and Women* or *The Ring and the Book* to some of the Zola-like achievements of the 1870s, or the early realism of *Pippa Passes*, it will have fulfilled a good deal of its purpose. His life and poetry during his earlier years and his marriage to Elizabeth have customarily and understandably attracted the greater interest. Yet his later life is in many ways the more intriguing and illuminating, as well as offering his greatest single masterpiece in *The Ring and the Book*.

To regard the sixteen years of his courtship and marriage to Elizabeth as being a digression from the main course of Browning's life is scarcely tenable. However, such a view has an element of truth, insofar as it suggests he was less modified and less enraptured, perhaps, by the experience than might be supposed. The Browning of 1861 is still, in almost every respect, very much the Browning of 1844. The underlying continuity of character, the importance of the well-guarded 'life within life', is central to this. I have, therefore, made it the subject of a general discussion in Chapter 3, 'The Madhouse and the Shrine'. It is at this stage of Browning's life that the voices of the inner world were to become disturbingly audible in his poetry and it is therefore a convenient point at which to consider them in general.

No purpose would be served in the bibliography to this life by reprinting a large selection of the material listed in the *New Cambridge Bibliography of English Literature* and the annual volumes of *The Year's Work in English Studies*. On the other hand, a more extended reading of non-literary material is a useful illumination of those topics which held the attention of Browning and his contemporaries. Consequently the notes to this biography are full and the bibliography concise.

For access to material upon which this book is based, I am particularly indebted to Mr Vincent Quinn, Keeper of Special Collections, Balliol College, Oxford; the Ashmolean Museum and the Bodleian Library, Oxford; the British Library; the London Library; the Victoria and Albert Museum; the Libraries of University College, London, and of the University of Wales Institute of Science and Technology, Cardiff. To the Master and Fellows of Balliol, I am grateful for permission to quote from the unpublished correspondence of Benjamin Jowett and the Browning family.

My thanks are due to Dr Park Honan who read the typescript of the book and made most perceptive and valuable comments upon it, and to my wife who endured the unravelling of Browning's mental complexities. The passage of the book from manuscript to published volume was made easy to the author by the patience and editorial professionalism of Ms Linden Lawson and Ms Jane Cary, no less than by their enthusiasm. Like all his biographers, I owe an immeasurable debt to the diligence of those compilers of Browning correspondence in the last ninety years, whose work has been the foundation common to all lives of the poet during that period.

The revisions which Browning carried out on his poems, notably in the case of his earlier work, resulted in a number of variant readings being perpetuated. To avoid confusion, so far as possible, I have followed the texts of those editions most easily available at the time when this book was written. These consisted of the Everyman's Library volumes published by J. M. Dent for most of the poetry; and for the pieces not reprinted there, the collected edition of Browning's poetry published by Smith, Elder in 1896. Only with the Penguin edition of 1981 are all the poems currently made available in a single edition.

I

'Poor Old Camberwell!'

One afternoon towards the end of the 1830s, Thomas Carlyle rode out on horseback from Cheyne Row. Yellow and thin, as he described himself, he found this form of exercise the most beneficial for a man to whom literature had refused 'both bread and a stomach to digest bread'.[1] Crossing the Thames by the old wooden Battersea Bridge, he left behind him the smoke and the high black architecture of London. Fields and woods, as yet unspoilt, lay a little way south of the river on the way to Wimbledon Common.

The tall strong-featured figure, dark-haired under a wide-brimmed hat, was familiar in the literary society of the day. On this occasion, as he remarked, he encountered another horseman who was very different in appearance and manner. Carlyle recalled him as a beautiful youth with striking features and a head of dark flowing hair. Recognizing the older man, the youth stopped and began to speak eagerly in praise of the Scottish philosopher and all his works. Carlyle observed him with a characteristically dour scepticism, noting the fashionable clothes, especially the green riding-jacket. The jacket alone suggested an inclination for 'the turf and scamphood' rather than a serious interest in literature. He confessed himself 'anything but favourably impressed'.[2]

As time passed and he met the young man again, Carlyle's opinion of him improved. He wrote of 'a neat dainty little fellow', praised his modesty, his simple speech and manners, finding in him 'much ingenuity, vivacity and Cockney gracefulness'.[3] For a period of forty years, until the death of the older man, the friendship between Thomas Carlyle and Robert Browning was to remain one of the firmest between the major literary figures of the Victorian period.

The disparity between Browning's public image and the private reality of his life became a paradox of his early years and his maturity alike. Those who saw him in youth took him for a racing man or a dandy, an impression he fostered by reading sport and scandal in *Bell's*

Life in London as keenly as he read the *Westminster Review* or the *Examiner*. He once found his poetry referred to in *Bell's* while reading it for the details of a particularly sensational murder in Islington.[4]

Years later, those who met him casually would take him for a banker or a bon viveur. Again, it was an impression he cultivated, disowning the greater reality by proclaiming firmly, 'I'm not a literary man'.[5] Others might resemble an accepted model, whether of moderate conformity, like Tennyson, or of bourgeois rebellion, like Shelley and Swinburne. Browning stood apart, independent of conformity and rebellion alike. Given the circumstances of his birth, perhaps it could scarcely have been otherwise.

He was born on 7 May 1812, the son of one Robert Browning and the grandson of another. The Brownings traced their ancestry to East Woodyates in Dorset during the later seventeenth century, but it was only with the poet's grandfather that their immediate history began. Robert Browning, the grandfather, was born in Dorset in 1749. At the age of twenty he moved to London, where he had been appointed to a clerkship in the Bank of England. Nine years later he married Margaret Tittle, whose family had considerable wealth from their plantations on the West Indian island of St Kitts. Their son, the second Robert Browning who was father of the poet, was born in 1782.

By a stroke of patronage and a fortunate marriage, the first Robert Browning established himself as a gentleman of substance. Indeed, both wealth and position were consolidated in 1784 when he was appointed Principal Clerk of the Bank-Stock Division. Small wonder that he should stand firmly for Church, king, and the established order. To that allegiance he held tenaciously against threats from European revolution and subversive schemes for ruining the owners of West Indian plantations by emancipating their slaves. In the finer things of life, too, he was a level-headed Hanoverian gentleman who announced that the Bible and *Tom Jones* contained all that was worth reading.

Even the blow which fell when Margaret Tittle died after eleven years of marriage was not insupportable. At forty-five he chose as his second wife Jane Smith, twenty-three years old and well provided for. By her he had a second family of nine children. To disencumber himself of his son Robert, he sent the young man out to St Kitts to administer the Tittle plantations. It was hardly to be imagined that the boy would find such an opportunity distasteful, let alone that he might repay his father by a rash and ungrateful act of rebellion.

But the second Robert Browning, the poet's father, was shocked and sickened by the system of slavery. His son wrote many years later: 'I have never known much more of those circumstances in his youth . . . in consequence of his invincible repugnance to allude to the matter – and I have a fancy, to account for some peculiarities in him, which connects them with some abominable early experience.'[6]

Despite his father's refusal to discuss that experience, the poet had no doubt as to its nature. When questioned, his father would close his eyes and show 'exactly the same marks of loathing that may be noticed while a piece of cruelty is mentioned . . . and the *word* "blood", even, makes him turn pale'.[7]

If the cruelties of the slave system were revolting, so was the dismissive official blandness towards slaves. On the island of Antigua, for instance, an aide-de-camp beat a pregnant slave woman with a cart whip. When she tried to make a complaint, he beat her again. The only person punished was the abolitionist bookseller, John Hatchard, who was condemned and fined in the Court of King's Bench in 1817 for publishing the scandal.[8] In 1846 Robert Browning the poet still bitterly recalled 'freemen who have a right to beat their own negroes'.[9]

Indeed, the poet always retained a pride in his father who, as his mother told him, 'conceived such a hatred to the slave system in the West Indies . . . that he relinquished every prospect, – supported himself, while there, in some other capacity, and came back, while yet a boy, to his father's profound astonishment and rage'.[10] As the youngest Robert Browning remarked: 'If we are poor, it is to my father's infinite glory.'[11]

The unwilling expatriate returned to England from St Kitts. He had no qualifications beyond a well-developed taste in painting and a natural ability as a caricaturist. To devote himself to art was his principal ambition, but he reckoned without his father's resentment or his stepmother's jealousy. The eldest Robert Browning refused to subsidize art and, at his wife's insistence, declined to afford his son a university education. In his grandson's view, the old man was an unforgiving patriarch towards his son and 'continued to hate him till a few years before his death'.[12]

Nothing was to be done for the second Robert Browning by his family. Ironically, his salvation came from a director of the Bank of England for whom he had worked in St Kitts and who, in 1803, nominated him to a clerkship in the bank. So, condemned to follow his father's profession, he was obliged for half a century to 'consume his life after a fashion he always detested'.[13]

Yet this was not quite the cautionary tale that it might seem. A Bank of England clerkship was not an onerous appointment. Nor was the poverty of the second Robert Browning more than comparative. True,

3

he never attained such wealth as his father had possessed, but he lived comfortably enough among the fields and hills of rural Camberwell. Moreover, his hunger for learning was appeased by the acquisition of a large and varied library. His knowledge spread quickly in the spheres of ancient and modern literature, art and history. The learning he displayed was both eclectic and profound. Indeed, in such chosen subjects as the French Revolution or the letters of Junius his scholarship was almost intimidating.

Yet the second Robert Browning was too much the figure of the benign and gentle scholar to intimidate anyone. His son called him 'tender-hearted to a fault'. Dante Gabriel Rossetti thought him 'lovable beyond description . . . a complete oddity . . . innocent as a child'.[14] One of his friends, W.J. Stillman, summed him up succinctly and astutely: 'He had the perpetual juvenility of a blessed child. If to live in the world as if not of it indicates a saintly nature, then Robert Browning the elder was a saint; a serene, untroubled soul, conscious of no moral or theological problem to disturb his serenity, and as gentle as a gentle woman.'[15]

His other-worldliness was evident in domestic affairs as well as in public life. Sarianna, his daughter, remarked that if she had gone to her father while he was engrossed in his library and said, 'There will be no dinner to-day', he would have looked up from his book and replied, 'All right, my dear, it is of no consequence'.[16]

In 1811, secure in his clerkship at the bank, the second Robert Browning took a wife. She was Sarah Anna Wiedemann, of German descent, whose father was a Dundee shipowner. She and her sister had come south to Camberwell, where they both found husbands. Sarah married Robert Browning, and Christiana married John Silverthorne, a local brewer. The Browning marriage was unusual in at least two respects. Sarah was a Congregationalist, a member of the York Street Chapel in Walworth. At thirty-nine she was also ten years older than her bridegroom. Any possible division in matters of religious opinion was overcome by Robert Browning renouncing the established Church in favour of the York Street congregation. The consequence of Sarah's age was that she bore only two children, Robert Browning the poet in 1812 and his sister Sarianna two years later.

Mrs Browning, in the eyes of those who knew her intimately, possessed a serenity to equal her husband's. It came perhaps from a tranquil religious faith and a love of music, for she was an accomplished pianist. An early glimpse of Browning as a child shows his enchantment in listening to her, and his cries of 'Play! Play!' when the music stopped. Her enthusiasm, if not her technical ability, was communicated to him.

4

It found expression in several of his poems about keyboard composers of the seventeenth and eighteenth centuries, no less than by his use of Schumann's *Carnaval* in *Fifine at the Fair*.

In her private religious belief Mrs Browning tempered faith with humanity. She was, for instance, a subscriber to the London Missionary Society whose conditions of membership involved acceptance of 'those views of doctrinal truth which for the sake of distinction are called Calvinistic'. Yet hers was no benighted Calvinism of the kind which her son consigned to 'Madhouse Cells' in his poem 'Johannes Agricola in Meditation'. Johannes gloats over the burning of the God-loving and virtuous in hell while knowing that he, one of the Elect, can blend 'All hideous sins, as in a cup,' and yet be saved. The one book in the household bearing Mrs Browning's signature endeavoured to meet the moral objections of such a creed. It was Elisha Coles's *Practical Discourse of Effectual Calling and Perseverance* (1677), an attempt to include all believers among the Elect.

Just as her husband joined the congregation for morning service at York Street, Walworth, so Mrs Browning made her concession to the established Church on Sunday evenings. It was then that the family attended Camden Chapel, Camberwell, where a fashionable Anglican preacher, Canon Henry Melvill, began his ministry in 1830.

After their marriage in 1811, the Brownings settled in Southampton Street, Camberwell, a Georgian Arcadia where suburbanization had scarcely begun. London, whose development had been predominantly north of the Thames, was a distant prospect of towers and spires, three miles away across the intervening meadows. Fields, orchards, the wooded mounds of Herne Hill and Dulwich Hills, were to be the landscape of Browning's childhood. It was above Camberwell, on Herne Hill, that Browning's contemporary John Ruskin passed his boyhood, a child's Garden of Eden as he recalled, lying a few miles south of the Strand:

> The view from the ridge on both sides was, before railroads came, entirely lovely: westward at evening, almost sublime, over softly wreathing distances of domestic wood; – Thames herself not visible, nor any fields except immediately beneath; but the tops of twenty square miles of politely inhabited groves. On the other side, east and south, the Norwood hills, partly rough with furze, partly wooded with birch and oak, partly in pure green bramble copse, and rather steep pasture, rose with the promise of all the rustic loveliness of Surrey and Kent in them, and with so much of space and height in their sweep, as gave them some fellowship with hills of true hill-districts.[17]

5

Though the orchards and pastureland of his most famous poetry were a reality in the Camberwell of Browning's youth, much of the area was occupied by graceful houses and their gardens. Friern Manor had been built in 1725 by Lord Bolingbroke and it was there, the visitor was assured, that Alexander Pope had written 'a part, if not the whole, of his Essay on Man'.[18] The house and gardens of Grove Hill had been honoured in the time of Dr Lettsom by visits from James Boswell and Lord Shelburne. The gardens had been much admired: 'The whole was arranged with considerable taste, and ornamented with inscribed pedestals and statues, suitable to the various localities which they occupied.'[19] No less impressive was Champion Lodge, Camberwell, to which George IV, as Prince of Wales, had been a visitor.

To this extent the landscape of Browning's childhood was not one of wild and romantic nature, nor even of nature put to useful agricultural purposes. It was nature as parkland, discreetly populated and tastefully ornamented. The eighteenth century had not yet quite died in Camberwell, though the expansion of its population which almost doubled every decade from 1800 to 1840 was soon to alter that. But still, in Browning's childhood, the civilized Arcadia of the Augustans, the ideal of *rus in urbe*, was more evident than has been suggested. Combined with the choice of reading in his father's library it was to have a significant effect upon his own tastes.

Nor was Arcadia to be complete without art and education in their more overt forms. Beyond Camberwell, at a little distance, lay Dulwich, famous both for its college and its gallery which had been bequeathed for public exhibition in 1810, long before the opening of the National Gallery. In Camberwell itself, plentifully supplied with schools and with pulpits for well-patronized preachers like Canon Melvill, literary and philosophical societies were founded with Athenian earnestness.

By the time that Browning reached manhood, it was precisely the Arcadian and Augustan qualities that brought destruction on the area. It was first fashionable, then popular. Twenty years before Browning's birth, armed guards had had to walk beside the coaches crossing the open land towards London. All too soon, as Ruskin lamented, the railways which put the footpads out of business brought a havoc of their own. Yet to Browning in his first published poem, *Pauline* (1833), the magic of a child's landscape was still vivid. He recalls sun on a pool, a scene haunted by half-caught glimpses of Ovidian nymphs and satyrs. Where the pond gathers,

> ... the trees bend
> O'er it as wild men watch a sleeping girl,

6

And thro' their roots long creeping plants stretch out
Their twined hair, steeped and sparkling; farther on,
Tall rushes and thick flag-knots have combined
To narrow it; so, at length, a silver thread
It winds, all noiselessly, thro' the deep wood,
Till thro' a cleft way, thro' the moss and stone
It joins its parent-river with a shout.

With river gods, no less than with nymphs and satyrs, the young
Browning populated this early world of his imagination. Nature unin-
habited had little appeal for him in this respect. When asked bluntly if
he cared for nature, the answer was one whose truth is corroborated by
his poetry. 'Yes, a great deal,' he said, 'but for human beings a great
deal more.' [20] As G. K. Chesterton remarked, most poets finding themselves in a wagonette of trippers would have been quieted and exalted
by escaping into the fields. 'The speciality of Browning is rather that he
would have been quieted and exalted by the wagonette.' [21]

Like Shelley, whose classicism he shared and who was the idol of his
adolescence, Browning populated his poetic landscapes in youth with
figures of legend. Sometimes in *Pauline* these are the recognizable figures
of antiquity like Agamemnon or Andromeda. Often they are the Shelleyean ghosts of 'Alastor' or 'The Witch of Atlas'. As Baudelaire was to
remark of the Salon of 1846, there are as many forms of romanticism as
there are romantics. For Browning its appeal was not in Wordsworthian
solitude but in the visions of *Pauline*.

As some world-wanderer sees in a far meadow
Strange towers, and walled gardens, thick with trees,
Where singing goes on, and delicious mirth,
And laughing fairy creatures peeping over.

Much later in his life a young admirer remarked to him: 'There is no
romance now except in Italy.' Browning thought for a moment. 'Ah,
well,' he said, 'I should like to include poor old Camberwell.' [22]

It was into the household in Southampton Street, with a modest retinue
of page-boy and servants, that Browning and his sister Sarianna were
born. In his early childhood the family moved to a second house in the
same street, where they remained until the move to Hatcham, New
Cross, in 1840. Browning was 'a handsome, vigorous, fearless child, and
soon developed an unresting activity and a fiery temper'. [23] To most
contemporaries the temper manifested itself as impulsiveness rather
than ill-humour. The harmony of family life showed how easily his

energy was harnessed to acquiring knowledge and the temper subdued by enlightened indulgence.

Until his own marriage to Elizabeth Barrett thirty-four years later, Browning continued to live under his parents' roof in what he described as 'a great delight ... in this prolonged relation of childhood'.[24] The nature of that relationship was described by him in a rare cry of intercession to Elizabeth at the thought of their wedding being kept a secret from his parents. 'Because, since I was a child I never looked for the least or greatest thing within the compass of their means to give, but given it was, – nor for liberty but it was conceded, nor confidence but it was bestowed.'[25]

The fond pride which he cherished for his father's rebellion over the matter of slavery was matched by an affectionate and easy devotion to his mother. During all the years in which he lived as a man under the same roof, 'it was his rule never to go to bed without giving her a good-night kiss. If he was out so late that he had to admit himself with a latch-key, he nevertheless went to her room.'[26]

Browning's friend and contemporary, Alfred Domett, left one of the most vivid pen-portraits of the future poet and his parents, though not much to the advantage of Robert Browning senior. On his visits to Southampton Street, Domett saw the obvious pride of Mrs Browning in her son and his gentle love of her. Once, Domett recalled, 'in the act of tossing a little roll of music from the table to the piano, he thought it had touched her head in passing her, and I remember how he ran to her to apologize and caress her, though I think she had not felt it'. Browning's father remained in Domett's memory as a *'dry adust'* man, small in build and reserved in manner, with an enthusiasm only for his books and engravings. Later still, he confessed to Domett that his son's poetry – *Paracelsus* and *Sordello* – was *'beyond* him', despite his natural pride in the young man's progress. The two children and their parents seemed to Domett 'a most suited, harmonious and intellectual family'.[27]

Thomas Carlyle, making a more businesslike appraisal of the household, described its occupants as 'people of respectable position among the dissenters, but not rich neither'. Mrs Browning he noted as 'the true type of Scottish gentlewoman', and agreed with Domett about the pride of the parents in their only son, who was 'the very apple of their eyes'.[28]

It was perhaps to be expected that Mrs Browning, married at an age when the time for childbearing had so diminished, should have been indulgent towards an attractive and intellectually precocious son. It proved, of course, to be more than mere indulgence, an aspect of what Browning himself later called 'my father and mother's childlike faith in goodness'.[29] This gentle and placid affection which was so much part of Mrs Browning's nature seemed to convey itself with ease to the animal world beyond the limit of human communication. Sarianna, for example, remembered how their mother would 'lure the butterflies in the garden to her, and domestic animals obeyed her as if they reasoned'.[30] Such sympathies, even without the accompanying skill, were to be inherited by her son.

Browning's own attitudes, whether in politics or poetry, owed much to the religion of his childhood. The Congregationalism of the nineteenth century was a milder and less dogmatic form of the religion of the Independents, which had first appeared in England in the reign of Elizabeth. That Puritan belief which led its believers through persecution to exile in New England and then, briefly, to power and influence under the Cromwellian Commonwealth was suitably modified by its inheritors. Yet whether as Puritanism or Nonconformity, it retained the same emphasis upon the independence of individual congregations. Religious duty was owed to God and conscience, rather than to the hierarchy of the church.

The implications of such a belief were political and intellectual as well as theological. However, in an age when dissenters were more aptly described as Nonconformists than as Puritans, there was a further important distinction between the religion of the Brownings and other non-Anglican denominations. Unlike Methodism, its closest and most popular rival, it was not a new growth, conditioned by the society of the eighteenth century. Its origin and its sense of tradition led back to a darker age of persecution and fanaticism, to an opposition to the established order which had been paid for by mutilation, exile, and even death. It was possible to be a Methodist and to think of religion in terms of Nonconformity. In its externals, Congregationalism might seem to differ only a little from this; but, to a family like the Brownings, a Puritan ancestry of belief remained a predisposing factor in their attitude to politics, education, and literature, as much as towards Christian doctrine itself.

Puritanism, in this context, was a positive cultural force, sharing little of the repressive narrow-minded prudery with which the term was popularly associated. Moreover, its original harshness had been softened over a period of two centuries. In consequence, neither of Browning's parents regarded Puritanism or Nonconformity as requiring the bleak intellectual tyranny of the seventeenth century at its worst, or the suffocating respectability sometimes evident in the later Victorian period. In Browning's youth their religion was, with good reason, a

9

force for political reform and cultural enlightenment. The relics of an earlier persecution remained on the statute book. As late as 1812 they were subject to penalties for attending their own chapel by the Conventicle Act of 1670. Long after this they endured the common fate of political disqualification, and until 1854 Oxford and Cambridge were open only to members of the Established Church. The religion of Browning's childhood was a significant ingredient in the education of an outsider.

Faith in goodness and a belief in the power of knowledge determined much of the parental 'indulgence' shown to Browning. A child's enquiring mind was always to be stimulated rather than stifled. The fact that a publisher of Shelley's poem *Queen Mab* was convicted of blasphemous libel for issuing it did not deter Mrs Browning from getting Shelley's works at her son's request.[31] Ignorance was never preferable to knowledge. As Browning was to make Aprile say in *Paracelsus*, reflecting his own upbringing,

> ...no thought which ever stirred
> A human breast should be untold.

A generation later, Edmund Gosse, the son of a gifted Puritan father, dared to ask his parent about the old Greek gods. They were, he was told, 'the shadows cast by the vices of the heathen.... "There is nothing in the legends of these gods, or rather devils, that it is not better for a Christian not to know."'[32] Browning was to look back over half a century to his father as friend, teacher and companion; 'my father, best of men, most indefatigable of book digesters!'[33] From respect and inclination he retained an ill-defined allegiance to the Nonconformist belief of his parents throughout his life. His father was to him a 'wonderful child's friend', while Gosse lamented; 'What a charming companion, what a delightful parent, what a courteous and engaging friend my Father would have been, and would pre-eminently have been to me, if it had not been for this stringent piety which ruined it all.'[34]

To Browning, his father remained this loving companion who had opened the treasures of his library to an eager child, who read the whole of Dryden's *Essay on Satire* to him as they walked up Nunhead Hill, who placed no prohibition on books or learning, and who introduced him to Homer at five years old. The last event was to be celebrated by Browning in his poem 'Development', published in his last collection, *Asolando* (1889). Yet even before the introduction to Homer, it seems, Browning was composing verses of his own. His sister Sarianna recalled him 'as a very little boy, walking round and round the dining-room table, and spanning out the scansion of his verses with his hand on the smooth mahogany'.[35]

'Development' has a double value in the understanding of Browning's character. It shows, quite simply, how his father, 'that instructor sage', introduced him to a new world of beauty and excitement. More important, it establishes the extraordinary consistency of Browning's beliefs throughout life, the independence and self-reliance of his mind, the splendid obstinacy with which he rejected criticism of his own poetry, the Bible, the works of Homer or Shelley. The opening of 'Development' describes how the introduction to Homer began:

> My Father was a scholar and knew Greek.
> When I was five years old, I asked him once
> 'What do you read about?'
>   'The siege of Troy.'
> 'What is a siege and what is Troy?'
>   Whereat
> He piled up chairs and tables for a town,
> Set me a-top for Priam, called our cat
> – Helen, enticed away from home (he said)
> By wicked Paris, who crouched somewhere close
> Under the footstool, being cowardly,
> But whom – since she was worth the pains, poor puss –
> Towzer and Tray, – our dogs, the Atreidai, – sought
> By taking Troy to get possession of
> – Always when great Achilles ceased to sulk,
> (My pony in the stable) – forth would prance
> And put to flight Hector – our page-boy's self.

Three years later, when Browning and his friends were still 'playing at Troy's Siege', his father introduced him to Pope's translation of Homer. Later still, the child was eager to read the original text.

> 'Quite ready for the Iliad, nothing less?
> There's Heine, where the big books block the shelf:
> Don't skip a word, thumb well the Lexicon!'

This piece of progressive education, which took place between 1817 and 1824, was followed by a minor tragedy. The twelve-year-old child encountered a work by the German critic Wolf, his *Prolegomena in Homerum* (1795). Homer, it seemed, had never existed. The poems were fragments handed down by oral tradition. There had never been a Troy or its inhabitants. 'Why must he needs come doubting, spoil a dream?' wailed the child. It was the same cry that was to echo years later over the criticism and desanctifying of the Bible by David Strauss and his followers. Browning was to deal summarily with Strauss in *Christmas-Eve* as the exponent of a loveless creed. In the case of Wolf and Homer, his childhood dream was to be more publicly exonerated.

Despite its story of a child's disillusionment, 'Development' is a celebration of the downfall of pedants like Wolf and Strauss. Tradition and belief, beauty and dream, had been vindicated. In 1873 the archaeologist Heinrich Schliemann discovered not only Troy but what was then believed to be King Priam's treasure. Three years later, at Mycenae, he uncovered a number of graves, flesh still visible on the skeletons, and reported that he had at last looked upon the face of Agamemnon. Wolf, like the biblical critics, was worsted. In his lifelong faith, religious and artistic, Browning had triumphed.

As a child he was made free of his father's library. His unsupervised reading might strike horror into a modern child psychologist. The beauties of Homer apart, there were also such passages as those in Book XXII of the *Odyssey*. After death or torment inflicted upon his betrayers – men and women – Odysseus gives Melanthius up to vengeance. The infant Browning read how the feet of hanged women still fluttered like birds' wings as Melanthius was emasculated, nose and ears lopped off, likewise hands and feet, these 'morsels' being fed to dogs in front of him before he was put to death.

For such ghastliness he had been well prepared by other items of childhood reading. Chief of these was Nathaniel Wanley's *Wonders of the Little World: or, A General History of Man in Six Books* (1678). Among its anecdotes of piety the work contained much that was grotesque or terrifying. With great relish Wanley devotes chapters to monstrous births and abortions. Lazarus 'had a little Brother growing out at his breast ... voided no excrements, but by the mouth, nose, and ears'.[36] Among milder examples was the woman who gave birth to two fish, which 'as soon as they came out of her Womb, did swim in the Water as other Fish'.[37] More awesome was the concubine of Pope Nicholas III who gave birth to 'a Monster, which resembled a Bear'.[38]

To the child's imagination Wanley also offered a chapter 'Of such Persons as have changed their Sex', including a spirited account of a girl who leapt a ditch, ran screaming home to report that 'her Bowels fell out', but exhibited instead 'the hidden evidences of a man'.[39] To complete the child's knowledge of the world there was a formidable section on torture and execution. He read, for example, a description of how a man might be severed at the waist, his upper half kept alive on 'an hot Iron, or Plate of Copper, that sears up the Veins; whereby they keep him in sense of intolerable pain so long as they can'.[40] Persia supplied the ingenious device by which a man's body was enclosed in two troughs, head, hands and feet protruding. By forcing him to eat, 'pricking his Eyes with Needles' if he refused, his executioners ensured that within the human waste of the troughs 'there are worms engendered, which eat into his body'.[41]

Browning was later to face accusations that much of his poetry contained material that was morbid or horrible. In his childhood reading the cause of this was not far to seek. Indeed, 'the good old style of Wanley', as he called it, left its mark upon his poetry in more specific ways. From the epigraph to *Pauline* in 1833 to the character of Paracelsus, passages from *The Ring and the Book* or stories like 'The Pied Piper of Hamelin', and even 'The Cardinal and the Dog' in 1889, the debt to Wanley is direct and clear.

For good measure, his Browning grandfather who lived until 1833 became reconciled to his son after the unpleasantness over St Kitts. The old man would appear in Southampton Street from time to time, where he would divert the child from his books by telling stories. The favourite was that of Elizabeth Brownrigg who tortured her apprentices and was at last hanged before a large and enthusiastic crowd at Tyburn in 1767 for the murder of one of them. The point of the story, as the child heard it from his grandfather, was that many people whose surname was Brownrigg changed it to Browning in the wake of this scandal. In fantasy, Mrs Brownrigg was almost one of the family.

Despite the niceness of his feelings over cruelty to slaves, it seems evident that even Browning's father shared something of this taste for the macabre. He had, for instance, developed an enthusiasm for the study of anatomy. A dead rat, awaiting dissection when business was slack, had been discovered in his desk at the Bank of England. He disappeared unaccountably from the company on his wedding day and was found contentedly anatomizing a duck. If this morbidity of taste was inherited by three generations of Brownings, it is not surprising that the graveyard humour of Thomas Hood should have been among Sarianna's favourite reading.

The literary education which Browning acquired from his father's library was not exclusively confined to the grotesque and the ghastly. From its contents he imbibed a range of learning which was both oddly assorted and yet formidable. Finding the fifty volumes of the *Biographie Universelle*, bought on publication in 1822, he set about reading them through. He had been taught French as well as Latin and Greek, and a tutor, Angelo Cerutti, was employed to teach him Italian. He was also to learn German, at the University of London, when he was sixteen.

His father was an admirer of Pope and the eighteenth century, while Browning in the first place was drawn to neglected poets of an earlier period, including Quarles' *Emblems* and the poetry of Donne. Indeed, with alarming precocity he proceeded to set to music Donne's song *Goe, and catche a falling starre*. This sign of promise was nurtured by his parents with equal eagerness. John Relfe, musician-in-ordinary to the king, was procured as his teacher.

Yet there was one other area in which his father's library was perhaps the richest of all. Not only did it contain a fine collection of prints, that of Caravaggio's *Perseus and Andromeda* being the child's favourite: there were two books whose influence was more immediate.

The first of these was Vasari's *Lives of the Painters*, whose accounts of Fra Lippo Lippi and Andrea del Sarto were to be the raw material of some of Browning's most famous poetry. The second was a work of surreal enchantment attributed to Gerard de Lairesse.

Gerard de Lairesse (1640–1711) was a Flemish painter afflicted by blindness. When bereft of sight he composed his treatise on *The Art of Painting in All its Branches*. Apart from his observations on technique, Lairesse spends much of the book creating pictures in his imagination. His inspiration is Ovid's *Metamorphoses*. He shows in effect how to take a pleasant rural scene and turn it into a wonderland of legend, populated by the creatures of myth, the temples and statues of a pastoral idyll. The impact of this device upon the imagination of a child among the hills and orchards of Camberwell was immediate. As Browning wrote on the fly-leaf of his father's copy: 'I read this book more often and with greater delight when I was a child than any other: and still remember the main of it most gratefully for the good I seem to have got from the prints and wonderful text.'

Almost seventy years later, in *Parleyings with Certain People of Importance in Their Day*, Browning recalled the dreamlike spell of Lairesse's neo-classical visions:

> Beyond
> The ugly actual, lo, on every side
> Imagination's limitless domain
> Displayed a wealth of wondrous sounds and sights
> Ripe to be realized by poet's brain
> Acting on painter's brush!

Most vividly of all he remembered a walk with Lairesse, described in the sixteenth chapter of *The Art of Painting*. The blind artist took as his route a pleasantly wooded area of the kind familiar to Browning and his father on their walks. In his imagination the scene becomes 'the *Seat of blessed Souls ... beautiful and orderly*'.[42] Against the green trees stands a superb fountain of white marble with figures upon it. Beyond it a broad level path is edged with stone and ornamented by tall vases of flesh-coloured marble carved with dancing girls. At the crossroads the sign-post is a statue, half-man and half-satyr, facing the way in which the travellers must go. Close by, a naked nymph on a marble plinth sheds water from the vase she holds. A tomb supported by marble sphinxes proves to be the grave of Phaeton, for 'a Piece of a Chariot, and half a Wheel in the shape of a Star' are unearthed close by.[43] Yet to come are a bridge, a herdsmen's village and a fine temple. The appeal of this 'game' to an imaginative child was not only immediate but profound.

By the time he reached manhood Browning was an authority on a number of unlikely subjects, whether through Lairesse and Wanley or through the study of minor figures in the history of painting and the literature of mediaeval Europe. Nor was this knowledge acquired at the expense of more orthodox education in the literatures of Greece, Rome, France and England. He was to be the translator of Aeschylus and Euripides, the admirer of Balzac, and an enthusiast for the lesser-known poetry of John Donne and Christopher Smart.

Cecil Lang suggests that with the exception of Milton, Swinburne was the most learned of England's major poets. In the area of literature, classical and general, this is certainly tenable. In a wider context Browning's learning proved more daunting. It extended over literature in half a dozen languages, biblical scholarship, the philosophy of Plato and Kant, the lives and works of little-known mediaeval or Renaissance figures. Beyond that, it embraced obscure composers, theories of music and language, the minor details of Provençal or troubadour culture, medicine and zoology. To all this was added a healthy appetite for contemporary politics, religious controversies, culture, international affairs and criminal proceedings. Moreover, he had also an exceptionally retentive memory. As he wryly concluded, he was unable to forget anything 'but names, and the date of the battle of Waterloo'.[44]

Those who met him in later life were apt to come away stunned by the ease and range of his expertise. His father's friend John Kenyon marvelled at the young man's inexhaustible knowledge. In 1846 the historian Alexander Kinglake confessed himself 'quite astounded' by the range of Browning's learning. After all other topics had been covered, it appears, the breeding of animals was discussed. Whereupon, as Browning was reminded, 'you discoursed as scientifically on the training of greyhounds and breeding of ducks as if you had never done anything else all your life'.[45] The knowledge which he displayed was profound as well as broad. Dante Gabriel Rossetti, recalling visits to the Louvre with Browning, wrote: 'I found his knowledge of early Italian art beyond that of any one I ever met – *encyclopaedically* beyond that of Ruskin himself.'[46] It might be argued that Ruskin conceded something of the kind, writing in *Modern Painters*, when he referred to Browning's poem 'The Bishop Orders his Tomb at St Praxed's Church':

> I know no other piece of modern English, prose or poetry, in which there is so much told, as in these lines, of the Renaissance spirit, – its worldliness, inconsistency, pride, hypocrisy, ignorance of itself, love of art, of luxury, and of good Latin. It is nearly all that I said of the central Renaissance in thirty pages of the 'Stones of Venice' put into as many lines, Browning's being also the antecedent work. The worst of it is that this kind of concentrated writing needs so much *solution* before the reader can fairly get the good of it, that people's patience fails them, and they give the thing up as insoluble.[47]

Praise from such men was gratifying enough. Yet in his final sentence Ruskin describes the flaw of learning which almost destroyed Browning as a poet. The trouble was, as G. K. Chesterton remarked, that the young Browning acquired his store of scholarship 'in the same casual manner in which a boy learns to walk or to play cricket'.[48] Browning found it hard to realize that other men and women fell far short of him in this respect. In many of his poems, notoriously *Sordello*, he assumes that his readers will be adequately informed in the subject matter of the poem, and accordingly makes no concessions. In the case of *Sordello* the reader must be familiar with the minutiae of Italian history in the thirteenth century, the politics and struggles of Verona or Mantua, the manners of the troubadours, and the geography and culture of mediaeval Italy and Provence.

Far from offering explanations, as Westland Marston confided to William Michael Rossetti in 1850, Browning worked in an opposite direction. He deliberately condensed his narrative verse so that 'if an exclamation will suggest his meaning, he substitutes this for a whole sentence'.[49] This habit of condensation and his over-estimate of his readers' erudition were jointly responsible for the charges of obscurity which clung, however unjustly, to his general reputation. The magnificent gallery of *Men and Women* or the superb humanism of *The Ring and the Book* were too easily forgotten by the reader who struggled in the toils of *Sordello*.

By contrast with the Tennysonian gloom of Somersby Rectory, the patrician caste of the Swinburne family, the alternate poverty and gentility of Dickens' childhood, the house in Southampton Street was a home of ungrudging affection and modest prosperity. The presence of the parents, signified by book-filled shelves and the rich themes of Beethoven on the piano, exuded security and contentment. Sarianna, plain and a little solemn, grew closer to her brother as time passed. Page-boy and servants, two dogs, a cat, the pony, and a variety of Browning's own pets – monkeys, owls, hedgehogs, magpies, snakes and an eagle – made up the population of domestic life. It was a household of unassuming happiness by Browning's later accounts.

The great world beyond the garden trees and the hedge was represented in the first place by the larger Browning family, notably two of his father's half-brothers, Reuben and William. Uncle Reuben, his nephew's favourite, had been placed by the grandfather in Rothschild's bank. From this position of influence in the 1850s and 1860s he was to issue several publications, addressing the nation on such subjects as bank notes and the currency, income tax and stamp acts.

William Shergold Browning, the elder of the two, was an author of a different kind. He had begun with a Bank of England clerkship and then, through the grandfather's friendship with Nathan Rothschild, had gone to work for Rothschild's bank in Paris. His historical novel *The Provost of Paris* was published in 1833, and a more successful three-volume novel, *Hoel Morvan: or, the Court and Camp of Henry V*, appeared in 1844. Like his half-brother and nephew he had a scholar's interest in history as well. His *History of the Huguenots during the Sixteenth Century* appeared in a number of editions between 1829 and 1845.

Beyond the figures of his family, Browning's first experience of the world came from his schooling. He was sent briefly to a kindergarten near Southampton Street only to be removed, according to family legend, because he was too clever. The lady who ran it was accused by other parents of neglecting their children while 'bringing on Master Browning'.[50] Whether a child who was writing poems in the manner of Ossian by this time really needed bringing on was another matter.

Next he was sent to the junior department of Peckham School as a weekly boarder, returning home from Saturday until Monday. The classes were run by the Misses Ready, whose brother, the Reverend Thomas Ready, was owner and headmaster of the main school. To this senior school Browning moved when he was about ten years old, remaining until he was fourteen.

Though he endured separation from his parents during the week, this was much less than the loss of home life experienced by contemporaries who were dispatched to more famous schools for much longer periods. Peckham School was little more than a stroll from Southampton Street, closer than Dulwich Gallery or the hills on which he walked with his father.

As a young man Browning indulged the middle-class privilege of recalling his education as a time of mental and physical misery. There was the bullying of a gifted younger boy by his elders and the constant threat of punishment by the master.

> Yet when a schoolfellow of mine, I remember, began translating in class Virgil after this mode, 'Sic fatur – so said Aeneas; lacrymans – *a-crying*' ... our pedagogue turned on him furiously – 'D'ye think Aeneas made such a noise – as *you* shall presently?' How easy to conceive a boyish half-melancholy, smiling at itself.[51]

From his days in the junior school Browning remembered the Misses Ready brushing the hair of the boys to the rhythms of Isaac Watts' hymns which they sang as they worked.

> Lord, 'tis a pleasant thing to stand
> In gardens planted by Thy hand....
> Fools never raise their thoughts so high.
> Like *brutes* they live, like BRUTES they die.[52]

Some years later, walking with Alfred Domett past the wall of the school playground, Browning delivered his final verdict on Mr Ready's establishment: 'some remark expressive of the disgust with which he always thought of the place'. And for Domett's benefit he recited an epigram which he had composed after leaving there:

> Within these walls and near that house of glass,
> Did I, three years of hapless childhood pass –
> D——d undiluted misery it was![53]

Perhaps it was, though his unsympathetic sister added that even Browning himself had conceded that 'the boys were most liberally and kindly treated'.[54]

By contrast with the excitement and enchantment of his father's library, the routine of construing, chanting, memorizing classical texts was an appalling tedium. In April 1828 Robert Browning the elder enrolled his son in the newly founded London University. He vouched for the boy's character and 'unwearied application for the last six years, to the Greek, Latin & French Languages'.[55] The university had been founded by those, including Nonconformists, who were to be excluded from Oxford and Cambridge on doctrinal grounds for a further twenty-six years. Browning, at his own insistence, was among the first students when classes began in the autumn of 1828. He was entitled to his place not least because his father was a £100 shareholder in the new educational venture.

Browning's enthusiasm lasted for six months. After a week he left his lodgings and returned to Camberwell, though continuing to travel to his classes from there. In the following spring he withdrew from the university altogether. His contemporaries missed his appearance, 'a bright handsome youth with long black hair falling over his shoulders'.[56] Soon he was exploring new and more scientific paths of knowledge, perhaps a corrective to the prodigies and monstrosities of Wanley's *Wonders of the Little World*. He attended the lectures of Dr James Blundell at Guy's Hospital, the celebrated physician sharing at least with Wanley a special interest in midwifery.

This was the sum of his formal education. In a wider context he was the spiritual charge of George Clayton, minister of the York Street congregation. Despite the stories of Browning as an adolescent showing an open indifference to the services and being rebuked publicly for his inattention, Clayton was a man who held considerable fascination. He combined, it was said, 'the character of a saint, a dancing master, and an orthodox eighteenth-century theologian in about equal proportions'.[57] He was certainly a man of education, culture and tolerance, for all the tedium of his long extempore prayers 'which were newspapers entering into every particular of births, marriages, and deaths, and foreign travels of deacons and the like'.[58]

Browning's later account of the working-class chapel in *Christmas-Eve* – the fat old woman, the consumptive lad, the man with his head bandaged in a handkerchief, the greasy cuffs, and 'the preaching-man's immense stupidity' – was hardly a portrait of the smart York Street congregation. A more likely original was the Reverend Joseph Irons of Camberwell Grove. Alfred Domett recalls the game in which they would see how far down the street they could hear him 'bawling his sermon'. At a gratifying distance they caught the thundering power of his words loud and clear. 'I am very sorry to say it, beloved brethren, but it is an undoubted fact that Roman Catholic and midnight assassin are synonymous terms.'[59]

To the more sophisticated York Street congregation, as to those who heard Canon Melvill at Camden Chapel, the performances of the preachers amounted to a spiritually superior type of drama. Ruskin, like Browning, heard Melvill's sermons regularly, admiring them as 'sincere, orthodox, and oratorical on Ciceronian principles. He wrote them from end to end with polished art, and read them admirably, in his own manner.'[60] To one like Browning, who was to find so much inspiration in the dramatic monologue, the sophistication of George Clayton, the elegance of Henry Melvill, even the stentorian qualities of Mr Irons offered models of their kind.

In the far-removed area of visual art, Browning's education was both domestic and public. His father's taste was in Dutch genre paintings, combined with a talent that produced caricatures in the manner of Gillray or Cruikshank upon such subjects as the 1832 Reform Bill. Browning himself had shown some gift for caricature at school but in painting his taste was for a classicism that appealed little to his father.

At home he rescued the print of Caravaggio's *Perseus and Andromeda* from its neglect, installing it in his own room. At Dulwich Gallery his individual preferences were never in doubt. When Elizabeth Barrett believed that he had slighted the gallery, Browning excused himself by recalling the magnificence of its paintings in his childhood memory.

> It is just as if I had spoken contemptuously of that Gallery I so love and am so grateful to – having been used to go there when a child, far under the age allowed by the regulations – those two Guidos, the wonderful Rembrandt of Jacob's vision, such a Watteau, the triumphant three Murillo pictures, a Giorgione music-lesson group, all the Poussins with the 'Armida' and 'Jupiter's nursing' – and – no end to 'ands' – I have sate before one, some *one* of those pictures I had predetermined to see, a good hour and then gone away ... it used to be a green half-hour's walk over the fields.[61]

Expert opinion was later to decide that the Rembrandt and the Giorgione were not by those artists after all. But like Wolf and his criticism of Homer, there could be no place for expert opinion in the memory of a childhood idyll.

Two groups of friends held pride of place in Browning's adolescence. One of these consisted of the sisters Sarah and Eliza Flower, his elders by a number of years. Before that he was the companion of three 'wild youths', his Silverthorne cousins, with whom he shared the green walks and woods of Camberwell.[62]

Of the three cousins it was James Silverthorne, three years older than Browning, who became the closest friend. The two shared interests in art, which Silverthorne hoped to make his career, as well as in music and literature. It was James Silverthorne who apparently introduced Browning to the poetry of Shelley, with remarkable consequences, and in whose company Browning enjoyed his first experience of the London theatre.

To Elizabeth Barrett in 1845 Browning described the excitement of being in the gallery with Silverthorne for the German Opera's first production of *Fidelio* in London, the even greater delight of a large white-haired, red-cheeked German gesticulating in his frenzy – and the amusement of the two young men on finding him there again when they went back the next week.[63] There were memories, too, of going to Richmond with Silverthorne to see Edmund Kean as Richard III, and to *Hamlet* before that.

James Silverthorne was the only witness at the wedding of Browning and Elizabeth Barrett. He never became an artist but instead went into the family business and ran the brewery. He died in 1852 at the age of forty-three and was mourned by Browning as Charles in the poem 'May and Death'. Much of what the poem commemorates is tactfully implicit, but there are memories of returning from the magic of Kean's performances, the excitement after the theatre of

> ... a pair of friends
> Who, arm in arm, deserve the warm
> Moon-births and the long evening-ends.

Most of all it is a poem of the Camberwell woods in spring, a memory of the scene familiar to Browning and his cousins, where one plant

> ... starts up green
> Save a sole streak which, so to speak,
> Is spring's blood, spilt its leaves between.

The friendship with the Silverthornes, despite its shared artistic enthusiasms, had the quality of adolescent *bonhomie*, turning later into a deeper affection. The case of Sarah and Eliza Flower was very different. With Browning their relationship was sentimental, passionate, even perhaps morbid. It seems that he was twelve years old when he first met them. Eliza would then have been twenty-one and Sarah nineteen. Mrs Sutherland Orr, who was Browning's friend and after his death published a biography relying a good deal on his surviving sister, is quite clear that despite the difference of nine years in age Browning fell in love with Eliza Flower. He 'conceived a warm admiration for Miss Flower's talents, and a boyish love for herself'.[64] Since he remained close to the sisters until he was sixteen, such a thing is not impossible. He had before him the difference in his parents' ages and, indeed, was six years younger than his own future wife.

The two sisters, despite their comparative youth, were figures of some importance in the world of early nineteenth-century Nonconformity. Their own father, Benjamin Flower, had been a martyr to the vested power of the House of Lords, which in 1799 had fined and imprisoned him for a libel on one of its members, the Bishop of Llandaff. There had been no trial and, of course, no jury. This spectacle of the Established Church and an unreformed parliament acting in a manner worthy of the Tudors and the Stuarts was an object-lesson to the world of political and religious dissent.

At the death of their father in 1829 the two orphaned sisters became wards of W. J. Fox, a Unitarian minister and journalist who was to prove Browning's literary godfather. He was a contributor to the *Westminster Review*, editor himself of the *Monthly Repository*, to which John Stuart Mill and Harriet Martineau, as well as Browning, were contributors. His friends included the actor Macready and the critic John Forster.

Fox's career and reputation had been remarkable. As a preacher he was so compelling that his followers built the famous South Place Chapel for him in 1824. All too soon he was disowned by his flock. This was in part due to his unorthodox opinions but no less to the scandal of his domestic life. Eliza, the elder of the Flower sisters, moved in and replaced Mrs Fox, who nevertheless remained a member of the *ménage*. Eliza ran the household until her death in 1846, acquiring contemporary fame as the writer of political songs and of music to *Hymns and Anthems* for South Place Chapel.

Eighteen twenty-four was both the year of Fox's triumph at South Place and of Byron's death. At twelve years old, Browning had written his first poem of significance, 'Incondita', which had been composed both in admiration and imitation of the dead romantic hero. His mother made a copy of the poem and his parents approached several London publishers in hope and expectation. The poem was politely declined. Mrs Browning showed it to Eliza Flower who, in turn, showed it to Fox.

Fox, by now an arbiter of literary taste as well as a preacher, reported that 'Incondita' was promising but, it was said, he found in it 'too great splendour of language and too little wealth of thought'.[65] Browning himself, always sensitive to the follies of his early work, later retrieved and destroyed such copies of the poem as had survived.

Although Fox was to be Browning's literary patron, he received a letter in 1827 from the younger sister, Sarah Flower, which must have made him regret that either of the two girls had ever set eyes upon the future poet. Though Sarah was twenty-two and Browning only fifteen, she announced that he had converted her to atheism. 'The cloud has come over me gradually,' she confessed, adding later: 'It was in answering Robert Browning that my mind refused to bring forward argument, turned recreant, and sided with the enemy.'[66]

Even if he mixed profligacy with piety to the extent alleged by his critics, Fox had reason to be alarmed at Sarah's intellectual apostasy. He need not have worried. She recovered her faith and became the author of one of the most famous hymns in the English language, *Nearer, my God, to Thee*. But what had happened to Robert Browning, the contented child of Nonconformity, to make him such a persuasive atheist in his early teens?

If one word could answer the question, it was 'Shelley', but that was an over-simplification. In 1826, according to Browning, his cousin James Silverthorne presented him with Shelley's *Miscellaneous Poems*. These were issued by William Benbow, who had been variously prosecuted for seditious libel and obscenity in respect of other items on his list.[67] To the beauty of the poems, combining romantic and classical appeal as Lairesse had done in landscape, was added the sense of political and doctrinal persecution. Shelley, renouncing his patrician and orthodox background, was by proxy at least to share the political and religious disqualifications which lay, however mildly, upon the Brownings.

It would have been strange if Browning, at fourteen, had remained indifferent to Shelley's genius. In 1827 he persuaded his parents to enquire through the columns of the *Literary Gazette* where other poems of Shelley's could be bought. This took Mrs Browning to the office of Hunt and Clarke in York Street, Covent Garden. Among the volumes which she purchased for her son was the *Posthumous Poems* of 1824, including 'Alastor' and 'The Witch of Atlas'. Whether she acquired *Queen Mab*, 'Mr Shelley's Atheistical Poem: very scarce', is an open question. Like Thomas Paine's *Age of Reason* it was circulated by deists and atheists as a defiance of the blasphemy laws, though it was successfully prosecuted until 1840.

To a teenage poet who had good reason to despise the cynical corruption of pre-reform politics, Shelley offered a banner of liberty under which it was a privilege to march. As Mrs Shelley was to write in her preface to the collected edition of the poems in 1839: 'the younger generation rising around ... cannot remember the scorn and hatred with which the partisans of reform were regarded some few years ago, nor the persecutions to which they were exposed'.[68] To the young rebel there was also an intoxicating violence in some of Shelley's language. Part of the preface to *Hellas*, denouncing 'those ringleaders of the

23

privileged gangs of murderers and swindlers, called Sovereigns', was even suppressed until Buxton Forman's edition of the poet's works in 1892.

How agreeable, too, to identify oneself at that age with Alastor, described by Shelley as 'a youth of uncorrupted feelings and adventurous genius', whose experience of 'all that is excellent and majestic' leads him on to become the perfect poet.[69] How well this accorded with Browning's own ambition 'to be a Poet, if not *the* Poet'.[70]

As for the atheism which Browning acquired from Shelley, it was as exclusively moral as the short-lived vegetarianism. In later years, particularly in his *Essay on Shelley* in 1852, Browning regarded the older poet's atheism as being temporary, as his own had been. It was a mere moral anger against God for the imperfections of the world, an anger that would have been subdued had Shelley lived to grow into a fuller understanding.

> Nor will men persist in confounding, any more than God confounds, with genuine infidelity and an atheism of the heart, those passionate, impatient struggles of a boy towards distant truth and love, made in the dark, and ended by one sweep of the natural seas before the full moral sunrise could shine out upon him.[71]

In his adolescence Browning had read Voltaire as well as Shelley. Yet the atheism which he embraced was not the cool witty demolition of belief by Voltaire's cruel precision. It was the honest moral indignation of Shelley, whose anger in *Queen Mab* requires the existence of a God to berate and abuse. Shelley, the moral atheist of the Regency, caricatured the Deity as Gillray's prints had lampooned the Prince of Wales, or Cruikshank's contemporaries caricatured politicians like Sidmouth and Castlereagh. Looking upon the sufferings of the world in *Queen Mab*, Shelley sees the constant threat of hell for those who had endured torments enough on earth, and heaven as a reward for the servile. His denunciations are aimed against a God who appears like a celestial and omnipotent Lord Liverpool.

> A vengeful, pitiless, and almighty fiend,
> Whose mercy is a nick-name for the rage
> Of tameless tigers hungering for blood.

When Browning insisted that Shelley, had he lived, would have matured in understanding and abandoned his youthful unbelief, he was describing his own case. Before his teens were over he had returned to Christianity in much the same form as he had left it. A quarter of a century later, in Italy, Browning laconically observed the attraction that Catholic church decoration and ritual held for his own infant son. He remarked blandly that 'it is as well to have the eyeteeth and the Puseyistical crisis over together'.[72]

In his own youth it seems that the problems of adolescence and the atheistical crisis were over together. Yet this was not quite true. The experience through which he had passed was surely the stuff of poetry to a young romantic prepared to lay bare his soul to the world. At the age of twenty Browning had written a poem which he termed 'A Fragment of a Confession'. It was far in advance of the early 'Incondita' and, indeed, this time there was to be no difficulty with the London publishers. The poem might now make its own way. When it was finished, in the autumn of 1832, Christiana Silverthorne, Mrs Browning's sister and mother of the three Silverthorne boys, said to her nephew: 'I hear, Robert, that you have written a poem; here is the money to print it.'[73]

2

A Fragment
of a Confession

'By-the-bye, did you ever happen upon Browning's *Pauline?*' Joseph
Arnould asked Alfred Domett in 1847, 'a strange, wild (in parts singu-
larly magnificent) poet-biography ...'.[1] Fifteen years earlier, when the
poet's aunt Mrs Silverthorne offered to pay for its publication, that was
precisely the type of poem most likely to do justice to its author's private
personality and public reputation.

Ambitious, 'supremely passionate' in his own estimate, darkly handsome in a manner both romantic and urbane, Robert Browning in the
first decade of manhood combined an air of youthful fashion and future
promise.[2] The most vivid impression of him as a young man in the reign
of William IV was recorded by the daughter of W. J. Fox, recalling his
visits to her father.

> I remember when Browning entered the drawing-room, with a quick light
> step; and on learning from me that my father was out, and in fact that
> nobody was at home but myself, he said: 'It's my birthday to-day; I'll wait
> till they come in,' and sitting down to the piano, he added: 'If it won't
> disturb you, I'll play till they do.' ... He was then slim and dark, and very
> handsome; and – may I hint it – just a trifle of a dandy, addicted to lemon-
> coloured kid-gloves and such things: quite 'the glass of fashion and the mould
> of form.' But full of ambition, eager for success, eager for fame, and, what's
> more, determined to conquer fame and to achieve success.[3]

As Elizabeth Barrett Browning later confided to her sister Arabel,
there was a tradition in her husband's family that 'a Browning can fail
in nothing'.[4] Nonconformist beliefs in the virtues of industriousness and
self-improvement, stimulated by the challenge of achievement against
hostile prejudices, had a part to play in this. Yet the thrust of poetic
ambition was not always attractive. It made him self-centred, capable
of a degree of self-possession which verged upon arrogance, and bred in
him a literary self-righteousness which tolerated neither adverse criticism nor hesitant acceptance.

By the autumn of 1832 it seemed to Browning there was nothing that was impossible to him in the arts. He had conceived what he later called 'a foolish plan' to produce under different names 'this poem, the other novel, such an opera, such a speech, etc. etc.'. As for *Pauline*, 'The present abortion was the first work of the *Poet* of the batch.'[5] He soon modified his ambition to the production of 'a series of monodramatic epics'.[6]

In one respect, at least, all such things were possible to him. His father was not rich by the standards of those whom Byron had called England's wealthiest sons, yet he had money enough to provide for Sarianna and to ensure that if his son chose the life of a poet he would never starve. When the possibility of a career was discussed, the young Browning had asked 'to see life in the best sense, and cultivate the powers of his mind'. At all costs he would not 'shackle himself in the very outset of his career by a laborious training, foreign to that aim'.[7]

The father, remembering the vindictive philistinism of his own parent, granted the request. Browning from then on felt that he had been bequeathed a sacred trust, which was financial as well as poetic. He managed his life with a banker's fastidiousness, showing, as his wife described it, a horror of 'owing five shillings five days, which I call quite morbid in its degree and extent'.[8] Nor was it merely in matters of money that there was faith to be kept or a debt to be discharged. Throughout his life the obligation to work as a poet lay upon Browning's conscience. The motives for such industriousness as led to his last book appearing on the very day of his death were varied. Yet in his own mind, one of them was clear beyond doubt.

> It would have been quite unpardonable in my case not to have done my best. My dear father put me in a condition most favourable for the best work I was capable of.... He secured for me all the ease and comfort that a literary man needs to do good work. It would have been shameful if I had not done my best to realize his expectations of me.[9]

In the shadow of such decisions and obligations *Pauline* was written and published anonymously. Originally, Browning recalled, it was conceived as part of his scheme to be poet, musician, and even actor. Not only was that scheme abandoned but *Pauline* remained incomplete, 'A Fragment of a Confession', once intended to rival Byron's *Childe Harold's Pilgrimage* or Wordsworth's yet unpublished *Prelude* as a statement of the romantic soul.

The poem is dated 'Richmond, October 1832', a reference to its conception rather than its completion. On that evening Browning had gone to the theatre in Richmond to see the great, though ailing, Ed-mund Kean in one of his last performances as Richard III. Under the influence of the tragedian's fading power, the young man conceived his grandiose scheme of which *Pauline* was the first project – '*que de châteaux en Espagne!*' wrote the middle-aged poet in his copy of the book.

Wordsworth, Byron, but most of all Shelley served as exemplars for the poem. Browning chose to describe to his make-believe mistress Pauline what Wordsworth was later to call in the *Prelude* 'The Growth of a Poet's Mind'. His admiration of learning and antiquity; his youthful atheism and adulation of Shelley, 'Sun-treader'; the cynicism engen-dered by unbelief; the recovery of faith in God and the joy of passing with Pauline into an idyllic land: these stages of his development pro-vided a ready framework for more than a thousand lines of blank verse.

To the young romantic of the early 1830s the movement in whose wake he followed offered two major forms of poetic expression. Since the publication of Rousseau's *Confessions* in 1781 the description of inner experience, thinly disguised or without any disguise whatever, had become a fashionable mode of composition. Its rival was the drama for, as Victor Hugo remarked in the Preface to *Cromwell* (1828), 'the drama is the distinguishing characteristic of the third epoch of poetry, of the literature of the present day'.[10] Shelley had used both the confessional and the dramatic form. Seven years before Hugo, though the *Defence of Poetry* was not published until 1840, he had made the same choice. 'The drama being the form under which a greater number of modes of expression of poetry are susceptible of being combined than any other, the connexion of poetry and social good is more observable in the drama than in whatever other form.'[11] It was quite natural that Browning, having tried one mode of romantic expression in *Pauline*, should later regard drama as a self-evident alternative.

Who was Pauline in relation to the poet? It was a question any reader of the poem was likely to ask upon its publication in March 1833. Browning, despite his appearance and manner of a romantic dandy, showed no sign of passionate involvement with a woman. Ambition of his kind appeared to preclude sexual love. Referring to his literary début he explained to his future wife: 'My whole scheme of life ... was long ago calculated – and it supposed *you*, the finding such an one as you, utterly impossible.'[12] Soon afterwards he added that he had 'for many years now made up my mind to the impossibility of loving any woman'.[13]

By introducing such a figure in a confessional poem, placing an intermediary between himself and the reader, Browning was bound to invite speculations from biographers and critics alike as to the identity of his secret mistress. One or both of the Flower sisters proved to be favourite candidates. She is almost certainly an invented figure, enabling Browning to give some degree of objectivity to what would otherwise be a direct self-revelation to the reader. Perhaps more to the point is the type of mistress she appears to be, as described in the opening lines of the poem.

> Pauline, mine own, bend o'er me – thy soft breast
> Shall pant to mine – bend o'er me – thy sweet eyes
> And loosened hair, and breathing lips, and arms
> Drawing me to thee – these build up a screen
> To shut me in with thee, and from all fear,
> So that I might unlock the sleepless brood
> Of fancies from my soul, their lurking place,
> Nor doubt that each would pass, ne'er to return
> To one so watched, so loved, and so secured.

Unless the lines are mere clichés of a romantic embrace, which seems unlikely, the figure of imagination is as much maternal as sexual. The opening of the poem describes her leaning over the poet as a mother might do with a child, forming 'a screen/To shut me in with thee'. Such phrases are as suggestive of a child's comfort in its mother as of a young man's happiness with his mistress. Even the remorse for youthful atheism and cynicism has the quality of a son's contrition.

> I had been spared this shame, if I had sate
> By thee for ever, from the first, in place
> Of my wild dreams of beauty and of good.

The place where he might have sat 'from the first' and avoided the fall occasioned by intellectual pride was no doubt at his mother's side in York Street Chapel under the suave approval of the Reverend Clayton's gaze.

In the development of Browning's mind, *Pauline* marked the most intense moment of his admiration for Shelley as a poet and a personal romantic god.

> Sun-treader – life and light be thine for ever;
> Thou art gone from us – years go by – and spring
> Gladdens, and the young earth is beautiful,
> Yet thy songs come not – other bards arise,
> But none like thee – they stand – thy majesties,
> Like mighty works which tell some Spirit there
> Hath sat regardless of neglect and scorn.

Even the recovery of faith involves Browning in no rejection of Shelley. 'Sun-treader, I believe in God, and truth,/And love.... Thou must be ever with me.' Anticipating the argument of his *Essay on Shelley* nineteen years later, Browning sees the older poet's anger against God as entirely compatible with a religious belief into which he would have grown – had he lived. Moving into the light of a new love of God, he carries Shelley with him.

The landscapes and moonscapes of Shelley, the caves and ruined temples haunted by figures of myth, found their reflection in the poetry of his young admirer. No less, the heroes of Shelley's poems 'Alastor' or 'Prince Athanase', which influenced the style of Browning's poetry, offered easy and agreeable patterns for self-identification by the young aspiring romantic. So, in 'Alastor':

> There was a Poet whose untimely tomb
> No human hands with pious reverence reared,
> But the charmed eddies of autumnal winds
> Built o'er his mouldering bones a pyramid.

'Prince Athanase' also invited the reader to assume the fancy dress of a young doomed romantic:

> There was a youth, who, as with toil and travel,
> Had grown quite weak and gray before his time;
> Nor any could the restless griefs unravel.

It does not belittle Shelley's poetry now to see him as a bad model. Tennyson had imitated Keats in 'Mariana' and was admired for it. But Shelley was a poet of strange, fragmented landscapes, vague emanations of light, of spheres and cycloramic vistas. In this aspect he anticipated some of the qualities of the Surrealists. Like them, he was a good stimulus but a bad pattern for imitation.

Some of Browning's images and descriptions, the allusions to Plato or Prometheus, were overtly Shelleyean. Others were drawn, in the first place, from the treasures of his own childhood, like the coveted print of Caravaggio's *Perseus and Andromeda*,

> ... so beautiful
> With her dark eyes, earnest and still, and hair
> Lifted and spread by the salt-sweeping breeze.

Despite the hostility of the critics, *Fraser's Magazine* in December 1833 dismissing Browning as The Mad Poet of the Batch, the poem was redeemed by the pictorial freshness of those descriptions recalling personal experience. Not surprisingly, one of these was an account of imagined glories to which he was led by the riches of his father's library.

> They came to me in my first dawn of life,
> Which passed alone with wisest ancient books,
> All halo-girt with fancies of my own,
> And I myself went with the tale, – a god,
> Wandering after beauty – or a giant,
> Standing vast in the sunset – an old hunter,
> Talking with gods – or a high-crested chief,
> Sailing with troops of friends to Tenedos.

Yet Browning soon had cause to wince over the poem's worst defects, the self-importance of a youth who believes his commonplace adolescent experiences have a unique public value.

> I am made up of an intensest life,
> Of a most clear idea of consciousness
> Of self.

Such passages stood high in the list of those which the poet, in his fame, would rather not have written. Bad poetry in the eighteenth century was dull or grandiose; in the romantic period it was more embarrassingly pretentious. 'Will you and must you have *Pauline?*' he pleaded with Elizabeth Barrett. 'It is altogether foolish and *not* boylike.'[14]

Something was saved from the wreck of this first book's hopes. W. J. Fox, to whom Browning had sent the poem, reviewed it in his *Monthly Repository* as 'a hasty and imperfect sketch' which was none the less cause enough to give a 'glorious leap' and shout 'Eureka!' at the prospect of what the young poet would one day achieve. Allan Cunningham in the *Athenaeum* also found fault with the structure of the poem, but generously praised its 'nature, passion, and fancy in individual passages'.[15] It was Cunningham's notice which Browning later said 'gratified me and my people far beyond what will ever be the fortune of criticism now'.[16]

The most important review was never published. John Stuart Mill was to have written a notice for the liberal Sunday paper, the *Examiner*. The review was never completed, but the notes which Mill had made were written in his copy of the book. This was sent back to Fox, who in turn showed the comments to Browning. 'With considerable poetic powers,' Mill concluded, 'the writer seems to me possessed with a more intense and morbid self-consciousness than I ever knew in any sane human being.'[17] The character of Pauline, in Mill's view, was a mere fiction, and he doubted the sincerity of Browning's hatred of his own past selfishness. All the same, 'the psychological history of himself is powerful and truthful – *truth-like* certainly, all but the last stage'.[18]

The more extravagant forms of romantic self-display were not to the taste of the great Utilitarian. Browning felt, as he later said, that his early poems had been 'so transparent in their meaning as to draw down upon him the ridicule of the critics, and that, boy as he was, this ridicule and censure stung him into quite another style of writing'.[19] If reviewers from now on complained of the obscurity of his poetry, it seemed they had only themselves to blame. Moreover, his hypersensitive reaction to a mixed press turned him from a confessional into a dramatic poet. When his *Dramatic Lyrics* appeared in 1842 he made a point of announcing in the advertisement that the poems were 'always Dramatic in principle, and so many utterances of so many imaginary persons, not mine'. In the years after *Pauline* his romantic allegiance had not changed, but he had chosen its alternative mode of expression.

The reputation for morbidity and an attraction to madness was another matter. His interest in the darker paths of human behaviour grew until many of his readers found that the chatter of the madhouse and the intent voice of the obsessive were uncomfortably close to the surface of some of his finest poems. Even in *Pauline* the hint of romanticism grown sick is readily exploited. The girl's blood is as important to him as the other accoutrements of her beauty.

> How the blood lies upon her cheek, all spread
> As thinned by kisses; only in her lips
> It wells and pulses like a living thing.

All of which leads to assurance of the supreme gratification in love: 'As I might kill her and be loved for it.' Though it was not then public knowledge, Browning in his early twenties had written poems of a type to shock – or in some cases to intrigue – his contemporaries, bringing him artistic praise and moral misgivings in equal measure.

Pauline's epitaph came almost fifteen years later when Browning received a letter from a young man who called himself 'a most enthusiastic admirer of your works'. In the British Museum the young man had encountered the anonymous *Pauline*. Surely, 'this beautiful composition ... presents a noticeable analogy to your first acknowledged work *Paracelsus*'. The correspondent, Dante Gabriel Rossetti, thus confronted him with the poem's authorship.[20]

Browning's groan of despair at not being able to suppress *Pauline* as he had done his boyhood 'Incondita' was tempered by the genuine admiration of his early work which grew up in the 1850s and 1860s.

England's late Georgian culture in the 1830s had wearied of romantic posturings. To a later generation, notably the Pre-Raphaelites and their sympathizers, the pictorial qualities of *Pauline*, the description of the girl and of Andromeda, or the orchards and woods of Camberwell, offered gems of light and colour. That these admirers thought far more highly of the poem than its author did was a measure of the effect the critics had had upon him. He was never to allow himself to be so browbeaten by the reviewers again.

It had cost Mrs Silverthorne £30 to pay for the printing and advertising of *Pauline*. As Browning later learnt, not one copy was sold. For all his self-confidence and ambition, the experience of publication had scarcely been encouraging. He had put before the world this analysis of a poet's soul with all the frankness and romantic sensibility of a Shelley or a Byron. The world yawned, politely or otherwise, and turned its back.

The thrust of energy in Browning's personality, the need for occupation, was a characteristic of his entire life. Now there were discussions as to what alternative profession he might pursue. It was possible, after all, to be a man of affairs and write a good deal of poetry at the same time. He seemed most suited either for a career at the Bar or else as a diplomat. The first of these choices he regarded with professed repugnance and later lampooned in the characters of his lawyers in *The Ring and the Book*. 'I desire to be very rich, very great,' he wrote to Elizabeth Barrett, 'but not in reading Law gratis with dear foolish old Basil Montagu, as he ever and anon bothers me to do.'[21] Browning's interest in crime and the behaviour which engendered it was profound. The practice of law had no appeal for him.

Diplomacy was not treated with the same scorn. Edmund Gosse, observing Browning in old age, saw how easily the excitement of travel had taken the place of the excitement of writing.[22] In 1835 Browning applied to accompany a mission to Persia and, after his marriage to Elizabeth Barrett, invited Monckton Milnes to find him a post as a British diplomat at the Vatican.

Nothing came of these applications, but there was no doubt of his enthusiasm for the glamour and intrigue of diplomacy. His only taste of it came after the disappointment over *Pauline*, a visit to Russia in the spring of 1834. It was through his Uncle Reuben's connections at Rothschild's bank, probably in the course of loan negotiations with Russia, that the chance occurred. The Russian consul-general in London, the Chevalier de Benkhausen, was to visit St Petersburg for three months or so in the spring of 1834. He agreed to take Browning as his secretary.

The party left London at the end of February, travelling across Holland and northern Germany. To his family Browning described 'the endless monotony of snow-covered pine-forests, through which he and his companion rushed for days and nights at the speed of six post-horses'.[23] The remote tracts of eastern Europe, hardly known at all in English experience, left their impression on his imagination. Forty-five years later, in 'Ivàn Ivànovitch' from *Dramatic Idylls*, he wrote of a similar journey.

> Through forestry right and left, black verst and verst of pine,
> From village to village runs the road's long wide bare line.
> Clearance and clearance break the else-unconquered growth
> Of pine and all that breeds and broods there.

The spring that had begun in the west was scarcely visible in the villages of Lithuania or Russia,

> Snow-whitened everywhere except the middle road
> Ice-roughed by track of sledge.

The capital city to which he came was the St Petersburg of Dostoevsky's 'White Nights', which with the coming of spring 'reveals herself in all her might and glory, in all the splendour with which heaven has endowed her, in the way she blossoms out, dresses up, decks herself out with flowers'.[24] The grandeur of the city, its royal residences and the treasures of the Hermitage, was summed up by the pageant which Browning watched when the ice on the Neva was broken and the tsar drank the first glass of water from it. But the colour and vivacity of the peasants' life remained with him too. He wrote to Elizabeth Barrett of material for a play – never to be written – 'a fair on the Neva, and booths and droshkies and fish-pies and so forth, with the palaces in the back ground'.[25]

When Browning returned to London in the summer of 1834 he had enjoyed his first and last experience of diplomacy. Yet his life was full and even busy with all the occupations of a man about town. Indeed, 'this light rational life I lead', as he called it, might have beguiled a lesser man into indolence.[26] There was little danger in that for one who, in his wife's words, was 'descended from the blood of all the Puritans and educated by the strictest of dissenters'.[27]

Yet such Puritanism was not incompatible with a casual and agreeable life among young men of talent and ambition. One such group in

Camberwell, to which Browning belonged, was the Colloquials. It was a provincial counterpart of the more famous Apostles at Cambridge, in which Tennyson, Arthur Hallam, Monckton Milnes and the more obvious heirs to established power were members. In another sense it was the forerunner of the Old Mortality at Oxford, twenty years later, founded by Swinburne and the natural rebels against established power.

The Colloquials were provincial but not impoverished. They met in one another's houses and established their own journal, the *Trifler*, in 1835. Browning contributed to this a facetious answer to an essay on debt and two epigrams on the dullness of his old headmaster, Thomas Ready. Yet the Colloquials were far removed from the patrician independence of the Apostles or the Old Mortality. There was a cosiness and domesticity about their meetings. A younger brother of one member recalled the pride of the parents, especially the mothers, in their clever sons, and how 'my mother liked us to be in the drawing-room on the evenings when those young men used to come in for tea after their debates'.[28] Among the Colloquials were two contemporaries who became Browning's friends. Unlike him, they were members of the Established Church and had therefore followed more straightforward careers.

Joseph Arnould, two years his junior, had been educated at Charterhouse and Wadham College, Oxford, where he won the Newdigate Prize for poetry, took a first, and became a fellow until his marriage in 1841. Then, having been called to the Bar at the Middle Temple, he later went to India, becoming a judge of the Bombay supreme court in 1859. His admiration and affection for Browning is recorded in the letters that Arnould wrote in the early 1840s. To Arnould, Browning was 'a true friend ... an energy of kindness about him.... He is a noble fellow. His life so pure, so energetic, so simple, so laborious, so loftily enthusiastic. It is impossible to know and not to love him.'[29]

Browning's closest friend among the Colloquials was Alfred Domett, a year his senior. Domett was educated at St John's College, Cambridge, and, like Arnould, was called to the Bar at the Middle Temple in 1841. Like Arnould, too, he left England for a life in the colonies, becoming prime minister of New Zealand in 1862–3. On his sudden emigration in 1842 Browning made him the subject of 'Waring'.

> What's become of Waring
> Since he gave us all the slip ...?

Before then, Domett had already travelled in Italy, Austria, Canada, the United States and the West Indies. He returned to England from New Zealand in 1871 and resumed the friendship with Browning which

35

lasted until Domett's death in 1887. Like Browning and Arnould, Domett was a poet, best known for his *Ranolf and Amohia, a South Sea Day Dream* (1872).

Until he was over thirty, Browning's friendships were mainly with companions of this kind. A few, Domett and Arnould among them, became his lifelong natural friends. In a wider sphere he lived as though a member of an extended club made up of the affable, intelligent and prosperous young men of his acquaintance. In terms of Victorian achievement they would not take the most glittering prizes of fame and high office, reserved for Monckton Milnes, Tennyson and the protégés of the Apostles. But in the colonies or in the middle ranks of public life at home their success was undoubted and ungrudged. This was a consideration that occupied Browning's thoughts more than he cared to admit, the haunting contrast in his case between the soaring reputation of Tennyson and his own recognition withheld, year after year and decade after decade.

While the profession of the law, which he despised, provided him with such companions, that of diplomacy introduced him to another who was to have an immediate effect upon the direction of his poetry. It was in the summer of his return from Russia that Browning met the Count Amédée de Ripert-Monclar. Monclar at twenty-six was a full-faced young man with the high dome of intellect, a type clearly defined for Browning, who showed a wry and sceptical interest in the current quack science of phrenology. Monclar was not an exile, despite the antipathy of the new regime of Louis Philippe, but became a regular visitor to England in the 1830s. He had an interest in finance and a pretension to authorship, the former of which brought him to Reuben Browning, who in turn introduced him to his nephew.

Like James Silverthorne, Monclar was a congenial literary mentor. More than that, his urbanity and cosmopolitan taste enabled him to illuminate by a French and European insight the literature and art with which Browning had long been familiar. Guiding him to Balzac and a new generation of realists in France, Monclar became a most valued acquaintance. At another level he renewed Browning's enthusiasm for a life of diplomacy, since Monclar was secretly acting as a contact between Bourbon exiles in England and the royalists in France. To the excitement of Russian travel there was now added the spice of revolutionary intrigue.

Before the summer of 1834 was over, Monclar led his friend towards a new conception of human character in poetry. He first suggested the life of Paracelsus as a suitable subject for poetry, then had second

thoughts and advised against it 'because it gave no room for the introduction of love'.[30] His reservations came too late. Browning saw in the
story of Paracelsus, a name adopted by the sixteenth-century physician
Theophrastus Bombast von Hohenstein, all that was needed to justify
himself after the failure of *Pauline*.

There was much in the character of Paracelsus which appealed
directly to Browning. The sixteenth-century physician had been a seeker
after curious knowledge and, in one legend, sought the elixir of life
which he believed to exist in the East. By seeking knowledge and the
good of humankind at the expense of love, he broke the cardinal rule of
Shelleyean romanticism. Yet in his inevitable fall he was as much the
romantic victim as Goethe's Faust, Shelley's Prometheus, or even
Milton's Lucifer in the eyes of Blake and Shelley.

Paracelsus owes much to Alastor, described in Shelley's preface as
one who 'drinks deep at the fountains of knowledge and is still insatiate'.
Too late, he sees that the power of knowing is acquired at the expense
of the power to love. 'Blasted by disappointment,' as Shelley puts it in
the preface to his own poem, 'he descends to an untimely grave.' His
tragedy lies in forfeiting love by intellectual and spiritual arrogance, the
fate avoided by the narrator of *Pauline* who recognized his errors before
they destroyed him.

This time there was to be no question of presenting the poem as its
author's confession. However intriguingly the self-centred Paracelsus,
with his uncompromising ambition, his hunger for learning and fame,
might seem to be the young Browning in fancy dress, the identification
was not admitted. The poem was cast in the form of a verse drama, not
adapted to the stage. Its five acts presented Paracelsus at the crises of
life: determined to seek knowledge at all costs; confronted by the poet
Aprile, the spirit of love, and spurning him; realizing the failure of his
life; turning to grosser pleasures; his final thoughts and reconciliation in
the shadow of approaching death.

Of the three other figures in the drama, the poet Aprile with his
devotion to love and beauty, even at the expense of knowledge, is
another representation of Browning's idol Shelley. Festus and Michal,
the male and female friends of Paracelsus, have a parental role, advising,
cautioning, agreeing with him at first, commiserating and comforting
when that seems more appropriate. There is little justification for
reading the poem as a direct reference to Browning's thoughts about
himself, yet in the opening scene with Festus and Michal anxiously
advising on the choice of life there is the distinct air of a family confer-
ence in Southampton Street.

37

If the poetic drama he wrote is ill suited to the stage this is largely because it reflects the great central preoccupation of Browning's art, the anatomy of the human mind and the conduct it dictates. In general, the greater the degree of morbidity involved, the more he relished it. *Pauline* might have been simply a romantic confessional poem. By the time that he wrote the preface to *Paracelsus* in March 1835, the tone of clinical enthusiasm and the glint of the literary scalpel were in evidence. He clearly sets out his intention 'to reverse the method usually adopted by writers whose aim is to set forth any phenomenon of the mind or the passions'. There will be, he promises, no characters or action required to demonstrate the psychology of his hero. Instead, 'to create and evolve the crisis I desire to produce, I have ventured to display somewhat minutely the mood itself in its rise and progress, and have suffered the agency by which it is influenced and determined to be generally discernible in its effects alone.'

All of which was only to say that *Paracelsus* became what the twentieth century, in general usage, calls psychological drama. Had it been remarkable for nothing else, its hopes would have been slight. By contrast with *Pauline*, Paracelsus' successive mental states are succinctly delineated in his pursuit of knowledge, from 'A ready answer to the will of God' to 'an arrogant self-reliance' and 'A monstrous spectacle ... A being knowing not what love is'.

No less than in its shrewd analysis of motive and belief, the poem appealed by the sheer descriptive brilliance of many pictorial images, whether in the calm sunlit garden at Würzburg or the gorgeous evening panorama of Constantinople.

> Over the waters in the vaporous west
> The sun goes down as in a sphere of gold
> Behind the outstretched city, which between,
> With all that length of domes and minarets
> Athwart the splendour, black and crooked runs
> Like a Turk verse along a scimitar.

The power and concision of such writing shone out among the run of mediocre poetry which characterized the mid-1830s. In his description of the poem's only female character, Michal, for example, Browning anticipates something of the Pre-Raphaelite qualities by linking her elusive beauty with the easy appeal and background of a Victorian genre painting.

> ... Michal's face
> Still wears that quiet and peculiar light,

Like the dim circlet floating round a pearl
      . . . And yet her calm sweet countenance,
Though saintly, was not sad; for she would sing
Alone. . . . Does she still sing alone, bird-like,
Not dreaming you are near? Her carols dropt
In flakes through that old leafy bower built under
The sunny wall at Würzburg, from her lattice
Among the trees above, while I, unseen,
Sate conning some rare scroll from Tritheim's shelves.

Many of the ingredients in such images are the stuff of which popular Victorian painting was made: the light on the girl's face, the lattice above, the leafy bower and trees, the young man reading as the notes of the song reach him. To many of Browning's middle-class readers it was to seem an idealized glimpse of home, the suburban idyll to which they, like he, might aspire.

Indeed, the Würzburg garden at sunset in Act I of *Paracelsus* had its counterpart in the enclosed summer garden at Camberwell. Outside the smoky little room, as he called it, where Browning worked, the insect worlds of hedge and wall presented the substance of poetry.

        This kingdom, limited
Alone by one old populous green wall,
Tenanted by the ever-busy flies,
Grey crickets, and shy lizards, and quick spiders,
Each family of the silver-threaded moss. . . .
Yon painted snail, with his gay shell of dew,
Travelling to see the glossy balls high up
Hung by the caterpillar, like gold lamps.

As clearly as any letter or diary, such passages show the private summer world of 1834 upon which Browning looked as he worked in the solitude of his room in Southampton Street.

Paracelsus was a success with the critics, a poem of which Browning remained proud. 'By the author of *Paracelsus*' was the description of himself on the title-pages of his subsequent books for many years to come. Its pictorial qualities were simply enjoyed. Moreover, the poem discusses life's fundamental questions in terms calculated to appeal to the thinking man of the 1830s who need not regard himself as a scholar. It was popular, as Tennyson's philosophizing was popular. Its dialogues discussed the qualities of love and their relation to human experience. It developed a post-romantic idea of nature as an extension of human thought rather than the object of it. In dealing with human perfectibility, it did so in a popular manner that had more in

39

common with Macaulay's political optimism than with the strictly evolutionary *Origin of Species*.

A publisher was found for *Paracelsus*, Effingham Wilson of the Royal Exchange. The book was issued in August 1835. Though the *Athenaeum* pontificated on the foolishness of young men imitating Shelley, there was favourable notice elsewhere. W. J. Fox was enthusiastic in the *Monthly Repository*. There was praise from Leigh Hunt's *Journal* in November and from a biographer and critic of Browning's own age, John Forster. In the *Examiner* for 6 September 1835 Forster guessed that the author of *Paracelsus* was a young man, since his name was new. 'If so, we may safely predict for him a brilliant career, if he continues true to the present promise of his genius. He possesses all the elements of a fine poet.' Six months later, in the *New Monthly Magazine* for March 1836, there appeared an article on 'Evidences of a New Genius for Dramatic Poetry'. This too was the work of Forster, and much of it was devoted to Browning. 'Without the slightest hesitation,' it concluded, 'we name Mr Robert Browning at once with Shelley, Coleridge, and Wordsworth .... he has in himself all the elements of a great poet, philosophical as well as dramatic.'[31]

Forster's acclaim was in part the battle-cry of a young generation on the verge of replacing its predecessor in popular esteem. Unlike *Pauline*, *Paracelsus* bore Browning's name upon its title-page, a formal announcement of the poetic career which he now pursued with all the meticulously applied zeal of a banker.

Paracelsus won Browning his first literary fame from the reviewers. It also launched him into the cultural society of London during the declining years of William IV. His proud patron, W. J. Fox, gave a dinner at his home in Bayswater on 27 November 1835 at which the principal guest was the great successor to Edmund Kean, the tragedian W. C. Macready. It was a spirited gathering, Fox enlivening the meal by vigorously defending his view that Lady Macbeth was best portrayed as a delicate, fragile creature on the stage rather than a figure of demonic strength.

After dinner, Browning arrived and was brought in to be introduced. Macready, echoing the views of so many others, noted: 'he looks and speaks more like a youthful poet than any man I ever saw'.[32] Macready in his middle forties had a strong square-jawed handsomeness, a mercurial temper and generosity, which might well have matched Browning's own. In friendship or hostility the two men had much in common.

At their first meeting, after Fox's dinner, the sympathy between them was immediate. Macready was frankly admiring in respect of Browning's achievement, in such a manner that the younger man could hardly fail to be flattered. He sent the great actor a copy of *Paracelsus*. In portentous cadences of a kind to still the pit and gallery, Macready duly prophesied 'the writer can scarcely fail to be a leading spirit of his time'.[33]

The story of the friendship between Browning and Macready belongs to another chapter. Yet in itself it led the younger man to further acquaintanceships and to lasting sympathies. He was invited to dinner at the tragedian's Elstree home on 31 December 1835. That morning he went to the Blue Posts in Holborn and took the coach to Edgware and Elstree. While waiting at the Blue Posts he noticed one or two other young men among the passengers looking at him with curiosity, particularly 'a tall, ardent, noticeable young fellow'. They rode in silence together to Elstree and then, of course, found themselves Macready's guests. 'Did you see a little notice I wrote of you in the *Examiner*?' asked the tall young man. He was Browning's admirer John Forster.[34]

Between Browning and Forster friendship prospered easily, though its future course was less smooth. Both were precocious and ambitious. Yet between one who was critic and historian and a second who was a poet, there was no direct sense of rivalry. Admiration and gratitude were easily exchanged. Moreover, Forster counted Charles Lamb and Leigh Hunt among his older friends, winning their sympathy for Browning as well.

This entrance into literary society had been effected through the good offices of W. J. Fox. But Fox did more than that. In his Bayswater sitting-room 'with its chintzes and black-framed engravings', Browning read *Paracelsus* aloud to selected visitors. Unlike Tennyson's incantatory style of reading, Browning delivered his own lines with an incisive sense of timing and drama, much in the manner of an actor. These recitations attracted a certain notice. Through Mary Cowden Clarke, the daughter of Fox's neighbours, and her husband Charles, the young poet-actor was introduced to Edward Moxon.

Moxon, at thirty-four, was already on his way to becoming the most celebrated of London publishers. He was also the husband of Charles Lamb's adopted daughter. So far, Browning had found encouragement from Fox, and admiration from Macready and Forster. What he lacked, perhaps, was a man with commanding sense of the literary and financial realities of publication. Moxon's success in both spheres was illustrated by the authors whom he had brought to fame by the time of his death in 1858. They included Wordsworth, Shelley, Southey,

Tennyson, Landor and Coventry Patmore. Of all the friendships that resulted from *Paracelsus*, that with Moxon was among the most important to Browning as a poet.

The change which all these acquaintanceships wrought in Browning's life was seen most clearly on 26 May 1836. It was the occasion of a famous supper party after the first night of a new tragedy, *Ion*, at Covent Garden. The author was Thomas Noon Talfourd, poet, barrister and MP, future judge, literary journalist, and editor of Charles Lamb's papers. He was also to defend Moxon on charges of blasphemous libel arising out of the publication of Shelley's poetry.

Browning was invited to the select *Ion* supper as a friend of Fox and Macready. When the guests sat down he found himself opposite Macready. Yet it was the figures of the elderly men on either side of Macready to whom he paid most attention. On the left was Walter Savage Landor, on the right William Wordsworth. For the first of these Browning was to develop an admiration which turned into veneration. For the second he felt an irradicable distaste.

Talfourd showed an engaging mixture of vanity and generosity. He was eagerly binding congratulatory messages on *Ion* into splendid volumes and was now upon the second book of them. Yet as his turn came to propose a toast he announced the Poets of England, coupled with the name of Robert Browning, the youngest guest. It was at this point that Wordsworth himself leant across and said (with 'august affability' as Browning recalled): 'I am proud to drink your health, Mr Browning!'[35]

To a young poet of twenty-four it might seem that the gods of an older generation had smiled upon him. Yet while the approval of Landor was treasured by Browning, his personal feelings for Wordsworth were rarely disguised. The Laureate was, after all, the man who had deserted the cause of both revolution and reform, becoming a placeman of the ministry of Lord Liverpool, that most despised of Tory governments in the recent past. Talfourd brought the two poets together at his house on future occasions, but to little purpose. Wordsworth with his 'slow talk' and ageing conservatism was far removed from the impulsive, searching spirit of Browning's mind. The poet of *Paracelsus* 'never got over the somewhat chilling and awful personal bearing of the old man'.[36] The spectre of the renegade romantic and revolutionary, laden with the honours of treason, was to be exorcised five years before Wordsworth's death in Browning's 'The Lost Leader', from *Dramatic Romances and Lyrics* (1845).

> Just for a handful of silver he left us,
> Just for a riband to stick in his coat.

However unfairly, this was the caricature of the great rebel, with his laureateship and his time-server's pension, which he presented to his disillusioned followers. The thoughts of the poem, if not its lines, ran through Browning's head as he studied the hollowed wreck of poetic idealism by the light of Serjeant Talfourd's candelabra.

> Shakespeare was of us, Milton was for us,
>> Burns, Shelley, were with us – they watch from their graves!
> He alone breaks from the van and the freemen,
>> He alone sinks to the rear and the slaves!

Though Wordsworth had his sinecure and pension long before, the final apostasy of the laureateship was still eight years in the future at the time of the *Ion* supper. Conversation developed, Mary Russell Mitford seizing the opportunity to offer to write a play for Macready. This 'pert audacity' was briskly snubbed.[37]

Yet to have a play written for him was a sop to any actor's vanity. Having put down Miss Mitford, Macready turned to Browning. 'Write a play, Browning,' he said expansively, 'and keep me from going to America!' Browning was not the least taken aback by the suggestion, having already considered such a possibility. 'Shall it be historical and English?' he suggested. 'What do you say to a drama on Strafford?'[38]

This proposal for a theatrical success was not quite as outlandish as it might sound. The bi-centenary of events connected with the Civil War was being celebrated. John Forster, now Browning's close friend, had just published the first of his *Lives of the Statesmen of the Commonwealth*, which continued to appear until 1839. The *Life of Strafford* was issued three weeks before the *Ion* supper with some assistance from Browning himself.

The supper party at Talfourd's house broke up, poet and actor going their ways to think further of the possibilities of Strafford's life as a stage success. In retrospect it seems inconceivable that it could have matched the expectations that were built upon it. Indeed, its appearance was the first act of that tragi-comedy which was Browning's infatuation with the theatre.

3
The Madhouse and the Shrine

To the world of the 1830s Browning had appeared in two poetic guises which, though apparently differing in themselves, had in common their imitation of other men's styles and attitudes. Such qualities as were admired in *Pauline* and *Paracelsus* were pleasing rather than original. To begin a personal confessional poem in 1832 was at least thirty years too late for originality. To hail poetic drama as the form of the future in 1835 was, again, merely to echo the triumphs of other men. That all this should be reinforced by an uncritical imitation of Shelley was likely to confirm the scepticism of reviewers, marking Browning as a poet who looked backward to the fashions of the recent past rather than to the future.

The success of *Paracelsus*, even his coming début as a dramatist at Covent Garden, scarcely altered this view of Browning's poetry or indeed of his personality. He remained the pattern-book figure of the young romantic dandy.

Yet the world had been misled. There was a more disturbing aspect of Browning's poetry and personality which had so far been hidden scrupulously from the reading public of the decade. It remained protected more or less from intrusion for the rest of his life, even perhaps from Elizabeth Barrett. At a time when his early poetic reputation stood in need of whatever assistance he might lend it, he would only publish the first evidence of certain darker preoccupations anonymously.

In January 1836 two poems appeared in Fox's *Monthly Repository*, the author's signature given only as 'Z'. They were 'Porphyria' (later called 'Porphyria's Lover') and 'Johannes Agricola in Meditation', paired in *Dramatic Lyrics* (1842) as 'Madhouse Cells'. As Edmund Gosse remarked, it seems extraordinary in a decade whose poetry was so drably predictable that two pieces of such power and originality should pass without notice.

Browning, in his early twenties, captures the voices of true lunacy in a manner which makes King Lear's fantastic dress of flowers, or hallucinations of mice and cheese, seem abysmally contrived. Johannes Agricola, the sixteenth-century Antinomian, is earnest and ecstatic in the knowledge that he is one of God's Elect. His sins, past and future, are irrelevant. He bursts upon the reader at the opening of the poem with a neurotic's ecstasy.

> There's Heaven above, and night by night,
>   I look right through its gorgeous roof.

Coveting predestination with relish and a plaintive reasonableness, he talks with a madman's certainty.

> For I intend to get to God,
>   For 'tis to God I speed so fast.

Nor is Johannes to be dismissed simply as a theological joke. Ecstasy of faith comes principally from seeing the damned in hell, the good and the pure whose lives merely compounded their fate, 'all their striving turned to sin', since they were not among God's chosen saints.

> I gaze below on Hell's fierce bed,
>   And those its waves of flame oppress,
> Swarming in ghastly wretchedness;
>   Whose life on earth aspired to be
>   One altar-smoke so pure!

The eternal torment of the good and the devout is cause for gleeful self-congratulation. But like Browning's other lunatics, Johannes explains the logic of his position with the patient, obsessive reasoning of the truly mad.

> God, whom I praise; how could I praise,
>   If such as I might understand,
> Make out, and reckon on, his ways,
>   And bargain for his love, and stand,
> Paying a price, at his right hand?

The second 'Madhouse Cell' contained a more famous patient, Porphyria's lover. He, like Johannes, addresses the reader in words of patient reasonableness. The first part of the poem is his gentle erotic idyll, the girl kneeling at the grate and the fire blazing up, the removal of her outdoor clothes and the loosening of her damp hair. He was content to lie inert, head pillowed on her bare shoulder, longing only to imprison the moment and the girl for ever, safe from all possible rivals.

45

> Porphyria worshipped me; surprise
>> Made my heart swell, and still it grew
> While I debated what to do.
> That moment she was mine, mine, fair,
>> Perfectly pure and good: I found
> A thing to do.

Those last six words, 'I found a thing to do', once again catch the bright simple inspiration of the insane:

>> . . . and all her hair
> In one long yellow string I wound
> Three times her little throat around,
> And strangled her. No pain felt she;
> I am quite sure she felt no pain.

He had only wanted to lie passively beside her, which he can now do without any fear that she will attempt to leave, merely tightening the braid from time to time to bring the colour back into her cheeks. The murder is no more to him than a practical joke at the girl's expense. She had wished to give herself to him for ever and, chortling like Johannes Agricola, he adds,

>> . . . she guessed not how
> Her darling one wish would be heard.

Later in Browning's life there were to be warning voices which deplored his enthusiasm for dissecting human conduct in search of the evil and the sickness which lay within it. 'I wish I could apprehend the attraction of this subject to you,' wrote Julia Wedgwood of *The Ring and the Book*; 'I thought I shared your interest in morbid anatomy.'[1]

Madness and obsession are among the principal themes of Browning's poetry by his own definition. In *Pippa Passes* (1841) he defines insanity as the inability to see that one's own mental state is deranged.

> I think my mind is touched – suspect
> All is not sound: but is not knowing that,
> What constitutes one sane or otherwise?

Both 'Madhouse Cells' are the voices of insanity by this criterion, the declarations of lunatics convinced by their own interior logic. It applies in great measure to the speakers of other poems like 'Cristina', or to the arguably psychopathic voice of the duke in 'My Last Duchess' and Caponsacchi in *The Ring and the Book*. At the level of obsession, the speaker of 'Soliloquy of the Spanish Cloister' is imprisoned by his own unbrotherly hatred, Pictor Ignotus, in the poem of that title, by his philosophy of art.

The idea expressed in *Pippa Passes* of two separate worlds of conscious-ness, one containing the sane, the other occupied by lunatics and criminals – the morally insane – is aptly illustrated by one of Browning's own dreams. In this, he told William Allingham, he had been watching Edmund Kean play *Richard III*. During the ghost scene there was a 'stupendous line', the finest in the play: 'And when I wake my dreams are madness – Damn me.'[2] The significance of the line was that it was not Shakespeare's but Browning's own, released by his subconscious mind in sleep.

In 1856 an equally famous Victorian, Lewis Carroll, also defined madness in similar terms as the inability to identify the mind's relation to external reality.

> Query: when we are dreaming and, as often happens, have a dim conscious-ness of the fact and try to wake, do we not say and do things which in waking life would be insane? May we not then sometimes define insanity as an inability to distinguish which is the waking and which the sleeping life? We often dream without the least suspicion of unreality: 'Sleep hath its own world', and it is often as lifelike as the other.[3]

Browning's interest in 'morbid anatomy', as Julia Wedgwood termed it, the amount of his poetry which is put into the mouths of the mentally or morally alienated, is one of his most striking characteristics. That it should have begun in the 1830s was no coincidence.

Quite simply, psychiatry in the early nineteenth century had taken a form which brought the minds of lunatics within the realm of literature. Browning was to take unique advantage of this. The treatment of madness until the end of the eighteenth century had consisted largely of restraints, punishment, and the cruellest physical remedies. In litera-ture, the madman was represented by the figures of King Lear or Middleton's *Changeling*, to be pitied or feared rather than understood. Then, in 1806, there appeared in England *A Treatise on Insanity*, trans-lated from the French of Philippe Pinel. At the Bicêtre asylum in Paris, Pinel had extended the doctrine of the Revolution to unchaining the lunatics in his care and substituting a new treatment of 'moral therapy'. Enquiry and benevolence were to replace the former brutalities. Within a few years, alienists in England were following the same path, followed in their turn by poets and novelists.

By the 1830s the new study of phrenology had lent its support to moral therapy. If the nature of the individual brain could be determined by the contours of the skull, the work of therapy would be immeasurably assisted. Browning boasted of the two skulls which he kept in the room where he wrote. They constituted a humorous *memento mori*. Yet, as he explained to his future wife, they were also phrenological specimens.[4]

These historical developments were the occasion rather than the cause of Browning's preoccupation with the interior world of the self-deluded and the psychopath. Even without that, he showed an enthusiasm for the observation of criminal mentalities. Nathaniel Wanley and other items of childhood reading had gone some way to whet his appetite. He supplemented these sources by the reading of criminal trials or, for instance, by a visit to the collection of the famous detective Vidocq, 'knives and nails and hooks that have helped great murderers to their purposes'.[5]

In literature, as much as in the science of mentality, he was a child of his time. Victor Hugo, in his preface to *Cromwell*, had already pointed out that the grotesque was a distinguishing feature – even *the* distinguishing feature – of romantic art in the second quarter of the nineteenth century. 'Madhouse Cells' might almost have been written to prove him right. Classicism, in Hugo's view, had separated tragedy and comedy, never allowing them to engender this third and most interesting type of the grotesque. 'Antiquity', he concluded, 'could not have produced *Beauty and the Beast*.'[6]

It was not remarkable that a poet should keep his private creative life and his public appearances well separated. What caused the comments in Browning's case, during his last thirty years, was the absolute distinction between the interior world of his days and the embarrassment of the bonhomous philistinism with which he 'dinnered himself away' in fashionable society, night after night. Henry James devised a theory of two Brownings, as if he were a literary Jekyll and a philistine Hyde. Gladstone's daughter Mary, meeting him at dinner, knew that this could not be the poet Browning. 'He talks everybody down with his dreadful voice, and always places his person in such disagreeable proximity with yours and puffs and blows and spits in yr. face. I tried to think of Abt Vogler but it was of no use – he couldn't ever have written it.'[7]

There could have been no more fascinating subject for a dramatic monologue than Browning's own account of the two conflicting dispositions which he bore within him. Yet, if Burne-Jones was to be believed, the truth was clear enough. According to Mary Gladstone, Burne-Jones reassured her when he 'called Browning's outside "moss", and said the works of a man were his real self'.[8]

However, the resolution of that psychological conflict merely lays the way open to a moral one, of which 'Madhouse Cells' was the first example. Browning was the public Liberal and the anti-vivisectionist, nobly abhorrent of cruelty towards human beings or animals: but the human potentiality for cruelty and oppression in its most bizarre forms fascinated him as strongly as it had Nathaniel Wanley two centuries before and perhaps more than any other single theme in his own work. As Alfred Domett reported, Browning collected those instruments which were devised for the infliction of pain or death.[9] Humanitarianism did not inhibit him, for instance, from allowing Half-Rome in *The Ring and the Book* to discuss with relish the brutal refinements of the dagger which stabbed Pompilia and her parents, the wounds now on display upon the chancel steps. That Genoese weapon is equipped with tiny hook-teeth which spring open as the blade enters the flesh and rip wide the wound as it is drawn out again.

The deeper fascination for Browning lay in the moral incongruity of such horrors, and the problems which they posed about the aberrations of the human mind. In his poem 'A Forgiveness', in *Pacchiarotto and How he Worked in Distemper* (1876), he combines the study of mentality and morality, as if to encompass all mankind in a madhouse cell. The poem meditates on one of the oddest works of man's hand. Knives, guns, whips, daggers, are employed to cause death or suffering. Why, then, are they made with such loving and decorative art, as if they were the finest expression of the human spirit?

> I think there never was such – how express? –
> Horror coquetting with voluptuousness,
> As in those arms of Eastern workmanship –
> Yataghan, kandjar, things that rend and rip,
> Gash rough, slash smooth, help hate so many ways,
> Yet ever keep a beauty that betrays
> Love still at work with the artificer
> Throughout his quaint devising. Why prefer,
> Except for love's sake, that a blade should writhe
> And bicker like a flame?

Browning devoted some fifty years to considering that last question in one form or another. In doing so he touched upon a most sensitive nerve of moral philosophy in the world of new philanthropic pretensions. Was it not enough, in the course of war or crime, that men and women should be put to death or tortured? Why was it necessary that the implements used should be embellished with such affection by the artist or craftsman?

It was a distinctively modern misgiving. The shield of Achilles and

49

the weapons of the besieging Greeks had not caused Homer such moral qualms: nor could there be equivocation on the part of those who abominated such devices altogether. The terms in which Browning writes are those of a post-romantic age. Yet what is 'Horror coquetting with voluptuousness,' in 'Porphyria's Lover' or *The Ring and the Book*, but the literal counterpart to Hugo's metaphor of *Beauty and the Beast*?

In the closed world of his poetic imagination, the moral beauty of sexual love and the moral bestiality of the psychopath drew Browning's most powerful responses. That this should be the case was in part a matter of personality, in part the romantic inheritance. The decades before Browning's birth, no less than those of his youth, had been a period of philanthropic aspiration in European culture and society alike. Yet the moral disturbance which the Marquis de Sade provoked in literature was seen no less in the great canvases of Delacroix or a painting like Goya's *The Throat-Slitting* of 1810–12. Beauty or voluptuousness, in Goya's painting, for example, is represented by the captured woman in the cave, kneeling bound and naked but for her stockings. The two bandits are naked too and the events preceding this moment are powerfully suggested. The horror or brutality is summed up by the dead body of the woman's husband or companion, the bandit who drags back her head by the hair, the better to apply his knife to her throat now that he has no further use for her.

To an earlier or a later age, such scenes (whether by Goya or Browning) were better not depicted. A gentler age would find them unendurable, a more barbaric age might think them mundane. It was in the romantic period and its aftermath that the moral conjunction of philanthropy and savagery fused with such power in the darker dramas of poetry or visual art.

Browning did not seek to justify his preoccupation with the tyrant, the cheat, or the psychopath in such terms. He shared with the romantics a curiosity about the odder freaks and motives of personality, the deviant paths that led by one route to love or holiness, by another to righteous cruelty or moral cynicism. Yet he saw himself no less as a beneficiary of the great Puritan tradition which endorsed his enthusiasms with the theological imperative of Original Sin. By his own account, it was this that gave the impetus to his religious and literary creeds. Puritanism offered an intellectual framework to a study of human oddity which might otherwise have seemed merely the inquisitiveness of the dilettante. At the heart of such faith was a central tenet. In 'Gold Hair: A Story of Pornic' from *Dramatis Personae* (1864), he describes it simply and specifically.

Original Sin.
The Corruption of Man's Heart.

Browning was not a formally religious poet any more than he was a pure romantic idealist. His role was to diagnose the corruption or the moral incongruity of human conduct, to be the pathologist rather than the healer. To that extent he has more in common with Sade than with Wordsworth, a greater affinity with Nathaniel Wanley than with Bunyan.

In 'Ned Bratts', published in *Dramatic Idylls* (1879), Browning elaborates the moral paradox about the beauty of implements designed to cause death or pain. As a dispassionate observer he describes men and women crowding eagerly to watch seventeenth-century Puritans branded on the face, or flogged, or having their noses slit off, 'just leaving enough to tweak'. He calls the occasion 'things at jolly hightide, amusement steeped in fire'.

A reader of his poetry might reasonably wonder whether such ferocity appealed only to the figures of the poetry and not to the author. Observers of his impatient energy and bitter invective noted how hostility was apt to be expressed in images of physical violence. In imagination, if not in reality, it was Browning himself who appeared to prefer his excitement 'steeped in fire'.

'Madhouse Cells' offered the first perspective of that inner world whose privacy Browning guarded with an intensity which a contemporary like Henry James found intriguingly eccentric. As a matter of literary necessity, much of his time was spent within this sphere, the 'life within life' of which Alfred Adler speaks in *Individual Psychology*, and which Adler regards as the characteristic refuge of the supremely ambitious – spiritually, intellectually, or morally. The criminal, the neurotic, the pietist and – more happily – the artist are Adler's chosen categories of those who live within the self-devised moral laws of such a retreat.[10]

To apply Adlerian theory or any comparable thesis to Browning is misleading; yet the image which Adler employs fits with a double aptness the enigma of Browning's privacy. By the common consent of his contemporaries he lived a life within life. It also happens that those groups whom Adler cites as doing the same – the criminal, the neurotic, and the pietist – are among the principal subjects of analysis in his poetry. That he was supremely ambitious he never denied, determined to be a poet, 'if not *the* Poet', and measuring his progress intently against that of his near-contemporary, Tennyson.

If it served no other purpose, the inner world of his creations, however mad or bad they might seem to others, offered a safe release for an uneasy mental energy which abounded in him. His own wife observed this clearly and wrote of her misgivings in the last year of her life. She feared then that his creative will had failed him and that if he could not create he must destroy, as his 'vital energy ... strikes its fangs into him'.[11]

Into the voices of his criminals, lunatics, saints, and lovers went some of that energy which was apt at other times to reveal itself in personal flashes of hatred, violence, and prurience over matters of love and death. Browning had a gift for invective which shocked some and put others in fear of his repartee. With no elegance but a good deal of effect, he dismissed the spiritualist D. D. Home as 'a dungball', Edward Fitzgerald as a brute, a blackguard, and as Tennyson's 'lick-spittle'. Physical threats and crudity of metaphor characterized the tone of other hostilities. He meditated publicly in the *Athenaeum* on the comparative satisfaction of kicking or spitting upon the dead Fitzgerald. He promised to rub the faces of certain literary critics in their own excrement. In 'At the "Mermaid"' he compared Austin's poetry to breaking wind. With Disraeli he exchanged dinner-table spite – each behind the other's back – notably in Browning's semi-public limerick:

> We don't want to fight,
> By Jingo, if we do,
> The head I'd like to punch
> Is Beaconsfield the Jew.[12]

The forces of Browning's 'life within life', however fine their poetic creations, were apt to appear unattractive. In his correspondence to Isa Blagden he was to reveal the fascination of primitive life in Brittany, listening to a woman on her deathbed just beyond a thin partition; sharing a house with a man who slept in one room with his daughters and a pretty servant girl; being able to see up the girl's short tunic as she stooped to gather washing and to note that she wore nothing underneath. By the laws of his private world, such topics were entirely proper to address to a favoured female correspondent in the first decade of his long bereavement.

The determination with which Browning guarded his private world was a topic of literary gossip in the 1870s and 1880s, yet it was no less apparent in the 1830s and 1840s. Until he was thirty-four he lived under his parents' roof, largely withdrawn from the world beyond his immediate family. 'Browning – lives at Peckham because no one else does!'

Leigh Hunt explained to William Allingham.[13] Association with others was often through the formal structure of groups like the Colloquials or the salons of men like Bryan Proctor, rather than through the development of exclusive or individual affection.

After the departure of Alfred Domett for New Zealand in 1842, it was to be a frequent theme of Browning's correspondence that he lived in isolation at Hatcham, seeing no one for months at a time and, of his own choice, refusing invitations. Moreover, by 1845 he had never been drawn to fall in love with any woman and had concluded that such a thing would be impossible for him. Yet he wrote these words as a man who equalled any contemporary poet in the subtle analysis of sexual emotion, notably in the erotic suggestiveness of *Pippa Passes*. It was almost as if he feared that the reality of woman might prove stale after his own creation of her, as if in a decisive area of his experience, art had triumphed over life. Nothing less than the Muse incarnate, in the shape of Elizabeth Barrett, would alter that.[14]

Such were the enigmatic messages of love and hate, ambition and frustration, which emanated from this private domain. As a matter of upbringing and personal dedication, Browning had lived from childhood in a literary structure, at first of other men's works but increasingly of his own. The exterior world of Camberwell's woods and fields was transformed by the inner experience of the landscapes of Gerard de Lairesse. Nunhead Hill became an Arcadian setting for Dryden's discussion of satire. It was a moral universe as self-sufficient in its way as those of Johannes Agricola, Porphyria's lover, or for that matter of Alfred Adler's description.

The literary structure of this private world into which Browning withdrew from dinner parties and salons had an importance beyond the poetry which he wrote or meditated. It extended into correspondence through which Browning, even more than most contemporaries, was able to pursue friendship and love at the level of literature. He was not a distinguished letter-writer, yet friendship for Alfred Domett in New Zealand and love for Elizabeth Barrett a few miles away were brought equally within the scope of the pen.

Unlike the reality of personal encounter, the letter was a form in which the writer created both his own persona and that of the recipient. He might love or befriend on his own terms, free from interruption or prevarication. To visit Elizabeth Barrett regularly and frequently did not invalidate the need for letters in which a further dimension of their love was revealed. In *Sordello*, Browning was to offer a theory that denied the existence of beauty until it had been created by a divine lightning-flash of love in the soul of the admirer. By the literary device of correspondence, Browning aided the creation of his own Elizabeth Barrett, to whom he gave his adoration. To profess his love for her on the evidence of what she had written became entirely logical. By his own theory she was in part the creation of his inner world, as the people of his poetry were in their entirety. In the light of this, it was not illogical that he should see his love and his destiny in a woman with whom he had exchanged correspondence, whose poetry he had read, but whom he had never spoken to nor seen.

After her death, the secure retreat of a literary structure gave him purpose and consolation. *The Ring and the Book* was both the story of the Roman murder and an account of how Browning wrote the poem itself. More specifically than at any other time he made himself and the 'life within life' a subject of his writing. The revelation was a qualified one, however; the processes of that life were described, but not its content.

Whether any other person, however greatly adored, could share fully in that most private world was open to doubt. Elizabeth herself believed that an artist must 'either find or *make* a solitude to work in'.[15] Could there be a shared solitude for two poets, however absolute their faith in one another? In the end it was impossible, even for Browning with Elizabeth. There were creatures of his private domain, like Mr Sludge, whose very existence might have hurt and offended her. There was the dark drama of cruelty and innocence in *The Ring and the Book*. As Browning told Julia Wedgwood, Elizabeth remained aloof from its possibilities in principle and would have disapproved of it in practice had it been written during her lifetime.[16]

The extent of her exclusion in the last years of her life can only be surmised. Elizabeth was apt to complain to those closest to her that Browning was writing nothing. It may have been true that the themes of his later poetry were for a time suppressed; yet something was being written, if only 'Mr Sludge, "The Medium"'', whose length is that of a major poem. Much more was being meditated. The devotion of Browning to Elizabeth is not called in question by this withdrawal. With the omens of her approaching death he began to establish an independence for himself, his eyes upon the life which must follow. At that point, though perhaps long before it, the door had closed again upon the recesses of his darker preoccupations. Perhaps, indeed, it had never opened.

After her death the figure of Elizabeth was enshrined in that inner privacy, a memorial which appeared as much his own creation as the Elizabeth Barrett of their correspondence in 1845-6. There was to be a certain oddity in Browning's veneration of the shrine. He was quick to sense trespassers and sacrilege, which was understandable; but its dead saint became a personal totem of his privacy in a manner that was not always to his credit. Having compromised himself with Lady Ashburton, for instance, Browning was quick to involve Elizabeth and to destroy his proposal of marriage by informing her ladyship that his heart lay buried in Florence. By the same device he was able to enjoy a series of platonic friendships with women in his last twenty-eight years, secure from the ultimate assault upon his literary retreat.

In the light of this, the myth of 'two Brownings' in the 1870s and 1880s is not remarkable, however insubstantial in the face of the evidence. Edmund Gosse and Mary Gladstone discovered the truth, which was as simple and unsurprising as Burne-Jones had supposed. Gosse had been overawed by Browning the social 'tiger', and Miss Gladstone was repelled by his manner. Neither was admitted to the inner world of the shrine or the madhouse cells, yet both of them glimpsed what lay behind the outer walls. They did so by persuading Browning to talk about his poetry, the very thing which the Browning of dinner-table gossip would not do. By this path they came to what Burne-Jones had called Browning's 'real self', and they found that it was, indeed, the poetry.[17]

The lacquered carapace of the romantic dandy in the 1830s was as much a protection of that domain as the loud voice and bonhomie of the fashionable dinner-table in the world of Henry James and Gosse. 'Madhouse Cells' in 1836 contained those monsters of a private world whose kin were to be found in *The Ring and the Book* and *Red Cotton Night-Cap Country* thirty or forty years later. For all the attention which a confessional poem like *Pauline* invites, it is less informative about Browning's interior world than the plaintive lunacy of Johannes Agricola or Porphyria's lover. It is not the least surprising that *Pauline*, as a first poem written in the first person, should have been published anonymously by its young and uncertain author. That 'Madhouse Cells', appearing after the success of *Paracelsus* – whose authorship was acknowledged – should also be anonymous is a different case. It seems a clear indication of the particular significance he attached to the two later poems. Withholding his identity, he awaited the public reaction to the display of his two moral and spiritual monsters. For the time being, he waited in vain.

4
Macready

The partnership into which Browning and Macready entered was to endure through a series of progressively greater disillusionments until its final dissolution seven years after Serjeant Talfourd's supper party. During that period most of Browning's literary talent was employed in writing for the London stage, while much of his emotional energy became engaged in his various disputes with Macready as actor-manager.

Both men, at their best, were capable of great generosity and enthusiasm. At their worst they were equally given to vanity and self-righteousness. Had their enterprise prospered easily, this temperamental similarity might have mattered less. In the difficulties which they soon faced it was to be the rock upon which friendship struck. Browning showed the impatience of the young romantic for whom the theatre offered both success and self-advertisement. Macready had the religious arrogance of one who implores God to improve him in wisdom and conduct, and feels instantly assured that the improvement has been effected.

Above all, Macready was master in his own house, which was to be Covent Garden Theatre. Three days after the famous supper party, for instance, he recorded in his diary his absolute command of audience and players at that evening's performance of *Julius Caesar*.

> Went to the theatre; the audience was rather noisy through the early scenes, but I was not disposed to yield to them. I do not think that my reception was quite so long as Kemble's, or I did not use sufficient generalship with it; but I acted Cassius in my very best style, and made the audience feel it. I was good; I was the character; I felt it. The audience were rapid and vehement in their applause; I was first and most loudly called for at the end of the play.[1]

Macready had moved to Covent Garden after inflicting violence on Alfred Bunn, lessee of Drury Lane Theatre, a few weeks before the *Ion* supper. Bunn felt, probably rightly, that most of his audience would prefer Shakespeare's *Richard III* if the last two acts were omitted. As manager, he gave orders for this. Macready stormed from the stage at the end of the truncated version and burst in upon Bunn shouting: 'You damned scoundrel! How dare you use me in this manner?' As Bunn tried to rise, the outraged tragedian struck him 'a backhanded slap across the face'. He dug a fist into Bunn, who then managed to get the little finger of Macready's left hand into his mouth and bite it. The prompter and the rest of the cast arrived to Bunn's shrieks of, 'Murder! Murder!' and Macready shouting, 'You rascal! Would you bite?'[2]

The truth was that Mr Bunn preferred wild animal shows to classic dramas. Animals paid better and were on the whole easier to deal with than human performers. Macready later withdrew to become the manager of Covent Garden, yet the omens were scarcely propitious for a congenial partnership with the impetuous young poet.

Even before the name of Strafford was mentioned at Talfourd's supper, Forster had visited Macready on 16 February 1836 to tell him that Browning proposed to write a play about Narses, Justinian's military commander. In the state of the London theatre it hardly appeared that such a project could be commercially successful. As Macready knew, orange peel, nutshells and empty porter bottles littering the house were a surer sign of prosperity than favourable notices in the *Examiner* or the *Athenaeum*. Often the behaviour of audiences was worse still. A typical Drury Lane disturbance was caused by a man in a tier-box singing loudly until the police were called. He leapt down into the orchestra, and the audience who had been shouting 'Turn him out!' now fought the police on his behalf. The leader of the orchestra enterprisingly struck up *God Save the King!* to restore order but the notes were lost in the uproar. A five-act tragedy on an obscure Roman general was unlikely to thrive in such a cultural climate.[3]

No more was heard of Narses. Indeed, it was more than two months after Talfourd's supper party that Macready noted in his diary on 3 August, 'Forster told me that Browning had fixed on Strafford for the subject of a tragedy; he could not have hit upon one that I could have more readily concurred in.'[4] Unlike Narses, Strafford was a figure of some interest as England began to celebrate the bi-centenary of those events that led first to his rise as chief adviser to Charles I, then to his death on Tower Hill as parliament turned against him and the king deserted his favourite.

Nor was there any doubt that history, in fact and fiction as well as on the stage, enjoyed its first true popularity in the early nineteenth century. The novels of Scott were evidence of this and a contributing factor to the success of the vogue. As Scott remarked in the Dedicatory Epistle to *Ivanhoe* (1819), the public was ready to receive the treasures of the past, 'translated into the manners, as well as the language, of the age we live in'.[5] Historical writing had earlier been a matter of annals and memoirs or, in Gibbon's case, an account of a more distant civilization. The early Victorians were to discover the drama and humanity of their past, to find that it was, as Carlyle remarked in *Past and Present* (1843), 'a world, and not a void infinite of gray haze with fantasms swimming in it'.[6] Perhaps the final proof of its appeal came on 7 November 1848 when Ludgate Hill was jammed with the carriages of booksellers struggling to reach the offices of Longman in Paternoster Row. It was publication day of the first volume of Macaulay's *History of England*, a book destined to have a greater commercial success in its time than the works of either Byron or Scott himself.

There was even better reason than this to expect the triumph of a play based upon Strafford's downfall. In May 1836 a life of Strafford, written by John Forster, had been published and well received. Forster had been ill earlier in the year and Browning assisted him in the composition of the final chapters. Through this act of friendship, Browning's idea for a poetic tragedy based on Strafford's life began to take shape. He worked at it in the autumn of 1836, quieting Macready's alarm over a rumour that the whole play had been written in ten days at the end of September. A month later it was almost finished and, with the fourth act still incomplete, Browning brought it to Macready on 19 November.

Macready told the young man to sit down and write a synopsis of the missing scenes. While this was being done he went off to the Garrick Club where Talfourd, Charles Kemble and others were at dinner. Returning from this conviviality, he took the manuscript, hired a cab for his country house at Elstree, bought two cigars 'and smoked to Edgware'.[7] Reading through *Strafford* in mellow mood, he was favourably impressed. During the next few days he read it again and found his natural enthusiasm tempered by the first cold misgivings. 'I find more grounds for exception than I had anticipated,' he noted. 'I had been too much carried away by the truth of character to observe the meanness of plot, and occasional obscurity.'[8] Even when the missing scenes were supplied, on 20 December, Macready still thought it 'not up to the high-water mark'.[9]

Bluntly, Macready foresaw the commercial failure of *Strafford*, a reverse which must affect him both as an actor and as one who had invested money in Covent Garden. He delayed for as long as possible, devoting his energies instead to the already popular dramas of Bulwer-Lytton. Not until 19 March 1837, when time was forcing a decision upon him, did he read *Strafford* again. 'Read *Strafford* in the evening, which I fear is too historical; it is the policy of the man, and its consequence upon him, not the heart, temper, feelings, that work in this policy, which Browning has portrayed – and how admirably!'[10]

While undecided, he read the play to David Webster Osbaldiston, still manager of Covent Garden. To his surprise and relief, Osbaldiston was delighted with the piece, 'caught at it with avidity, agreed to produce it without delay on his part, and to give the author £12 per night for twenty-five nights, and £10 per night for ten nights beyond'.[11] After that there was no question of further delay. Indeed, as Macready heard, John Forster was trying to persuade Longman to publish it in time for the first performance. Longman agreed, and so it seemed Browning had found both a sympathetic actor-manager and a commercial publisher.

Yet the misgivings over what Macready called 'the dangerous state of the play' persisted. He and John Forster endeavoured to rewrite parts of it, to Browning's instant annoyance. As a compromise, it was agreed that Browning himself should carry out the revisions. Macready found them 'mere feeble rant – neither power, nor nature, nor healthful fancy – very unworthy of Browning'.[12] Nothing would save the play now, he concluded, but the brilliance of the acting.

The row between the two men was still far from breaking out openly. As the printed edition of *Strafford* went to press in April, Browning added a dedication; '... in all affectionate admiration to William C. Macready, Esq. by his most grateful and devoted friend, R. B.'. Both the gratitude and devotion were under increasing strain as the rehearsals progressed. By the day of the first performance on 1 May 1837, Browning described the state of affairs to Fox as 'perfect gallows'.[13] For all that, the play was well received on the first night, Macready as a Vandyke portrait of Strafford being repeatedly called for by pit and galleries. There were demands for the author's appearance too, but these went unregarded.

The play ran for five nights, at a time when even a theatrical success would be measured by no more than a run of a week or two. The reviews were mixed, the best coming from the *Morning Herald*, whose notice on 4 May was one of unqualified enthusiasm, describing *Strafford*, as a play, as 'the best that had been produced for years'.

In truth, *Strafford* was a somewhat pedestrian drama of political conspiracy. Especially in its last act, it falls short of tragic nobility if only because the verse alternates between flat modernity and overwrought Shakespearean rhetoric. Tied to history, the play was doomed to end indecisively, Strafford unable to choose between escape and martyrdom until it is too late. His exit, tottering out to execution, moaning, 'O God, I shall die first – I shall die first!' is one of the most banal moments of the entire play. In general, the burden of historical events in *Strafford* weighs too heavily on the poetic pretensions. The greater tragedy was that Browning should have applied so much of his early life to work of this kind.

Because *Strafford* was not the total failure that Macready had feared, Browning chose to follow it with a series of other plays, more or less historical. In itself this was not perhaps remarkable at a time when verse drama seemed likely to be one of the major literary forms of the nineteenth century. If Browning was led into a blind alley, he was by no means alone. Tennyson and Swinburne, notably the latter, were his companions in seeking a revival of Elizabethan glories on the English stage, or even a continuation of romantic poetic drama in the manner of plays like Shelley's *Hellas*. John Forster had already prophesied the development in his 'Evidence of a new Genius for Dramatic Poetry' in the *New Monthly Magazine* of March 1836. Works little known to the twentieth century, like C. J. Wells' *Joseph and his Brethren* (1824), were regarded as patterns for the future by Swinburne and Pre-Raphaelite admirers into the 1860s and 1870s.

It was not to be. Thomas Lovell Beddoes, author of *The Bride's Tragedy* (1822) and the posthumously published play *Death's Jest-Book*, watched without enthusiasm the indiscriminate imitation of the Elizabethans and Jacobeans into which the poetic drama of the 1830s and 1840s degenerated. Of the great playwrights imitated he wrote, 'they are ghosts – the worm is in their pages.... Just now the drama is a haunted ruin'.[14] From the distance of German exile Beddoes also enquired after the health of English poetry; 'What are the votaries of the Muse doing yonder? What is Cosimo de' Medici? Paracelsus? Strafford? and Sergeant Talfourd's Ion or John?'[15]

Despite the scepticism of Beddoes and those who had been practising the art since the 1820s, Browning continued to suppose that verse drama might be the most popular poetic medium of the mid-nineteenth century. After the moderate success of his first play he wrote to a friend, Fanny Haworth, that he was going 'to begin thinking a tragedy (an Historical one, so I shall want heaps of criticisms on *Strafford*) and I want to have *another* tragedy in prospect'.[16] Describing the two, he called the second 'a subject of the most wild and passionate love, to contrast with the one I mean to have ready in a short time'.[17]

In spite of his enthusiasm and commitment to the scheme for dramatic writing, Browning was on the verge of a shivering sand in which so much of his early genius and energy were to be lost. Because the public was interested in history, he equated this with his own taste for the little-known and curious stories of the past. The downfall of Strafford had an obvious and even topical appeal to the audiences of 1837. No one could say that of the two dramas with which Browning followed it.

King Victor and King Charles, the historical tragedy promised to Miss Haworth, was a story dug out of the fifty volumes of his father's *Biographie Universelle*, describing the rulers of Savoy and Sardinia in the early eighteenth century. King Victor Amadeus II had abdicated in favour of his son Charles. Thinking better of this, Victor attempted to regain his crown, a course of action which ended in his imprisonment and death. Like *Strafford*, the play is a drama of court conspiracy and intrigue. Yet the extent to which Browning misjudged his public is clear from his note to the readers, 'acquainted, as I will hope them to be, with the chief circumstances of Victor's remarkable European career'.

Macready received the play and read it with dismay. Better than anyone, he knew what the effect of such a topic would be on the eaters of oranges and the crackers of nuts who had been won with difficulty from the more exciting pleasures of Mr Bunn's performing animals. The Covent Garden management was heading for bankruptcy and the theatre's salvation lay in plays like Bulwer-Lytton's *The Lady of Lyons*, which ran for night after night and made no more demands upon the audiences than a nodding acquaintance with the most elementary human passions.

King Victor and King Charles was, in Macready's words, a great mistake. 'I called Browning into my room and most explicitly told him so, and gave him my reasons for coming to such a conclusion.'[18] The play was, of course, rejected and remained unperformed. After the disagreements during the production of *Strafford*, this rebuff brought Browning and Macready to a point where they openly voiced their mutual criticisms.

For all that, the hope of a great success in verse drama still flickered among Browning's ambitions. He plunged back into the depths of the *Biographie Universelle* and found an even more unlikely story for a popular play. *The Return of the Druses* is a melodrama of love and death among a Lebanese religious sect during the Middle Ages. Why Browning should have imagined that this piece could hold the stage for a single night is not apparent. Possibly, protected as he was from personal financial need, he found it more difficult to appreciate that the theatre was first and foremost a commercial venture rather than a showcase for imaginative scholarship or historical ingenuity.

Macready received the manuscript of the play in August 1840 and read it with unrelieved despondency: 'Read Browning's play, and with the deepest concern I yield to the belief that he will *never write again* – to any purpose. I fear his intellect is not quite clear. I do not know how to write to Browning.'[19] Far and away the worst aspect of the matter, for Macready, was that Browning himself was supremely self-confident and had no apparent realization that he had done anything but write a great theatrical success. On 27 August 1840, a few weeks after sending the play to Macready, he paid a personal call while the actor-manager was in his bath. 'Browning came before I had finished my bath, and really *wearied* me with his obstinate faith in his poem of *Sordello*, and of his eventual celebrity, and also with his self-opinionated persuasions upon his *Return of the Druses*. I fear he is for ever gone.'[20]

Macready had rejected *King Victor and King Charles* in September 1839. He sent back *The Return of the Druses* in September 1840. That autumn, still undeterred, Browning began work on another poetic drama, *A Blot in the 'Scutcheon.*

By this time, however, there was no doubt that he had learnt something of the theatre's commercial needs. Gone were the scholarship and the recondite historical details. *A Blot in the 'Scutcheon* was a straightforward drama of secret love and family honour in a patrician household of the eighteenth century. Henry, Earl Mertoun, seeks the hand of Mildred Tresham from her brother, Thorold, Lord Tresham. Henry and Mildred are secretly lovers already, he paying nightly visits to her room. Though the marriage proposal is favourably received, Thorold is disturbed by news of a man's secret visits to his sister. He confronts the disguised figure and kills him in a sword-fight. Mildred dies upon hearing of Mertoun's death. Thorold dies too, of poison, with the arms of his dead sister about his neck.

The play nicely combines a sexual drama of domestic life which might have come from the pen of Samuel Richardson with the melodrama of early Victorian theatre. Even the most cursory description of the play shows the directness of its appeal to the audiences who had crowded Covent Garden for *The Lady of Lyons* or the Haymarket for *Money*. Indeed, Browning was conscious that he had gone a considerable way to meet the commercial taste of the theatre, describing the new play to Macready as 'a sort of compromise between my own notion and yours'.[21] He promised that 'There is *action* in it, drabbing, stabbing, et autres gentillesses'.[22]

Macready, with memories of the two previous plays in his mind, was reluctant even to read the new manuscript. He delayed for nine months and then, in September 1841, read it at John Forster's request. Macready had given up any part in the management of the ailing Covent Garden and was now manager of the Haymarket. His primary concern was to keep this theatre in turn from bankruptcy and he could simply not make up his mind whether Browning's new play would assist him in this. The plot was appealing and yet he had doubts. In these circumstances he sent the manuscript to Charles Dickens, a friend of Forster's and himself, a man who had a shrewd appreciation of popular taste and theatrical possibilities.

It was 25 November 1842 when Dickens replied at last. He had been deeply moved by the drama, finding it 'full of genius, natural and great thoughts, profound and yet simple and beautiful in its vigour ... And I swear it is a tragedy that *must* be played: and must be played, moreover, by Macready.'[23] Macready allowed Dickens' view to decide him, especially when the great novelist added, 'And if you tell Browning that I have seen it, tell him that I believe from my soul there is no man living (and not many dead) who could produce such a work'.[24] At the time, neither Macready nor Forster felt inclined to tell Browning either what Dickens had said or even that he had seen the manuscript.

From the first reading of the play at Drury Lane on 28 January 1843 there was anger on Browning's part and resentment on Macready's. Macready, who was not present, heard that when the prompter, Willmott, read the play to the actors, they received the tragedy with hoots of laughter. Macready summoned Browning and, with a certain satisfaction in seeing his own worst expectations fulfilled, informed the poet of the reception his work had provoked. When Browning demanded to know who had read the play, he was told that it had been Willmott. Willmott, said Browning, was nothing but 'a broadly comic personage with a wooden leg and a very red face, whose vulgar sallies were the delight of all the idle jesters that hung about the theatre'.[25]

Worse was soon to follow. Though Macready made amends by reading the play to the actors himself, he accompanied this with an announcement that he would not be appearing in the production. The part of Tresham would be taken by another actor, Phelps. Browning assumed that this was a deliberate insult to his play, calculated to make him withdraw it. He refused to be drawn into the trap. For the time being he agreed that Phelps should take the principal role. Towards the end of his life, Browning recalled how Macready saw that his plan had failed and said that he would after all take the part. 'I beg pardon, sir,' said Browning firmly, 'but you have given the part to Mr Phelps, and I am satisfied that he should act it.'[26] At these words, Browning told Mrs Orr, the great actor flew into a sudden rage, screwed up his copy of the play and threw it on the floor of the green-room.

There was, of course, some truth on both sides. Macready knew that Phelps was ill and had himself decided to understudy the role of Tresham. At the same time he was seriously worried about parts of the play, and told Browning that the second act needed to be rewritten for the stage. He disclaimed any intention of appearing in the play himself, unless an emergency should require it. 'I *could not* play this part of Browning's unless the whole work of the theatre stopped. ... I thought it best to reduce it to its proper form – three acts, and let Phelps do it on all accounts.'[27]

There came a flying visit from Browning who was rude to the door-keeper, refusing even to give his name, and appeared before Macready 'in a very great passion'. Macready observed that the contretemps with the doorkeeper had ensured that the young poet's dignity was mortally offended. 'I fear he is a very conceited man,' the hard-pressed actor-manager concluded.[28]

Then came the sensitive question of rewriting a play with which its author was already well satisfied. 'Browning, however, in the worst taste, manner, and spirit, declined any further alterations.'[29]

Despite so much bitterness on both sides, the play was well received at the opening performance at the Haymarket on 11 February 1843. Helen Faucit appeared as Mildred, and Phelps took the role of Tresham so well that at least one young member of the audience, W.J. Fox's daughter, believed to the end of her life that she had seen the part acted by Macready himself.[30] Browning's friend Joseph Arnould reported:

> The first night was magnificent. ... Poor Phelps did his utmost, Helen Faucit very fairly, and there could be no mistake at all about the honest enthusiasm of the audience. The gallery (and this, of course, was very gratifying, because not to be expected at a play of *Browning*) took all the points quite as quickly as the pit, and entered into the general feeling and interest of the action far more than the boxes – some of whom took it upon themselves to be shocked at being betrayed into so much interest for a young woman who had behaved so improperly as Mildred.[31]

Despite the moral misgivings of the more affluent patrons, Arnould described the first night unequivocally as 'a triumph'. He went again with his wife on the following night, when the gallery was full but the boxes exhibited a 'desolate emptiness'. What was regarded as the scandalous subject matter of the play, nightly visits by the hero to the bedroom of the heroine, had deterred the more influential part of the audience. As for the third night of the production, said Arnould, 'It was evident at a glance that it was to be the last'.[32] *A Blot in the 'Scutcheon* was now played in the deserted grandeur of the Haymarket, 'the miserable, great, chilly house, with its apathy and emptiness'.[33]

The final curtain fell on the play, and on Browning's hopes as a dramatist, on 15 February 1843. Three days later the *Athenaeum* issued a stern rebuke. Browning's only achievement had been to 'pain and perplex'. The play was 'a very puzzling and unpleasant piece of business ... the acts and feelings of the characters are inscrutable and abhorrent. ... A few of the audience laughed, others were shocked, and many applauded; but it is impossible that such a drama should live even if it were artistically constructed, which this is not.'

Forty-two years later, when the play was produced in America, Browning remarked that if his inclination to write for the theatre had met with half the encouragement shown by his American enthusiasts, he might have continued 'for better or worse, play-writing to the end of my days'.[34]

The squabble over *A Blot in the 'Scutcheon* marked the end of his friendship with Macready. Eight years earlier he had written to the famous actor after the *Ion* supper: 'The admiration I have for your genius is too assured and "thorough-shine" to admit certain misgivings which commonly attend a less absolute conviction.'[35] With a self-abasement which he might more properly have made before the ghost of Shelley, he offered his dramatic talents for the sole and greater glory of Macready. To fail would be its own recompense. To succeed would bring him the supreme reward, that of 'my name pronounced along with yours'.[36]

Dead poets might be more conveniently worshipped in this fashion than living actors. Shelley was what Browning chose to make him, sun-treader or a potential convert to Christianity who would neither argue nor criticize. Macready, however, was the idol who repaid admiration by demanding the rewriting of plays, who would snub Browning by refusing his card – let alone his visit – who crumpled up *A Blot in the 'Scutcheon* and threw it on the green-room floor. Browning was over thirty, past the age for indiscriminate hero-worship. Time would have cured him of this anyway. As it happened, Macready accelerated the process. In the conflict between adulation and impatience of criticism, the victor was no longer in doubt.

65

Though there could be little further prospect of Browning's success in the theatre, there was one piece of unfinished business, which he described to Alfred Domett three months after the abortive run of *A Blot in the 'Scutcheon*. He had met the second son of Edmund Kean, Charles Kean, who was making a reputation by his flamboyant stage productions. Kean expressed interest in a play of Browning's, *Colombe's Birthday*, which may have been written before the failure of *A Blot in the 'Scutcheon*. The poet read the play aloud to Kean and his wife, who was to take the part of Colombe if the play were produced. Kean was polite and even flattering, assuring Browning that he would be delighted to produce the drama. Then came a displeasing condition of acceptance. Pressure of other engagements would mean that *Colombe* must wait rather more than a year before Kean could put it on the stage. It was not performed by him. Only in 1853, when Browning was in Italy, did it run for seven nights at the Haymarket with Helen Faucit in the principal part.

Once again, Browning had taken his play from the by-ways of European history, setting it in the Duchy of Juliers and Cleves during the seventeenth century and making the operation of the Salic law the basis of its plot. Colombe, the duchess, must yield her sovereignty to a male claimant, Prince Berthold. He offers her a marriage of convenience which will enable her to retain it. Colombe, in love with a lawyer, Valence, refuses, prizing love above power. At least the triumph of love gave the play a human appeal lacking in some of Browning's earlier drama. Even Berthold's cynicism is penetrated by the woman's choice.

> All is for the best!
> Too costly a flower were you, I see it now,
> To pluck and set upon my barren helm
> To wither.

By the time that *Colombe's Birthday* was finished Browning was thirty-one. Though he had written other poetry, including dramatic poetry not intended for the stage, the bulk of his literary and personal energy had been devoted to establishing himself in the London theatre. At its best it was a congenial and sociable literary medium, so long as friendships could be preserved. The supper parties and the clubs which were an extension of theatrical society appealed to that aspect of Browning's character which marked him as a widower many years later. He was seen as the great diner-out who loved to be lionized by his hosts and hostesses. It was an oversimplified truth, and it was no less true of Browning in the early 1840s before his marriage. The only difference was that as a young dramatist he found it harder to persuade society to lionize him than was to be the case in the days of his fame.

The balance of loss and gain which his experience of the theatre represented was now evident. *Paracelsus* had shown his ability to write dramatic verse before the first play. His plays developed this in requiring a sharper definition of character, a more vigorous and even colloquial dialogue, a greater sense of place and atmosphere. The benefits of this were shown as early as *Pippa Passes* no less than in the later dramatic monologues. Yet the years of apprenticeship to the stage also represented the loss of a period in which some of his best poetry might have been written. Browning was increasingly apt to measure his own success against that of Tennyson, three years his elder. As *A Blot in the 'Scutcheon* closed after three nights and *Colombe's Birthday* was yet unperformed, Tennyson's collected *Poems* of 1842 went through one reprint after another to satisfy public demand. A civil list pension was almost in his grasp and the laureateship was but a few years away.

Browning's last experience of the theatre for the time being had also shown the divergence between his own taste and that of the public.[37] On 15 February 1843 the *Athenaeum* had made plain that *A Blot in the 'Scutcheon* was an affront to contemporary sexual morality – a criticism paralleled by the *Spectator's* remarks on *Pippa Passes* on 17 April 1841. The play was unpleasant and abhorrent, to use the *Spectator's* terms; a few people in the audience laughed and many were shocked. The laughter was a natural enough defence at a time when, as Edmund Gosse learnt from his father, the portrayal of sexual feeling was acceptable only when viewed 'in a ridiculous light'.[38]

Yet it was one of Browning's strengths, not least in his earlier poetry, that he dealt forthrightly with the sexual relationships of men and women. In these terms he wrote more powerfully and suggestively than any poet in England since John Donne two and a half centuries before. The reaction of audiences and critics alike had assured him that such things were unwelcome even in the milder treatment suited to the stage. In 'A Light Woman', which appeared in *Men and Women* (1855), the speaker describes how he seduced a friend's mistress. Then, in a laconic conclusion aptly recalling the reception of *A Blot in the 'Scutcheon*, the poet adds his wry farewell to such dramas.

> And, Robert Browning, you writer of plays,
>   Here's a subject made to your hand!

In the long term even Macready was forgiven. Talking to Domett in 1885 Browning referred to his friendship and quarrel with the great

67

actor. 'Ah, a sad business,' he said, 'but it is all over and past long ago.'[39]

For the immediate future it was Joseph Arnould who made the shrewdest prediction. Though referring to *A Blot in the 'Scutcheon*, its appreciation of Browning's energy and ambition rendered it true of his entire experience of the London theatre. 'I am sure in whatever way he regards it,' wrote Arnould to Domett, 'whether as a failure or a partial success, the effect on him will be the same, viz. to make him still to work, work, work.'[40]

5
Sordello: The Scapegoat

During a performance of *Strafford*, its author was approached by a
stranger who enquired if he was the same Browning who had written
Romeo and Juliet and *Othello*. The question was at first received with the
glowering suspicion of one who detects a joke aimed against him. Then
he discovered that the two plays mentioned were not Shakespeare's but
burlesques upon them. There was a sizeable audience in the 1830s who
would not be diverted from wild animal shows and pantomimes by the
originals but might none the less pay to see Shakespeare ridiculed.[1] For
all that it was a discouraging comment on Browning's own reputation
by the age of twenty-five.

Within three years of that date, while his theatrical career and poetic
progress ran parallel, the name of Robert Browning became not so
much famous as notorious. While his plays either failed to reach the
stage or to run for more than a few nights when they did so, a worse fate
still dogged his poetry. He became the object of easy laughter among
the literary world and of public scorn in the columns of the reviews.

The cause of this merriment and derision, as well as a good deal of
honest exasperation, was *Sordello*, published in March 1840. Any critic
who subsequently wished to show the impossibility of admiring Browning had only to mention *Sordello*, it seemed, in order to raise sympathetic
sighs of despair. There was often a fine irony in this. Ezra Pound, for
instance, found room for a scathing reference in the *Cantos*, poems in
which he himself went on to include such devices as Chinese ideograms,
thereby confounding the reader's comprehension to a far greater degree
than Browning had ever done.[2]

'Who will, may hear Sordello's story told,' was Browning's promise
in the poem's first line. Yet the story of *Sordello*'s creation was quite as
remarkable in its way as the story which the poem itself purported to
describe.

Browning's enthusiasm for Italy had never been in doubt, certainly not since Angelo Cerutti with his lively and scholarly mind had been engaged as Italian tutor when Browning was sixteen. Italy was already the country to which the boy owed a strong allegiance in terms of neo-classical art and literature. Seen in that light, it was the land whose artistic glories had been opened to him by Vasari and whose literature appeared to be embodied in the sublime visions of Dante. If the dreams and landscapes of Gerard de Lairesse could be realized anywhere, it was surely among the contrived Arcadias of Roman or Palladian villas.

It is possible that Browning worked on *Sordello* for seven years from the publication of *Pauline* in 1833. By April 1835 he was able to write to W. J. Fox describing it as 'a more popular' work than *Paracelsus* which was to appear that year.[3] The problem in tracing the evolution of *Sordello*, indeed the problem for Browning in writing it, was that the periods of composition alternated with other demands on his time from Macready and the theatre. It seems likely that for a variety of reasons *Sordello* was written or re-written four times between 1833 and 1840, emerging as a poem of almost six thousand lines in six books. In size and scope it might have been the first major poem of the Victorian period, comparable in stature to Milton's *Paradise Regained*, Pope's *Dunciad*, or the great single works of the English romantics.

No one, of course, received it in that way. The first, though not insurmountable, problem lay in the subject of the poem. Sordello was a Mantuan poet and warrior of the early thirteenth century whom Browning had discovered from at least two sources. The first of these was Dante's *Purgatorio* in which he is several times mentioned. In the famous translation of 1812 by Henry Francis Cary, the meeting of Virgil and Sordello in canto VI is described.

> 'Mantua', the shadow, in itself absorb'd,
> Rose towards us from the place in which it stood,
> And cried, 'Mantuan! I am thy countryman,
> Sordello.' Each the other then embraced.

There was little enough basis in this for Browning's story. He went again to the volumes of the *Biographie Universelle* in his father's library. Its columns offered him a compound of fact, legend and fabrication which had gathered about the name of the troubadour warrior. Very little indeed was known about Sordello beyond question. This in itself rendered him an attractive subject, a hero who could be moulded to the poet's purposes. The disadvantage, of course, was that the readership of early Victorian England knew little about Sordello and cared even less.

Browning saw the matter in another light, as he described it in the dedication of *Sordello* to Joseph Milsand in Browning's *Collected Poems* of 1863. Modernity was the essence of the work. Like Shelley in 'Alastor', Byron in *Childe Harold*, or Wordsworth in *The Prelude*, 'The historical decoration was purposely of no more importance than a background requires; and my stress lay on the incidents in the development of a soul'. The last five words almost exactly repeat the sub-title of Wordsworth's poem. *Sordello* was no mere historical exercise. It was to carry forward the work of the romantics, to adapt the great statements of experience in their major writings to the psychological requirements of the mid-nineteenth century.

To this end there would be a subtle and haunting evocation of Sordello's childhood in the castle of Goito near Mantua. A true romantic's vanity and ambition, not far removed from Browning's own, would inspire Sordello to oust the minstrel Eglamor from the Lady Palma's court at Mantua and take his place. Like Paracelsus, he finds ambition a worthless impulse in itself. Retirement gives him leisure to analyse, in terms that are post-romantic rather than mediaeval, the psychology of love and beauty; the nature of art and perception, including the role of poetic inspiration; the internal struggle between a man's humanity and his poetic obligations; and the necessary role of evil in the world. Surely, it seemed, these were the topics that would appeal to intelligent readers in the 1840s, regardless of the costume in which the poet clothed them. For good measure it was even possible to invest Sordello with a degree of nineteenth-century liberalism. At a time when Italy lay divided between the Guelf cause allied to Pope Henricus III and the rival Ghibellines supporting the Emperor Frederick II, it appears to Sordello that the former is the more democratic and admirable party. Force of circumstance has made him a leader of the Ghibellines, but in the last book of the poem he is caught between the claims of power and democracy. At his death he proves to be a democrat worthy of Lord John Russell or Gladstone, the badge of the autocratic Ghibellines crushed under his foot.

There was surely no reason, then, why Browning's historical poem should not have the type of success enjoyed by the more remote subjects of Byron, like *Manfred*, which commended themselves by a lively and dramatic approach to the intellectual fashions of the nineteenth century.

In May 1836, writing to Macready after the *Ion* supper, Browning described the poem as 'nearly done: I allow myself a month to complete it'.[4] This was probably a reference to the second version. At this stage it may well have been a far more straightforward poem than it proved to be four years later. Unhappily, there now occurred one of those freaks that bring despair to any author.

Early in 1837, before Browning had committed his new work to a publisher, there appeared the *Plays and Poems* of Mrs Busk. The first lines of the opening page blasted Browning's hopes and labours like a bolt from heaven.

> Listen, Fair Dames and Gallants Gay,
> Who love the Poet and his Lay,
> And Italy's harmonious clime,
> Soft nurse of painting, music, rhyme, –
> Come listen to the tale I tell
> Of him who sang and loved so well,
> The Mantuan Troubadour, renown'd Sordel!

There were two thousand lines of this tinkling ditty in a style imitated from Sir Walter Scott. Nor was it simply a matter of pre-empting Browning's subject. Mrs Busk did so in a manner which reduced *Sordello* to the verse of the nursery or the schoolroom. Reviewing the book on 22 July 1837, the *Athenaeum* asked unkindly of the tale: 'Is this founded upon the same subject as that chosen by the author of *Paracelsus* for his announced poem?'

Edmund Gosse once remarked: 'It was part of Mr Browning's essentially masculine order of mind to be in no wise disheartened or detached from his purpose by this indifference of the public.'[5] In the same spirit he was not to be deterred by Mrs Busk and her *Sordello*. He set about writing the six books of his poem for a third time, putting as much distance as possible between his own and the style and subject matter of his rival. Mrs Busk's poem was vacuous, melodious, as lightly ornamental as embroidery. Therefore, Browning must be historical, intellectual and violent.

The dangers inherent in this third version which he produced were clear enough. On 23 December 1837 he called upon Harriet Martineau and told her, '*Sordello* will soon be done now'. But, as Miss Martineau added, in describing the third version, Browning 'must choose between being historian or poet. Cannot split interest. I advised him to let the poem tell its own tale.'[6]

Unfortunately, that was precisely the course which the appearance of Mrs Busk's poem had ruled out. It was no part of the young romantic's inclination to trip tastefully along in the footprints of dame-school rhyming.

Because of the hostility which it generated in its final form it might be assumed that *Sordello* deteriorated with every version that Browning produced. Perhaps, though, the merely historical poem which Miss Martineau glimpsed was the worst of all. Several months later there occurred an opportunity by which Browning was able to save *Sordello*, in part at least, from being the poetic ruin which seemed its destiny.

In 1837, under the auspices of his Uncle William at Rothschild's bank, Browning had paid a visit to Paris. A year later a Rothschild shipment to Trieste offered him the means of fulfilling a far greater ambition: his first journey to Italy. The voyage may even have been dictated by a need to refurbish *Sordello* for the last time, since Lombardy and its hill towns were the object of his travels.

He sailed from St Katharine's Docks on 13 April 1838 on the *Norham Castle*. For the first week of the seven-week voyage the ship was delayed in the English Channel by gales and snow. There followed a stormy crossing of the Bay of Biscay, Browning being so sick that he could not even reach the deck without the guiding arm of the ship's captain, Matthew Davidson. Then, after a fortnight of misery, the *Norham Castle* passed Cape St Vincent, cleared the Straits of Gibraltar and exchanged Atlantic gales for the heat of the North African coastline.

'I did not write six lines while absent,' Browning told Fanny Haworth, '(except a scene in a play, jotted down as we sailed thro' the Straits of Gibraltar).'[7] Yet in his mind the final form of a major poem was taking shape, for he promised her at the same time: 'You will see *Sordello* in a trice, if the fagging fit holds.'[8]

Any drama which he might have written on the voyage paled by comparison with the macabre reality around him. Off Algiers the *Norham Castle* encountered a wrecked smuggler, floating keel uppermost. Captain Davidson had her made fast. Then, by means of a capstan-rope around her stanchions, the crew of the British ship righted her. Browning watched the gruesome scene with relish. As the smuggler turned suddenly upright, he counted 'one dead body floating out; five more were in the forecastle, and had probably been there a month under a blazing African sun'.[9] It intrigued him to see the attitudes in which the smugglers had died, one with his hands still clasped rigid in prayer.

The looting began, the English crew swarming on to the wreck, carrying away tobacco, cigars and bales of cloth. 'I cannot restrain my men,' Captain Davidson explained to Browning, 'and they will bring the plague into our ship, so I mean quietly in the night to sail away.'[10] The men pitched the corpses into the sea as they sought out their booty. Captain Davidson, who burnt disinfectants as a precaution, turned sick with the sight and smell. Browning proved to have a stronger stomach on this occasion. That evening the wreck was cut loose in a scene of mingled horror and glory, as he recorded it; the hulk 'reeled off, like a mutilated creature from some scoundrel French surgeon's lecture-table, into the most gorgeous and lavish sunset in the world'.[11]

Next day there was heavy rain, washing the fear of contagion from the decks of the *Norham Castle*. Browning landed at Trieste on 30 May and took the steamer for Venice. With him he carried his own loot from the Algerian smuggler, items which were a characteristic choice: 'two cutlasses and a dagger . . . intended for use.'[12]

For two weeks he remained in Venice, spellbound by its grandeur and decay, the market scenes and the bare-legged girls by the bridges of quiet canals, cameos which were to appear in *Sordello* itself.

> That Bassanese
> Busied among her smoking fruit-boats? These
> Perhaps from our delicious Asolo
> Who twinkle, pigeons o'er the portico
> Not prettier, bind late lilies into sheaves
> To deck the bridge-side chapel, dropping leaves
> Soiled by their own loose gold-meal? Ah, beneath
> The cool arch stoops she, brownest-cheek! . . .
>   . . . Nay, that Paduan girl
> Splashes with barer legs where a live whirl
> In the dead black Giudecca proves sea-weed
> Drifting has sucked down three, four, all indeed
> Save one pale-red striped, pale-blue turbaned post
> For gondolas.

From Venice he travelled inland to the fortified hill town of Asolo with its commanding view northwards across the Brenta Plain towards the Alps. Fifty-one years later the enchantment of the mediaeval town – the ruined castle and walls, the superb panorama of Lombardy – had lost none of its power. It was to be celebrated in his last collection of all, *Asolando* (1889).

> Lost from the naked world: earth, sky,
> Hill, vale, tree, flower, – Italia's rare
> O'er-running beauty crowds the eye.

The magic of Asolo itself was almost eclipsed by the castle of Goito, the scene of Sordello's childhood, facing northward towards Mantua from its hillside. In turn, it was to form the basis for a haunting and evanescent description in the final version of Browning's poem. If, as he told Fanny Haworth, he wrote virtually nothing during his travels in

Italy, he gathered enough from what he saw and heard to add a new and truly inspired dimension to the poem in its existing form.

His journey took him to Romano, across the valley from San Zenone degli Ezzelini, one of whose lords, Alberic, is hideously murdered at the end of Browning's story.

> ... I think grass grew
> Never so pleasant as in Valley Rù
> By San Zenon where Alberic in turn
> Saw his exasperated captors burn
> Seven children with their mother, and, regaled
> So far, tied on to a wild horse, was trailed
> To death through raunce and bramble bush.

Far removed from the gentility of Mrs Busk's tale, this was the historical account with all its savagery intact, written by a man who had stood at the place of such atrocities and who was told there how 'Alberic's huge skeleton' had been 'unhearsed' when a burial mound burst open five months before.

Bearing with him the images of his journey, Browning went back to Verona, which he was to use as yet another setting in his poem. From there he returned overland to England, across the Tyrol and down the Rhine.

The summer of 1838 was devoted to completing *Sordello* in its final form. At last the great poem, a chronicle of the inner life of the hero which might replace the failed *Pauline*, was ready for publication. The problem, of course, was to find a publisher. Browning's acquaintance Edward Moxon agreed to issue it but only on condition that the poet's father should pay the costs. This method of financing a book, even through a reputable publisher like Moxon, was still relatively common and Robert Browning the elder agreed at once to the arrangement. His son's poetry was not greatly to his own taste, which still led him back to the lucid cadences of Pope, but the pride and affection with which he watched the young man's progress were unquestionable.

Sordello, a Poem in Six Books, appeared as a volume of 253 pages early in March 1840. Unusually for Browning, it was written in rhyming couplets and was a verse narrative rather than the dramatic form in which he had done his best work so far. Yet of all his poetry to date, none had been launched upon the world with fuller expectation of success than this.

The result was one of the greatest literary disasters in the history of English poetry. Not only did *Sordello* itself fail, it dragged down

Browning's uncertain reputation with it. To live down the failure and farce of his poem took him more than twenty years. If the book's impact on the reading public could be judged by sales, the arithmetic of failure was painfully clear. Fifteen years later, with the publication of *Men and Women*, only 157 copies of *Sordello* had been sold out of the original edition of 500. Eighty-six further copies had been given away but half the edition remained in stock.

Worse than this was the reception *Sordello* received among its few influential readers. Some were inclined to uncomprehending resentment, others to mirth. Of the more famous reactions, Carlyle alleged that his wife had read the six books of the poem and was none the wiser as to whether Sordello was a man, a town, or a book. It is scarcely credible that she could have been in any doubt, but the literary world now turned waggish at Browning's expense. Tennyson claimed that he understood only the first line, 'Who will, may hear Sordello's story told', and the last line, 'Who would has heard Sordello's story told', and that both statements were lies. More famous still was the account of the journalist Douglas Jerrold who, recovering from a serious illness, was presented with the poem as his first piece of convalescent reading. With deepening dismay he grappled with Browning's verse until the fearful truth dawned upon him. The terrible secret which his family had kept from him was that his illness had brought insanity in its wake. 'My God!' he cried. 'I'm an idiot. My health is restored but my mind's gone. I can't understand two consecutive lines of an English poem.' Pale as death he handed the book back to his relatives at the bedside and saw, in turn, a look of complete bewilderment come over each face as they read it. With a sigh of profound relief, he went back to sleep. The story is always told of *Sordello* without the most important qualification. Douglas Jerrold was a distinguished contributor to *Punch* and a renowned wit. Given the way in which *Sordello* became a laughing-stock, he might have found it hard to resist a good deal of elaboration upon the truth of his first acquaintance with the poem.[13]

Following this lead, Harriet Martineau enlisted herself in the ranks of those who were so confused by the poem that they thought themselves ill. The reviewers were more robustly constituted. Those who bothered with the book at all dismissed it in terms of forthright common sense. Obscurity and affectation seemed evident to them all, and the *Spectator* on 14 March 1840 bluntly attributed this to Browning's 'crudity of plan and self-opinion'. It was once more left to Swinburne, Rossetti and the Pre-Raphaelites to find descriptive beauties in the poem which were too little apparent in 1840. Such admiration was in part the rebellion of a

younger generation against the dull and ponderous tastes of its predecessors. It was also an overdue act of justice.

By the age of twenty-eight Browning had evidently destroyed his reputation as a poet, while his plays were being rejected by Macready. Yet
there was more to the story of *Sordello* than that. At its best it showed a
poetic quality in advance of any of his writing for the theatre. If, during
his twenties, he wasted his talents as a poet, he did so to a far greater
extent by writing for the stage than in *Sordello*.

The faults of the poem were clear enough. Browning had entirely
disregarded Wordsworth's warning in the preface to his *Lyrical Ballads*
as to the taste of a new and more democratic age: 'To this knowledge
which all men carry about with them, and to these sympathies in which,
without any other discipline than that of our daily life, we are fitted to
take delight, the Poet principally directs his attention.' For answer, it
seemed, Browning had demanded a minutely detailed knowledge of
rivalry and politics in thirteenth-century Europe and a yet greater
familiarity with the warring courts and cultures of mediaeval Italy. Nor
did this prevent him from describing *Sordello* to Fox as a popular poem
in conception.

Even the reader who had access to a library as extensive as Browning's
father's would still have been stopped short by such passages as that at
the end of the third book, which begins:

> My English Eyebright, if you are not glad
> That, as I stopped my task awhile, the sad
> Dishevelled form wherein I put mankind
> To come at times and keep my pact in mind
> Renewed me.

English Eyebright was not, as it might sound, the name of a plant or a
bird but the nickname which Browning had privately given to his friend
and correspondent Euphrasia Fanny Haworth, being a literal English
rendering of her first Christian name.

There was, moreover, the problem of the style – or, more accurately,
styles – in which Browning chose to write. They varied from the Virgil-
ian simile as Dryden used it in the seventeenth century to a versification
which would pass for Gerard Manley Hopkins'.

> My transcendental platan! mounting gay
> (An archimage so courts a novice-queen)
> With tremulous silvered trunk, where branches sheen

77

> Laugh out, thick-foliaged next, a-shiver soon
> With coloured buds, then glowing like the moon
> One mild flame, last a pause, a burst, and all
> Her ivory limbs are smothered by a fall,
> Bloom-flinders and fruit-sparkles and leaf-dust,
> Ending the weird work prosecuted just
> For her amusement.

An age accustomed to the transparent ease of Hood, Mrs Hemans, or the young Tennyson regarded the compression and energy of such writing as wilful obscurity. Not so the young men of the 1860s who were to bring Browning to popularity at last. Yet even a historical perspective could scarcely excuse his style at its worst. The willing reader, beginning *Sordello*, encounters a discontinued sentence after twelve lines which leads to another of tortuous complexity, twenty-four lines long, likely to send him back to 'Casabianca' or 'The Lady of Shalott' with the least possible delay.

Samuel Johnson's famous remark on Richardson's fiction, that anyone who reads the novel for its story is likely to hang himself, might well be applied to *Sordello*. Yet the most apt comparison is perhaps with Edmund Spenser's *Faerie Queene*, like Browning's a poem of strange and haunting beauty in some of its passages though daunting to most readers in its entirety. Contrary to its critical reputation and reception at the time, *Sordello* contains some of the finest poetry of its day, a good deal that Tennyson might have envied and some which opens poetic landscapes beyond any of his own. Edmund Gosse, one of the shrewdest judges of his age, found in it 'passages of melody and insight, fresh enough, surprising enough to form the whole stock-in-trade of a respectable poet'.[14]

By contrast with Mrs Busk, Browning dwelt upon violence and eroticism as historical realities, the trades of torture and murder practised by men

> anointed, then, to rend and rip –
> Kings of the gag and flesh-hook, screw and whip.

Yet it was the pictorial qualities which Gosse and the Pre-Raphaelites before him admired, like the portrait of Adelaide of Goito which is almost a Rossetti painting in words.

> – Nor Adelaide bent double o'er a scroll,
> One maiden at her knees, that eve his soul
> Shook as he stumbled through the arras'd glooms
> On them, for, 'mid quaint robes and weird perfumes,

> Started the meagre Tuscan up (her eyes
> The maiden's also, bluer with surprise).

In one sense, the final version of *Sordello* was Browning's committal to verse of his Italian journey. This is true of his account of the bare-legged girls in Venetian backwaters, conveyed with the casual suggestiveness of a Fox Talbot photograph. If one other example serves to illustrate this, it is his description of the castle of Goito, the scene of his hero's childhood. Again, his picture is subtle and suggestive, full of images of light and darkness, hazy, half lit, with an air of menace and veiled sensuality.

> Pass within:
> A maze of corridors contrived for sin,
> Dusk winding-stairs, dim galleries got past,
> You gain the inmost chambers, gain at last
> A maple-panelled room: that haze which seems
> Floating about the panel, if there gleams
> A sunbeam over it will turn to gold
> And in light-graven characters unfold
> The Arab's wisdom everywhere; what shade
> Marred them a moment, those slim pillars made,
> Cut like a company of palms to prop
> The roof, each kissing top entwined with top,
> Leaning together.

By hidden ways the reader is brought to the secret chamber of the enchanted castle.

> A vault, see: thick
> Black shade about the ceiling, though fine slits
> Across the buttress suffer light by fits
> Upon a marvel in the midst: nay, stoop –
> A dullish grey-streaked cumbrous font, a group
> Round it, each side of it, where'er one sees,
> Upholds it – shining Caryatides
> Of just-tinged marble like Eve's lilied flesh.

Like Sordello, Browning was intrigued by the eroticism of the naked girls undergoing their eternal penance, holding up the font like slaves.

> The font's edge burthens every shoulder, so
> They muse upon the ground, eyelids half closed,
> Some, with meek arms behind their backs disposed,
> Some, crossed above their bosoms, some, to veil
> Their eyes, some, propping chin and cheek so pale....

> So dwell these noiseless girls, patient to see,
> Like priestesses because of sin impure
> Penanced for ever, who resigned endure,
> Having that once drunk sweetness to the dregs.

Such passages in Browning's poetry highlight his visual technique, that of detailed description and spatial awareness. It is what T.S. Eliot, comparing Milton with Shakespeare, called the ability to make the reader conscious of being in a particular place at a particular time.[15] Significantly, it was precisely the manner in which Browning's mentor Gerard de Lairesse executed his imaginary paintings. People and objects were described to the reader even more directly in their relations than if they had been on a stage set. In poetry the comparable quality exists in Shakespeare, Donne, or Browning. It is much rarer in Milton, Shelley, or Tennyson.

Because it is both precise as a stage-setting and yet at the same time naturalistic, Browning's poetry shows frequently a quality which the twentieth century might recognize as cinematic in its own terms. This was to be true, for example, of the first section of *Pippa Passes*, the lover and the mistress getting out of bed to admire the view from the window. If it is allowable to think of his work in such terms, then the description of the secret apartments at Goito, the strange and evocative décor, is perhaps reminiscent of nothing so much as Jean Cocteau's film fairy-tale, *La Belle et Le Bête*.

Nor is it merely a matter of evocative description, since Browning constantly accompanies this by psychological analysis of conduct associated with it. The naked girls, doomed to bear their burden of penance, lead on to his consideration of the relevance of love to beauty. It was a topic soon to be relevant in the most intimate affair of his whole life. Beauty, he concludes, cannot be loved for itself without breeding a mere frustration in the lover. Instead, it is the lover who creates beauty in the woman and by so doing creates her, as God created Eve. The lover is woman's creator. The poet is a supreme creator. Hence, the poet is the truest lover of all. In a striking image, Browning describes the simultaneous perception of love and beauty by divine sanction:

> ... fresh births of beauty wake
> Fresh homage; every grade of love is past,
> With every mode of loveliness; then cast
> Inferior idols off their borrowed crown
> Before a coming glory: up and down
> Runs arrowy fire, while earthly charms combine

To throb the secret forth; a touch divine –
And the scaled eyeball owns the mystic rod:
Visibly through his garden walketh God.

After nearly a century and a half, agreement on the excellence or failure of *Sordello* remains unlikely. The traditional view of literary criticism is represented by T. R. Lounsbury who, in 1911, dismissed the poem as 'a colossal derelict upon the sea of literature'.[16] Yet an age which has come to terms with poetry as diverse and complex as that of Rainer Maria Rilke and Ezra Pound is scarcely bound by such a judgement. Edmund Gosse's claim that *Sordello* contains, among its complexities, enough beauty to form the entire stock-in-trade of a poet is surely an exaggeration. None the less, what it exaggerates is an essential truth.

In 1862, writing in his *Estimate of the Value and Influence of Works of Fiction in Modern Times*, the idealist philosopher T. H. Green concluded that literature could not represent human life in all its slow and minute progressions.[17] From a subjective standpoint it seemed that Browning in *Sordello*, no less than James Joyce in *Ulysses*, sought to disprove such a thesis. The public or critical objections to both poem and novel were much the same – linguistic, allusive and organizational complexity: yet *Sordello* was important in Browning's development as a poet precisely because it allowed him to be speculative and suggestive, to dwell at' length upon the landscape of the mind and the springs of action that lay within it. The magic castle of Goito was as much a secret vision as the Arcadia of Gerard de Lairesse. By contrast, the dramas written for Macready had trained Browning to be specific, objective, and to adopt the idiom of external reality. The two lines of development were to be richly fused in the work which lay ahead.

6
Bells and Pomegranates

The effect of *Sordello* upon Browning's reputation reflects the changed literary world of the 1840s. A growing readership of books and the technology of mass printing had transformed the social context of poetry since Wordsworth and Coleridge issued their *Lyrical Ballads* in 1798 or the first canto of Byron's *Childe Harold* appeared in 1812. Apart from the value of its literature, the poetry and authors of the romantic movement were news in themselves. Upon the public interest in this, and in the related issues of political or economic reform, rose the new reviews of the first quarter of the nineteenth century – the *Edinburgh*, the *Quarterly* and the *Westminster* – with such contributors as Macaulay, Mill, Bentham and John Wilson Croker. Reputation in itself became increasingly a marketable commodity, raising Byron to international fame and condemning Keats to more than twenty years of posthumous obscurity.

By 1840 this new world of magazines and reviews, the trade of instant judgement, was securely established to serve the wider readership of the early Victorian period. Even twenty or thirty years earlier, *Sordello* might have been left to fade from the public memory. By 1840 the scale of its disaster was of sufficient interest to remain fresh in the reader's mind, to the lasting damage of Browning's standing as a poet. *Sordello* was both little read and well known.

Not that he was dismayed even by this. As the hostile reviews burst upon him, he wrote to Eliza Flower in March 1840: 'I have a head-full of projects – mean to song-write, play-write forthwith.' He then suggested that she might care to set to music the lyrics of his next publication, *Pippa Passes*.[1]

For all this self-confidence, the gruff rebuttal with which he met his critics, his endurance was severely tried. In 1830, at the age of eighteen, he was already writing to Christopher Dowson, a friend from the Colloquials, of his 'very indifferent health and very uncertain spirits'.[2]

By 1841 it was brain and liver fever which had reduced him to 'the shade of a shade'.[3] The chief and characteristic disorder was a series of headaches treated by a doctor who 'has piloted me safely through two or three illnesses, and knows all about me'.[4] To Elizabeth Barrett in 1846 he described how his bouts of feverishness were the prelude to his headaches.[5] Ironically, invalid though she was, it was his health which concerned her during that year. Gently she reproved his injudicious conduct. 'I heard yesterday that "Mr. Browning looked very pale as he came upstairs". Which comes of Mr. Browning's writing when he should be walking! – now doesn't it?' He had, it seemed, condemned himself to what he described vaguely elsewhere as 'vertiginousness' and 'a dizzy head'.[6]

The suggestion that Browning had inherited his mother's affliction, trigeminal neuralgia, was natural enough. A congenital defect, allowing insufficient room to the nerve as it passed through the floor of the skull, would have predisposed him to the severe attacks of pain in the upper face and near the eyes. A later age was to cure the malady temporarily by injections of alcohol or, indeed, permanently by cutting the trigeminal nerve near its origin.

There was, however, a quite different explanation in which, once again, Alfred Adler was to illuminate intriguingly an aspect of human personality which relates to Browning's condition. In 1911 Adler published his paper on *The Psychic Treatment of Trigeminal Neuralgia*, based upon his own success in treating three sufferers from the complaint. In each case, he found that neurosis rather than physiology had precipitated their chronic illness.

Positive proof of Browning's illnesses in his twenties and early thirties could not possibly be deduced from Adler's account. Yet that account offers a parallel which is, to say the least, a worthwhile topic of speculation. The personality most predisposed to trigeminal neuralgia from psychological causes, writes Adler, is one distinguished from youth by 'ambition, *conceit*, desire to know everything, to discuss everything, to be distinguished for bodily strength, beauty, distinction in dress'. In this catalogue, at least, every item applied to the youthful Browning, by his own account and by those of his contemporaries. In such a personality, Adler continues, the natural instincts 'take in him the form of the *ideas of greatness*, frequently actually modifying and obstructing the sexual instinct'. The characteristic of this 'obstruction' was that the subject should fail to find suitability in the women of his acquaintance rather than that he should notice his own inhibitions.

Though only a parallel and not a proof, it is interesting to see how

Adler's notion of ideas of greatness indulged at the expense of sexual feeling corresponds to the theme of *Paracelsus* – ambition pursued at the expense of love. Browning, unlike Adler's patients, possessed a clear insight into his own situation.

Last of all, Adler describes the role of the neuralgic headaches in the patient's conduct. The desire for recognition in society is coupled with a subconscious fear that this will not occur. The headaches, subconsciously generated, are therefore the means of avoiding society.[7]

Quite apart from Adler's thesis, a modern view of Browning at thirty is likely to emphasize the unresolved conflicts which remained as he passed from his twenties into his thirties. His supremely ambitious nature was confronted by the apparent collapse of his reputation as a poet. What *Paracelsus* had done for him was quickly undone by *Sordello*. In itself it was not remarkable at that time that Browning should be unmarried at thirty-four, still in parental pupilage at Camberwell: yet he was not one of nature's virgins, as by common consent another great figure of the 1830s, John Henry Newman, was held to be. Browning's careful and suggestive analysis of physical love between men and women had become a chief characteristic of his poetry by that age and, in thought at least, a major preoccupation. To compound whatever frustrations he might feel at thirty-four there was one statistical consideration. His family had been, on the whole, long-lived. However, diseases which were later to be simply cured or prevented lay in murderous ambush in the future of many young Victorians. Early working-class deaths decreased the overall life expectancy. Yet Browning at thirty-four was not, statistically at least, on a threshold of love and literature. He was just six years short of the average age of mortality for the Victorian period.

It is more tempting, because more intriguing, to regard the neuralgic headaches as outward manifestations of the conflicts engendered inside that 'life within life' behind Browning's bluff exterior manner; but the balance of doubt remains. The headaches became fewer and slighter after his marriage to Elizabeth Barrett, which might be seized upon to show that mere sexual frustration had played a large part in their origin. Unfortunately, as Adler remarks of cases other than his own cures, trigeminal neuralgia – whether of psychological or physiological origin – was alleviated by going to a warmer climate. It must remain a matter of speculation whether Elizabeth or Italy, or perhaps both, should be regarded as the successful therapy in Browning's case.

Before this, it was perhaps consideration of health which was among the causes of the Browning family's move from Southampton Street, Camberwell, to the greener pastures of Hatcham, near New Cross, in December 1840. Though they were hardly more distant from the centre of London than before, it seemed that there was less danger of Hatcham being swept away in 'the Railway "sirocco"', as Elizabeth Barrett termed it.[8]

As yet there was no intention that he should leave his parents' home. Indeed, the move brought the family closer to his grandfather's second wife, whose attitude towards them was reported to combine a natural curiosity with a waspish distaste. A room was set apart for Browning's work, its window opening on to a view of chestnut trees, holly hedge, and lambs bleating in the fields.[9] The room itself was adorned with a pair of skulls, in one of which Browning housed his pet spiders. 'Last year I petted extraordinarily a fine fellow,' he told Elizabeth Barrett in 1845, 'a great fellow that housed himself, with real gusto, in the jaws of a great scull, whence he watched me as I wrote.'[10] The two skulls were prized possessions, an open concession to Browning's taste for the macabre and a source of amusement when his visitors noticed their gruesome presence. 'Phrenologists look gravely at that great scull, by the way, and hope, in their grim manner, that its owner made a good end. He looks quietly, now, out at the green little hill beyond.'[11]

If the two skulls and similar bric-à-brac were to some extent a self-advertisement by the author of 'Madhouse Cells', there was no doubt of his genuine enthusiasm for the other item of decoration in his room, the print of Perseus and Andromeda which he had treasured since childhood. It was here that Carlyle depicted Browning at thirty working in his dark blue shirt and trousers, delighting in this 'picturesque bit of ghastliness', as the poet described his *memento mori*.[12]

That apart, Hatcham was close enough for Browning to record that he would walk to London and back, while inviting visitors to 'conquer the interminable Kent Road, pass the turnpike at New Cross, and take the first lane with a quickset hedge to the right'. There they would find the Brownings' garden, 'and trees, and little green hills of a sort to go out on'.[13] The influence of this pleasant garden view upon such poems as the two 'Garden-Fancies' and 'Home-Thoughts, from Abroad' was simple and direct.

In the early 1840s Browning moved a good deal in the more patrician literary society of London while privately expressing his alienation from it. 'I am dull, in every sense, this dull evening,' he wrote to Alfred Domett in New Zealand in 1843, 'and you are veritably *nearer* to me than the people in the city five miles off. Some call me over from time to time (*there* lies note the last, which I stopped this to say "no" to); but these are away – so are not you.'[14]

Chief among those who might have been Browning's patron, influential enough to have won him a civil list pension or a sinecure diplomatic post, was Richard Monckton Milnes, later Baron Houghton. Friend of Tennyson and Hallam, Conservative turned Liberal, traveller in the Levant who evinced a more than passing interest in the possibilities of harem ownership, Milnes attracted admiration and ridicule in equal parts. His *Life and Letters of John Keats* in 1848 restored the reputation of a forgotten romantic. He got Tennyson his pension and fed the Sadean enthusiasm of the young Swinburne from his library of pornography at Fryston. He lolled like a dandy on his bench in the House of Commons and even on the gravest topics the fatuousness of his style was known to provoke laughter. His breakfast parties, which Browning attended and where Swinburne passed out drunk, were the great events of fashionable intellectual society. As his friend Carlyle remarked acidly, if Jesus Christ returned to judge the world Monckton Milnes would be sure to invite Him to breakfast.

In Harley Street there was the less frenetic literary salon of 'Barry Cornwall', Bryan Proctor, whose circle included Leigh Hunt, Charles Lamb and Dickens. All were introduced to Browning and remained sympathetic to his work.

More important still was the developing relationship with Carlyle through Browning's visits to Cheyne Row. Despite his cantankerousness and pessimism, Carlyle remained the dour formidable intellect among all those whom Browning knew in the early 1840s. Indeed, he had penetrated the disguise of the young man-about-town and concluded that Browning 'among the men engaged in England in literature just now was one of the few from whom it was possible to expect something'.[15] Such qualified enthusiasm from Carlyle was rare enough to be worth more than ecstatic encouragement from any other contemporary.

Although he met men who admired his poetry, Browning felt no obligation to like them or their work in return. In Carlyle's case his attachment was profound and enduring. 'I dined with dear Carlyle and his wife (catch me calling people "dear", in a hurry, except in letter-beginnings!)' he wrote to Fanny Haworth in 1841.[16] He also retained his affection for Bryan Proctor, a barrister as well as a poet, a commissioner in lunacy whose professional experience was well matched with Browning's own curiosity about the labyrinth of human madness. However, he failed to reciprocate Dickens' enthusiasm for *A Blot in the 'Scutcheon*, expressed privately. 'Dickens is not asleep, but uproarious,' he wrote to Domett of the novelist's apparently limitless success, 'and (I think) disgusting, in his Pecksniffs.'[17] As for his most likely source of preferment, he could only report that 'Milnes is, or was, in Egypt or Syria'.[18]

Edward Moxon's premises were also a venue for authors of varying condition. Thomas Campbell, once the great Scottish romantic poet and now in his declining years, was to be seen 'in a kind of maudlin drowse over the fire in Moxon's shop'. Browning, fascinated by the sight of the great poet in decay, asked if it really was Campbell in the Dover Street shop. 'Very likely Campbell,' said Moxon airily; 'he does not know where to go to kill time, and we take no notice of him.'[19]

Unlike almost all Browning's other literary acquaintances, Moxon was a publisher and therefore able, at least, to put the poet's work before the reviewers and the public. Like many early Victorian publishers he had been won over to the idea of publication in parts, which had proved so successful in the case of Dickens' novels, and to the more economic format of cheap type and double-column pages. He had found that this method answered well in bringing out his editions of Elizabethan dramatists. If Browning agreed, and if his father was still prepared to meet the costs, it would be possible to issue plays or collections of poems in this form for about £16 a time. After the expensive failure of *Sordello*, in commercial terms, it was an idea which commended itself to the Browning family.

Moxon's sympathetic attitude towards the young poet was to some extent a recognition of the moral support which Browning had offered during the greatest crisis in the career of the celebrated publisher. In 1839 Moxon had published Shelley's *Poetical Works*, omitting the passages of *Queen Mab* that secured the conviction of William Clark in 1821. However, these were restored in the popular edition of 1840 at the insistence of the poet's widow. Henry Hetherington, an atheist radical, protested that now 'there was one law for the "low booksellers of the Strand" and another for the aristocratic booksellers of Dover Street'.[20]

The government reluctantly indicted Browning's publisher for blasphemous libel. In 1841, Moxon and three booksellers stood in the dock at the Central Criminal Court.[21] Browning, who had assisted in preparing the edition of Shelley, could only lend moral support. Another friend, Serjeant Thomas Noon Talfourd, led the defence. One passage cited from *Queen Mab* in the indictment typified the rest.

> From an eternity of idleness
> I, God, awoke; in seven days' toil made earth
> From nothing; rested, and created man:

> I placed him in a Paradise, and there
> Planted the tree of evil, so that he
> Might eat and perish, and My soul procure
> Wherewith to sate its malice, and to turn,
> Even like a heartless conqueror of the earth,
> All misery to My fame.

Before Lord Denman and the Queen's Bench judges, Talfourd argued that such passages were no more blasphemous than the speeches put by Milton into the mouths of the fallen angels in *Paradise Lost*. None the less, the jurors found Moxon guilty. Denman suggested pointedly that, for the future, the answer to such books lay in 'confuting the sentiments themselves' rather than in criminal prosecutions. He merely bound Moxon over in his own recognizances to be of good behaviour. *Queen Mab* was never prosecuted again.[22]

The poor sales of *Strafford* had dissuaded Longman from taking on any more of Browning's work. Despite the failure of *Sordello* in 1840, Edward Moxon was prepared to lend his name, if not his money, to the more economically produced editions of the poet's work between 1841 and 1846.

The eight parts published during this time were given the collective title of *Bells and Pomegranates*, which in itself brought charges of obscurity from the *Athenaeum*. It happened to be an unidentified allusion to the bells and pomegranates on the robe of the High Priest in *Exodus*, xviii, 33–34.[23]

Eight parts of *Bells and Pomegranates* were published, four of them being the plays which Browning had already offered to Macready or Charles Kean. The other parts were *Pippa Passes* (1841); *Dramatic Lyrics* (1842); *Dramatic Lyrics and Romances* (1845), and a pair of verse dramas not intended for the stage, *Luria, and A Soul's Tragedy* (1846).

In the dedication to Serjeant Talfourd, Browning describes *Pippa Passes* as 'the first of a series of Dramatical Pieces, to come out at intervals'. More specifically, while walking in Dulwich Wood after his return from Italy, he had conceived a simple and poignant idea. In the setting of Asolo, rich in its associations with the crime and political intrigues of the past, he would describe a young girl, a figure of innocence moving untouched through a world of murder, adultery, assassination and prostitution. The setting, however, would be modern.

It remains an irony of Browning's reputation that the poem should be known for the simple optimism of Pippa's lyricism rather than for the uncompromising realism of some of its major scenes. From the opening portrayal of the adulterous Ottima and her lover Sebald to the political intrigue and the dark designs of enforced prostitution, its most striking achievements were of a quite different order.

If *Pippa Passes* caused moral misgivings to such reviewers as the critic of the *Spectator*, it was largely because Browning in 1841 chose to describe sexual infidelity in a manner which still shocked many readers in the 1880s. Ottima rises naked from the bed with 'Those morbid, olive, faultless shoulder-blades', wheedling Sebald as he opens the shutters. When they discuss the murder of her husband and Sebald tries to make Ottima call herself a whore, the poem is far closer to the world of Maupassant or Zola than to the decorative eroticism of *Sordello* where, as in a Boucher painting, 'Venus' kiss-creased nipples pout/Back into pristine pulpiness'.

In this first main scene of *Pippa Passes* Browning enters a world of post-romantic modernism. If, like Donne, he uses the details of ordinary life to heighten sexual suggestion, he also develops a naturalistic quality which parallels the camera in its loving description of objects and decoration. So Ottima speaks as she watches her lover open the shutters awkwardly.

> Mind how you grope your way, though! How these tall
> Naked geraniums straggle! Push the lattice –
> Behind that frame! – Nay, do I bid you? – Sebald,
> It shakes the dust down on me! Why, of course
> The slide-bolt catches. – Well, are you content,
> Or must I find you something else to spoil?

The reader, too, is admitted to a world of adult sexual preoccupations unknown to virtually all contemporary poetry, Tennyson's included. For instance, Sebald recalls how the peasants laughed after old Luca married young Ottima, because the closed shutters indicated that they spent the mornings in bed making love.

> O, I remember! – and the peasants laughed
> And said, 'The old man sleeps with the young wife!'

This was not so much a subject for the 1840s as an anticipation of Maupassant's novel *Une Vie* (1883) in which Jeanne is embarrassed by the amusement of the hotel staff when her husband takes her to bed in the afternoons. Henry Vizetelly was prosecuted and imprisoned in the year of Browning's death for issuing that novel in England.[24]

There is also an immediacy in the naked Ottima drawing Sebald close behind her to admire the view:

> Ah, the clear morning! I can see St Mark's:
> That black streak is the belfry. Stop: Vicenza
> Should lie ... There's Padua, plain enough, that blue!
> Look o'er my shoulder – follow my finger –

Unlike Sebald she has little regret at her husband's death. When her lover says of the old man,

> 'Faith, he is not alive
> To fondle you before my face!

Ottima replies with a wanton provocation,

> Do you
> Fondle me, then!

Even Sebald's remorse for their crime is expressed in terms of his sensuous appreciation of Ottima's beauty.

> I would give your neck,
> Each splendid shoulder, both those breasts of yours,
> That this were undone!

Into this scene of guilt and desire drifts the pure innocence of Pippa's most famous lines.

> *God's in his heaven –*
> *All's right with the world!*

As moral admonition or macabre irony, the intrusion is equally effective. It impels Sebald to exclaim to his mistress:

> Go, get your clothes on – dress those shoulders!

The poem is populated by characters as evocative in their way as any in a novel. Jules the sculptor dreams of modelling his mistress Phene naked upon horseback. Luigi is torn between his own safety, his mother's pleading, and the moral duty of assassination to help free Italy from the Austrian tyranny imposed on her by Metternich. Among them all is the comic, sinister character of the dissolute young Englishman, Bluphocks, a useful tool of the Austrian police, with his doggerel on quack medicines which might almost have come out of an interior monologue by Leopold Bloom in James Joyce's *Ulysses*. '*Hebe's plaister – One strip Cools your lip. Phoebus' emulsion – One bottle Clears your throttle – Mercury's bolus – One box Cures....*' The concluding words omitted are presumably '*the Pox*'.

With a bluntness that Dickens dared not use, for instance in describing the profession of Nancy in *Oliver Twist*, Browning records the conversation of the young Asolo prostitutes who sit on the cathedral steps and talk of their clients.[25] One is currently being kept by a man 'Greyer and older than my grandfather'. With skill as well as tact, Browning portrays these girls as credible and sympathetic figures. The one in question talks quite naturally of the old man,

> Feeding me on his knee with fig-peckers,
> Lampreys, and red Breganze-wine, and mumbling
> The while some folly about how well I fare,
> To be let eat my supper quietly.

The poem is open to the interpretation that none of these dramas happened anywhere but in Pippa's mind and imagination as she walked through Asolo on the one day which was her holiday from working in the silk mill. But whatever the interpretation, the poem marked Browning's greatest achievement to date, the modernity and characterization which were to typify most of his finest work in the future. With *Pippa Passes* he had at last come of age.

John Forster loyally praised the poem in the *Examiner* on 2 October 1841 but elsewhere there was a mixture of incomprehension and moral disapproval. In print, let alone on the stage, the subjects of Browning's poems were scarcely welcome to those who regarded the evangelical piety of Robert Montgomery, author of poems on such subjects as 'The Effects of Indiscriminate Novel-Reading', as the highest form of art. By comparison with Montgomery, said Elizabeth Barrett firmly, her spaniel Flush was more of a poet 'by the shining of his eyes!'[26] None the less, the moral climate was such as to make *Pippa Passes* an object of censure by periodicals like the *Spectator* of 17 April 1841. 'In one scene, a young wife and her paramour discuss their loves, and the murder of the "old husband" needlessly, openly, wantonly, tediously, and without a touch of compunction, sentiment, or true passion.' It was of little use to point out that in reality this was precisely the manner of such discussions or that, in this case, the weight of sin made the perpetrators see death as a welcome salvation.

At thirty years old the young romantic had still to make his way as a poet. To compound the impression of gloom, he lived in a self-made literary isolation, an inward life devoid of friends. The row with Macready had strained his relationship with Forster as well. In 1842 the most enduring of his affections among the Colloquials was with Alfred Domett. But Domett had already decided upon a life in New Zealand. Describing his departure in 'Waring', Browning was able to treat the

incident with an ironic melancholy, though the strength of his affection
and the gentle reproach were never far below the surface of the poem.

> I left his arm that night myself
> For what's-his-name's, the new prose-poet
> That wrote the book there, on the shelf –
> How, forsooth, was I to know it
> If Waring meant to glide away
> Like a ghost at break of day?

Despite the disguise of 'Waring', Browning's true feelings were put
on public display in the course of the informal, intimate verse.

> Meantime, how much I loved him,
> I find out now I've lost him:
> I, who cared not if I moved him,
> Who could so carelessly accost him,
> Henceforth never shall get free,
> Of his ghostly company.

The letters which Browning wrote to Domett after this speak for
themselves in describing that sense of loss. 'I have a sort of notion you
will come back some bright morning a dozen years hence and find me
just gone – to Heaven or Timbuctoo,' he wrote as his friend sailed for
New Zealand.[27] Four months later, still under his parents' roof, he
added, 'I have seen nobody this long time, not Cris. Dowson even –
Arnould never since our parting night'.[28] By the following year he was
still writing to Domett in the same vein. 'I go out but seldom, so keep
meaning to see Arnould and other friends instead of seeing them.'[29] In
October 1843 he added, 'I make no new friends, which sometimes seems
a pity'.[30] 'I want to hear about you often, if but in scraps and notelets,'
he wrote a month later, adding a plea that was nicely balanced between
earnestness and facetiousness: 'take ship, in heaven's name, and come
here in the cursed six months! There you walk past our pond-rail
(picking up one of the fallen horse-chestnuts), and now our gate-latch
clicks, and now – '[31]

The close and essentially benevolent male friendships of the earlier
nineteenth century put Domett in somewhat the same relationship to
Browning as Hallam was to Tennyson. But whereas death was celebrated by *In Memoriam*, Domett's twenty-nine-year absence was more
lightly lamented in 'Waring' and a number of private letters.

Death was soon to deprive Browning of two of the closest friends of
his adolescence and early manhood, the Flower sisters. Both were seriously ill with tuberculosis. Eliza died in 1846 and her younger sister,

now married as Sarah Flower Adams, died two years later. It was in 1845 that he had to write his last letter to Eliza, the object of his early affections, who was by then too ill to receive his visit. There was no pretence between them as to the inevitable course of her sickness.

> Of your health I shall not trust myself to speak: you must know what is unspoken. I should have been most happy to see you if but for a minute – and if next Wednesday, I might take your hand for a moment. –
>   But you would concede that, if it were right, remembering what is now very old friendship.
>   May God bless you for ever[32]

There were two clear remedies for such personal sorrows as this, both of which Browning adopted. The first lay in dedication to work, a resolve natural to one of Browning's upbringing. By contrast, there was the cure for loneliness offered in the agreeable but emotionally un-demanding company of fashionable society. As a widower, Browning was to be conspicuous by his appearance at the dinner tables of London's hostesses, at patrician house parties and the private recitals of celebrities like Clara Schumann. To the surprise and even dismay of his friends he shone as wit and raconteur among the rich and the famous. Again, it was Browning the bachelor who served an apprenticeship which was to make Browning the widower a lion of London's seasons in the 1860s and 1870s.

Joseph Arnould described the young poet in the metropolitan society of the mid-1840s. 'Glorious Robert Browning is as ever, but more genial, more brilliant, more anecdotal than when we knew him four years ago.'[33] Yet the geniality and the anecdotes were accompanied by an appeal to both the intellect and sophistication of his hosts. 'Browning's conversation is as remarkably good as his books, though so different: in conversation anecdotal, vigorous, showing great thought and reading, but in his language most simple, energetic and accurate.'[34] At a grow-ing distance, Arnould watched Browning 'from one height scaling another'.[35]

Among the houses outside London where he was now made welcome was Bettisfield Park in Flintshire. Here he visited Sir John Hanmer, member of parliament and Tory, 'born so, and bred so'. They discussed politics and poetry, including Hanmer's own volume of 'pretty poems', *Fra Cipollo and other Poems*, from which Browning took the epigraph for *Colombe's Birthday*. But in Hanmer's case politics had a more immediate relevance. To Browning's delight he deserted the Tory ranks and voted for the abolition of the Corn Laws, a move intended to feed England's poor more cheaply by abolishing the duty on imported grain.[36]

93

Despite the time and industry which Browning spent on his longer poems and plays, he had also been at work on shorter poems for about eight years. Most of these remained unpublished. On 22 May 1842 he told Domett that he had decided to 'print a few songs and small poems which Moxon advised me to do for popularity's sake'.[37] In Browning's case 'small' was a comparative term, applied as it was to a poem like 'The Pied Piper of Hamelin', written for Macready's son and numbering over three hundred lines. Even so, Moxon's advice seemed well timed in the light of Browning's reputation as the author of obscure and often impenetrable poems of almost epic length.

Dramatic Lyrics, a collection of sixteen pieces, was published in yellow paper wrappers during November 1842. It was followed three years later by *Dramatic Romances and Lyrics*, containing twenty-two further poems in the same format. This pair of books made up the whole of Browning's shorter poems before the appearance of *Men and Women* in 1855.

Taken together, the two collections look back to the 'prolonged relation' of Browning's childhood as well as forward to the interests and preoccupations of his maturity. 'Cavalier Tunes', for instance, belong very much to the world of the parlour and the piano with their thumping rhythms and boisterous choruses.

> *Marching along, fifty-score strong,*
> *Great-hearted gentlemen, singing this song!*

Their titles, 'Marching Along', 'Give a Rouse' and 'Boot and Saddle', no less than the later and more famous 'How they brought the good news from Ghent to Aix', indicate their tone. Though far removed from the obscurities of *Sordello*, they bred another reputation, that of Browning the trite and insensitive optimist. As he later complained, if his poetry were free from charges of incomprehensibility, it was unfairly characterized by such lines as '*Bang, whang, whang* goes the drum, *tootle-te-tootle* the fife'. As much as 'The Pied Piper of Hamelin', which he termed 'A Child's Story', such pieces as 'Cavalier Tunes' were homely if not childish amusements. They lie like forgotten toys among the literary possessions of a man of thirty.

Indeed, life at Hatcham was more specifically commemorated by two 'Garden-Fancies' in the second collection. The female figure in the first of them, 'The Flower's Name', might be taken for the poet's mistress, though it is hard to dissociate Browning's mother from the memory of the garden she had created.

Here's the garden she walked across,
    Arm in my arm, such a short while since:
Hark, now I push its wicket, the moss
    Hinders the hinges and makes them wince!
She must have reached this shrub ere she turned,
    As back with that murmur the wicket swung;
For she laid the poor snail my chance foot spurned,
    To feed and forget it the leaves among.

In her reverence for the lowest forms of animal life, the woman described is characteristically of the Browning family. The view from the poet's window seems unmistakably that of the early Victorian summer garden which Mrs Browning tended.

Down this side of the gravel-walk
    She went while her robe's edge brushed the box:
And here she paused in her gracious talk
    To point me a moth on the milk-white flox.
Roses, ranged in a valiant row,
    I will never think that she passed you by!
She loves you noble roses, I know;
    But yonder, see, where the rock-plants lie!

Many of the poems in the two books reflect the learning acquired from his father's library, though less formidable here than in the earlier, longer poems. 'Artemis Prologuizes' is a tribute to Euripides, while the history and culture of Europe from the troubadours to Napoleon are employed elsewhere. Yet even in a poem like 'The Flight of the Duchess', inspired by a boyhood memory of a snatch of a song, Browning's style shows a modernity of subject and treatment far beyond the 1840s.

That's one vast red drear burnt-up plain,
Branched thro' and thro' with many a vein
Whence iron's dug, and copper's dealt;
Look right, look left, look straight before, –
Beneath they mine, above they smelt,
Copper-ore and iron-ore,
And forge and furnace mould and melt,
And so on, more and ever more,
Till, at the last, for a bounding belt,
Comes the salt sand hoar of the great sea shore.

As a poetic landscape, the equivalent of this lies not in the 1840s, nor indeed in the Victorian period as a whole, but in the industrial waste-lands of W. H. Auden or Stephen Spender ninety years in the future.

Even apart from the two 'Madhouse Cells' reprinted there, the two collections clearly show the future direction of his poetry. Two of the dramatic monologues, 'My Last Duchess' and 'The Bishop Orders his Tomb at St Praxed's Church', are among the most accomplished of all Browning's poems. He had, of course, served his apprenticeship as a writer of dramatic verse, and the effect of this appears in the chill concision of the Duke's hints or the deathbed lewdness of the worldly prelate. That apart, the impact of the monologue was all the greater since it removed any means for the poet to conciliate the reader. Browning's achievement was precisely in showing the worst that could be said or done without such palliation. Having murdered his first wife, the Duke is permitted to buy a replacement. The Bishop, guilty of a full range of the deadly sins, approaches his end mouthing piety and aiming a sneer at the dead rival who would have taken his mistress from him.

'Madhouse Cells' might have served Browning as a more general title. The Duke, the Bishop, the speaker in 'Soliloquy of the Spanish Cloister', occupy private universes not far removed from those of Porphyria's lover and Johannes Agricola. 'Cristina', which Browning placed immediately before 'Madhouse Cells' in *Dramatic Lyrics*, is less famous but yet a superb exercise in the plausible interior logic of the insane. The speaker believes that when the promiscuous Queen Cristina of Sweden glanced at him for an instant, she fell irretrievably in love. She has, of course, never looked at him since, but that moment's glance is now her whole life to her. The poem describes the reaction of an amorous prude to a promiscuous woman, carried to an extreme which is only possible in the pathetic, insistent reasoning of the mad.

> She should never have looked at me,
>   If she meant I should not love her!
> There are plenty ... men, you call such,
>   I suppose ... she may discover
> All her soul to, if she pleases,
>   And yet leave much as she found them:
> But I'm not so, and she knew it.

From this rational basis the speaker convinces himself that what was in truth the supreme obsessive moment of his own life was really that of Cristina's.

> Doubt you whether
> This she felt as, looking at me,
>   Mine and her souls rushed together?

Elsewhere the poems of the two collections are coloured by Browning's use of the grotesque in a wider sense, never more so than in describing the love of men and women. 'The Laboratory' is a monologue by a girl, addressed to the alchemist who is preparing a poison to kill her rivals. She rewards the old man with her jewels, gold and sexual promise. Browning, with his interest in the criminal mind, shrewdly identifies the sense of power enjoyed by the poisoner over his victims, later to be exemplified in the case of Dr Thomas Neill Cream.

> Soon, at the King's, a mere lozenge to give
> And Pauline should have just thirty minutes to live!
> But to light a pastile, and Elise, with her head,
> And her breast, and her arms, and her hands, should drop dead!

The poem is characterized throughout by the exhilaration of the girl who is certain to succeed in her purposes.

A companion poem to this, 'The Confessional', links love and death in circumstances which are no less gruesome. The girl's memory of love is recalled through the intervening experience of being tortured by the Inquisition.

> This poor wrenched body, grim and gaunt,
> Was kissed all over till it burned,
> By lips the truest, love e'er turned
> His heart's own tint: one night they kissed
> My soul out in a burning mist.

The exact nature of sexual ecstasy is left skilfully if suggestively imprecise while revealing that the girl herself was shocked by its intensity. Similarly, the heroine of 'In a Gondola', accepting death as the price of love, urges her lover:

> 'Tis said, the Arab sage
> In practising with gems can loose
> Their subtle spirit in his cruce
> And leave but ashes: so, sweet mage,
> Leave them my ashes when thy use
> Sucks out my soul, thy heritage!

In such poems Browning was of course treading dangerous ground. Erotic realism was no more palatable to the reading public of the early 1840s simply because it was mingled with murder or torture in an historical setting. The obscurity of *Sordello* was scarcely to be redeemed by this any more than by the secrets of the madhouse or the cool logic of the criminally insane.

It detracts nothing from the finest poems of the two collections to say that the poetry in general gives the impression of Browning striving after an effect. At their best the poems combine realism with the power and colour of dramatic verse. Elsewhere the combination of sexuality and horror, for instance, comes too close to melodrama. As it happened, *Dramatic Lyrics* went almost unnoticed in the press. John Forster loyally reviewed it in the *Examiner* on 25 November 1842. Yet even he implied, as kindly as possible, that the sense of striving after effect was the book's greatest weakness. 'In a word, Mr Browning is a genuine poet, and only needs to have less misgiving on the subject himself.'

The publication of the second collection, *Dramatic Romances and Lyrics*, in November 1845 produced little further response from the reviewers. Once again it was the *Examiner* which offered the greatest encouragement. Of Browning's poems it wrote: 'They look as though already packed up and on their way to posterity; nor are we without a confident expectation that some of them will arrive at that journey's end.'

The noblest reward was not a review at all. Among the copies of *Dramatic Romances and Lyrics* which Browning had sent out was one to Walter Savage Landor, who combined the vigour of classicism and the rebelliousness of a romantic in a manner which made him second only to Byron as a hero of the new generation. By way of a reply, Landor sent a poem to the *Morning Chronicle*, which published it on 22 November 1845.

> To Robert Browning
>
> There is delight in singing, tho' none hear
> Beside the singer: and there is delight
> In praising, tho' the praiser sit alone
> And see the prais'd far off him, far above,
> Shakespeare is not our poet, but the world's,
> Therefore on him no speech! and brief for thee,
> Browning! Since Chaucer was alive and hale,
> No man hath walkt along our roads with step
> So active, so inquiring eye, or tongue
> So varied in discourse. But warmer climes
> Give brighter plumage, stronger wing: the breeze
> Of Alpine highths thou playest with, borne on
> Beyond Sorrento and Amalfi, where
> The Siren waits thee, singing song for song.

Browning had anticipated Landor's invitation in the final lines of the poem. In the autumn of 1844 he sailed to Naples, arriving in September. On 4 October he had reached the Siren Isles, which suggests that Landor in his poem may have been referring to this visit. He crossed the Piano di Sorrento, finding there both the setting and occasion for his

poem 'The Englishman in Italy'. In these lines the poet comforts a girl
while the Sirocco blows. The descriptions of the lush southern autumn
are in terms sensuous enough to derive from Keats.

> We shall feast our grape-gleaners (two dozen,
>> Three over one plate)
> With lasagne so tempting to swallow
>> In slippery ropes,
> And gourds fried in great purple slices,
>> That colour of popes....
> And end with the prickly-pear's red flesh
>> That leaves thro' its juice
> The stony black seeds on your pearl-teeth.

Browning left no other account of his visit to southern Italy but the
poem is alive with images of the population in that area – the fishermen,
the screaming naked children as 'brown as shrimps', and the grape
harvesters.

He travelled north to Rome, where he visited the grave of Shelley,
and then to Leghorn to call on Edward John Trelawny, friend and
companion of Byron and Shelley, the last man to see Shelley alive.
During the conversation, Trelawny stoically bore the pain of a surgeon's
probe locating a bullet in his leg from an ancient wound. By the end of
1844 the traveller was back in England. In consequence of his visit to
the church of San Prassede in Rome, he carried with him impressions
that were soon to be transformed into one of the most brilliant and
compelling examples of the dramatic monologue, the inspired humanism of 'The Bishop Orders his Tomb at St Praxed's Church'.

While Browning's poetry continued to show the fascination of Italy
and the Renaissance, his Italian journey reflected his growing identification with liberalism in English politics. As the speaker of 'The Englishman in Italy' explains to the Italian girl,

> ... in my England at home,
>> Men meet gravely to-day
> And debate, if abolishing Corn-laws
>> Is righteous and wise
> – If 'tis proper, Sirocco should vanish
>> In black from the skies!

Summing up the situation in England, he had already told Domett,
'Here everything goes flatly on, except the fierce political reality (as it
begins to be). Our poems, &c., are poor child's play.... There is much,
everything, to be done in England just now.'[38] As it happened, his own

contribution was through his poetry – in the form of the attack on Wordsworth's apostasy in 'The Lost Leader', on the Corn Laws in 'The Englishman in Italy', and on political dilettantism in 'Waring'. Though he remained, in poetry and disposition, committed to an active part in the controversies of his time, Browning shared with many contemporaries a belief that the existing Corn Laws were the chief impediment to social peace. If the threatened revolution of the Chartists was not to become a reality, if the vitriol-throwing or murder was not to characterize industrial warfare, a quick and simple remedy was needed to feed the starving workers of the new cities. He and others might be forgiven for seeing in the abolition of tax on imported grain a speedy and obvious remedy. Hence the enthusiasm with which he saw that abolition, announcing in 1845 that 'times are mending here – Peel turns Liberal, "with other delights"'. One of those delights was Carlyle's sympathy with such views as Browning's; 'the intensity of his Radicalism, too, is exquisite'.[39]

In respect of his own future, Browning was determined to the point of defiance to follow through what he had begun. By the age of thirty he already had that well-developed resentment of criticism which, for almost half a century, drove him to turn against reviewers in language which was often crude and generally ill judged. For the time being his bitterness was voiced privately, as in a letter to Domett in 1843.

> They take to criticising me a little more, in the Reviews – and God send I be not too proud of their abuse! For there is no hiding the fact that it is of the proper old drivelling virulence with which God's elect have in all ages been regaled. One poor bedevilling idiot, whose performance reached me last night only, told a friend of mine, the night before that, 'how in *reality* he admired beyond measure this and the other book of Mr B.'s, but that *in the review*, he thought it best to,' &c., &c. This Abhorson boasted that he got £400 a year by his practices! But New Zealand is still left me![40]

He also complained that there was something approaching a plot against him to prevent good reviews from appearing. When R. H. Horne praised him in the manuscript of an article for the *Church of England Quarterly* for October 1842, Browning swore that 'some wiseacre of a sub-editor has been allowed to travel over and spoil [it] in as many points as he has touched'.[41] The result was, in Browning's view, to dull the praise and sharpen the criticisms, 'so that instead of flaring heaven-high, as Carlyle would say – I only range with the gas-lamps in ordinary. Read and laugh, for thereto I send it!'[42]

It seemed a measure of Browning's insecurity, as regards his literary reputation at this time, that he vacillated between scorn of his critics when they disliked his work and a hasty acceptance of those who praised him. 'Were you never discouraged at the indifference of the public and the hostility of the critics to your writings?' W. G. Kingsland asked him. 'Never,' said Browning firmly. 'Why, I had the approbation of Fox, and Mill, and Forster, and was content with their verdict.'[43]

To the world at large Browning even turned his alleged 'incomprehensibility' into a joke, as if it had been invented solely by his detractors in the reviews and magazines. 'After all, writing unintelligible metaphor is not voted as bad as murder,' he remarked lightly upon the reception of *Sordello*.[44] It was once again in private, a fortnight after his thirtieth birthday, that he anticipated another 'ten or dozen years' of literary apprenticeship. 'I don't expect to do any real thing till then.'[45]

The fortitude and consistency of Browning's character was never more clearly shown than in such resolves. He had outlived the span of Keats and Shelley, almost that of Byron, and of Wordsworth in the years of achievement. To a young romantic there was every reason to regard the time of promise as past. Even Tennyson, his near contemporary, was approaching the meridian of a career and the gradual decline of his powers. For all the disappointments which attended nearly a dozen of his books at their first appearance, not to mention the collapse of his ambitions as a dramatist, Browning continued to show a confidence and self-reliance which had more in common with the faith of his childhood than with the romantic revival. In his attitude to the future of his own poetry, no less than in the scorn which he showed to his critics, he behaved with an inspired arrogance. Those who observed his conduct might have been forgiven for supposing that he truly did, after all, regard himself as one of God's Elect.

In other terms he showed the dedication of a soldier or an ascetic. It was a private resolve to show himself worthy of the trust which his family and the dead gods of the romantic movement had placed upon him. From this confinement he sprang upon the world periodically with the energy of a schoolboy set free. Then he was the dealer in informed anecdote and the expansive gossip of the fashionable dinner table. Into such a life and such a frame of mind there now intruded the poetry and the personality of Elizabeth Barrett. In itself, such an intrusion was unremarkable. The cause for surprise, misgiving or dismay among those who knew him was Browning's response.

The events in themselves were simple. Elizabeth Barrett was six years older than Browning. In 1844 she had reached that stage in her literary career where there was a call for an edition of her collected poems.

Moxon agreed to publish this in two volumes. However, it was then discovered that the poems as they stood could not be satisfactorily distributed in the two volumes without leaving the first one rather short. Miss Barrett therefore added another poem, 'Lady Geraldine's Court-ship'. The subject of the poem was to be familiar in Tennyson's *Maud* or *Aylmer's Field*, not to mention a spate of popular fiction. It was the love of the hero, in this case a poet, for a woman who was his social superior.

> She was sprung of English nobles,
> I was born of English peasants.

For the poet, however, love was to prove triumphant. On her Sussex estate, grand enough to rival Goodwood or Petworth, the hero, Bert-ram, read to Lady Geraldine a selection of other men's poetry.

> Or at times a modern volume, – Wordsworth's solemn-thoughted idyl,
> Howitt's ballad-verse, or Tennyson's enchanted reverie, –
> Or from Browning some 'Pomegranate', which, if cut deep down the middle,
> Shows a heart within blood-tinctured, of a veined humanity.

It was a nicely turned compliment but little more than that. Browning and Elizabeth had never met, though they had each known of the other for some time. Dining at Serjeant Talfourd's house in 1839, Browning had encountered an amiable elder guest, John Kenyon. Not only was Kenyon second cousin to Elizabeth Barrett, he also proved to have been a schoolfellow of Browning's father. Up to that point Kenyon was not even sure that Robert Browning senior was still alive and one of his first questions to the son was to establish the fact.

Robert Browning senior remembered his old friend. Next morning he drew a sketch of Kenyon as a schoolboy which his son at once recognized as the guest at Talfourd's dinner table. Kenyon was now the friend of Wordsworth, Landor and Southey. Not surprisingly he took a personal and literary interest in the career of his invalid cousin, Miss Barrett. He also had considerable admiration for Browning, though with reservations over the 'muddy metaphysical poetry'.[46] Yet even in this he made the significant connection between the young early Victorian and the fashion begun two centuries before by John Donne.

As early as 1841 John Kenyon had suggested to his cousin that she might care to receive a visit in Wimpole Street from the author of *Sordello*, 'one of the lions of London who roared the gentlest and was best worth my knowing'. But, as she explained, 'I refused then in my blind dislike to seeing strangers'.[47] She and Browning had still not met on 10 January 1845 when he wrote to return the compliment paid him in 'Lady Geraldine's Courtship'. 'I love your verses with all my heart, dear Miss Barrett.'[48] They were the first words he had addressed to her and the impulsive tone was surely to be forgiven in one who had received the first flattery from Elizabeth. Yet in the careful etiquette of early Victorian England, what followed in that letter – written by a man to a woman who was a nominal stranger – was utterly astonishing. 'I do, as I say, love these books with all my heart – and I love you too.'[49]

7
'The Sleeping Palace'

It seemed that no two people of their kind could have been more differently situated than Browning and Elizabeth Barrett at the time of their first meeting in 1845. He was, if not acclaimed as a poet, at least well known in the literary salons of his day. By the standards of the time he had travelled widely, from St Petersburg to Naples, from the coast of North Africa to Paris and the Rhine. He moved with apparent ease in the groups that gathered about Monckton Milnes or the poet-politician John Hanmer, as well as in the more intimate gatherings of Carlyle or Bryan Proctor. If his career as a dramatist ended in failure, it still made him temporarily a figure of the London theatre, the partner of Macready and the protégé of Moxon.

Only to those who knew him intimately was it apparent that Browning, in his own way and for quite different reasons, lived a life that was in some respects as solitary as Elizabeth Barrett's.

In her father's house at 50 Wimpole Street Elizabeth Barrett, at thirty-nine years old, endured the greater imprisonment of bodily sickness. 'I lie all day, and day after day, on the sofa, and my windows do not even look into the street,' she wrote eighteen months before their meeting.[1] Browning's isolation was voluntary.

There were obvious points of similarity between them. Whatever the difference in their reputations, both were established among the poets of the day. Their families both adhered to an evangelical Christianity, spurning alike the charm of the Oxford Movement's catholicism and the bleak intellectualism of Strauss's *Life of Jesus*, to be translated by George Eliot in the year of their marriage. Each family owed its wealth in part to the slave plantations of the West Indies. Elizabeth was the first Barrett for some generations not to have been born there. Her family still marvelled at a great-great-grandfather who 'flogged his slaves like a divinity'.[2] Above all it was in their literary and intellectual precocity that they had most in common. '*I* was precocious too,' Elizabeth wrote, 'and used to make rhymes over my bread and milk when I was nearly a baby.'[3] She was writing French heroic tragedy by the age of ten. Alone at first, then with the aid of a tutor, she learnt Greek and Hebrew. At a similar age she shared Browning's boyhood enthusiasm for the gods and heroes of Homer. Her first poem, *The Battle of Marathon*, an imitated epic in four books, was published when she was fourteen. It was issued in an edition of fifty copies at her father's expense.

Perhaps the most profound similarity between the two future lovers went far beyond any of this. For separate reasons each was dedicated to the profession of poetry. It is not necessary to equate the frustrations suffered by Browning with the tragedy of Elizabeth Barrett's existence in order to see that for each of them this absorption in work and literary ambition was not merely a dedication but the sole path to salvation from the dissatisfactions of their lives.

Elizabeth had been born in 1806, the eldest of eleven children. Now that the family had settled in England again, her father Edward Moulton Barrett built a country house, Hope End, near the Malvern Hills. Its rather oriental domes, stained glass and gardens of white roses acknowledged the fashions of Georgian decoration without paying exclusive tribute to any one of them. Among the security and affluence of these surroundings, Elizabeth's childhood was passed.

In the light of what was to follow, the name of Hope End has a gloomy resonance. The death of Elizabeth's mother put Edward Moulton Barrett in supreme and direct charge of his family, despite the arrival of an aunt as a maternal substitute. Posterity was to depict him as the tyrant of the sick-room and the bane of his children's lives. While there was ample justification for this view, it was less than the whole truth.

He was as proud as any Browning of his child's literary achievements and intellectual promise. When he opened his own library to Elizabeth he did so with reservations, perhaps feeling these proper in the case of a daughter. 'Don't read Gibbon's history,' he told her, 'it's not a proper book. Don't read "Tom Jones" – and none of the books on *this* side, mind!' As Elizabeth recalled with a lightly malicious satisfaction, 'I was very obedient and never touched the books on *that* side, and only read instead Tom Paine's "Age of Reason", and Voltaire's "Philosophical Dictionary", and Hume's "Essays", and Werther, and Rousseau, and Mary Woolstoncraft.'[4] If Mr Barrett was concerned that his daughter might imbibe an anti-Christian rationalism from such writings, he need not have worried. The effect of Paine, Voltaire and Hume was that of a timely inoculation against religious unbelief. What she acquired from the romantics was more immediately dangerous, a pronounced sympathy for the rights of women.

If some of his contemporaries are to be believed, Mr Barrett's personality changed markedly as he crossed the threshold of Hope End or his other houses. He was, it was said, 'a very pleasant man in society but a perfect martinet in his own home'.[5] His support for political enfranchisement and the Reform Bill of 1832 showed a liberal self-interest. It was the equally famous measure of the following year – the abolition of slavery in the British colonies – which brought him close to financial ruin. In the difficulties which he faced he became more taciturn, gloomy and inflexible.

During her twenties Elizabeth's health declined. Despite stories of a riding accident in her youth and a spinal injury, she was actually suffering from consumption, as tuberculosis was generally known. Hope End was sold and the family moved to Sidmouth in 1832. There was a period in London, during which she met her cousin John Kenyon and, through him, Wordsworth and Coleridge. Her father found the money, in 1833, to pay for the publication of her translation from Aeschylus and her own shorter poems as *Prometheus Bound and Miscellaneous Poems*.

In 1838, when her health had deteriorated still further, she was sent to Torquay, where in July 1840 her eldest brother, Edward, known as 'Bro', was drowned in a boating accident. It was five years before Elizabeth could survey calmly the aftermath of that tragedy and its effect upon her. Writing of her grief, she used words and sentiments which might easily have come from Browning himself, whom she was not to meet for another two years. 'I do believe that I should be *mad* at this moment, if I had not forced back – damned out – the current of rushing recollections by work, work, work.'[6]

Despite the supposed benefits of sea air, following the rupture of a blood vessel in her lungs, she was glad to leave Torquay. 'I go to rescue myself from the associations of this dreadful place. I go to restore to my poor papa the companionship of his family.'[7] She returned to the fogs and dampness of London in 1841, to the house in Wimpole Street, with an optimism over her physical health which was to prove ill founded. 'My case is very clear: not tubercular consumption, not what is called a "decline", but an affection of the lungs, which leans towards it.'[8]

Her spiritual progress during four years of invalid life in Wimpole Street, confined to one room and even to the sofa within it, is chronicled in her own words. At first the burden of grief had crushed her. 'But the truth is, my faculties seem to hang heavily now, like flappers when the spring is broken, and a separate exertion is necessary for the lifting up of each – and then it falls down again.'[9] When John Kenyon suggested to her that Browning should pay a visit during 1841, he was not to know that she had just written to Mrs Martin, a family friend and neighbour at Hope End. 'Perhaps it is hard for you to *fancy* even how I shrink away from the very thought of seeing a human face – except those immediately belonging to me in love or relationship.'[10]

This was three years after the tragedy at Torquay. A few months later, however, she confided to her former tutor, H. S. Boyd, that one flame of enthusiasm still flickered in her mind. 'Part of me is worn out; but the poetical part – that is the *love* of poetry – is growing in me as freshly and strongly as if it were watered every day.'[11] The recovery was slow but certain. 'Once I wished *not* to live,' she wrote in March 1842, 'but the faculty of life seems to have sprung up in me again, from under the crushing foot of heavy grief.'[12] Six months later she was able to tell Mrs Martin that her physical health had improved in proportion and that 'the spitting of blood . . . which more or less kept by me continually, *stopped quite* some six weeks ago'.[13] It was possible to believe that her health might improve permanently, though she was still unable to think of leaving the Wimpole Street house for a drive except in the warmth of summer.

Her illness followed the pattern of tuberculosis, a steady decline interrupted by temporary improvements. However, the decline would have been slower and the improvements more marked almost anywhere other than in the sooty air of central London.

With the improvement in health came the first cries of impatience at her predicament, their tones echoed from memories of Mary Wollstone= craft and the rights of womanhood. 'Do you think I was born to live the life of an oyster, such as I *do* live here?' she demanded.[14] 'I still sit in my chair and walk about the room,' she reported, describing her improved health, 'But the prison doors are shut close, and I could dash myself against them sometimes with a passionate impatience of the needless captivity.'[15]

It was into this life and into this frame of mind that there was interjected the first message from a man of whom she already knew and whose poetry she already admired. 'I love your verses with all my heart, dear Miss Barrett . . . and I love you too.'

The manner in which the correspondence between Browning and his future wife began was described by him in one of the letters themselves, written in November 1845. He had returned to England from Italy late in the previous December to find that Kenyon had sent Sarianna

Browning a copy of Elizabeth's collected *Poems*. In 'Lady Geraldine's Courtship' he found the flattering reference to *Bells and Pomegranates*.[16] There was of course no means of conveying his thanks but by letter. As Kenyon explained to him, 'my cousin is a great invalid, and sees no one, but great souls jump at sympathy'.[17] There was no doubt of that. Elizabeth answered his first letter, by return, on 11 January 1845, her words fulfilling Kenyon's prediction. 'Sympathy is dear – very dear to me: but the sympathy of a poet, and of such a poet, is the quintessence of sympathy to me.'[18] She had refused her cousin's offer to bring Browning to her in 1841, a lost opportunity at which he hinted in his first letter. Now she was evasive, not refusing but postponing the occasion. Warning him that he might be disappointed and even bored by her, she added: 'Winters shut me up as they do dormouse's eyes; in the spring, *we shall see*: and I am so much better that I seem turning round to the outward world again.'[19]

During the next four months, until their first meeting at Wimpole Street on 20 May 1845, they exchanged letters several times a week. At first it was clear that Elizabeth feared Browning's interest in her as merely the sympathy of one in robust health for an invalid woman. Spurning this, she went on to demand frankness from him and to insist that her feelings were not to be spared. 'Only *don't* let us have any constraint, any ceremony!' she wrote at the beginning of February. '*Don't* be civil to me when you feel rude.'[20]

In the period when they were merely correspondents, Browning had already opened a window upon a world which Elizabeth had scarcely glimpsed at all, and that not for the past seven years. He talked of his meetings with Carlyle and Dickens, described his workroom with its skulls, spiders and the print of Andromeda. All of this was written in a breezy boyish style, much as he used elsewhere to tell her jokes. 'Out comes the sun, in comes the *Times* and eleven strikes (it *does*) already, and I have to go to Town.'[21] At the end of February he was still writing in the same tone of youthful and confident enthusiasm, a style far removed from anything she had known in the years of grief. 'Real warm Spring, dear Miss Barrett, and the birds know it; and in Spring I shall see you, surely see you – for when did I once fail to get whatever I had set my heart upon?'[22]

Her response was still nervous, even apprehensive. 'I have not been very well,' she wrote on 20 March. 'This implacable weather! this east wind that seems to blow through the sun and moon!' More to the point, she added: 'You are Paracelsus, and I am a recluse, with nerves that have been all broken on the rack, and now hang loosely – quivering at a step and breath.'[23] Yet the tone of the correspondence was increasingly that of mingled admiration and gratitude on both sides. Browning spoke of 'the octaves on octaves of quite new golden strings you enlarged the compass of my life's harp with'.[24] By mid-April Elizabeth confessed the existence of silent, unwritten letters to him. If he knew of them, 'you would not think for a moment that the east wind, with all the harm it does to me, is able to do the great harm of putting out the light of the thought of you to my mind'.[25]

Not for a further month were they to set eyes on each other. A more sceptical age might have taken their professions of mutual admiration as no more than Browning's first enthusiasm for Macready, impulsive rhetoric soon tarnished in the air of reality. It was Browning who seemed to reverse their situations by suggesting that Elizabeth, not he, was the one who opened a window on to a richer life. He even sought to make light of her own sickness by writing often of the headaches and vertigo which prostrated him. Perhaps, in Elizabeth's improved state of health, the difference between them could be minimized.

Like many others, Browning misunderstood the true nature of her illness before seeing her. He believed that she had suffered a spinal injury and that she would be confined to her room and her sofa for the rest of her life. This might have explained her reliance on morphine, in itself a potential problem. There were those at the time, like Julia Ward Howe, and others since who were taken by the notion of Elizabeth Barrett Browning as a drug addict. The truth was simpler. As a cure for insomnia and to soothe the spasms of her lungs, she took muriate of morphia, 'what I call my elixir and I take it in a combination with aether and something else'.[26] Her strength of mind was sufficient to make the opiate her servant rather than her master. To see in her the image of a hopeless addict is preposterous, if only because she lacked the hopelessness which so frequently precedes the addiction.

Browning came to the house in Wimpole Street on 20 May 1845. The woman he saw was still the invalid of the sofa, six years his elder. By the standards of the twentieth century she had a strength of features, a handsomeness perhaps rather than beauty or prettiness, and the dark corkscrew ringlets which were fashionable in the 1830s and 1840s.

Between these two people there existed a natural sympathy and admiration bred by several months of correspondence. What no other person will ever gauge was how a spark was struck on that spring afternoon in Wimpole Street which fired admiration into love. Browning was now to experience the 'coming glory' described in *Sordello*, where

> ... up and down
> Runs arrowy fire, while earthly forms combine
> To throb the secret forth.

He was, it seemed, true to his vision, the poet creating beauty in his mistress by his love of her. So he declared his own feelings.

Elizabeth naturally and sensibly took a more cautious view. 'I began with a grave assurance that I was in an exceptional position and saw him just in consequence of it, and that if ever he recurred to that subject again, I could never see him again while I lived.'[27] The risk was too great that Browning was motivated by no more than a noble romanticism and chivalry, casting himself in anticipation as Caponsacchi in *The Ring and the Book* to rescue Pompilia from her domestic captivity. 'To my mind, indeed,' wrote Elizabeth the next year, 'it was a bare impulse – a generous man of quick sympathies taking up a sudden interest with both hands.'[28]

To put the matter beyond question, Browning wrote a letter after the first meeting in which he set down his feelings for Elizabeth. Thoroughly alarmed, she replied that these were words which he must '*forget at once, and for ever, having said at all*.... Now, if there should be one word of answer attempted to this; or of reference; *I must not* ... I *will not see you again*.'[29] In her own mind she thought of his love at first as infatuation but, as she recalled, the letters and visits persisted. 'So then I showed him how he was throwing into the ashes his best affections – how the common gifts of youth and cheerfulness were behind me – how I had not the strength, even of *heart*, for the ordinary duties of life.'[30]

Browning was unmoved. To judge by his remarks to Domett and others in the preceding three years, the loneliness in his own life could scarcely be redeemed by work alone. It was a common enough phenomenon. His contemporary the painter G. F. Watts, for example, reached his thirties as an industrious bachelor. He then sent plaintive letters to Georgy Duff Gordon confessing the melancholy and despondency which solitary work brought him, begging her 'to look out for, and if possible find me a wife'.[31]

The tragi-comic figure of Watts stands in marked contrast to Browning. In Browning's letters and conversations the predisposing cause of his love for Elizabeth is not hard to trace. The precipitating cause had much to do with that nobility, energy and passion which animated her even in sickness. To the appeal of that imprisoned soul Browning answered with all his heart. It would have been enough to respond with chivalry and generosity. As it happens, he responded by falling in love. 'He said that the freshness of youth had passed with him also, and that he had studied the world out of books and seen many women, yet had never loved one until he had seen me.'[32]

They shared not only interests in literature and a disposition towards Nonconformist Christianity but a sympathy for animals great and small. Elizabeth had an instinctive aversion to bats, but her other affections seemed limitless. 'Oh – and I had a field-mouse for a pet once, and should have joined my sisters in a rat's nest if I had not been ill at the time ... and blue-bottle flies I used to feed, and hated your spiders for them; yet no, not much.'[33]

In such outbursts and in Browning's own attitudes the lovers might well appear to have been in their first youth. To him, Elizabeth was Sleeping Beauty soon to be woken by her Prince, while the house in Wimpole Street and its garden seemed 'the strange hedge round the sleeping Palace keeping the world off'.[34] He was perhaps too courteous to identify the ogre in the same enchanted kingdom, yet as love ripened between them and the first plans were laid the forbidding shadow of Mr Barrett was never far off.

The meetings between them, Browning alone in the room with Elizabeth and the adored spaniel Flush, could never have been kept secret. Yet their relationship would only continue in this way, she explained, 'if we avoid making it a subject of conversation in high places, or low places'.[35]

At first Elizabeth saw her father as the mouthpiece of Dr Chambers, 'a part of whose office it is, Papa says, "to reconcile foolish women to their follies" '.[36] After they had corresponded for nine months, Elizabeth endeavoured to gauge the extent of her father's antipathy to such things for Browning's benefit. 'I might certainly tell you that my own father, if he knew that you had written to me *so*, and that I had answered you – *so*, even, would not forgive me at the end of ten years ... for the singular reason that he never *does* tolerate in his family (sons or daughters) the development of one class of feelings.'[37] Two weeks later, at the end of September 1845, she added a defence of her father which might under the circumstances seem remarkable. '*Don't* think too hardly of poor Papa. You have his wrong side ... his side of peculiar wrongness ... to you just now. When you have walked round him you will have other thoughts of him.'[38]

It was true that his contemporaries vouched for the amiability of Mr Barrett once he was outside his home, yet this hardly excused his conduct towards his daughter. It was proposed that she should spend the winter in Malta or Pisa to secure the improvement that had occurred in her health. The good to be obtained by a warmer climate was never in doubt. When she at length reached Italy and then returned to London in the month of August, five years after this, the contrast was formidable. 'I began to cough before we reached London. The quality of the air does *not* agree with me, that's evident.... coughed day and night, till Robert took fright, and actually fixed a day for taking me forthwith back to Paris.'[39] As the winter of 1845–6 drew on, Mr Barrett was silent on the subject of Pisa, then he seemed indifferent. Elizabeth's brother George, anxious for her health, pressed the matter. The consequence, as Elizabeth told Browning, was her father's decision that 'I "might go if I pleased, but that going it would be under his heaviest displeasure" '.[40]

Her feelings towards her father were central in Elizabeth's developing relationship with Browning. Yet those feelings were not defined as simple resentment or submissiveness. After the decision on Pisa, which condemned her to a winter of isolation and discomfort in London, she was understandably resentful. 'The bitterest "fact" of all is, that I had believed Papa to have loved me more than he obviously does: but I never regret knowledge.'[41] She was, however, a true child of her time, believing that parental indifference could never absolve her of a daughter's duty to love a father. Three months before the elopement she was to write, 'Yet in that strange, stern nature, there is a capacity to love – and I love him – and I shall suffer, in causing him to suffer'.[42]

To an outsider Mr Barrett might seem if not a subject for sympathy at least the victim of an obsessional neurosis; but in more practical terms he was the growing threat to Browning's love for Elizabeth. A year after their first correspondence she had to warn him urgently of the danger of 'a suspicion entering *one* mind'. After that, 'we should be able to meet never again in this room.... letters of yours, addressed to me here, would infallibly be stopped and destroyed – if not opened.'[43]

The worst of it was that with every visit which Browning paid, the cause for suspicion increased and that she, now forty years old and with a reputation as a poet now exceeding Browning's own, was as powerless as a child of ten in the affairs of the home. In March 1846 there was to be an angry scene with her father because Browning had visited her during the morning. By August, the month before the elopement, suspicion seemed to ripen into certainty. Before dinner Mr Barrett came to his daughter's room and found her lying on the sofa in a white dressing-gown, unlaced because she found it difficult to breathe in the sultry air. With an expression like thunder, as she said, he asked, 'Has this been your costume since the morning, pray?' 'Oh, no. Only just now, because of the heat.' 'Well, it appears, Ba, that *that man* has spent the whole day with you.' Rather feebly she explained that her visitor had intended to leave much earlier but had been prevented by the thunder showers.[44]

Elizabeth's caution towards her suitor prevailed throughout the spring and summer of 1845. In the autumn she responded at last to his 'noble extravagances' as he would have wished. 'How would any woman have felt ... who could feel at all ... having such words said (though "in a dream" indeed) by such a speaker?'[45] In the light of this acknowledgement she gave him her pledge. 'However this may be, a promise goes to you in it that none, except God and your will, shall interpose between you and me, ... I mean, that if He should free me within a moderate time from the trailing chain of this weakness, I will then be to you whatever at that hour you shall choose ... whether friend or more than friend .. a friend to the last in any case.'[46]

She was indeed to be freed from the weakness which afflicted her at that time, if only by a temporary alleviation. Their hopes of meeting in Pisa during the coming winter were soon to be frustrated. Yet from this point there was no question that, barring the triumph of tyranny in the shape of Mr Barrett or the deterioration of Elizabeth's health, the union of the lovers was assured.

During the twenty months of this courtship, Browning lived two lives. One was enclosed in the sick-room at Wimpole Street and the almost daily correspondence by which his visits were supplemented. The other related to the continuing appearance of *Bells and Pomegranates*, to his presence as a guest in literary salons or at the dinner tables of likely patrons, even to the choice of an occupation which might be necessary if he had to support Elizabeth financially.

Though the two lovers kept their secret closely, it was inevitable that the matters of Browning's other life – finance, patronage, literary prospects – should intrude into their exchanges. How were they to live? Elizabeth had money of her own, £8,000 in government stock and an income or £200 a year. Browning still had an allowance from his father, and in any case it was unthinkable to him that he should live on Elizabeth's money. It was time, perhaps, to put his patrons and admirers to the test. In June 1846, with Tennyson enjoying a civil list pension, Browning considered writing to Lord Monteagle, who professed to admire his poems. 'When you are minister next month, as is expected, will you give me for my utmost services about as much as you give Tennyson for nothing?'[47] It seems likely that he also mentioned this, perhaps less audaciously, to Monckton Milnes who had helped to get

Tennyson his pension. At all events, Browning wrote to Elizabeth five days later of 'the Embassy which Young England in the person of Milnes has promised me'.[48] Sir Moses Montefiore, who had successfully negotiated a removal of certain discriminations against Jews in Turkey in 1840, was being dispatched to Russia to end, by diplomatic pressure, the practice of sending Jews into internal exile. Browning was offered a post in this mission.

He turned down the offer for the best of reasons. It would have meant immediate separation from Elizabeth. Indeed, as she pointed out, a career in diplomacy would frustrate the very purpose it was intended to serve. Though the income would be welcome, 'if you are to do diplomacy for it, ... how do you know that you may not be sent to Russia, or somewhere impossible for me to winter in?' Since this was precisely what Milnes was offering, the matter ended there for the time being.[49]

During his courtship of Elizabeth, the last two numbers of *Bells and Pomegranates* appeared. The seventh, *Dramatic Romances and Lyrics*, was issued in November 1845, the eighth and last, *Luria, and A Soul's Tragedy*, in April 1846. As with the previous parts of the series, the cost of publication was borne by Browning's father.

Both pieces in the final part were verse dramas, though neither was suitable for stage production. *A Soul's Tragedy* was the first written, and in completing *Luria*, as Browning told Elizabeth in September 1845, he was making a conscious decision to turn his back on the writing of plays. 'That "Luria" you enquire about, shall be my last play – for it is but a play, woe's me!'[50]

Apart from the usual loyal review by John Forster in the *Examiner* on 25 April 1846, the volume went virtually unnoticed upon its appearance. It was now five years since the first part of *Bells and Pomegranates* – *Pippa Passes* – had appeared. From the wreck of its original hopes there survived three parts which contained some of the best, most vigorous and certainly the most original writing of the early Victorian period: *Pippa Passes, Dramatic Lyrics* and *Dramatic Romances and Lyrics*. To judge by their reception in the press, whatever poetic fire burnt in these pages was swamped by the dull wastes of verse drama and the over-shadowing reputation of *Sordello*.

In respect of the final part of *Bells and Pomegranates*, this was unjust. *Luria*, the tragedy of a Moorish general in the service of the Florentine army, immediately invited comparison with *Othello*. Not surprisingly, it suffered badly in consequence. By contrast, *A Soul's Tragedy* was a sad yet ironic study of the corruption of revolutionary purity and the cynicism of those who manipulate it. Though set in sixteenth-century

Italy, its relevance was more obviously to Italian politics of the nineteenth century. Its caustic analysis of tyrants and revolutionaries alike
is far closer to Shavian drama than to the liberalism of early Victorian
England.

The first act, in verse, is largely devoted to the opportunist revolutionary Chiappino seducing Eulalia, the mistress of his friend Luitolfo
who is even then pleading for Chiappino before the Provost of Faenza.
When Luitolfo returns, having killed the Provost on Chiappino's behalf,
Chiappino sends him away and puts on the bloodstained clothing
himself. He thus acquires both his friend's mistress and a reputation as
the people's champion.

The second act, in prose, introduces the voice of authority in the
shape of Ogniben, papal legate from Ravenna, a worldly and weary
politician upon whom Shaw could scarcely have improved. 'I have seen
three-and-twenty leaders of revolts,' he remarks confidently. When
Chiappino defies him in the name of 'a pure Republic', Ogniben is
unperturbed. 'And by whom do I desire such a government should be
administered, perhaps, but by one like yourself?' The astonished leader
of the rebellion finds himself urged towards a position of power by the
authority against whom he had revolted. His way to marry Eulalia and
inherit Luitolfo's goods is made clear. When Luitolfo returns, it is to
hear with dismay Chiappino's defence of his own conduct. 'Now, why
refuse to see that in my present course I change no principles, only re-
adapt them and more adroitly?' It is Ogniben, papal legate and man of
the world, who emerges as the dominant character if not the hero of the
drama. His advice to Chiappino even embraces the treatment of Eulalia. 'Do you want your mistress to respect your body generally? Offer
her your mouth to kiss – don't strip off your boot and put your foot to
her lips!'

Finally, of course, Ogniben urges the sensible necessity of compromise
in moral principles. 'There is Truth in Falsehood, Falsehood in Truth.'
Had David and Goliath only realized it, they had far too much in
common to make their fight either necessary or desirable.

Chiappino, overcome by the even greater cynicism of Ogniben, goes
into exile. Ogniben ends the play with the paradoxical, cynical urbanity
which gives his character its stamp of the devil's advocate in a drama of
Bernard Shaw's. 'And now give thanks to God, the keys of the Provost's
Palace to me, and yourselves to profitable meditation at home. I have
known *Four*-and-twenty leaders of revolts!' If, as Gosse remarked, it was
astonishing for two poems like 'Madhouse Cells' to appear almost
unnoticed among the limp and nondescript verse of the 1830s, it was no

less surprising that a piece like *A Soul's Tragedy* should have been published unnoticed and virtually unreviewed in 1846. In many respects, and at a very general estimate, it was about eighty years ahead of its time.

Browning's contemporaries could hardly be expected to judge him in terms of the future development of literature. As it happened he not only made his resolution to end his career as a dramatist but found it easy to abide by. In the year in which *Luria and A Soul's Tragedy* appeared, he and Elizabeth were to leave England for Italy. If for no other reason, this voluntary exile put an end to his ambitions as a playwright, far removed from the world of Macready, Charles Kean and the necessary contacts with the world of the London stage. From 1846 onwards poetry and diplomacy were the only two professions which, it seemed, were still possible to him.

Even before their commitment to one another in September 1845, Browning had warned Elizabeth not to 'stop up all the vents of my feeling'.[51] The terms in which he declared himself the following month were more florid and rather more controlled than Elizabeth's. 'I feel that if I could get myself *remade*, as if turned to gold, I WOULD not even then desire to become more than the mere setting to *that* diamond you must always wear.'[52] Though there was no doubt of the feeling between them, it was Elizabeth who spoke most simply of love and Browning who wrote in terms of extreme admiration less directly and with slightly more reserve. He could not match Elizabeth's extreme of gratitude. 'I never thought that any man whom *I* could love, would stoop to love *me*.'[53]

In more practical terms, after the understanding between them in September 1845 they had to decide how and when their lives should be joined. During the coming months of winter, once her father had made it impossible to go to Pisa, nothing could be done. It would scarcely have been feasible to move her from the house in Wimpole Street. At the same time, an indefinite delay would mean that sooner or later Mr Barrett would decide that his daughter should receive no more visits or letters from Browning.

Yet while the threat to their plans from Mr Barrett seemed to grow, the impediment to them of Elizabeth's ill health diminished. The winter of 1845–6 was unusually mild and even in February she was able to make her way as far as the drawing-room, 'and took Henrietta by surprise as she sate at the piano singing'.[54] By May she had been driven to the Botanical Gardens, a clear improvement on the past summer's outing which stopped short of Regent's Park. In June, for the first time in five years, she was able to walk to the drawing-room and then write her letters there. Soon came drives to the Serpentine, to Westminster Abbey, and even to the slums of Shoreditch to buy back Flush from the dog-stealers who were holding him to ransom. Her sister Henrietta 'cried out in loud astonishment' at the visible gain in health. Mr Barrett seemed displeased by the change. 'She is mumpish, I think,' he said.[55]

They discussed Italy and the means of getting there. Though, by June 1846, Elizabeth's health was better than it had been for at least five years, such a journey was almost unthinkable for one who had rarely been able to leave her room since her arrival at Wimpole Street in 1841. It was possible to sail from Brighton to Rouen, and so drive to Paris. In July Browning had planned a further route. By joining the Loire south of Paris they could travel by river and canal to Marseilles and so by sea to Leghorn, which was within two hours' drive of Pisa. The long ordeals of a rough sea voyage via Gibraltar, or an arduous coach journey, could both be avoided.

Whatever Elizabeth's feelings, Mr Barrett had to be deceived. As for her sisters, both Arabel and Henrietta had told her by the beginning of 1846 that they guessed the truth of her feelings for Robert Browning. 'We are as safe with both of them as possible,' she assured him.[56] Her brothers too had their suspicions but she judged it best to say nothing to them. Browning's parents were of course told, and showed nothing but kindness and enthusiasm for their future daughter-in-law.

Elizabeth had another valuable friend, though not yet a confidante, in the art critic and essayist Anna Jameson. Mrs Jameson, ten years her elder, was later to be known affectionately to the Brownings as 'Aunt Nina'. It was she who was to be their companion and assistant in the difficult task of moving Elizabeth from Paris to Italy.

A month before the wedding Elizabeth wrote: 'By the time all this is over, we shall be fit to take a degree in some Jesuits' college – we shall have mastered all the points of casuistry.'[57] Occasionally their subterfuge was aided by chance or coincidence. In May 1846 there was a rumour in society and then an announcement that Mr Browning was to marry Miss Campbell. The prospective bridegroom was assumed by a number of people to be the poet of *Sordello*, and in that form the rumour reached the Barrett household. He was, in fact, another Browning who lived near Regent's Park, but the confusion was welcome.[58]

In the final weeks it was Browning who urged the need to act quickly, while Elizabeth seemed inclined to delay. Yet Mr Barrett's suspicions could not be contained for ever. Indeed, by the end of August the visits to Wimpole Street were growing more perilous. 'I altogether agree with you,' wrote Browning, '- it is best to keep away - we cannot be too cautious now at the "end of things".'[59]

But what was the end to be? The plan that they devised was at first sight bizarre. They would marry secretly, Elizabeth giving the appearance that she had merely been out for a drive. She would then return to her usual life at Wimpole Street until an elopement could be arranged. If the truth were discovered before that elopement, Mr Barrett might turn his daughter out of the house but he could not forbid her to join her husband.

September began ominously. Flush was abducted by the dog-stealers, and Elizabeth's attention was diverted to his fate until the ransom had been paid and Flush returned five days later. By then, Browning was in bed under his doctor's orders with an attack of 'the old *vertiginousness*, or a little worse'.[60] He recovered from this by 8 September only to receive a letter from Elizabeth two days later which caused him the greatest alarm.

Mr Barrett had decided that the house in Wimpole Street was to be cleaned and painted. He had sent his son George to find and rent another house for a month at Dover, Reigate or Tunbridge. The lovers would thus be separated and, by the time the month was over, the onset of winter might imprison Elizabeth until the following summer. Indeed, if the winter were severe and her health deteriorated, she might never leave her prison alive. Still she hesitated. 'It seems quite too soon and too sudden for us to set out on our Italian adventure now.'[61] Browning had no such misgivings. He replied the same day, Thursday 10 September, reminding her that if she were taken from London their marriage must wait another year. 'You see what we have gained by waiting. We must be *married directly* and go to Italy. I will go for a licence to-day and we can be married on Saturday.'[62]

On Saturday morning, accompanied by her maid Wilson, Elizabeth went to the cab-stand in Marylebone Road. 'I staggered so, that we both were afraid for the fear's sake.'[63] They called at a chemist's shop for some sal volatile to steady them and so arrived at St Marylebone Church just before eleven o'clock. Browning was there with his cousin, James Silverthorne, and the wedding was surely one of the strangest on record. When it was over, husband and wife parted without a word. Elizabeth drove alone to the house of H. S. Boyd at Hampstead, the friend who had taught her Greek in her youth. There she awaited her two sisters, having sent her maid back to Wimpole Street to fetch them. Neither Arabel nor Henrietta knew anything of the marriage and had been alarmed by Elizabeth's disappearance. Perhaps they feared that she had eloped in earnest. In their company she now drove as far as Hampstead Heath and then home at length to Wimpole Street.

As they drove past St Marylebone Church again, she wrote, it all seemed like a dream. She had left her father's house that morning as Elizabeth Barrett Moulton Barrett. The first two names were Christian names and the last two regarded in the family as surnames. Upon her return she had therefore become the authoress whose name and celebrity were soon to eclipse her husband's: Elizabeth Barrett Browning.

The following day John Kenyon paid a visit to Wimpole Street. With his eyes appearing to fill the entire lenses of his spectacles, he asked Elizabeth, 'When did you see Browning?' and then, 'When do you see Browning again?'[64] Almost guiltily she began to feel that the secret had been discovered. She was paralysed by apprehension of having to write, sooner or later, such words as: 'Papa, I am married; I hope you will not be too displeased.'[65]

Still no date had been set for their journey to Italy. But on 15 September Mr Barrett announced that the family would move on the following Monday, 21 September, to Little Bookham, six miles from the nearest railway and more than a mile from the nearest coach. Elizabeth was still inclined to wait until she had written all the letters to announce her marriage to friends and family. Browning saw that to delay until she was moved to Bookham might be to frustrate all their plans. He made arrangements for them to leave England four days hence, on Saturday 19 September. Accompanied by her maid, Elizabeth was to meet him at Hodgson's bookshop between 3.30 and 4.00. They would take the train from Vauxhall station and the night boat from Southampton to Le Havre.

It was not the best route, perhaps, and the crossing was a bad one. They took the coach for Rouen and then another for Paris. Elizabeth was so weak that Browning had to carry her from the vehicle. But at least in Paris there was accommodation to be had and the sympathetic assistance of Mrs Jameson who was now their companion.

Partly by coach and partly by river steamer they travelled south to Avignon and Marseilles. Not only was Browning now obliged to lift and carry his wife, she was also so weak and thin that, as Mrs Jameson remarked, the jolting of the carriages bruised her badly. At Marseilles a French ship took them first to Genoa and then to Leghorn. A short railway journey brought them at last to Pisa on 14 October.

Browning's first task was to find a home for himself and his bride. He took an apartment in the Collegio Ferdinando, close to the Campo

Santo of Pisa with its cathedral, baptistry and leaning tower. There was still no thought of Florence. Until the following spring, Pisa seemed to be their journey's end. In its mild winter, English invalids sought relief for their chests and lungs. 'Mrs Jameson says she "won't call me *improved* but *transformed* rather",' wrote Elizabeth three weeks after their arrival.[66] Yet for Browning, no less than for his wife, the long childhood was over. For the first time he faced with full independence a life that was remarkable for its perils as well as for its promise.

8
Casa Guidi

The journey which the Brownings made to Florence in the spring of 1847 was intended as the beginning of a tour through northern Italy. Its objects were the art of the Renaissance and the romantic splendours of Italian scenery which later artists like Salvator Rosa had made so fashionable. That Browning and his wife should have been enchanted and detained by the charm of Florence was not surprising. A large number of their compatriots and contemporaries had suffered the same agreeable fate.

To many Victorian writers and artists, no less than to their predecessors, the image of that city in its river valley among the Tuscan hills was scarcely less than a premonition of paradise. The red tiling of Brunelleschi's graceful cathedral dome, the marbled face of Giotto's bell-tower, the palaces and gardens, galleries and river-walks were an enticement in themselves. For the connoisseur, the Tribune and the Uffizi housed collections that no city in the world could surpass. And all this was contained not in a metropolis as smoky as London or as gaudy as Rome, vast and oppressive, but in a congenial city whose green surroundings might compare with Oxford or Bath.

Perhaps not until the 1920s in Paris could any continental city boast such a large and impressive colony of those who were leaders in the culture of England and America. Dickens, Thackeray, George Eliot and Henry James were distinguished visitors. The sculptors Hiram Powers and William Wetmore Story and the novelist Nathaniel Hawthorne were among the Americans who came. The Villino Trollope housed another famous family – mother and sons. From the age of the great romantics there were such survivors as Walter Savage Landor and Seymour Kirkup. The Foreign Office stationed an English minister, Lord Holland, in the city. Charles Lever, the novelist, was English consul at La Spezia but preferred to live in Florence. The Hollands' villa sheltered the painter G. F. Watts, who left several likenesses of the coquettish Augusta, Lady Holland. His canvas of her lolling on a 'day-bed' is recognizably and more obviously an intimate glimpse of her ladyship sprawling obligingly in her boudoir.

Naturally, the Brownings were both sympathetic to the cause of Italian liberty, Elizabeth referring to the odious sound of Austrian drums in Lombardy. From the settlement imposed upon Italy by the Peace of Paris in 1815, Florence was under the rule of its Grand Duke, Leopold II. Ineffectual, shabby and reformist, he presided over a court which was as much Firbankian as tyrannical. Even in this respect, Florence had a stronger appeal than almost any other part of northern Italy. It was said that an English visitor throwing a bowl of soapy water out of his hotel window had drenched the Grand Duke. Hurrying down to apologize, the visitor was assured by the duke that he would be forgiven rather than that the ducal repose should be disturbed by threatening letters from Lord Palmerston.

There was an easy-going and cosmopolitan society in Florence which attended the grand ducal drawing-room, the masked ball and carnival, opera and recitals at the Pergola. In the summer it was possible to escape the extreme heat and the mosquitoes by retiring to the wooded hills, those around Bagni di Lucca being Browning's choice. If the winter were too severe, the visitors moved south to Rome for the worst months.

Above all, however, it was the enchantment of the city itself – river, bridges, palaces and gardens – which exercised the greatest spell upon those who remained there. Sophie Hawthorne was delighted with the gas-lamps upon the Lungarno, making a cornice of glittering gems that converged in the distance, the reflection of the illuminated border below providing 'a fairy show'.

> Florence is as enchanting as I expected. It is a place to live and be happy in – so cheerful, so full of art, *so well paved*. It is delicious weather today, and the air is full of the songs of birds. The merlins are in choir over against our terrace, in a wood of the Torrigiani gardens. The marble busts, on their pedestals, seem to enjoy themselves in the bosky shade. The green lizards run across the parapet, and to exist is a joy.[1]

To her friend Miss Mitford, Elizabeth Barrett Browning was to write in 1854: 'I love Florence, the place looks exquisitely beautiful in its garden-ground of vineyards and olive trees. ... Such nights we have between starlight and firefly-light, and the nightingales singing.'[2] Browning himself described the city many times, though often through the conduct of its dead citizens. 'Old Pictures in Florence', from *Men and Women,* contains one of the most succinct yet brilliant views, taken on a spring morning.

> In the valley beneath, where, white and wide,
> Washed by the morning's water-gold,
> Florence lay out on the mountain-side.
>
> River and bridge and street and square
> Lay mine, as much at my beck and call,
> Through the live translucent bath of air,
> As the sights in a magic crystal ball.

It was in such a season and by such a light that Browning and Elizabeth first saw the city. Far from being a stage in a journey, it was their only true home for the rest of their life together, and in Elizabeth's case a final resting-place.

However great their enthusiasm for travelling in Italy, it was to be expected that they should find a permanent home there. Quite apart from Elizabeth's health, there could be no question of returning to live in England. Mr Barrett had been outraged at the discovery of his daughter's marriage, resolute in his bitterness. He announced to the household in Wimpole Street that she had deceived him. From that day he spoke of her as if she were dead. The letters she sent to him, even those in black-edged envelopes indicating death and mourning, remained unopened. When she visited England they were all returned to her with their seals unbroken. For the time being her brothers were obliged to share this sense of outrage, but with Arabel and Henrietta she and Browning corresponded freely and affectionately.

At the same time, Elizabeth's health was a factor in restricting the amount of travelling that could be undertaken. The warmer climate had eased the effects of her consumption, but she had become pregnant early in her marriage and suffered a miscarriage at Pisa about a month before setting out for Florence. Though this obliged her to rest for several weeks, she made light of it in a letter to her sister Henrietta. 'Pray don't think that I was in danger of dying on Sunday week – it is only my imagination which suggests cases. The Doctor assured Robert that there was no danger. Everybody wonders to see me recovering my strength now by handfuls, or heartfuls.'[3]

For just over a year, until they rented their apartment in Casa Guidi, the Brownings lived in successive sets of furnished rooms in Florence. Though, as Elizabeth insisted, it was cheap to live in Italy, the living was done largely on her own money. There were those friends of hers, like Miss Mitford, who resented this greatly, regarding Browning as indolent and effeminate, the worst possible choice as a husband.[4]

Browning himself felt uneasy at bearing less than an equal share of the financial burden. He had already been obliged to borrow £100 from his parents to cover the cost of the journey to Italy. There was, of course, still no probability that he could provide an income from his poetry. So, having rejected Monckton Milnes' offer of a diplomatic post in Russia the previous year, he applied again before leaving Pisa for Florence in an attempt to find a more congenial appointment. There were proposals for sending a British diplomatic mission to the Vatican. Far from separating the Brownings, such a climate would be ideal for Elizabeth during the winter, even if they were advised to find a cooler lodging in summer. He wrote to Milnes, asking for an appointment, assuring him that he would be 'glad and proud to be secretary to such an embassy' and that he would 'work like a horse' to justify his place.[5] Milnes might well have secured Browning the post but, as the whim of government changed, the enthusiasm for a mission to the Vatican cooled and it was never sent.

It was in May 1848, just over a year after their arrival, that the Brownings confirmed their residence in Florence by taking a lease on the unfurnished rooms in Casa Guidi, almost opposite the Pitti Palace. To Miss Mitford, Elizabeth wrote enthusiastically of 'six beautiful rooms and a kitchen, three of them quite palace rooms and opening on a terrace'. As for their life together, 'Robert and I go out often after tea in a wandering walk to sit in the Loggia and look at the Perseus, or, better still, at the divine sunsets on the Arno, turning it to pure gold under the bridges'.[6]

There were two aspects of the truth of the Browning marriage, each one emphasized appropriately to the correspondent. To the sceptical Miss Mitford, Elizabeth wrote of being 'deep in the fourth month of wedlock; there has not been a shadow between us'. She repeated this in stronger terms to Miss Mitford almost eighteen months later.[7] Yet to her confidante Mrs Jameson, 'Aunt Nina', she admitted in December 1847, looking about her 'with a sort of horror, seeing that this is not heaven after all. We live just as we did when you knew us, just as shut-up a life. Robert never goes anywhere except to take a walk with Flush, which isn't my fault, as you may imagine: he has not been out one evening of the fifteen months.' Not that this was evidence of tedium, for 'what with music and books and writing and talking, we scarcely know how the days go'.[8]

The change in Browning seemed absolute. From the brilliant talker of the dinner table and the purveyor of informed anecdote, whom Arnould had observed, he was now the recluse who was content to be alone with Elizabeth in that nearly claustrophobic intimacy which pervades his poetry of sexual love in *Men and Women*. The dandy of the immaculate suiting and the yellow gloves was now the casual dresser in 'unmentionable plaids', as his wife remarked, the man who loathed the very sight of fashionable shops. 'He bought a pair of boots the other day (because I went down on my knees to ask him, and the water was running in through his soles), and he will not soon get over it.'[9] As for gloves, whatever their colour, he declined to buy them.

As a husband, Browning appeared anxious, affectionate and resolute in putting Elizabeth's least interest before any of his own. If they quarrelled at all it was in terms of the most gentle absurdity, as Elizabeth described to Henrietta in November 1847.[10]

'I do wish, Ba, you wouldn't do so and so.'
'Well, I won't do it any more.'
'Don't say such words to me, Ba.'
'Why, what ought I to say, then?'
'Say that you will do as you please as long as you please to do it.'

The idyll of married love entered a new phase towards the end of 1848 with the discovery that Elizabeth was pregnant again. She was to suffer several miscarriages and on this occasion, as she wrote to Mrs Jameson during the pregnancy, Browning 'wished to heaven that the living creature would exhale and disappear in some mystical way without doing me any harm'.[11] In the light of the later affection lavished on the child, it is instructive to find this indication that sex was, foremost in Browning's view, an expression of his love for Elizabeth and only secondarily, and indeed dangerously, a means of parenthood.

The boy who was to be christened Robert Wiedemann Barrett Browning – and known as 'Pen', short for Penini – was born at Casa Guidi on 9 March 1849. Despite Browning's misgivings during the pregnancy, the safe arrival of the child left both parents overjoyed. That he was indulged and spoilt was perhaps not unexpected. The intimate 'tete-à-tete' between two lovers, as Elizabeth described it, was now expanded to include the one other person who could ever be admitted to it, their only child.

Before the month of March was over, Browning's happiness was overthrown by news from England. His mother, whom he had not seen for two and a half years, and whom Elizabeth had never met, died suddenly of a heart attack. His sister Sarianna, knowing the effect that the news would have upon him, wrote two preparatory letters after her mother's death, saying only that she was 'not well' and then 'very ill'. Elizabeth watched her husband anxiously, aware that he had 'loved his mother as such passionate natures only can love'.[12] The letter announcing Pen's birth arrived at New Cross before Mrs Browning's death, but she was already unconscious and never received the news. The coincidence of birth and death afflicted Browning with terrible force, 'and just because he was *too happy* when the child was born, the pain was overwhelming afterwards'.[13]

During the spring and early summer Browning seemed 'worn and altered', his joy in the birth of Pen diminished to a mere fondness.[14] He read and re-read Sarianna's letters and was found weeping over them. For him, he swore, it was impossible to visit England again and it would break his heart to see his mother's garden once more.

Elizabeth was understandably alarmed by his deterioration and fancied that the most likely cure would be a change of scene. In their first summer they had gone to Vallombrosa only to find that the abbot refused admittance to female guests and that, with their companion the journalist G. S. Hillard, they were obliged to return to Florence. Then, in 1848, they had gone to the Adriatic coast during the summer. The advantage of a cooler resort during summer would benefit them both. By this time Browning had been ill with an ulcerated throat and owed his cure to a visitor to Florence, the ex-Jesuit 'Father Prout'. Prout, a humorous journalist whose real name was Francis Mahony, prescribed a diet of eggs and port wine which proved effective. Now, at Elizabeth's insistence, they were to leave Florence for the summer to complete the recovery.

Just before their departure, on 26 June, Pen was baptized in the French Evangelical Protestant Church, which was in fact the chapel of the Prussian legation in Florence. It was Elizabeth's suggestion, as Browning told Sarianna, that the child should have their mother's maiden-name, among others. For himself, 'I have been thinking over nothing else, these last three months, than Mama and all about her'.[15]

After leaving Florence, driving north along the coast from Pisa to Lerici and back, they found themselves at length in the resort of Lucca. Lying between Florence and Pisa, this offered summer accommodation in the height and coolness of the hills at Bagni di Lucca, reached on the backs of donkeys by winding mountain paths. The summer and early autumn were passed in this 'eagle's nest', as Elizabeth called it, in one of the highest villas of Bagni di Lucca. All about them rose the mountains with their vine terraces, while the river ran swiftly below through wooded banks and under the arches of old bridges.

There were no mosquitoes, no Austrian drums nor carriages, Elizabeth wrote. 'Robert and I go out and lose ourselves in the woods and mountains, and sit by the waterfalls on the starry and moonlit nights.' They met no one 'except a monk girt with a rope, now and then, or a barefooted peasant'.[16]

In the quiet summer of Bagni di Lucca, Browning's grief grew less acute and his attention turned increasingly towards his infant son who was to be the object of so much affection. When Pen, rolling over and over on the floor, accidentally hit his head against it, Browning threw down his newspaper and exclaimed, 'Oh, Ba, I really can't trust you!' Then, wrote Elizabeth, 'Down Robert was on the carpet in a moment, to protect the precious head. He takes it to be made of Venetian glass, I am certain.'

She herself was sufficiently recovered in health to make an excursion on horseback five miles into the mountains for a summer picnic, following the dry torrent courses beside precipitous ravines. 'We dined with the goats, and baby lay on my shawl rolling and laughing.'[17]

Though Browning told the story with variations over the years, it was almost certainly at Bagni di Lucca that he first saw a sonnet sequence of Elizabeth's, later to be published as *Sonnets from the Portuguese*. As far back as 22 June 1846 she had written to him from Wimpole Street: 'You shall see some day at Pisa what I will not show you now. Does not Solomon say that "there is a time to read what is written." If he doesn't, he *ought*.'[18]

At Lucca the sonnets were still untitled, a collection of forty-four poems in which Elizabeth had enshrined her adoration for her lover before their marriage, the last sonnet dated two days before the wedding. One morning, after they had discussed the propriety of expressing personal love in poems that might be publicly read, Elizabeth said: 'Do you know I once wrote some poems about *you*. . . . There they are, if you care to see them.'[19] Writing of the incident fifteen years later, after Elizabeth's death, Browning found it so clear in his mind that he could recall her precise tone and gesture, even the mimosa beyond the window at which he was standing.

The manuscript book which she gave him contained poems, like the forty-third sonnet 'How do I love thee? Let me count the ways', which were rich in a devotion simply expressed. Others, like the thirty-eighth sonnet, captured the charmed intimacy which survived even the rigours of the sick-room and the interior gloom of the Wimpole Street house.

> First time he kissed me, he but only kissed
> The fingers of this hand wherewith I write;
> And, ever since, it grew more clean and white . . .
> Slow to world-greetings . . . quick with its 'Oh, list,'
> When the angels speak. A ring of amethyst
> I could not wear here, plainer to my sight,
> Than that first kiss. The second passed in height
> The first, and sought the forehead, and half missed,
> Half falling on the hair. Oh, beyond meed!
> There was the chrism of love, which love's own crown,
> With sanctifying sweetness, did precede.
> The third upon my lips was folded down
> In perfect purple state; since when, indeed,
> I have been proud and said, 'My love, my own.'

As the subject of one of the great love poems of the Victorian period, Browning was both exalted and humbled. It was unthinkable that such private moments should become the property of the world. But it was unthinkable, too, that some of the noblest sonnets since Shakespeare in their direct expression of love should be condemned to oblivion. A compromise was reached. The poems were to be published as if written to the sixteenth-century Portuguese poet Camoens by his mistress Catarina. The appropriate title was chosen and the sequence appeared in Elizabeth's *Poems* of 1850.

The existence of the sonnets throws an interesting light upon the Browning marriage as it existed in its poetry. Browning wrote a good deal of love poetry, the best of which was to appear in *Men and Women*. Rarely does it make direct reference to his life with Elizabeth, with the notable exception of the last poem, 'One Word More'. His analysis of the relationships between men and women, their loves and modes of coexistence, playfulness and passion, cold awakening and ultimate solitude, is more penetrating than it seems in his wife's poetry. Yet she was to excel him in the almost intimidating frankness of adoration as the sonnets expressed it.

To this extent their poetry reflects a more guarded commitment on his side than on hers. Browning, more than Elizabeth, found the need of some exterior framework or fiction through which to express the truths of a love that was sexual and spiritual. As in poetry, so in life. At first it had been Browning who strove to convince Elizabeth that love between them was possible. By 1849 she had long accepted that conviction and was, by the nervous ebullience of her temperament, the dominant partner in the marriage. Physical frailty alone was apt to give a misleading impression.

Returning to Florence in the autumn of 1849, they were both preoccupied during the winter which followed with the preparation of new volumes of poetry. Elizabeth was collecting and revising such poetry as she had written since 1844, to be published by Moxon in 1850. She had also written the first half of *Casa Guidi Windows* in 1848, expressing her support for Italian liberty. But the revolutionary hopes had grown bitter. Leopold II had been restored to power in Florence with a guard of white-uniformed Austrian troops. In a second part of *Casa Guidi Windows*, in 1851, she was to describe the disappointment of her political expectations.

Browning, no less than Elizabeth, devoted the winter of 1849–50 to a long poem on a topical subject. Yet it was far removed from the causes which she supported so eloquently at the time. In *Christmas-Eve and Easter-Day* he joined that flourishing debate in which Christians, sceptics and honest doubters had become embroiled by the mid-nineteenth century. He antedates by more than a decade poets like Matthew Arnold, whose 'Dover Beach' laments the 'melancholy, long, withdrawing roar' of the Sea of Faith, and is the near-contemporary of Clough's supposition in the streets of Naples in *Easter Day*, that

> Christ is not risen, no –
> He lies and moulders low;
>   Christ is not risen.

The religious debate was well in its stride long before this. Strauss's *Das Leben Jesu*, the historical criticism of the New Testament to extract from it the figure of Christ as a supreme human being and no more, was available in George Eliot's translation of 1846. In fiction, the loss of religious belief was a fashionable theme from J. A. Froude's *Nemesis of Faith* in 1849 until Mrs Humphrey Ward's *Robert Elsmere* in 1888. However, no single author achieved such celebrity in the discussion as Tennyson with *In Memoriam*, published in the same year as Browning's new book. Tennyson gave most readers precisely what they wanted, a reaffirmation of faith after a tasteful airing of the alternatives.

> There lives more faith in honest doubt,
> Believe me, than in half the creeds.

Browning's position was clear from the start. After his adolescent 'atheism' he reverted to the faith of his parents. In Florence he attended

the services of the Church of Scotland which approximated to it. Now
he contributed to the debate that absorbed men's minds a statement of
the three practical choices confronting the intellectual world. In doing
this he combined a colour of description with a suppleness of argument
in poetry. In contrast to the lyricism of the late romantics, he put verse
at the service of philosophy in a manner more common in the age of
Dryden and Pope, while employing the eye of the novelist in his noting
of human types.

Christmas-Eve, for the book consists of two separate parts, offers three
possibilities to the reader. There is the Nonconformist chapel with its
unprepossessing preacher and shabby congregation. Higher in the social
and political admiration of the world there is St Peter's, where the Pope
celebrates the Mass of the Nativity on Christmas Eve. Last and most
recent is the cold lecture-room at Göttingen where the rationalist professor delivers his bleak and comfortless address to his listeners.

Browning chose to describe Mount Zion chapel in terms which are
reminiscent of Dickens, despite his disapproval of *Martin Chuzzlewit* and
Pecksniff. In the rain gusting across the common, the members of its
plebeian congregation appear. They include the fat weary woman with
flapping umbrella, a prematurely aged sister-turned-mother nursing a
baby and a 'female something', white-lipped and rouged in dingy satins.
There is the shoemaker's lad with his consumptive cough and

> ... a tall yellow man, like the Penitent Thief,
> With his jaw bound up in a handkerchief.

As if recollecting the stentorian Mr Irons, the pastor of Camberwell
Grove, Browning adds to the chapel's other vices 'the preaching-man's
immense stupidity'.

In describing his experience of the chapel sermon, he addresses
the reader with the easy informality of a seventeenth-century verse
letter, explaining why any man of sense would have found the ordeal
intolerable.

> My old fat woman purred with pleasure,
> And thumb round thumb went twirling faster
> While she, to his periods keeping measure,
> Maternally devoured the pastor.
> The man with the handkerchief untied it,
> Showed us a horrible wen inside it,
> Gave his eyelids yet another screwing,
> And rocked himself as the woman was doing.
> The shoemaker's lad, discreetly choking,

Kept down his cough. 'Twas too provoking!
My gorge rose at the nonsense and stuff of it,
And saying, like Eve when she plucked the apple,
'I wanted a taste and now there's enough of it,'
I flung out of the little chapel.

The irony, as it later appears, is that the narrator is guilty of intellectual snobbery rather than endowed with the power of rational disagreement in this case. If there is a target for satire, it is himself. Yet he also stands against chapel Calvinism, resolute for free will, even the freedom for evil. His later poetry shows good and evil as necessary to human existence. This was a doctrine which he had long known from Bernard de Mandeville's *Fable of the Bees* (1714), a book whose subtitle was self-explanatory: *Private Vices, Public Benefits*. Vices, as Mandeville argued, were necessary to the stability of the social and economic order. In *Christmas-Eve* Browning puts the argument in terms of free will.

Able, His own word saith, to grieve Him,
But able to glorify Him too,
As a mere machine could never do.

One of the weaknesses of Browning's poem is that it requires God to appear like a Victorian magician and provide, as it were, a magic carpet to ferry the narrator about Europe. The fact that this is later revealed as a mere dream scarcely overcomes the objection. By the use of this device, however, the poet is next set down in Rome, where the Mass of the Nativity is celebrated in St Peter's amid scenes of gorgeous theatricality.

In this setting too one of the poem's chief delights appears as Browning's enthusiasm for visual description. Colour and depth succeed the darker caricature of Zion Chapel, as if the influence of Rembrandt had been replaced by Bellini or Raphael. Like Gerard de Lairesse, Browning is consumed by the enchantment of painting in words.

Men in the chancel, body, and nave,
Men on the pillars' architrave,
Men on the statues, men on the tombs
With popes and kings in their porphyry wombs,
All famishing in expectation
Of the main-altar's consummation.
For see, for see, the rapturous moment
Approaches, and earth's best endowment
Blends with heaven's: the taper-fires
Pant up, the winding brazen spires
Heave loftier yet the baldachin;

> The incense-gaspings, long kept in,
> Suspire in clouds; the organ blatant
> Holds his breath and grovels latent,
> As if God's hushing finger grazed him,
> (Like Behemoth when He praised him)
> At the silver bell's shrill tinkling,
> Quick cold drops of terror sprinkling
> On the sudden pavement strewed
> With faces of the multitude.

Despite a temporary admiration of the professed political enlightenment of Pius IX, Browning's own feelings for Rome and the papacy were less than flattering. 'I would not live there for the Vatican with the Pope out of it,' he told John Forster in 1854.[20] Yet, as in 'The Bishop Orders his Tomb at St Praxed's Church', the fascination of the ritual and the opulence is unmistakable. Indeed, in *Christmas-Eve* Browning allows that all the errors of Rome cannot make him believe 'That no truth shines athwart the lies'.

Last of all, in the Christmas Eve lecture at Göttingen, the narrator's wry scepticism, suspended during the glories of St Peter's, returns again. The subject of the lecture by 'The hawk-nosed, high-cheek-boned Professor' is, of course, 'The myth of Christ'. Of the sallow, turbercular professor, the poet says, 'God forbid I should find you ridiculous', and yet that is precisely what happens. This 'loveless learning' is sardonically summed up by Browning, no admirer of critics anyway, as 'The exhausted air-bell of the Critic'. The professor is allowed to talk nonsense for a while about the Idea and the Individuum, the possibility that Christ 'was and was not, both together'. Finally and dismissively, the poet himself considers the evidence for the claim that Christ's morality was all in all.

> What is the point where Himself lays stress?
> Does the precept run 'Believe in Good,
> 'In Justice, Truth, now understood
> 'For the first time?' – or, 'Believe in ME,
> 'Who lived and died, yet essentially
> 'Am Lord of Life?'

The argument of the poem, no less than Browning's personal preference, leads towards an inevitable choice. Of the three possibilities offered to the poet, it is Mount Zion Chapel that brings him closest to God and truth. Despite its unprepossessing inhabitants, that Nonconformist faith is unhampered by the interposition of priesthood and ceremonial between God and man. For all its imperfections, it enshrines a love totally absent from the irrational rationalism of Göttingen anthropology. Only the narrator's fastidious snobbery had prevented him from seeing the divinity in it at first.

By the end of *Christmas-Eve* Browning has made amends for whatever adolescent disrespect he may have shown the York Street congregation of his youth, turning against its rivals with a directness worthy of the Presbyterian Tract Society at that time. He hopes for the enlightenment of Pius ix,

> Turn'd sick at last of the day's buffoonery,
> Of his posturings and his petticoatings,
> Beside the Bourbon bully's gloatings
> In the bloody orgies of drunk poltroonery!

And for the rationalist professor, the caricature of David Strauss,

> May Christ do for him, what no mere man shall,
> And stand confessed as the God of salvation!

In arguing the merits of a religious faith, Browning employs a sophistication and urbanity, a range of political and topical allusion, which had not been applied to the subject with such skill since Dryden wrote *Religio Laici* and *The Hind and the Panther* in the 1680s. The same qualities characterize *Easter-Day*, which completed his publication of 1850.

The second poem meditates on the theme that was universally acknowledged as the most absorbing in the intellectual world of mid-Victorian England.

> How very hard it is to be
> A Christian!

The poem takes the form of an interior dialogue between a believer and a sceptic, the latter forced back step by step from his demand for absolute proof.

> Prove to me only that the least
> Command of God is God's indeed.

In that case would not he, like any man, court the most hideous martydom that even Nathaniel Wanley could devise:

> And give my body to be sawn
> Asunder, hacked in pieces, tied
> To horses, stoned, burned, crucified,
> Like any martyr of the list?
> How gladly, – if I made acquist,

> Through the brief minutes' fierce annoy,
> Of God's eternity of joy.

The theologians of 1850 were perhaps more likely to wince at this logic than their more distant successors. It was still familiar to them as the sardonic explanation offered by Edward Gibbon for the conversion of the Roman Empire to Christianity, 'Sapping a solemn faith with solemn sneer', as Byron termed it. 'When the promise of eternal happiness was proposed to mankind on condition of adopting the faith, and of observing the precepts of the Gospel, it is no wonder that so advantageous an offer should have been accepted by great numbers of every religion, of every rank, and of every province in the Roman Empire.'[21] *Easter-Day* shifted the ground further.

> You must mix some uncertainty
> With faith, if you would have faith *be*.

The argument of the poem apart, Browning shows the appeal of the Victorian religious debate to the intelligent reader who did not necessarily have pretensions to scholarship. It embraced many more subjects than religion, as *Easter-Day* shows. To argue about such matters was to enjoy an excursion through the more easily accessible areas of science, archaeology, literary and textual criticism, anthropology, historical and philosophical analysis. Because the proponents wished their views to reach a wide readership and therefore wrote often in general terms, the debate offered an education for everyman which was almost the Victorian equivalent of certain forms of mass publication and broadcasting a century later. What made the discussion still more compelling to its spectators was the awareness in each of its relevance to his individual life, death, salvation and immortal soul.

All this apparently worked to Browning's advantage. Like Tennyson or Newman, he had tapped a rich vein of middle-class interest. He exploited it with what seemed an effortless virtuosity in such poems as 'Bishop Blougram's Apology', 'Caliban upon Setebos', or the fine ironies of 'Cleon' and 'Karshish'. The subject in itself might be solemn, but it rarely called for solemnity of treatment. If Newman dealt with his religious ordeal by an intense and sublime pessimism in his *Apologia*, he also transformed it into one of the most witty novels of the early Victorian period – *Loss and Gain*, published in 1848. In such terms *Christmas-Eve and Easter-Day* might appear as Browning's *Apologia*. By the urbanity and wit of its successors he was closer in spirit to *Loss and Gain*.

In all this there lay a danger, scarcely evident as yet. As Browning reached his fame, his poems were searched, as those of Wordsworth and Tennyson had been, for evidence of a 'philosophy'. He was examined not as a poet but as a thinker, a philosopher, a theologian. When men like the Hegelian Sir Henry Jones scrutinized him with such expectations, they found him deficient. Being only human, they saw the fault as his, not theirs.

Towards the end of *Easter-Day*, Browning imagines himself at the Day of Judgement, faced with the promise of heaven but instead 'Choosing the world' as his eternal dwelling. It is of course a world of society, travel, art and beauty – something like an everlasting Grand Tour in the best of company.

> The statuary of the Greek,
> Italy's painting – there my choice
> Shall fix!

That such a desire, quickly overruled by divine revelation, should have surfaced in the winter of 1849–50 was perhaps an indication that Browning had been less changed by his marriage than he chose to believe. Of course, the handsome, fluent guest disgorging cleverness and anecdote at the dinner table had been replaced by the lover who lived in lone contented intimacy with his mistress. There was no suggestion that he regretted the exchange in any way. Yet the world outside gradually assumed the tempting appearance which it had done when he was working in the solitude of his room at Hatcham. There were dinners and parties among the most agreeable of men and women where Browning would be the centre of attention. There were galleries to be visited and journeys to be undertaken. From time to time it was possible for Elizabeth to accompany him into society. When she could not, he began to go on his own. It was rather at her insistence than his.

They had, in any case, made a number of mutual friends during their first years in Florence. G. S. Hillard, the American journalist who accompanied them on the abortive journey to Vallombrosa in 1847, remarked that 'a happier home and a more perfect union than theirs, it is not easy to imagine'. Browning he described as having a face 'full of vigour, freshness and refined power'. Elizabeth appeared a perfect match for this, 'the type of the most sensitive and delicate womanhood ... I have never seen a human frame which seemed so nearly a transparent veil for a celestial and immortal spirit'.[22]

Another early friendship in Florence was with the American sculptor Hiram Powers, best known for his statue of a chained and naked girl,

'The Greek Slave', which was to cause nervous comment at the Great Exhibition of 1851. Elizabeth saw in it only the evil of slavery, expressed in her own poem 'The Runaway Slave at Pilgrim's Point', and wrote a sonnet on the statue in these terms.

By 1849 the Brownings had made an enduring friendship with another young American, a sculptor and poet who had arrived in Italy with his wife. William Wetmore Story, a very cultivated and interesting person, as Browning thought him, was the son of Judge Story of the United States Supreme Court. He might almost have stepped from the pages of an early novel by Henry James, and it was indeed James who was later to edit Story's life and letters. Emelyn Story no less than her husband became an intimate friend of the Brownings. Elizabeth thought her 'a sympathetic, graceful woman, fresh and innocent in face and thought'.[23]

The two families were to share their lives, both in pleasure and vicissitude. They spent long evenings together in Florence and Lucca, as well as in Rome which was the Storys' destination. In 1854 Browning and Elizabeth took their turn in sitting by the bedside of the Storys' son Joe, who died of gastric fever. After Elizabeth's death, Browning's friendship with the family endured for the rest of his life.

A large number of the Brownings' friends were American, Elizabeth finding them 'very kind and earnest' as a race.[24] Among her own choices was Margaret Fuller, Marchesa d'Ossoli, who complimented Florence for being the Boston of Italy and who died in a shipwreck with her husband and child while returning to America in 1849. Among the more emancipated American ladies was Kate Field, journalist and feminist, and Hatty Hosmer, a young American sculptress who was to become 'a great pet' of the Brownings. It was Miss Hosmer who scandalized Rome by dressing like a boy and going about as freely in Italian society as any man would do. Included in their closest correspondents was the venerable name of James Russell Lowell, an early admirer of Browning's poetry, as Edgar Allan Poe was of Elizabeth's.

There was more than mere coincidence in this. Among those who knew him in London there was a sense that Browning was not quite English. There were even stories of creole ancestry which might account for his dark appearance. In Florence, those who met him casually were apt to think that he was indeed an American. It was his manner rather than his speech or appearance which suggested this. His enthusiasms and his conversation hardly seemed to fit the notion of the English gentleman. Story, writing to Charles Eliot Norton in 1861, remarked that 'Browning is by nature not an Englishman'. Without claiming him for the United States, Story with great accuracy described what it was that separated Browning from the educated men of his own country. 'Englishmen who think are rare,' he wrote, 'they are generally ganglions of prejudices, which they call opinions, and what ideas they have are generally narrow and bigoted.... Their education is never general, but special, and outside their speciality they are terribly barren.'[25]

So far as the verdict is a just one, it explains why Browning was so at ease with his American friends and, perhaps, why he was so sought after as an intellectual curiosity by the hostesses of London society. His religion and his upbringing had set him apart from the patrician Englishman whom Story seeks to typify and that alone made him an object of interest.

Other friendships formed in Florence indicate something of Browning's preference for those who moved outside the circle of fashionable society, however refreshed he might be by the knowledge that he was admired within it. Isa Blagden was to be another deeply loved and lifelong friend, his greatest support at the time of Elizabeth's death. She was probably of mixed race and possibly illegitimate, an exile from England and India alike. Not surprisingly, the figure of the exile or the expatriate appears among Browning's other friendships. Alfred Domett, Walter Savage Landor and the venerable Seymour Kirkup all partook of exile in different ways.

In Florentine society Seymour Kirkup was far more of a curiosity than Browning, for he was a survivor of an earlier culture and had known William Blake as well as Shelley and Keats. He lived as a gaunt and threadbare recluse in cavernous, dust-laden rooms near the Ponte Vecchio. With his hooked nose and long white hair he was taken by the local inhabitants for a practitioner of black magic, a belief strengthened by the fact that Kirkup had begun to dabble in the new art of spiritualism. Yet the hope he offered the Brownings was more tangible than messages rapped out on tables by the spirits of another world. When a young man, Kirkup had been sent to Italy as the victim of consumption. He survived there until the age of ninety-two, that most remarkable of figures who has conquered a fatal disease. Was there not hope, from his example, that Elizabeth's life might be far prolonged, if not saved, by the same climate?

In the spring of 1850 Browning was still furnishing Casa Guidi from such treasures as he could buy cheaply. Walking outside Florence one day he came across a pile of 'trash' in a corn shop and bought five age-darkened oil paintings which had been tossed aside there. He took them for an expert opinion to Kirkup, who at once pronounced them to be the work of Cimabue, Ghirlandaio, Giottino, saying of another that it was 'Giottesque, if not Giotto'.[26]

In the present state of Browning's finances, such a windfall might have been very welcome. Unfortunately, the paintings were not lost masterpieces. Kirkup shared with Landor a predilection for bestowing such names on acquisitions to please his friends. Swinburne, the luncheon guest of Landor in Florence, was horrified when his host insisted on presenting him with a Correggio which had belonged to Napoleon. He need not have worried – the picture proved to be 'a worthless daub'.

The summer of 1850 brought a crisis which overshadowed all financial considerations. Elizabeth suffered her fourth miscarriage and was gravely ill in consequence, so ill that the doctor expressed surprise to Browning at her recovery. As soon as she was well enough to be moved, he took her to the cooler and gentler air of Siena, having to lift her in and out of the train like a baby.[27] It was here that Pen began to express his infant intellectual preferences. He screamed to be taken into churches and, once inside, proceeded to kneel and cross himself before the eyes of his disapproving parents. 'One scarcely knows how to deal with the sort of thing,' wrote Elizabeth urbanely; 'it is too soon for religious controversy.'[28]

Despite her recovery from the miscarriage, her health was poor during the winter of 1850–51. Browning showed a natural restlessness for travel and society. They consulted routes and guidebooks to see if it would be possible to go together to Germany, Spain, Greece, even Egypt. It was not health but money which was the first stumbling-block. They had a reserve of £200 in the bank, totally insufficient for their plans.

So far as his literary income was concerned, Browning's career had hardly begun. In 1849 Chapman and Hall had published a collected edition of his poems, which consisted only of *Paracelsus* and *Bells and Pomegranates*. As yet, *Pauline*, *Strafford* and *Sordello* remained nothing but an embarrassment to their author. In 1850 the same publishers had issued his new book, *Christmas-Eve and Easter-Day*, at their own expense. It was published in April, well timed for an Easter sale. That was precisely the sale it achieved. Two hundred copies were sold initially and all interest in the book then declined.

The Brownings concluded by the spring of 1851, very logically, that they could only travel by letting their rooms in Casa Guidi and using the rent. In June they and Pen left Florence on a journey which was to last for almost a year and a half. They went first to Venice, Elizabeth spellbound by the drifting gondolas, the fantastic architecture, the coffee-drinking and music in the Piazza San Marco. By way of Milan they reached the lake steamers and crossed the St Gotthard between walls of snow. At Paris they met Tennyson and his wife who were just setting off for Italy and Florence. In whatever way they might appear as rivals, there was a cautious but growing friendship between the two men.

At the end of July 1851, in the loud optimism of that summer of the Great Exhibition, Browning, Elizabeth and their son, together with the maid Wilson, known as Lily, and the dog Flush returned to England after an absence of almost five years. One of Browning's first acts was to go to St Marylebone and, kneeling, to kiss the stones of the church in which he had married his wife.

9
Boulevard Life

Browning returned to England in his fortieth year. The comparative success of *Paracelsus*, still his most famous work, now appeared as a fleeting triumph of youth sixteen years in the past. A mere two hundred readers had bought *Christmas-Eve and Easter-Day* when the volume appeared in the year after the collected edition. Tennyson, against whom Browning was apt to measure his own success, had published *In Memoriam* some weeks later and that had already gone through five editions in little more than a year. Tennyson was also, of course, Poet Laureate by this time. Though the *Athenaeum* had canvassed Elizabeth's claims, Browning's name had not been mentioned.

Even that was not the worst of it. Five years of exile had produced only one book of new poetry, published in 1850. For a man with no other occupation, let alone one dedicated to being a poet, 'if not *the* Poet', it was an embarrassingly small output. There is no reason to doubt his sincerity in claiming that Elizabeth was the true poet and he only a clever writer. His most useful service to literature was apparently that of her guardian and comforter. 'If he is vain of anything, it is of my restored health,' Elizabeth wrote, adding: 'I have to tell him that he really must not go telling everybody how his wife walked here with him, or walked there with him, as if a wife with two feet were a miracle in Nature.'[1]

While in Paris they had both had misgivings about returning to England. Elizabeth was naturally apprehensive over her reception by the Barrett family and for a time wished Browning to make the journey alone. Though anxious to see his father and Sarianna, his eagerness was tempered by the thought of the house at Hatcham without his mother's presence.

They took lodgings in Devonshire Street, near the southern edge of Regent's Park. Elizabeth wrote to her father again, though no earlier letters had been answered. By way of reply she now received from him 'a very violent and unsparing letter', as well as all her own letters written to him during the previous five years, now returned with their seals still unbroken. 'What went most to my heart was that some of the seals were black with black-edged envelopes; so that he might have thought my child or husband dead, yet never cared to solve the doubt by breaking the seal.'[2]

Her sister Henrietta had married Captain Surtees Cook and was living in Somerset, but Arabel remained in Wimpole Street. Pen was taken there almost every day while Mr Barrett was out. Elizabeth herself visited the house. In Arabel's room while her sister dressed she heard her father on the stairs, his voice and his laughter, but she was never to speak to him.

Browning's own return to Hatcham was an occasion of pathos and farce. The memory of his mother and the consciousness of her absence now proved harrowing. Yet his father was about to become the object of scandal for his fervent courtship of a twice-widowed neighbour, Mrs Minny Von Muller. Now approaching the age of seventy, Robert Browning senior had written a number of imprudent and impassioned letters to this handsome middle-aged lady. Already in private and all too soon in public he was spoken of as a besotted dotard.

Old friendships were renewed during their eight weeks in London. There was a dinner with John Forster in Thames Ditton and an evening with Carlyle in Cheyne Row. Elizabeth admired Carlyle, whom 'I liked infinitely more in his personality than I expected to like him.... his bitterness is only melancholy, and his scorn sensibility. Highly picturesque too he is in conversation.'[3] There was also John Kenyon, who wished to be the Brownings' benefactor. The year before he had offered them money in order that they might travel but Browning had politely refused.

Their stay in London was comparatively brief. At the end of September, in company with Carlyle, they set out for Paris again. Browning had been greatly alarmed by the effect of London air on Elizabeth's lungs and the depression she suffered as a result of her father's continued bitterness. After they had gone, Browning's old friend Joseph Arnould wrote to Alfred Domett: 'I caught a glimpse of them while in town. He is *absolutely* the same man: her I like of all things – full of quiet genius.'[4]

They took an apartment on the Champs-Elysées, which at two hundred francs a month was no more expensive than their much shabbier lodgings in Devonshire Street. Elizabeth was delighted to find 'a southern aspect, and pretty cheerful carpeted rooms'.[5] Their evenings were spent at first with Carlyle who was on his way to visit one of the aristocratic bystanders of English literary society, Louisa, Lady Ashburton, with whom Browning's own life was later to be closely involved. In their own right the Brownings carried introductions to Lady Elgin, Mazzini, Victor Hugo and George Sand, though the promise of a meeting with Hugo was to be denied by political events.

During the autumn they moved in intellectual Parisian society. As the winter drew on it was often Browning alone who attended the salons and evening parties. When Elizabeth braved the comparatively mild weather of February 1852, she did so wrapped in furs and breathing with the aid of a respirator.

It was a meeting with George Sand, whom she greatly admired, which induced her to face such rigours. The great novelist sat with the immobility of an idol, receiving the admiration of male admirers in 'calm disdain'. Browning with his usual forthrightness remarked that 'if any other mistress of a house had behaved so, he would have walked out of the room'.[6] The more he saw of the society which gathered about George Sand, the less willing he was that Elizabeth should continue to be a part of it. Her sycophants consisted of 'crowds of ill-bred men who adore her *à genoux bas*, betwixt a puff of smoke and an ejection of saliva. Society of the ragged Red diluted with the lower theatrical.'[7] However little Browning matched the pattern of an Englishman, he had an Anglo-Saxon revulsion from the vanity and pretentiousness characteristic in so marked a degree of French literary society.

His disdain for the chic promiscuity of such company moved him to write 'Respectability', a lighter poem addressed to Elizabeth in their walks through the Parisian evening to a reception,

> Thro' wind and rain, and watch the Seine,
> And feel the Boulevart break again
> To warmth and light and bliss.

The poem is an urbane ironic argument in favour of married love which empowers them to caress in public and yet to be received at official functions.

> I know! the world proscribes not love;
> Allows my finger to caress
> Your lip's contour and downiness,
> Provided it supply a glove.
> The world's good word! – the Institute!
> Guizot receives Montalembert!
> Eh? down the court three lampions flare –
> Put forward your best foot!

Whatever his feelings about George Sand and her circle, Browning was that winter to form one of the great friendships of his life. In August 1851 Joseph Milsand, a critic who sought to introduce both contemporary English poetry and the writing of Ruskin to his countrymen, had contributed an article on Browning to the *Revue des Deux Mondes* in the series 'La Poésie anglaise depuis Byron'. Moreover, by the time that Browning met him in January 1852, Milsand was at work on another article, this time on Elizabeth's poetry.

That Browning should have taken at once to the French critic was not merely the result of Milsand's interest in his poetry and enthusiasm for it. Like Browning, Milsand was a Protestant. Like Browning, he abhorred the fast flashy society of the George Sand type, preferring life at home with his family. He was a man of conscience, with something approaching quietism. Towards Elizabeth he behaved with great consideration and to Pen Browning with instinctive gentleness. He was a man, in Elizabeth's view, for whose mind and conduct one felt a true reverence.

Life in Paris was far more than a succession of formal visits to eminent figures like Sand and Dumas. Browning's father and Sarianna arrived in November 1851, perhaps seeking shelter from the stormy resentment of Mrs Von Muller over the waning of her elderly suitor's impulsive admiration. In any case, the lease of the house at Hatcham was about to expire. To find a new home in Paris would put a discreet distance between Robert Browning senior and the loud indignation of Mrs Von Muller.

Overshadowing all other events was the *coup d'état* of December 1851, staged within earshot of the Brownings and showing for the first time a marked divergence in their views upon public affairs. Browning's inherent liberalism was affronted by the manner in which Louis Napoleon transformed himself from president of the Second Republic to supreme ruler of the Second Empire. Against the newly established emperor he increasingly directed all his natural suspicion of tyranny and established power. Whatever her reservations, Elizabeth continued to believe in the future Napoleon III. He brought to his empire a pledge of universal suffrage and the possibility, which later proved to be the case, that he would intervene in Italy to free the country from Austrian rule. 'The talk about "military despotism" is absolute nonsense,' she assured Mrs Jameson.[8]

Yet, as she described it to her brother George in a letter at the time, there had been military intervention close enough to the Champs-Elysées. In the rue de Richelieu the republicans were still holding out, facing the cannon and muskets of Louis Napoleon's guards. Browning, hurrying out alone to see for himself, was turned back from the area of danger.

On that day, 4 December, it was clear that the *coup* would be far from bloodless. The sounds of firing in the boulevards were clearly heard and cannons were drawn at full gallop down the Champs-Elysées to reinforce the positions of Louis Napoleon's troops. The Brownings' maid, Wilson, had taken Pen out into the avenue where he joined in shouting lustily at the soldiers. Once again, Lily Wilson was persuaded to take the child back into the safety of the apartment. 'The danger is, from the sudden sweep of the cannons,' Elizabeth explained to George, 'from which there would be no escape.' Her most immediate concern was that the president himself, who was with his men in the skirmishing, might be killed and that a state of anarchy would ensue. That night the fighting seemed to intensify. Refusing to go to bed, Elizabeth put on her dressing-gown and shawl and sat with Browning at the fireside until one o'clock in the morning. It was not that the Champs-Elysées was likely to become the scene of street-fighting, 'but simply that one shrank from going quietly to sleep while human beings were dying in heaps perhaps, within earshot'. By the next morning the quietness that followed the slaughter had settled upon the city.[9]

When it was all over, Browning remained aloof from the general enthusiasm. Elizabeth, on the other hand, reported the popular sympathy for Louis Napoleon as a leader who had delivered his people from a corrupt constitution. The public feeling had been displayed close at hand even before the fighting. 'The President rode under our windows on December 2, through a shout extending from the Carrousel to the Arc de l'Etoile.'[10] She admitted her disagreements with Browning in the matter but remained unmoved.

Her bland disregard for the danger to Pen was entirely retrospective and assumed for the benefit of her correspondents. Few Victorian children were more pampered and indulged than this unexpected and therefore cherished son. Both parents lavished upon him a degree of love which matched their gentle adoration of one another. He often appeared as an elaborate walking advertisement for the achievement of their married life. Even in an age when children were apt to be dressed as pantomime figures, Pen's appearance was truly conspicuous. In Paris, as Elizabeth wrote to her sister Henrietta, this sartorial passion ran to a white felt hat with feathers, white satin ribbons and blue satin sides, setting off golden curls, matching long white gaiters and pants. Contrary to the fears of child psychologists, the hermaphroditic appearance which he was obliged to assume until his mother's death when he was twelve was not the precursor of some terrible sexual catastrophe.[11]

Such grief as came to them during their winter in Paris was caused by tidings from England and the memory of old tragedies. At the end of 1851 Elizabeth's friend and correspondent, Mary Russell Mitford, had published her *Recollections of a Literary Life*. In this she had talked of Elizabeth and revealed the effect upon her of the drowning of her eldest brother, Edward or Bro, at Torquay in 1840. Worse still, in reviewing the book the *Athenaeum* seized upon the passage and quoted it at length as the most significant revelation made about the poetess.

When the *Athenaeum* reached Paris, Elizabeth's hypersensitivity on all such matters led to a near collapse. She could not bear to read the words. Later, at her insistence, Browning read them to her. The lingering grief for her brother was reanimated and she felt that a sacred and intimate memory had been violated to assuage public curiosity. Her letters to Miss Mitford were filled with the dismayed reproach of a friend to whom an unintended blow has been dealt. Yet the crisis passed and, indeed, the friendship survived in a somewhat impaired manner.

In the spring it was Browning's turn to receive a message from a world which, since his mother's death, had been almost dead to him. His cousin James Silverthorne, the companion of his youth who had introduced him to Shelley, Wagner and the London theatre, had been ill for some time. At the beginning of the previous year Elizabeth had written to Sarianna that Browning was in tears before he finished reading the letters which arrived in Florence describing Silverthorne's condition. In May 1852 Silverthorne died. Browning wished to go to England for the funeral but decided that Elizabeth, recovering from an attack of influenza, was not well enough to be left. It was not until the following month that they crossed to England and took lodgings in Welbeck Street, once again within a few minutes' walk of the Barrett house in Wimpole Street.

On this occasion Browning was far from empty-handed upon his return to England. Conscious of his wasted years in Florence, he set himself a resolution to be fulfilled at the beginning of 1852. It reflected characteristically his inherent Puritan belief that effort would produce achievement, that success was the reward of work, and that even in the sphere of poetry genius owed as much to diligence as to inspiration. He therefore resolved to dig himself out of his own predicament in the most logical manner. He would write a poem every day, come what might.

At twenty lines a day, 1852 would produce three or four books, each the length of *Christmas-Eve and Easter-Day*.

To anyone who held the romantic and inspirational view of poetry, such a scheme was ludicrous and deserved to fail. Yet if this were so, and if nothing could be done until inspiration struck, how was a work the length of *Paradise Lost*, *King Lear*, or for that matter *The Prelude* ever written?

As it happens, the Puritan method of composition was triumphant. How many poems which appeared in *Men and Women* were written in fulfilment of the resolution is uncertain because the dates of most are unknown. Only the result of the first three days is clear. On 1 January 'Women and Roses' was written, on 2 January ' "Childe Roland to the Dark Tower came" ', and on 3 January 'Love Among the Ruins'. If that was all the resolution produced, it more than justified itself. 'Love Among the Ruins' was the opening piece of *Men and Women*, a mesmeric poem of visual suggestion, two lovers depicted against the fading twilight images of ancient grandeur. ' "Childe Roland to the Dark Tower came" ' remains one of the most haunting and elusive visions in the entire Victorian period, defying total analysis yet perpetually evocative.

The reward of such endeavours was delayed for three more years until the appearance of the poems in book form. Even then the tribute was paid slowly and with something approaching reluctance.

The Brownings remained in London from June until October 1852, when the prospect of winter obliged them to go south again. It was for the most part a far more agreeable visit than that of the previous year, except for the last act in the farce of Robert Browning senior and Mrs Von Muller. Slighted as she felt herself to be, she brought an action in the Court of Queen's Bench for breach of promise. When the case was heard the London press fell hungrily upon the scandal and reported it with a mortifying wealth of detail. The ill-considered passion which Browning's father had poured out in his letters to Minny Von Muller was now read out for the benefit of the special jury and reported in the newspapers for the amusement of their readers. Never wavering in his loyalty to his father, Browning still felt the disgrace deeply. Nothing was spared the family; the letters and the courtroom references to a dotard in love were public property. Browning, with the support of Elizabeth, comforted his father. The jury found in favour of Mrs Von Muller and awarded her £800 damages. This was more than twice the defendant's annual salary. He withdrew to France, beyond the court's reach, and made his home in Paris with Sarianna.

Despite this, the three months which followed the case were convivial and enjoyable for Browning and Elizabeth. Mr Barrett was still un-relenting but Elizabeth had become reconciled with her brothers. With George, an Inner Temple barrister ten years her junior, she had resumed an intimate correspondence. Arabel was close by during the London visit, and Henrietta was still settled in Somerset with her husband, Captain Surtees Cook.

Early in their stay Henrietta came to London. Then there were evenings with the Proctors, visits to Carlyle, dinners and a drive with Monckton Milnes. They went to the christening lunch which Milnes held for his infant daughter, where the baby was obliged to sweep in, as Elizabeth termed it, in India muslin and Brussels lace. She was not well enough to attend the christening of Hallam Tennyson, to which the Laureate had invited them, but Browning went alone and was allowed to nurse the infant for a full ten minutes and even to toss it into the air.

There was lunch with the Ruskins, from which both Brownings came away deeply impressed by the goodness and intelligence of Ruskin himself. Observing Effie, however, Elizabeth concluded that she was pretty and elegant but incapable of intelligent effort. There was a meeting with Charles Kingsley, a more recent friend, and a dinner with Talfourd to which Browning went alone. To keep awake their enthusi-asm for Italian liberty, Mazzini came to Welbeck Street in July.

In his own right, Browning at last mended his quarrel with Macready. The occasion was Mrs Macready's death in September 1852. Browning's letter ignored the long disappointment of his theatrical writing, recall-ing the 'happy days when I lived in such affectionate intimacy with your family'.[12]

Before they left London, Browning received two visits from admirers, one old, the other young. W.J. Fox arrived at Welbeck Street where, perhaps understandably, he seemed far more intrigued by Elizabeth and the sight of Pen than by his former protégé. Of Elizabeth he observed that she talked beautifully of George Sand and 'silver-electroplated Louis Napoleon'.[13] To judge from his observation that she 'did not put her hand before her mouth', even the return to London had not brought on the spitting of blood by which Elizabeth was apt to gauge her state of health.[14]

The other visitor, who had first written to Browning five years earlier in order to tax him with being the author of *Pauline*, was Dante Gabriel Rossetti. Of the two visits it was probably Rossetti's which was the more gratifying to Browning. Despite the general indifference to his poetry, there were younger men, loosely grouped around the Pre-Raphaelites, who had begun to take it up. He also found Rossetti's combined enthusiasm for art and poetry congenial, though rather ungratefully he was to dismiss Rossetti's own poetry in 1875 on the grounds that he hated such affectation.[15]

On 16 September Elizabeth wrote to Henrietta in Somerset, warning her that 'this horrible climate is beginning to put out its gripes, and I must take care'.[16] Their departure, this time for Italy, could not be much longer delayed. Two days earlier Browning himself had written to Edward Chapman, at Chapman and Hall, asking for an account and any money due to him or Elizabeth, adding that he would have to leave London very shortly.[17]

As the first October fogs began to gather in the London air, Browning and Elizabeth took their leave. They travelled from Folkestone to Boulogne and stopped long enough in Paris to see Louis Napoleon's triumphal procession through the city on 16 October. A week later they set out, first by train, then by river steamer, for Lyons. They crossed the Alps by hired carriage, only to find that Elizabeth's breathing was distressingly laboured in the thinner air of the Mont Cenis Pass. It was necessary to stay first at Turin and then at Genoa to allow her to recover her strength. At length they reached Pisa and took the train to Florence, returning to the old uneventful life of Casa Guidi after so long an absence.

Writing to John Kenyon on 16 January 1853 Browning described the benefits of a mild May-like winter in Florence. Elizabeth had recovered from the journey, her cough was entirely gone, and they planned to visit Rome in a month or two.[18] Yet after a year and a half of travelling, the excitement of the *coup d'état* in Paris and the stimulus of so many meetings with friends, Casa Guidi might have appeared oppressive in its isolation from the world.

That it did not was in part the consequence of Browning's need for a period of tranquillity in which to make use of the material gathered during the months of travelling. There is no indication that he had planned such a sequence, rather that he now found himself in a mood to draw upon this experience in the pursuit of his greatest and most necessary ambition: to be a popular poet. On 24 February he wrote to Milsand: 'We live wholly alone here. I have not left the house one evening since our return. I am writing – a first step towards popularity for me – lyrics with more music and painting than before, so as to get people to hear and see.'[19]

Despite the seclusion which Browning implies, he and Elizabeth found two new friends that winter among the English colony in Florence. The first of these, Frederick Tennyson, was the eldest brother of the Laureate, an accomplished musician who had contributed to *Poems by Two Brothers* (1827). Having married Maria Giuliotti, daughter of Siena's chief magistrate, he settled in Florence. Tall with long fair hair, he was reputed to sit in the hall of his villa on the Fiesole road while forty hired musicians played to him. His eccentricities and his shyness, which Browning regarded as morbid in its intensity, gave him the reputation among Florentines of a mad, if benign, English milord. He was preoccupied by matters of religion, including the second coming of Christ. No one was surprised to find him a recruit for the fashionable practice of spiritualism.

The second new friend was more than twenty years younger. Robert Lytton, son of the novelist Sir Edward Bulwer-Lytton, was an *attaché* at the English legation in Florence. Indeed, he was a diplomat by profession who was to be Viceroy of India between 1876 and 1880. Like Seymour Kirkup and Elizabeth herself, Lytton developed an interest, soon turning to enthusiasm, in the phenomenon of 'table-rapping'. In 1848 two girls in Hyderville, New York, claimed that communication with the spirit world was possible by 'percussion sounds'. One of the two girls, the Fox sisters, later confessed that she had produced the sounds by cracking her knee-joints, but the new cult spread rapidly.

Elizabeth regarded Lytton, as she told Henrietta in November 1852, as 'a seer of visions, a great supernaturalist', and her faith was additionally confirmed by Hiram Powers who assured her that the rapping spirits in America were fully worthy of belief.[20]

Browning's own attitude towards such matters ranged from scepticism to frank distaste. The scorn came later and was directed against professional mediums like the American D.D. Home who enriched themselves at the expense of the gullible and the bereaved with performances which were all too close to stage conjuring. To be fair to Lytton and Tennyson, as well as Elizabeth, the earlier interest in table-rapping was more critical and questioning. Lytton's father, the novelist, accepted the possibility of such communication but suggested that it might well be the work of the living, exercising a form of telepathy. Elizabeth herself saw it only as an adjunct to certain biblical texts. 'We read of a prophecy concerning "angels ascending and descending upon the son of man." What if this spiritual influx and afflux is beginning? It seems to me probable – but we have to wait quietly and see.'[21] She was also impressed by the manner in which men had been converted from atheism by such manifestations, though she accepted that if good spirits could operate on men so might evil ones.[22] One such convert was

Seymour Kirkup, two years later. Browning, while not choosing to argue with Elizabeth's own belief, made no bones about denouncing Kirkup to her as a 'humbug'. Indeed, Elizabeth herself was still poised between scepticism and hope at the end of that time. 'A few solitary rappings will not satisfy me. . . . I suspend my opinion therefore about the Kirkup manifestations.'[23]

By April 1853 Browning's thoughts turned towards London again, where *Colombe's Birthday*, which Charles Kean had not produced after all, was receiving its first performance at the Haymarket Theatre with Helen Faucit in the title role. It ran for seven nights and was politely although not enthusiastically received. Yet its modest success seemed a good omen.

Soon after this, on 14 May, Elizabeth reported to Henrietta that the visit to Rome had been abandoned, with the heat of the summer growing, and that another journey to England was beyond their means. Browning was the more disappointed of the two, for after six months of Casa Guidi he thought wistfully of the 'blaze of life' which Paris and its society had been to him. To Sarianna and to John Kenyon, Elizabeth described him as having been 'demoralised' by his experience of Paris and reported that he pronounced Florence 'dead, and dull, and flat'.[24]

Yet the winter tedium of Florence had driven him to work on the new volume of poems. That summer, as the heat came like a tiger, in Elizabeth's words, they made excursions to Prato and Fiesole. In July the city had grown unbearable and they left Casa Guidi for Lucca, having taken the Casa Tolomei which stood high up in Bagni Caldi. In the calm of the terraced hillsides they remained until the cooler nights of October brought them back to Florence again.

What might have been three months of solitude was broken by visits from Lytton, Frederick Tennyson and the unexpected arrival of William Wetmore Story and his family from Rome. During the weeks that followed, the Brownings and the Storys lived high up in the hills, 'retired from the bustle of the Ponte below, where gossip simmers round the café, and we are leading the most *dolce far niente* of lives'.[25] Of the Brownings, Story wrote to James Russell Lowell: 'With them we have constant and delightful intercourse, interchanging long evenings together two or three times a-week, and driving and walking whenever we can meet. We like them very much – they are so simple, unaffected and sympathetic. Both are busily engaged in writing, he on a new volume of lyrical poems and she on a tale or novel in verse.'[26]

However impatient Browning may have been to return to the 'palpitating' life of the Paris boulevards, it seemed that Elizabeth had been proved right, as she wrote to Henry Chorley from Lucca. 'An artist must, I fancy, either find or *make* a solitude to work in, if it is to be good work at all.'[27] In their own case, at Lucca, the solitude extended to withholding poems from one another's scrutiny until they were finished. Yet such pieces as Elizabeth had seen from *Men and Women* seemed to her a match for the best that Browning had so far written.

To Browning himself the summer at Bagni Caldi was a memory of mountains, chestnut woods and moonlight.[28] Alone or in company with the Storys they crossed the hills, Elizabeth riding a donkey, and returned in the sunset or darkness among 'jagged mountains, rolled together like pre-Adamite beasts, and setting their teeth against the sky'.[29] In Elizabeth's accounts the figure of Pen at four years old is never long absent. Now, as she held him in her arms and said, 'God bless my child', he would hug her and reply, 'God bless mine Ba'.[30] In the close intimacy of the child and his parents he used their Christian names freely but not invariably. Browning's devotion to him had rivalled Elizabeth's. In order that Pen should not wake alone and frightened, he would sit by the sleeping boy while both Elizabeth and Wilson were out of the room. While his parents were occupied with their writing, Pen accompanied the maid and Ferdinando Romagnoli the manservant, as well as Flush, to the river and the lower slopes. As always he was dressed like the cherished object of Elizabeth's affection, his costume now including elaborate collars and pants of embroidered muslin.

There was only one matter in which Pen's wishes could not be granted. He was disappointed at having no brother to play with. Ignorant of the biological implications, he complained to his mother and made 'a very serious representation of disadvantages'.[31]

In the early autumn the Storys began their journey to Rome. Elizabeth, looking back on three months of work and friendship, wrote her own farewell to Lucca on 5 October. 'Such a summer we have enjoyed here, free from burning heats and mosquitos.... Mountains not too grand for exquisite verdure, and just kept from touching by the silver finger of a stream.' With Browning and the Storys she had again ridden on donkeyback the six miles up to Prato Fiorito. The effort had prostrated her for days afterwards. 'But who wouldn't see heaven and die?' Best of all, this appeared only a foretaste of the companionship to come. As cool autumn days began, the Brownings were also to travel south, sharing the cosmopolitan winter society of Rome with the Storys.[32]

Returning briefly to Florence, they set out by road for Rome. Upon their arrival, Browning was in a state of 'bilious irritability' and proceeded to cause Elizabeth the greatest distress by shaving off his finely groomed beard and whiskers. 'I *cried* when I saw him,' she wrote, adding: 'Of course I said when I recovered breath and voice, that everything was at an end between him and me if he didn't let it all grow again directly.' The beard was duly grown again, but to Browning's chagrin and to Elizabeth's amusement it grew white, 'which was the just punishment of the gods'.[33]

Yet the domestic comedy of the beard was soon eclipsed by tragedy and apprehension. Story's son and daughter were taken ill with fever. The little boy, Joe, succumbed almost at once, while the Brownings took the girl, Edith, and nursed her back to health. The gesture of friendship was the more commendable since Elizabeth was in great fear of the contagion touching Pen, 'those blue far-reaching eyes, and that innocent angel face emplumed in the golden ringlets'.[34]

For Browning at least there was consolation among the lively community of writers and painters in Rome. Thackeray was a visitor to the temporary home which they had set up in the Via Bocca di Leone, as were Fanny Kemble the actress and her sister Mrs Adelaide Sartoris. It was there, to the convalescent Edith Story, that Thackeray read an unpublished tale, *The Rose and the Ring*. Browning's own skill in amusing children was seen on a later visit to Rome. At one of Story's parties he read 'The Pied Piper of Hamelin' to the children, Hans Andersen read 'The Ugly Duckling', and Story, playing the flute, acted as piper to lead the assembly through the palatial Barberini apartments.

Though the Roman winter was mild enough for Elizabeth to go out during the day, visiting St Peter's and the Forum, it was as a rule Browning alone who went into the society of the capital after dark. He made the acquaintance of Hatty Hosmer, and met the English painter Frederic Leighton. There was also the ailing and elderly figure of John Gibson Lockhart, biographer of Scott and editor of the *Quarterly Review*, now in the last year of his life. Lockhart, like Landor, made enemies easily and almost unawares. Like Landor too, he formed an attachment for Browning. 'I like Browning,' he said guardedly, 'he isn't at all like a damned literary man.'[35]

The climate and the society of Rome in the winter of 1853–4 proved more to Browning's taste than those of Florence. As the spring came, his thoughts turned towards England and Paris. Yet the collection of poems which was to make up *Men and Women* was still incomplete – the distractions of Rome had ensured that – and it was financially out of the question to travel northwards again without a book to publish.

He had, on the eve of their departure from Rome for Florence, the air of a man who might belatedly be coming into the prime of his life.

'Robert is considered here to be looking better than he ever was known to look,' wrote Elizabeth to Sarianna. 'And this, notwithstanding the greyness of his beard, which indeed is, in my own mind, very becoming to him, the argentine touch giving a character of elevation and thought to the whole physiognomy.'[36]

While the question of Italy was in abeyance and while Elizabeth grew increasingly preoccupied by spiritualism, he had his own hobby-horse to ride. During that summer and autumn he watched with incredulity and then disgust the manner in which Lord Aberdeen's government committed England and its army to a disastrous war against Russia. Before much longer, as the invasion of the Crimea slowed down to a fruitless siege of Sebastopol, Elizabeth described him as frantic. He talked of England being disgraced in the face of Europe. 'When he is mild he wishes the ministry to be torn to pieces in the street, limb from limb.' She herself was content to suggest that the army should be led by 'properly qualified officers, instead of Lord Nincompoop's youngest sons'.[37]

In their accounts of one another, Browning and Elizabeth presented to the world much the same attitudes which had been evident between themselves during their courtship. Though each might rival the other in mutual love, it was Elizabeth who expressed her feelings the more fully and openly. Browning's affection appeared more practical and even more matter-of-fact. This degree of reserve gave him, as a public figure, an air of well-controlled vanity. With his fine grey beard, an expression of strength and nobility, he had acquired the decided look of a poet and philosopher which was to endure until his life's end. In all important respects he was as dedicated to the profession of poetry and as impatient of criticism as the young romantic of the dark flowing locks who had been so conspicuous in the salons of the 1830s: yet his good looks were now no less cultivated to suggest the pattern of the maturer sage.

By those for whom he cared he was greatly admired. Admiration, as he was later to admit, was very dear to him. The compliments of society in London and Paris, Rome or Florence had been extremely agreeable. Having his portrait painted in Rome led him to speak proudly of the 'magnificent' and 'marvellous' result.[38] That winter was, perhaps, unproductive, but the deference and appreciation shown him proved greatly to his taste. There were parties and dinners, congenial excursions and picnics in the Campagna. He had enjoyed the well-deserved flattery of young women like Hatty Hosmer, Miss Hayes and a certain house of emancipated ladies, as Elizabeth rather nervously thought them. Even in his extreme tolerance of awkward old men like Landor and Lockhart, it may be that Browning made allowances for characteristics in them which he felt developing in himself.

The self in which he took such pride was in this respect merely the shell of the poet. 'Choosing the world', its admiration and friendships, was a temptation more easily yielded to when yielding was temporary. From months of pleasant idleness he would return, with the stern conscience of the Puritan, and set to work again as if he had never intended to do anything else. His first loyalty, apart from Elizabeth and Pen, was to his work. Yet the New Year's resolution of 1852, to write poetry every day, was quite uncharacteristic. He worked with great intensity and at remarkable speed. But then, as Edmund Gosse observed, he might appear to turn his back on it for months and replace it as the mainstay of his life by the pleasures of travel or the congeniality of general society.[39] To be a bon viveur and a hermit seemed equally easy to him and equally to be indulged.

After the return to Florence from Rome in June 1854 until he and Elizabeth left for England a full year later, he seemed more withdrawn from the world than at any time in his life. There was not even a summer excursion to Lucca. To his friend Story he offered a concise and direct explanation as he moved from one mode of existence to another. 'I am trying to make up for wasted time in Rome and setting my poetical house in order.'[40]

10

'My Fifty Men and Women'

It was Elizabeth who provided the most buoyant summary of the winter's activities, writing to her sister Henrietta in April 1855. 'Robert's poems are magnificent, and will raise him higher than he stands. We are up early working, working. Penini's lessons I never neglect – then I write. – Then dinner – then I criticise Robert's MSS. Altogether I have scarcely breath for reading.'[1]

The truth was less exhilarating. In the colder air of a Florentine winter, Elizabeth's lungs had soon become affected. Browning talked desperately of warmer climates, including Egypt and the Sandwich Islands, said Elizabeth facetiously. During January he sat up night after night with her, tending the fire and boiling coffee, administering morphine to her as necessary. His 'tender patience' seemed inexhaustible, though as she reported, 'of course it was miserable for him'.[2] The symptoms alarmed him and yet they were not the worst kind. There had been no coughing of blood, no loss of voice, and comparatively little pain.[3]

By June all but one of the poems in *Men and Women* had been completed. At the same time there was a new threat in Florence itself where cholera was reported in the growing heat of the season. The effect of this was to hasten their plans for departure. Travelling to Leghorn, they embarked on a ship for Marseilles. Here they met Alfred Barrett, Elizabeth's brother, who was just beginning an unsanctioned marriage to his cousin Lizzie, formerly a ward of his father at Wimpole Street.

Arriving in Paris on 24 June they were at once embroiled in family business. Their apartment was in the same building where Browning's father and Sarianna had made their home, near the Invalides. During their stay, Browning and Elizabeth made speedy arrangements for the marriage of their maid Lily Wilson, who had become pregnant by the manservant, Ferdinando Romagnoli. On their arrival in England on 12 July, Lily was sent north to her family for the confinement while

Romagnoli, as seemed only just, undertook the bulk of the household chores during her lying-in.

They took a house in Dorset Street, near Portman Square, and discovered that their friends of 1851-2 had not forgotten them. Tennyson at once invited them to the Isle of Wight and Bulwer-Lytton to Derbyshire. Reluctantly the invitations were refused. Browning was to spend the next months on the revisions and proofs of *Men and Women*. After four years of work Elizabeth was near the end of her verse novel *Aurora Leigh*. Apart from such considerations they had not the money for travel. Robert Browning senior was now a fugitive from court orders and financial claims, hardly in a position to assist them. There was no question of any help from Mr Barrett. Indeed, as they were soon to find, he had cut Elizabeth out of his will entirely. Browning wrote to Edward Chapman repeatedly, asking for the latest account to be rendered and the sums due to himself and Elizabeth to be paid. In his own case the amounts were very small.

Mr Barrett, hearing of his daughter's presence in London, moved his household to Eastbourne for the summer. Up to that time Pen had been taken the short distance from Dorset Street to Wimpole Street, while Mr Barrett was out, so that he might spend the days with Arabel. On one occasion, while playing with his uncle George Barrett, Pen came face to face with his grandfather. Mr Barrett demanded whose child he was. George explained that he was Ba's child, and his father, dismissing the matter, changed the subject at once.

It was small wonder that Elizabeth thought the visit to England uncomfortable and unprofitable. They had neither the leisure nor the money to follow the Barretts to Eastbourne, though because Mr Barrett remained alone in Wimpole Street, it was safe to send Pen to the seaside with Arabel.

Within the limitations of their life in London they saw many friends and illustrious contemporaries. On 14 July Elizabeth's elderly cousin John Kenyon arranged a breakfast party at which they were to meet 'half America and a quarter of London'.[4] Rather ominously, Elizabeth added that the one American in England whom she most wished to meet was the medium D. D. Home. That wish was soon to be fulfilled.

Because his effect upon the Brownings - and upon Browning's choice of poetic subjects - was significant, it is necessary to say something about Daniel Dunglas Home. He was still a young man when he arrived in England from America in 1855. His expertise - whatever the explanation of the phenomena - was undoubted and he speedily acquired patrons. They included Lyndhurst, the former Lord Chancellor, Lady

Salisbury, the Duchess of Devonshire, Lady Londonderry, Landseer the painter, and Dr James Gully, the fashionable physician of Malvern.

In July 1855 he was the guest, at their home in Ealing, of Mr Rymer, a solicitor, and his wife, whose daughter had pretensions to being a medium. The sight and sound of Home was calculated to set Browning's teeth on edge. Here was a strapping young man who chose to behave towards his dupes as a wide-eyed baby even to the extent of calling the Rymers his papa and mama.

During fifteen years in Europe and England, Home appeared to produce the most astonishing manifestations at his seances. All too soon they were imitated by those who professed to be nothing but stage magicians. It was the easiest thing in the world to present a ghost through whose immaterial body swords could be passed or through whom a living man could walk. It required only some very simple lighting and a large sheet of plate glass behind which the performance took place. Indeed, as Robert-Houdin was soon to describe it in his book *The Secrets of Stage Conjuring*, such ghosts were only more sophisticated types of the images which railway travellers saw after dark when their reflections appeared outside the carriage window.[5]

The enthusiasm of Home's admirers was to reach near-hysteria during certain performances. One night in an upstairs room at Buckingham Place or Victoria Street – possibly both – he levitated, floated out beyond one closed window and back towards another. There were three witnesses, and the height above the street was variously given as thirty-five and eighty-five feet.

The incident was not explained. Home laughed and wondered what a policeman would have thought had he looked up and seen the floating body above him in the London night. Alas, it seems likely that the policeman would have seen nothing. Concealed from the witnesses, supported by the thick plate glass which stage magicians used, Home need not have left the room. He may have worked one of the great miracles of the nineteenth century. It seems more likely that only his reflected image passed into the night and back again. The principle would have been precisely the same as Robert-Houdin's 'Ghost Illusion'.

Such was the leading figure of spiritualism to whose seance at Ealing the Brownings were invited on 23 July 1855. In the presence of the Brownings and the other guests, Home went through his repertoire of tricks. The spirits played an accordion for him, less remarkable since a self-playing accordion was already on the market. Hands and arms from the spirit world manifested themselves. There were so many ways of producing the illusion that it is uncertain how it was done on this occasion. A skilful trickster, in the semi-darkness, could lay one hand only on the table, his neighbours on either side each thinking they were touching a separate hand. There were false hands which could be placed on the table while the medium remained free to manipulate the effects with one of his own. There were shoes which ended in gloved 'hands' and so enabled him, by moving his leg under the table, to produce a spirit hand in the air beyond.

Browning alleged that Home lay back in his chair in such a manner that he could stretch out his legs to produce effects of this type. He even claimed to have caught hold of the medium's foot under the table while Home was engaged in this particular deception.[6] During the remainder of the seance, the table was mysteriously lifted and Home, in a medium-istic trance, spoke as the dead child of the Rymers. The incident which was to cause most acrimony was the crowning of Elizabeth with a 'laurel wreath' of clematis which lay on the table. A spirit hand appeared and placed it on her head. This was presumably Home's own hand, which he was free to use by means of a conjurer's deception. When the hostility between them became public, after the publication of 'Mr Sludge, "The Medium"', Home described the incident in his own terms. Browning stood behind Elizabeth, he said, and 'seemed much disappointed' when the wreath was laid on his wife's head rather than his own. He had deliberately placed himself 'in the way of where it was being carried' in order that it should be put upon him.[7]

Browning's reaction to these events was severely practical. He asked the Rymers if he might attend another of Home's seances in the role of an investigator of these phenomena. His hosts told him that it would not be convenient. Robert-Houdin, the French stage magician, was also refused admission to Home's seances and other avowed sceptics were similarly turned away. Two of them wrote to Browning after the seance of 23 July 1855 and asked his opinion. He assured them bluntly that 'the whole display of "hands", "spirit utterances", etc., was a cheat and an imposture'. Finally, he confessed, he 'had some difficulty in keeping from an offensive expression of his feelings at the Rymers; he has since seen Mr Home and relieved himself'.[8]

This last remark was a reference to a visit by Mrs Rymer, her son and Home to the Brownings' house in Dorset Street several days after the seance. According to Home, Browning refused to shake hands with him. He was, said Home, pallid with rage and, as he harangued Mrs Rymer for her complicity in the fraud, his movements were 'like those of a maniac'. Elizabeth was visibly distressed and, as Home turned to make a hurried departure, she said, 'Dear Mr Home, I am not to blame. Oh, dear! oh, dear!' [9]

Between husband and wife the subject of spiritualism remained a difficult one. Browning was scarcely able to tolerate the mention of Home's name, and Elizabeth warned her sister Henrietta never to include it in her letters. Even in the most general terms the topic of spirit manifestations produced unease between them. Elizabeth was prepared to tolerate Browning's scepticism if he would in turn allow her the freedom to believe, 'which (thinking me very wrong), he can't do for me, or at least will not'.[10]

A far happier occasion than the Ealing seance was the evening of 27 September 1855 when the visitors to Dorset Street included Tennyson and two Rossettis – Dante Gabriel and William Michael. Tennyson had come to London from his home at Farringford on the Isle of Wight and spent two evenings with the Brownings. On 27 September, at what was one of the most impressive literary soirées of the Victorian period, Browning read 'Fra Lippo Lippi'. While Dante Gabriel Rossetti sketched him, Tennyson read *Maud* – 'my little *Hamlet*' as he fondly described it. Elizabeth was an observer of the occasion and her account, in a letter to Mrs Martin, the neighbour at Hope End, combined with that of William Michael Rossetti to preserve a record of the meeting. Apart from a few distinguished Pre-Raphaelites – Holman Hunt, Ford Madox Brown, Woolner – it seems that only Elizabeth's sister Arabel and Sarianna Browning were present.

Elizabeth gratefully recalled how Tennyson 'dined with us, smoked with us, opened his heart to us (and the second bottle of port), and ended by reading "Maud" through from end to end, and going away at half-past two in the morning'. After dinner Elizabeth and the other two women withdrew, leaving the men 'to discuss the universe'. Then, when they reassembled, Tennyson read. Dante Gabriel Rossetti spoke of the 'voice and vehemence' with which the more fiery passages were delivered; 'the softer passages and the songs made the tears course down his cheeks'. There was also an engaging vanity about the reading, as Elizabeth thought. 'He is captivating with his frankness, confidingness, and unexampled *naïveté*! Think of his stopping in "Maud" every now and then – "There's a wonderful touch! That's very tender. How beautiful that is!" Yes, and it *was* wonderful, tender, beautiful, and he read exquisitely in a voice like an organ, rather music than speech.'

Dante Gabriel Rossetti was an admirer of both poets and heard with delight the first reading of 'Fra Lippo Lippi'. Browning's performance was that of the actor rather than the verbal musician whom Tennyson had proved to be. He read 'with as much sprightly variation as there was in Tennyson of sustained continuity'. It was, Rossetti concluded, 'Truly a night of the gods, not to be remembered without pride and pang'.[11]

In August 1855 the printing of *Men and Women* began. While it was in the press, a month later, Browning added a dedicatory epilogue to the fifty poems that were contained in the two volumes. 'One Word More: To E.B.B.' is Browning's expression of regret that he has not been able to emulate Raphael and Dante whose entire lives and works were given to the worship of the women they loved.

This last poem was written in September. Though there was no question of lingering in London until publication day, which Chapman and Hall had fixed for 17 November, the Brownings remained until the printing was completed in early October. Then they returned to Paris. Neither Browning nor Elizabeth could doubt that this was his best work, which gave grounds for optimism at last. Yet the shadow of *Sordello* and the hostility of reviewers in the past was bound to cast a cloud upon the expectation with which they awaited the book's appearance. Despite this there was a tone of finality in the opening lines of the dedication to Elizabeth.

> There they are, my fifty men and women
> Naming me the fifty poems finished!
> Take them, Love, the book and me together.
> Where the heart lies, let the brain lie also.

The fifty-one poems of *Men and Women* represented the first collection of Browning's shorter work for ten years. 'The Guardian Angel', written at Fano during the Adriatic summer of 1848, is the earliest for which the date of composition is known. Inspired by Guercino's painting, it is a profession of love for Elizabeth, as is the last to be composed, 'One Word More'. In such a collection it was to be expected that Browning should employ a full range of his favourite subjects and styles: yet the two volumes of *Men and Women* are dominated by certain themes.

It is not invariably true that a poet's work forms a useful illustration of his life. Indeed, it is not always true of Browning. The major themes of *Men and Women*, however, illustrate his gift for the dispassionate analysis of those human preoccupations which in themselves are wont to generate most passion. Such is the case of the intimate relationships of men and women, of the mid-Victorian religious debate, or of the role to be played by a great artist. Even in those poems that present the polite society of the nineteenth century, like 'Up at a Villa – Down in the City', or of the seventeenth in 'A Toccata of Galuppi's', the tremors of revolution or the doom of mortality shiver below the equable, self-confident surface.

Almost half the poems in *Men and Women* describe the growth or decay of sexual love. A few are literal accounts of his love for Elizabeth, the rest are analytical and realistic in a manner which had first appeared in *Pippa Passes* fourteen years earlier. Browning's lovers are not the passionate and rhetorical figures of the romantic imagination. Their mutual infatuation is nourished and brought to fruition in a world of domestic gardens, sun-blinds and gaslit rooms. They part and grieve among furnishings and décor which might have set the scene in Wimpole Street or Camberwell. By contrast with most contemporaries, their world is as far removed as cinematic realism from the vibrant operatic laments which characterize certain passages in *Maud* or *Locksley Hall*.

> O my cousin, shallow-hearted! O my Amy, mine no more!
> O the dreary, dreary moorland! O the barren, barren shore!

In such poems as 'A Lover's Quarrel' the speaker remembers life with his mistress in terms of political reports in *The Times*, the interchange of sexual roles in a childlike game, the renewed excitement of seeing her dressed in different and more casual clothing for sledging. The dismissed lover in 'The Last Ride Together' contents himself with the thought that he has achieved more than the sculptor who carved a dead Venus from whom men turn 'To yonder girl that fords the burn!' Least of all does the betrayed Andrea del Sarto indulge in Tennysonian outbursts. With a weary resignation he surrenders Lucrezia to the young man waiting for her outside. 'Again the Cousin's whistle! Go, my Love.'

The erotic suggestiveness of Browning's love poetry owes much to an inspired combination of the intense and the casual. He employs the metaphor of 'mingling' or merging with his mistress as the device of sexual union, very much in the manner of Donne. In 'Two in the Campagna' it is more subtle and leads to an unfulfilled yearning for the mingling of souls as well as bodies. In 'Women and Roses', a slighter poem, the device is used with a directness which might have caused nervousness among some Victorian publishers. The speaker addresses a pretty woman who, it seems, is either undressing or being undressed in the course of their embrace.

> Eyes in your eyes, lips on your lips!
> Fold me fast where the cincture slips,
> Prison all my soul in eternities of pleasure!

G. K. Chesterton perhaps exaggerated when he wrote of Browning: 'A great number of his poems are marked by a trait of which by its nature it is more or less impossible to give examples.' He was scarcely guilty of exaggeration when he added: 'What the Nonconformist conscience has been doing to have passed Browning is something difficult to imagine.'[12]

Like a number of his contemporaries, Browning had made the transition from the mythological to the realistic and modern representation of his characters and situations. In doing so he had quietly crossed the frontier of a literary controversy. *Oedipus Tyrannus*, though it dealt with incest, was published by the Clarendon Press for the use of schoolboys. Shelley's *Cenci*, for the same reason, was banned by the Lord Chamberlain for a century. William Benbow was prosecuted for publishing obscene prints in his *Rambler's Magazine* in 1822. He was acquitted when the picture of a naked couple caught in bed by the woman's husband was shown to be Venus and Mars apprehended by Vulcan. In the other case the naked woman fondling a swan between her legs was identified as Leda. The Great Exhibition of 1851 admitted Hiram Powers' bound and naked girl because she was 'The Grecian Slave'. Another nude by J. A. Bell, complete with thigh-chains, was acceptable because she was Andromeda, and Professor Wickman's lightly embracing nudes because they were girls of the ancient world telling one another's fortunes.[13]

For all his use of historical subject matter, Browning was on the far side of the divide, where Verdi had caused one of the most recent shocks by presenting in *La Traviata* a study of sexual immorality in modern dress. *La Dame aux Camélias*, like *Madame Bovary*, had impressed both Browning and Elizabeth by its power. Though his portrayal of physical intimacy between lovers had a great strength and subtlety, Browning's poetry was open to much the same objection as the criticisms levelled against the work of the Belgian artist Félicien Rops, twenty-one years his junior. Of Rops it was objected that his nudes were morally and aesthetically impure in their realism. They bore the imprints of the corsets and the garters which they had just removed; when naked they even sat as if wearing skirts. Boucher and the great artists of the eighteenth century had painted women from the realms of mythology where clothes were not worn.[14]

Browning's skill was sufficient to dispense with explicit portrayals of the type in which Rops and his school specialized. Instead, he places his lovers in the reality of mid-Victorian fashion and décor. Intimacy and consummation of love are evoked by a glove, a fan, the curtains of a room, the cushions of an empty sofa bearing a faint perfume of the woman whose skirts have pressed casually against them.

'A Lover's Quarrel' is the man's account of a winter in a snowbound house with the mistress he has now lost. The intensity of their passion is suggested by the way in which love-making spread from the bedroom to the rest of the house and, in its growth, taught them new and even childish ways of occupying themselves with each other. When they rise from their embrace by the parlour inglenook, the obsessive clinging and caressing hardly cease.

> Then we would up and pace,
> For a change, about the place,
> Each with arm o'er neck.
> 'Tis our quarter-deck,
> We are seamen in woeful case,
> Help in the ocean-space!
> Or, if no help, we'll embrace.

The Times, with its account of Napoleon III, is cast aside and the speaker returns again to his mistress. There is the novelty of seeing her dressed in different clothes or of the two lovers playing like children.

> Teach me to flirt a fan
> As the Spanish ladies can,
> Or I tint your lip
> With a burnt stick's tip
> And you turn into such a man!

The image of unbroken physical contact and of each as the other's plaything heightens the sense of this enclosed intimate world, made free from intrusion by the snow. Though it is not autobiographical, 'A Lover's Quarrel' surely reflects the willing isolation of Browning and Elizabeth as lovers in the early years of their marriage.

The elusive and suggestive nature of love is taken one step further in 'Love in a Life'. The poem describes the man searching a deserted house for the woman he loves. The furniture, mirrors and decoration record her passing.

> Next time, herself! – not the trouble behind her
> Left in the curtain, the couch's perfume!
> As she brushed it, the cornice-wreath blossomed anew, –
> Yon looking-glass gleamed at the wave of her feather.

Love's existence is almost dependent upon the mundane objects of a life lived together and the impressions they preserve – visual, tactile and olfactory. The poem ends with the quest still in progress, its lines anticipating the numinous and transcendent suggestiveness of Rilke's early poems, half a century in the future,

> with such suites to explore,
> Such closets to search, such alcoves to importune!

The more famous and formal love poems of the collection, including 'Love Among the Ruins' and 'Two in the Campagna', share the haunting and evanescent vistas of Browning's pictorial qualities. While it is true that the scene matters much, it is presented in those neutral tones that a painter would employ for the indeterminate colours of distant sky and interior light. In the former poem the setting is 'the quiet-coloured end of evening' and the 'undistinguished grey' of daylight melting into dusk among the wreck of imperial grandeur. Characteristically it is the figure of the girl 'with eager eyes and yellow hair' upon whom the brilliance is lavished. The same neutral tones offer a setting for the latter poem as well, the Campagna presented as an endless frieze of feathery grasses.

> An everlasting wash of air –
> Rome's ghost since her decease.

So far as the theme of love can be summarized in *Men and Women*, it is done by Browning himself in a stanza from a short poem, 'In a Year'. The lines echo his own persistent curiosity and recurrent analysis in respect of love at the moments of its growth and decay.

> Was it something said,
> Something done,
> Vexed him? was it touch of hand,
> Turn of head?
> Strange! that very way
> Love begun.
> I as little understand
> Love's decay.

Among the themes of *Men and Women* religious belief, no less than sexual love, proves most absorbing to Browning when questioned by uncertainty. The comparative casualness of setting, and even of tone, which marks some of his love poetry is matched in the debates on religion by a well-calculated irony. Not all his readers found such treatment acceptable. Indeed, Elizabeth's sister Henrietta said bluntly that at least one of the poems, 'Karshish', was blasphemous.

Far from attempting blasphemy, Browning's effect in such poems as 'Karshish' or 'Cleon' was to strengthen Christian truth by revealing the folly of its critics. Five years earlier he had debunked David Strauss's strictly historical approach to New Testament events in *Christmas-Eve*. In 'Karshish' and 'Cleon' this process is continued more obliquely. It was common enough for the argument between the two sides to be pursued with scholarship, certainly with passionate conviction or sincere indignation. That a poet should employ irony and imagery, affecting amusement at and enjoyment of the great debate, was likely to irritate believers and sceptics alike.

'An Epistle, Containing the Strange Medical Experience of Karshish, the Arab Physician' – to give the poem its full title – describes an imaginary meeting in Palestine just before its invasion by the future emperor Vespasian in AD 66. Historical criticism is taken to its extreme possibility by allowing Karshish to examine the man who was the subject of one of Christ's miracles. Lazarus, raised from the dead many years before, is still alive even though his mind is now preoccupied by things that are not of this world.

Karshish is no sceptic nor scoffer. In the manner of any educated Victorian enquirer after truth, his attachments to science and religion are wholly compatible. Indeed, he appears far more critical of medicine than of religious belief. In a few lines the lawlessness and suspicion of Palestine are vividly indicated.

> Twice have the robbers stripped and beaten me,
> And once a town declared me for a spy.

The case of Lazarus, briefly, is that he deludes himself into thinking that he died and was brought back to life three days later 'By a Nazarene physician of his tribe'. Karshish offers a careful diagnosis of the original sickness and the present delusion.

> 'Tis but a case of mania – subinduced
> By epilepsy, at the turning-point
> Of trance prolonged unduly some three days.

Naturally, Karshish wishes to meet the physician who performed the alleged miracle. However,

> ... the learned leach
> Perished in a tumult many years ago,
> Accused, – our learning's fate, – of wizardry.

Karshish hears of the Crucifixion and the earthquake. As an historical critic he naturally gets them the wrong way round, believing that Christ was put to death for failing to prevent the earthquake rather than that it followed the execution. Of the claims that Christ was Son of God, Karshish remarks, 'The other imputations must be lies' – words not likely to reassure the middle-class reader of poetry in the 1850s.

By the end of the poem Karshish is a doubter. Unlike his Victorian successors he is not plagued by the thought that the New Testament events may be fictions but rather that they may be true. In this respect Browning offers a robust and ironic contrast to Matthew Arnold in 'Dover Beach' or Clough in 'Easter Day'.

In such discussions irony is not always incompatible with melancholy. So in 'Cleon' Browning presents a warm Hellenic world, luxury amounting to decadence, where death is an ever-present thought. The sunlit opulence of the islands, where the poet Cleon writes to thank his patron Protos for his gifts, is vividly evoked, making the advance of death upon its victims all the more poignant.

> The master of thy galley still unlades
> Gift after gift; they block my court at last
> And pile themselves along its portico
> Royal with sunset, like a thought of thee:
> And one white she-slave from the group dispersed
> Of black and white slaves (like the chequer-work
> Pavement, at once my nation's work and gift,
> Now covered with this settle-down of doves)
> One lyric woman, in her crocus vest
> Woven of sea-wools, with her two white hands
> Commends to me the strainer and the cup
> Thy lip hath bettered ere it blesses mine.

Cleon, in the first century A D, is merely the dilettante of his nation's cultural decline. The suggestion of Protos that immortality lies in an artist's works only spurs him to bitterness.

> 'Sappho survives, because we sing her songs,
> 'And Aeschylus because we read his plays!'
> Why, if they live still, let them come and take
> Thy slave in my despite – drink from thy cup –
> Speak in my place.

Only in the concluding lines is the precise date of Cleon's lament, and hence the poem's irony, fully revealed.

> And for the rest,
> I cannot tell thy messenger aright
> Where to deliver what he bears of thine

To one called Paulus – we have heard his fame
Indeed, if Christus be not one with him –
I know not, nor am troubled much to know.

Browning makes the arrogance of Greek learning in its decadence a
neat parallel for the dismissive intellectualism of the nineteenth century
as Cleon turns his scorn upon St Paul.

He writeth, doth he? well, and he may write.
Oh, the Jew findeth scholars! certain slaves
Who touched on this same isle, preached him and Christ;
And (as I gathered from a bystander)
Their doctrines could be held by no sane man.

Repeatedly in *Men and Women* Browning returns to attack the fallacy
that doubt or unbelief was either more honest or more intellectually
productive than religious faith. The doubt of doubt was to plague both
Karshish and Protos, perhaps even Cleon himself, as well as the preposterous young journalist Gigadibs in one of Browning's most impressive
poems, 'Bishop Blougram's Apology'.

'Bishop Blougram's Apology' stands apart from such poems as 'Karshish' and 'Cleon' in *Men and Women*. In its length alone it is a major
poem, one of the most accomplished as well as one of the most astonishing of the entire Victorian period. The subject matter is still the religious
debate, carried on between Blougram as a portrayal of Cardinal Wiseman, Archbishop of Westminster, and a sceptical young journalist,
Gigadibs. Whatever the subject, Browning's achievement is in his creation of Sylvester Blougram. In dealing with his brash young antagonist,
alone after dinner on a summer evening, Blougram's performance is
that of a virtuoso in argument. To Gigadibs, the worldly hypocrisy of
the bishop had appeared such an easy target. Yet every advance ends
with the ground cut from under him by an adversary who knows
Gigadibs' arguments better than the young man himself does, and who
has long since answered them. Every weapon which Gigadibs might
employ is effortlessly appropriated by his antagonist – common sense,
historical argument, knowledge of the world, shrewdness, intellectual
cunning, condescension, deceptive affability.[15]

In the person of Gigadibs, investigative journalism receives the
trouncing of all time, not least because it is soon Blougram who is
investigating his interviewer, revealing the vanity and greed for power
which lie under the honest exterior. The young man's well-prepared
arguments turn to dust at the first touch of Blougram's logic. Is

scepticism more honest or even more tenable than belief? Suppose Blougram agrees to disbelieve.

> Just when we are safest, there's a sunset-touch,
> A fancy from a flower-bell, some one's death,
> A chorus-ending from Euripides, –
> And that's enough for fifty hopes and fears.

Gigadibs, no less than Blougram, is caught in the trap of 'The grand Perhaps'. In the crucial image of the poem, Blougram sums up the futility of the sacrifice – in terms of religion and morality – which doubt and scepticism demand.

> What have we gained then by our unbelief
> But a life of doubt diversified by faith,
> For one of faith diversified by doubt?
> We called the chess-board white, – we call it black.

Nor is he slow to remind Gigadibs that without the moral imperative of religion, morality is no better than instinctive, 'blind, unreasoned-out'.

> Then, friend, you seem as much a slave as I,
> A liar, conscious coward and hypocrite,
> Without the good the slave expects to get,
> Suppose he has a master after all!

If Gigadibs hopes to fall back upon an intellectual ally like Strauss, he is soon disappointed. Blougram is even more familiar with Strauss and has long since seen the futility and sterility of the German critic's arguments.

> All Strauss should be
> I might be also. But to what result?
> He looks upon no future.

Blougram's technique is not unlike that of the stage-magician setting himself impossible tasks for Gigadibs' benefit and then performing them with flawless ease. How can an educated Victorian, a reader of Strauss and Fichte, possibly condone the superstitions of latter-day Catholicism in Italy or Spain?

> I pine among my million imbeciles
> (You think) aware some dozen men of sense
> Eye me and know me, whether I believe
> In the last winking Virgin, as I vow,
> And am a fool, or disbelieve in her
> And am a knave.

Eager to hear Blougram denounce himself one way or another, Gigadibs
is clearly shown that to believe in the Winking Virgin is, in truth, the
only alternative to blind superstition. No part of belief can be dispensed
with by the Church.

> First cut the Liquefaction, what comes last
> But Fichte's clever cut at God himself?

The poem is not without flaws. At times Blougram's self-confidence
is almost preposterous. The form of the dramatic monologue makes
Gigadibs a silent presence at the dinner table, playing with spoons,
exploring his plate's design and ranging the olive stones about its edge
as Blougram holds forth. To Browning, no less than to the reader, the
Bishop is a superb performer rather than a sympathetic character,
which distinguishes him from Fra Lippo Lippi or Andrea del Sarto.
Yet, through Blougram, Browning expresses the essential preoccupation
of his poetry.

> Our interest's on the dangerous edge of things.
> The honest thief, the tender murderer,
> The superstitious atheist, demireps
> That love and save their souls in new French books –
> We watch while these in equilibrium keep
> The giddy line midway: one step aside,
> They're classed and done with.

Society as a passing show, an arena for drama and scandal, is a theme
in Browning's poetry from *Pippa Passes* until the poems of the 1880s. His
preference was for elegant superficiality beneath which lurked the
causes of disturbance and destruction. In his early manhood the *vers de
société* of Winthrop Mackworth Praed illuminated the literary periodicals
with a mixture of sparkle and pathos in such poems as 'Good-night to
the Season' or 'The Last Quadrille'. Whether through debt or coincidence, there was a marked similarity between Browning's later observations of society and Praed's, of whom W. H. Auden remarked that his
serious poems are as trivial as his *vers de société* are profound.[16]

In *Men and Women*, no less than in his later work, Browning captures
the simultaneous facetiousness and melancholy of polite society in such
haunting rhythms as those of 'A Toccata of Galuppi's'. In the world of
Venetian vanities, 'Balls and masks begun at midnight, burning ever to
mid-day', Galuppi's music is the *memento mori* which sets the nerves
creeping. With perfect concision, at home as the observer of mortal
pretensions, Browning notes the bored revellers as they condescend to
give Galuppi's genius a casual moment's hearing.

> Well (and it was graceful of them) they'd break talk off and afford
> – She, to bite her mask's black velvet, he to finger on his sword,
> While you sat and played Toccatas, stately at the clavichord.

Upon its surface the poem catches the tone of condescending vulgarity with savage precision – 'I can always leave off talking, when I hear a master play'. The deeper echoes to the chords and flourishes of the verbal toccata are those of mortality, the funeral gondolas moving to the dank burial island of San Michele – 'Death came tacitly and took them where they never see the sun' – or the hopelessness of eternal life for those whose souls are worm-eaten by frivolity – 'What of soul was left, I wonder, when the kissing had to stop?' Such verses belie Browning's reputation as the robust and easy optimist. In their casual phrases he was able to chill the Victorian heart more effectively than Tennyson's lamentations had done. Characteristically, he achieves this while talking of frivolity rather than piety. That he should do so is both a reflection of his Puritan heritage and a tribute to his fascination with Blougram's 'dangerous edge of things'.

In its appeal, *Men and Women* shows a greater range than any of Browning's other collections. At one extreme there stands the popular ebullient underdog in 'Fra Lippo Lippi', a figure derived from the broad humane tradition of European comedy in Shakespeare or Beaumarchais, Fielding or Goldoni. The scapegrace painter-monk, caught by the watch at an alley's end 'Where sportive ladies leave their doors ajar', is Browning's most famous creation. The comedy of the poem is so forthright that it is in danger of being a mere recitation-piece. What saves it is Lippi's astute observation of his brothers in the cloister, his mockery of their moral pretentiousness, as much as the poem's serious commentary on the humanism of the Florentine Renaissance.

As 'poor Brother Lippo' explains himself, the starving child taken into the Carmine and made a monk as the price of regular meals, the saints of his pictures appear merely human, while his brothers in Christ show their moral fallibility. He observes them with amused tolerance, inviting ribald speculation over

> ... the Prior's niece who comes
> To care about his asthma.

Sociable, garrulous, indiscreet, bold and shrewd, Lippi is both a philosopher of the arts and a match for the men of the patrol or even Cosimo de Medici himself, as he shows by playing off one against the other. In a series of brief asides Browning sketches the torchlit scene of the arrest and the release, Lippi regarding the men of the guard first and foremost as possible subjects for religious painting.

> I'd like his face –
> His, elbowing on his comrade in the door
> With the pike and lantern, – for the slave that holds
> John Baptist's head a-dangle by the hair.

His voracious enjoyment of life makes him one of the most vividly realized of the gallery of men and women, with his full-blooded enthusiasm for the seduction of his female models, 'Like the Prior's niece ... Saint Lucy, I would say'. He is also credited with an anti-ascetic optimism which was all too soon to be typed as Browning's own.

> The world's no blot for us,
> Nor blank – it means intensely, and means good:
> To find its meaning is my meat and drink.

Optimism and obscurity were the contrary vices seen by many later critics in Browning's poetry. If 'Fra Lippo Lippi' laid him open to the first accusation, ' "Childe Roland to the Dark Tower came" ' certainly represented the other extreme in *Men and Women*.

'Childe Roland' was written in Paris on 2 January 1852. It remains one of the most enigmatic but compelling poems of the nineteenth century. Its obscurity lies not in technique or versification but in its strange deformed landscape and silent figures. At one level it may seem Shelleyean, at another it is an intriguing and allusive compound of legend and fairytale, mysticism and dream. In his own account, Browning describes how the poem 'came upon me as a kind of dream. I had to write it then and there, and I finished it the same day.... I did not know then what I meant beyond that, and I'm sure I don't know now. But I am very fond of it.' [17]

The fascination of the poem lies in the way in which it eludes total explanation. It has the landscape of a dream, barren and strangely lit. The symbolism of the dark tower and the other knights standing on the hillsides, 'met/To view the last of me', is suggestive rather than explanatory. At one level the poem depicts an implied ordeal of chivalry, Childe Roland in mediaeval literature having brought his sister back from elf-land under the guidance of Merlin. Yet if the poem, like Coleridge's *Kubla Khan*, is a record of a dream it embodies elements that had been in Browning's mind since childhood.

The tower itself recalls two others that were familiar in Browning's reading. The first is encountered by Aeneas in the sixth book of Virgil's epic, an iron tower on which Tisiphone sits while the sounds of torment rise beyond her. The second tower occurs in Dante's *Inferno*, Cantos VII and VIII, on the edge of the Stygian marsh. Both Aeneas and Dante are approaching the underworld, more specifically the realms of retribution and torment. Indeed, in the opening lines of Browning's poem 'That hoary cripple, with malicious eye' has a suggestion of Charon, though his aid in crossing the ghastly river is not required. A desolate landscape, the crossing of the river, the torments of the victims, the image of the dying man in the fifth and sixth stanzas of Browning's poem all suggest powerfully that 'Childe Roland' is a vision of individual death cast in the form of a dream. The landscape on the far side of the river is, like Virgil's or Dante's, that of nature in nightmare.

> Now blotches rankling, coloured gay and grim,
>   Now patches where some leanness of the soil's
>   Broke into moss or substances like boils;
> Then came some palsied oak, a cleft in him
> Like a distorted mouth that splits its rim
>   Gaping at death, and dies while it recoils.

The knight who fords the river does so in images of horror – the fear of treading on a dead man's cheek or tangling in the hair of a corpse. When the spear thrusts through a form like a water-rat, the shriek from the creature identifies it as a human baby. While the shape of a great black bird glides overhead, the comrades who have preceded Childe Roland are revealed standing on the hillside in a sheet of flame. To an age which produced so much poetry upon the subject of death in pietistic or consolatory vein, Browning's dream landscape and morbid imagery appeared striking but perplexing. It was both the achievement and the fate of Childe Roland's journey to be, like death itself, ultimately beyond explanation. By his own account Browning never intended it to be otherwise.

By the time that *Men and Women* appeared, Browning and Elizabeth had settled in Paris for the winter. As the reviews arrived from England, it was evident that Browning's stock had risen perceptibly but not by as much as he had hoped. There were a number of young admirers. The undergraduate William Morris contributed an enthusiastic review to the *Oxford and Cambridge Magazine* in March 1856. Dante Gabriel Rossetti privately described *Men and Women* as 'my Elixir of Life'. Cardinal Wiseman enjoyed a mild but pleasant revenge for Blougram. In the *Rambler* for January 1856, he indulgently prophesied Browning's early conversion to Catholicism.

By no means all the reviews were so bland, and some were distinctly unfavourable. This latter group was led by the *Athenaeum*, rarely impressed by anything appearing under Browning's name. On 17 November 1855 the journal complained of the poems' obscurity, enquiring: 'Who will not grieve over energy wasted and power misspent?' A former admirer, John Ruskin, expressed his disappointment to Browning in a letter and received a reply which told him to mind his own business.[18]

There was not even the consolation of financial success, for the sales of *Men and Women* had so far proved more disappointing than the reviews. Exasperated by this double slight to his best work, Browning's letters to Edward Chapman mingled appeals for money due with insults and threats against his critics. Never one to accept criticism easily, he now assumed a new degree of rancour towards those who failed to appreciate his work at its full value. This anticipated the savagery of his ripostes to men like Alfred Austin and Edward Fitzgerald in later years. For the present, such reviewers were dismissed as apes and swine (or 'grunters'). To Chapman he said reassuringly: 'Don't you mind them, and leave me to rub their noses in their own filth some fine day.'[19]

In his early forties Browning was already becoming that figure whom Edmund Gosse later described. The forceful opinion, the booming tenor voice, the greeting at twenty feet, the exhortation of friends and the bitter denunciation of enemies had now effaced entirely the wistful romanticism of his youth in Browning's public persona. That this was a protective shell against the world was clear to both Gosse and Henry James. In the privacy of his own mind Browning hungered for that popularity and that approval of the critics which he affected to despise. There was, indeed, one poem in *Men and Women* which took as its title the very word 'Popularity'. Inspired by the rediscovery of a great and neglected poet, by means of Monckton Milnes' *Life and Letters of John Keats*, it carried a double message. Other men, Tennyson included, had taken the colour of Keats' poetry and enriched themselves thereby.

> Hobbs hints blue, – straight he turtle eats.
> Nobbs prints blue, – claret crowns his cup.
> Nokes outdoes Stokes in azure feats, –
> Both gorge. Who fished the murex up?
> What porridge had John Keats?

All things considered, the question that shone with far greater clarity through these lines had a more direct application to their author in 1855. It was, surely, what porridge had Robert Browning?

After a brief spell of 'evil days and yellow satin sofas' in the rue de

Grenelle, where Elizabeth caught a bad cold, the Brownings moved in December to more agreeable apartments in the rue du Colisée, near the Champs-Elysées.[20] In Paris, it seemed, Browning was to be appreciated at once, however hesitant his acceptance in London. Milsand praised *Men and Women* in the *Revue Contemporaine* and a French translation of the poems was prepared for publication.

There was agreeable society in Paris, which Browning sampled more than Elizabeth. Though her bout of illness and spitting of blood ended in January, she was cautious during the remainder of the winter, relying to some extent on treatment with cod liver oil. Browning went alone to dinner with Monckton Milnes, who excelled himself on this occasion by netting George Sand, Cavour, and even a chair for Lamartine, though it was not occupied during the evening. Casting modesty aside, George Sand graced the occasion by appearing in a laurel wreath, lest her pre-eminence should be doubted. With Dante Gabriel Rossetti, Browning visited the Louvre and spent evenings discussing the painters of the Italian Renaissance. In June he was present at the baptism of the heir to Napoleon III, the Prince Imperial, who was destined to accompany his parents into exile and to die with the British army in the Zulu campaign of 1879.

It was after the baptism, by his own account, that Browning paid his visit to the Paris morgue, from whose raised observation walk he was able to study the corpses on metal surfaces, the water running down constantly over the copper to cool them, In consequence of this visit he wrote his poem 'Apparent Failure'. This short poem was said to be a favourite of Tennyson's among Browning's works – 'I *laik* that!' the Laureate announced in his Lincolnshire brogue.[21] Its lines are a tribute to Paris and, particularly, to

> ... the Doric little Morgue!
> The dead-house where you show your drowned.

Sardonically, Browning surveyed three of the drowned men and depicts them as a red republican thwarted by the Empire, a victim of cards and women, and a frustrated Napoleon. They afford amusement, not least the young man who was ruined by vice rather than by politics.

> Money gets women, cards and dice
>   Get money, and ill-luck gets just
> The copper couch and one clear nice
>   Cool squirt of water o'er your bust,
> The right thing to extinguish lust!

The macabre preoccupations of Browning's poetry had on the whole seemed dormant in *Men and Women*. Thereafter they were to be in the forefront of his work, not so much displayed as flaunted.

By July 1856 the Brownings had returned to England again, their visit motivated by the ill-health of John Kenyon, Elizabeth's cousin and their mutual benefactor. For several weeks they stayed at Kenyon's London house in Devonshire Place, though he and the Barrett family were to spend the summer separately on the Isle of Wight. Early in July Elizabeth completed her verse novel *Aurora Leigh*; Browning read 'this divine Book', as he called it, with unstinted admiration. It went straight to Chapman's printers and by September the first proofs were being corrected.

Because their stay in London was briefer, Browning and Elizabeth spent less time with their more famous contemporaries than had been the case in the previous summer. There was a breakfast party with Monckton Milnes in Upper Brook Street, however, at which their fellow guests included Nathaniel Hawthorne. Hawthorne was impressed by the apparent youthfulness of the Brownings, notably by the strong good looks of Browning himself with his dark head of hair scarcely touched by grey.

From London they went to the Isle of Wight to stay first with Arabel Barrett at Ventnor and then with John Kenyon at West Cowes. On hearing of Elizabeth's arrival in London, Mr Barrett had dispatched his family to Ventnor. As had become usual, he did not accompany them and the Brownings stayed with Arabel. Whatever resentment as a matter of filial obligation her brothers might once have felt towards Browning had long since disappeared. 'George and my brothers were very kind to Robert at Ventnor,' Elizabeth wrote, 'and he is quite touched by it.'[22]

The visit to their old friend John Kenyon, now seventy-two and ailing, took the form of a last farewell. He was pale and wasted, often struggling for breath and sometimes not well enough to share the company of his visitors. Elizabeth told Henrietta that a younger man might none the less have rallied. Even though the marks of death were upon him, she deluded herself that he might yet survive for some time. As it happened, he had scarcely ten weeks to live. On this final visit Elizabeth made Kenyon the greatest gift then in her power by dedicating to him her most celebrated work, *Aurora Leigh*.

At West Cowes she and Browning were still engaged with the proofs of the poem. On 22 September they were to begin a visit to Henrietta at Taunton. Henrietta's marriage to Captain William Surtees Cook in

1850 had also incurred Mr Barrett's displeasure, though not to the same degree as Elizabeth's marriage to Browning. Before their arrival at Taunton, Elizabeth wrote to her sister asking her not to change any other arrangements she might have made and politely warning her that both Brownings would be obliged to spend part of the time working on the proofs of *Aurora Leigh*.

By early October they were once more back in London at John Kenyon's house in Devonshire Place. The proofs were at last finished and they left for Paris on 22 October. They stopped briefly in Paris, travelled by steamer from Marseilles, and were back in the familiar comfort of Casa Guidi long before the publication of *Aurora Leigh* in London on 15 November. Elizabeth was never to see England again. When they had returned to Italy in 1856 it was left to Dante Gabriel Rossetti to write a wistful epitaph on their occasional summer visits. 'The Brownings are long gone back now,' he wrote in December, 'and with them one of my delights – an evening resort where I never felt unhappy. How large a part of the real world, I wonder are those two small people? – taking meanwhile so little room in any railway carriage and hardly needing a double bed at the inn.' [23]

I I
Choosing the World

The publication of *Aurora Leigh* appeared as the culmination of Elizabeth's poetic career. She had already described it as a novel in verse and, indeed, its romantic-didactic nature was never in doubt. Nor was its effect upon Browning and upon his estimate of his own work.

In its outlines *Aurora Leigh* seemed to be a compound of books by other men and women. Aurora, the narrator, is a poetess who was orphaned in Italy and brought to England. Of independent mind and means, she refuses the proposal of her cousin, the philanthropist Romney Leigh. Romney rescues a nearly destitute seamstress, Marian Erle, and arranges to marry her instead, to the chagrin of an unscrupulous admirer, Lady Waldemar.

Marian Erle fails to appear at the wedding, having been persuaded by Lady Waldemar of the unsuitability of the match. Many months later, Aurora Leigh meets Marian Erle in Paris and finds that the girl now has a baby. She had been drugged and raped, the child being the result of the crime against her. Under Aurora's care she is taken to live with her benefactress in Tuscany.

Romney Leigh, who has not after all married Lady Waldemar, arrives in Florence. Like Jane Eyre's Rochester, he has been blinded in a fire when the local malcontents, jealous of his city philanthropy, destroyed Leigh Hall. His first instinct is to marry Marian Erle and take her child as his own. Though still adoring him, she refuses on the grounds that her experience has destroyed her capacity for married love. Instead, and predictably, Aurora and Romney Leigh are united at last.

Jane Eyre was only one of the novels which offered a clear parallel to *Aurora Leigh*. Mrs Gaskell's *Ruth* describes the seduction of her innocent heroine and the girl's redemption by her love for the child she bears. The moral integrity of Marian Erle through all her sufferings is also strongly reminiscent of Fleur-de-Marie in Eugène Sue's *Mystères de Paris*.

Elizabeth had of course read all these novels and refers to them in her letters.

Its length and its digressions, giving the span of an epic poem to a story that will scarcely support it, have devalued *Aurora Leigh* in modern taste. Yet its descriptions of Paris and Florence and of Aurora's childhood in the Malvern Hills are excellent. To her contemporaries, moreover, Elizabeth offered that blend of melodrama and moralizing which so often seemed a prescription for popularity.

The reviews which greeted *Aurora Leigh* upon its appearance were not particularly favourable. They objected rather more to the unwieldy nature of the poem than to its subject matter, though the *Saturday Review* said bluntly that such topics were 'incapable of poetic treatment'.[1] Yet the reviewers were soon confounded by the sales of the book. They had felt, notably in the case of *Blackwood's*, that *Aurora Leigh* was too reminiscent of a third-rate fashionable novel. The consolation for its authoress was that it also won the market for such fiction. Within three and a half years *Aurora Leigh* had gone through five editions. It was not quite the level of popular success that Tennyson had enjoyed with *In Memoriam*, yet it was closer to that than to the small discriminating sale of a few hundred copies which had been the fate of Browning's own work.

Browning's estimate of his wife's poem as the most admirable which either of them had produced was never in doubt. Ruskin was restored to favour after his criticism of *Men and Women* by pronouncing *Aurora Leigh* as the greatest poem in the language, surpassed perhaps by the plays of Shakespeare but not by the sonnets.[2] The sincerity of Browning's own admiration was to be best demonstrated by the degree to which he became the imitator of *Aurora Leigh* after his wife's death. *The Ring and the Book*, *Fifine at the Fair*, *Red Cotton Night-Cap Country* and *The Inn Album* were all variants upon the novel in verse. In bulk, at least, they represented the greater part of his work during the remainder of his life.

It was well into the 1860s before Browning's own poetry earned even a substantial fraction of the sums that *Aurora Leigh* and Elizabeth's earlier poetry were providing, not least by their popularity in the United States. When Chapman and Hall paid £222 for the joint royalties in 1864, Browning's poetry accounted for £15 and Elizabeth's for the rest.[3] The money was welcome but by 1864 it had long ceased to be the principal support. On 3 December 1856, within a few weeks of the publication of *Aurora Leigh* which was dedicated to him, John Kenyon died. By the terms of his will Browning was to receive a sum of £6,500 and Elizabeth £4,500. When invested, the money brought them an annual income of £700 at a time when, as Elizabeth said, the royalties from their books – virtually from her books alone – were increasing.

Even had Elizabeth's health permitted it, she at least had no inclination to change her style of life. There was talk of going to Egypt for the winter but the old habits of financial prudence asserted themselves. With the necessary retinue of servants, Egypt would cost £28 a week, double the income from John Kenyon's legacy. They settled back into their familiar pattern of life at Casa Guidi varied by winters in Rome and the hot summer months in the hills at Lucca or Siena. In 1858, on their last journey from Italy together, they spent the summer on the English Channel coast at Le Havre.

Financial considerations apart, the death of John Kenyon was to Elizabeth more like the passing of a father than a cousin. She wept over the lock of white hair which had been cut from the old man's head soon after the last breath had passed from his body and which was sent to her as a keepsake.

By now Browning had reason to be apprehensive of the effect upon Elizabeth caused by news of sickness and death from England. There was no longer any question of her recovering as Kirkup had done in the warm Italian air. Her health had been irreparably undermined and she had already entered her last decline. From time to time she seemed better, in spirits at least, but the direction was never in doubt.

To the sorrow over John Kenyon there was soon added the news of her father's death on 17 April 1857. The bitterness and the desolation between them served only to make her grief more overwhelming. She was prostrated by it and Browning grew very alarmed. The only relief was of a most unexpected kind. Mrs James Martin, the former neighbour at Hope End, had written to Mr Barrett the previous year, urging him to forgive the children whom he had cast off at the time of their marriages. He replied that he had indeed forgiven them and had begun to pray for them and their own families. His forgiveness did not extend to receiving Elizabeth while she was in England, or restoring her to his will, or even in obliging John Kenyon's executors by giving them her address. However, at the time of his death, Mrs Martin's assurance offered one redeeming hope.[4]

There was no wavering in Browning's love and solicitude for Elizabeth. Yet at fifty years old her dark hair seemed to fall almost heavily about a face that was shrunk and lined from her sickness. Though he did not admit it, perhaps not even to himself, it was a countenance in which the prognosis might be clearly read.

As if in preparation for the time when he would be a widower, Browning launched himself still more energetically into the society of Florence and Rome. Elizabeth too had similar thoughts. Browning was six years her junior. At forty-four, with his strong good looks, he seemed more attractive than she had ever known him. Whatever his professions of eternal and romantic devotion, Elizabeth was a realist. Her brother George had written from England, urging her to safeguard Pen's interest in her part of John Kenyon's legacy should she die. Elizabeth felt this unnecessary. Browning could be trusted absolutely in matters of money, even if he could not be guaranteed to remain faithful in other respects. 'Robert will probably survive me,' she wrote; 'he may remarry . . being a man . . nay "being subject to like passions" as other men, he *may* commit some faint show of bigamy.'[5]

For the time being Browning's fame in Florentine society rested largely upon his visits three or four evenings a week to the Villa Brichieri, the home of Isabella (Isa) Blagden. The relationship between them and the manner in which Isa allowed him to display himself for the admiration of her guests reveals much of Browning in his middle forties.

Isa Blagden, thirty-eight years old and unmarried, was a figure about whom rumour and scandal gathered all too easily. She was said to be the illegitimate daughter of an English father and an Indian mother, though at her death her father's nationality was given as Swiss. Her slight build and dark, fine-featured face certainly supported the story of her Anglo-Indian origin. In an age free from the more sinister innuendoes of its successors, she believed that the personal intimacy of two women offered a mutual understanding 'seldom attained even in the holiest and truest marriage'.[6]

Browning and Elizabeth had been Isa Blagden's friends for several years before their return from England in 1856. She was 'Dearest Isa' to both of them, but as Elizabeth withdrew increasingly from society, it was Browning alone who enlivened the company at the Villa Brichieri. Among the other distinguished guests at these evening parties were the Trollope family, Lytton, Nathaniel Hawthorne and Kate Field. Yet it was Browning who appeared to be the prime source of verbal energy and anecdote. Frances Power Cobbe noticed the constant ripple of laughter about the sofa on which he generally sat. Next to him would be a female guest who had caught his eye, 'towards whom, in his eagerness, he would push nearer and nearer till she frequently rose to avoid falling off at the end'.[7]

Browning's enthusiasm for female company and friendship was never in question. To this extent his attitude to Isa Blagden is instructive. She was close to him, as to Elizabeth, and the only person to whom he could turn unreservedly at the time of his greatest bereavement. In the letters which the Brownings wrote to her, he expressed his love for Isa, though putting the word in inverted commas when it seemed necessary to avoid misunderstanding.

The nature of the love which he showed towards Isa might well have made the subject of one of his own poems. She was his companion and correspondent, though not his mistress, the object of an affection which lasted longer than the whole period of his courtship of and marriage to Elizabeth. It was as if his love for such women became a protection for him against the question of remarriage after Elizabeth's death. If he were to marry, surely it would have to be a marriage to one of these close female friends. Since that was impossible, the question need never be answered.

The value of Isa to him was more specific than that during Elizabeth's lifetime. Her admiration of him and the means which she afforded for his self-display appealed to a vanity in him which was less comic and self-deprecating than its expression allowed. 'I have just had two or three photographs made of my desirable self. Do you want them? Say "yes."' It was not the tone of a man to his mistress, rather of one who exercised an easy sense of superiority.[8] No less than an actor like Macready, he was good and he knew it.

At his age and in his situation he did not need to assert his dominance sexually, even if the emotional feminism of Isa Blagden had welcomed it. Instead he asserted himself by mingling kindliness with a bluff and boisterous presumption of possession. When he called her a goose, he added, 'I'll pluck all the pens from your wing till you squeal again!'[9] The occasion of the first squealing is not specified. In the same way he treated her to a violence of language which might have been regarded as vulgarity by other women. When Mrs Jameson, 'Aunt Nina', died and her sisters attempted to get up a subscription for their own support, he told Isa Blagden, 'I don't feel inclined to offer the least squeeze from my nipples'.[10] It was a coarseness of manner in which he liked to indulge more and more as time went by.

In the years to come, Browning was to set the same limit upon their love which had existed during Elizabeth's lifetime, a technique that he employed with other close female friends. When Isa took him by the hand, he reminded her that her other was still held by Elizabeth.[11] In consequence he was able to enjoy the luxury which became increasingly difficult as Victorian conventions were replaced after his death – intimate emotional frankness with a woman which was devoid of any risk of sexual involvement. He sought, in brief, the protective limits of vigorous flirtation.

All too soon Elizabeth was to be little more than a spectator or auditor of Browning's success in society, the invalid who retired to bed with a book in the room which Pen shared until her death when he was twelve years old. Yet in the respites from the progress of her disease she was still Browning's companion on certain occasions. The great set-piece among these was the masked ball at the opera during the carnival celebrations at Florence in February 1857.

The winter had been mild enough to permit this last formal appearance, she and Browning in their domino and mask occupying one of the boxes. There was dancing in the auditorium, during which an admirer tapped her shoulder and cried out, 'Bella mascherina!' Even Grand Duke Leopold came down from his box to join the waltzes. Later still the Brownings and the grandees returned to their boxes for supper at one o'clock in the morning, where Pen waited with a blue domino and pink trimmings. The servant Ferdinando produced galantine, sandwiches, rolls, cakes, ices and champagne. Presently the stuffiness of the air began to tell upon Elizabeth's lungs. She returned home in the carriage, leaving Browning to follow at four in the morning.

Among their former acquaintances in Florence, the Brownings still cultivated Robert Lytton and Seymour Kirkup. Indeed, Kirkup had now added mesmerism to the list of his interests. Browning arrived one day to find that the old man had literally entranced a pretty Italian girl who responded to every suggestion of the elderly hypnotist. The effect of this was spoilt when Kirkup shuffled into the next room to fetch a book and the 'mesmerized' girl turned to Browning with a friendly wink. Undaunted by Browning's scepticism, Kirkup introduced him to an Italian clairvoyant, Count Ginnasi of Ravenna. Browning wore no 'ornaments', not even a watch-chain, upon which the Count might exercise his art. However, his seamstress had omitted to put buttons on his shirt cuffs. For the first time he was wearing a pair of gold cuff-links which had been in his family for many years. The Count took one of the links and said, 'There is something here which cries out in my ear, "Murder! Murder!"' The cuff-links had indeed been taken from the body of Browning's great-uncle after he had been murdered by his slaves on the island of St Kitts eighty years earlier. These facts and his own possession of the cuff-links, Browning admitted, were known 'only to myself of all men in Florence'.[12]

Soon after their return from England in 1856, Elizabeth wrote of Kirkup as a tragic and pitiable figure. She need not have worried on this score. Though nearly seventy, he was to survive her by almost twenty years and, indeed, at the age of eighty-seven he was to embark on matrimony with Paolina Carboni who was then twenty-two.[13]

The Brownings in middle age were apt to feel a willing obligation towards their elders, Kenyon or Kirkup or W.J. Fox. During Elizabeth's last years the most trying tutelage was that which Browning endeavoured to exercise over Walter Savage Landor. Whether Landor was one of the great romantic rebels or merely a cantankerous bully depended very much on individual experience of him. He had been expelled from Rugby, sent down from Oxford, and driven into exile by his intemperate and libellous attacks on chosen enemies. In 1835 he left his wife in Fiesole, having reduced her to a state of chronic hysteria, and returned to England. By 1858 he was obliged to return to Italy to avoid the libel actions pending against him, having among other things imputed lesbianism to Mrs Yescombe, the wife of a clergyman. Despaired of by his friends, including John Forster who called him 'irritable, difficult to manage . . . apt to be driven wild with rage', Landor arrived in Florence in 1858.[14] His tone of address was well reflected by a short peremptory note in which he announced himself to the English minister, the Marquis of Normanby.

> We are both of us old men, my Lord, and are verging on decrepitude and imbecility, else my note might be more energetic. Do not imagine I am unobservant of distinctions. For you by the favor of a minister are Marquis of Normanby, I by the grace of God am
> Walter Savage Landor.[15]

The reunion between the eighty-three-year-old fugitive and his family at Fiesole was less than ecstatic and extremely short lived. Soon Landor had thrown himself upon the younger poet whose achievement in *Dramatic Romances and Lyrics* he thought was unrivalled since Chaucer. Landor arrived at Casa Guidi in full flight from his wife and sons. Browning went to Fiesole with Kirkup to attempt a reconciliation with Mrs Landor. When the lady arrived at Casa Guidi, Landor threatened to throw himself from his window if she was admitted, which his wife described as the best thing he could do. His daughter assured the Brownings that if a glass of water would save her father's life, she would not give it to him.

The literary world of Florence came to Landor's aid. He basked in the admiring society of Isa Blagden's villa. While Browning endeavoured to find a home for him, the Storys invited him to Siena. William Wetmore Story saw the old man in his predicament as a noble reincarnation of King Lear. The beautiful and emancipated young American,

Kate Field, shared with the Brownings the task of caring for him and Landor wrote a poem on the pleasure of being kissed by her.

After 1858 the Brownings spent their remaining two summers in Siena, where the Storys were also visitors. Close to their own villa they found a cottage and dutifully installed Landor there, as he acknowledged:

> You will have heard that I am now in a cottage near Siena, which I owe to Browning, the kind friend who found it for me, whom I had seen only three or four times in my life. Yet who made me the voluntary offer of what money I wanted, and who insists on managing my affairs here, and paying for my lodgings and sustenance. Never was such generosity and such solicitude as this incomparable man has shown on my behalf.[16]

Despite the heart-warming gratitude of such acknowledgements, it appears that on the very day of his arrival in the cottage Landor picked a quarrel with his landlady and threw his dinner, 'plates and all', out of the window.[17] The problem of finding a home for him was solved soon afterwards when Lily Wilson, by then Lily Romagnoli, left the service of the Brownings. With her husband she set up home in the Via Nunziatina in Florence, where Landor was her lodger until his death in 1864.

Landor, with his unpredictable conduct and his hearty contempt for Napoleon III, was more to Browning's taste than Elizabeth's. By the same token, such spiritualist sympathizers as the rich American couple David and Sophie Eckley were more to Elizabeth's taste than his. Indeed, Elizabeth innocently confessed to Arabel that Sophie Eckley had 'fallen in love' with her and adored her with 'a blind passion'. Yet she was quick to stress the delicacy and refinement of such feelings. Towards the Brownings the Eckleys showed a limitless generosity and a childlike devotion. Mr Eckley would try to give away everything he had in his pockets with tears and trembling in his voice. He would also lay his head under the Brownings' feet and invite them to walk over him, an experience which Sophie Eckley also wished to share. When the Brownings went to Le Havre in 1858, Sophie wept copiously at the prospect of even so brief a parting.[18]

There was a sad little ending to Elizabeth's friendship with the Eckleys who apparently feared that only their expensive presents and remarkable spiritualist experiences would make them welcome at Casa Guidi. Browning had long been suspicious of Sophie Eckley and the truth of her stories. After two years it was clear that she had fabricated almost everything in order to win Elizabeth's interest and affection.

The friendship which had been so carefully nourished ended abruptly in the winter of 1859. Browning informed Isa Blagden curtly that Sophie Eckley 'cheated Ba from the beginning – and I say, in the bitterness of truth, that Ba deserved it for shutting her eyes and stopping her ears as she determinedly did'.[19]

Though Florence and its society remained the setting for much of their life during Elizabeth's final years, the extremes of heat and cold were avoided by regular travel during the worst months of summer and winter. In August 1857, their first summer after returning from England, they had chosen Bagni di Lucca rather than the more sociable atmosphere of Siena to which the Storys had gone. Among their companions were Isa Blagden and Annette Bracken, a young woman with whom she was then living, and Robert Lytton from the English legation.

Elizabeth's relief was not only in escaping the heat of Florence. Browning had written little during the previous two years and now seemed to allow his interest to wander elsewhere. Apart from the attractions of Florentine society, he spent much of his time drawing and 'neglecting his own art', as she described it to Henrietta. At Lucca there were no models and no studio. 'Well – now poetry must have its turn,' she wrote, 'and I shall not be sorry for that.'[20]

Her hopes were unfulfilled. Soon after his arrival Lytton fell ill with gastric fever. Isa Blagden, whose love for this much younger man was strongly suspected, insisted upon nursing him in her own villa. 'Sentimentality and economy combined,' said Browning tersely, 'an imbecile arrangement.' Since her own villa was no more than twelve or fifteen feet away across the road, Browning too was conscripted for nursing duties. 'I have sate up four nights out of the last five,' he wrote on 18 August, 'and sometimes been there nearly all day beside.... Imagine what a pleasant holiday we all have!'[21] For his own health he went every morning at half-past six and bathed in a mountain stream, an experience so invigorating that he proposed to continue it until the end of his days.

The summer visit to Le Havre in the following year was no more productive than the stay at Lucca. They were accompanied by Robert Browning senior and Sarianna, both in Paris and Le Havre itself. Among their visitors were George Barrett and Elizabeth's younger sister Arabel. The fortitude of Arabel Barrett's character had no doubt been developed by her role as the spinster daughter who remained to look after her father until his death. To this she joined an interest in the Ragged Schools and an evangelical enthusiasm for good works.

Sea water had been prescribed as a means of arresting the decline in Elizabeth's health but she and Browning both detested the noise and squalor of the French port. They had, however, seen something of the Normandy coast, perhaps enough to give Browning that taste for the French resorts he patronized so frequently after her death. On their return to Florence there was a poignant contrast between the bluff vigour of Browning and the slow-moving, wasted figure of Elizabeth. Thackeray, convalescing in Paris, received a visit from Browning which did little to speed his recovery. 'Browning was here this morning,' he wrote. 'What spirits he has – almost too much for me in my weak state. He almost blew me out of bed.'[22]

By the time that they reached Florence again in October 1858 a chill autumn had already begun. There was no question of settling at Casa Guidi for the coming months. Instead, as in each of the three remaining winters of Elizabeth's life, they turned southwards for Rome. To Browning the change was welcome in itself. After the provincial amusements of Florence and the shabby parochialism of Le Havre, he returned to the society of Rome, patrician or bohemian, clever men and gifted women.

They returned to the apartment in the Via Bocca di Leone, where Elizabeth kept to her room, if not her bed, and Browning thrived. Even when he caught cold he still went out walking at six in the morning with the fountains frozen and the wind blowing hard from the cold hills. Elizabeth wrote to Isa Blagden in Florence, assuring her of his well-being. 'I must admit, however, that he is extremely well just now, to speak generally, and that this habit of regular exercise (with occasional homoeopathy) has thrown him into a striking course of prosperity,.as to looks, spirits and appetite.'[23]

If Browning was distraught or even worried by Elizabeth's condition, he concealed it from her as well as from the world, displaying everywhere his energy and high spirits. In the final winters in Rome he sought the company of painters like Frederic Leighton and William Page and figures of English public life including Odo Russell and Cardinal Manning. He cultivated such young women as Kate Field and Hatty Hosmer as well as a young Pre-Raphaelite, Val Prinsep, who led Browning into the revolutionary depths of bohemian society. Among American friends in Rome were Nathaniel Hawthorne and Story, under whose supervision Browning took up modelling in clay.

He was invited to dinner with the young Prince of Wales during the boy's visit to Rome in 1859, a summons issued at the Queen's request. During their last months in the city he went to one of the most splendid balls of the season. 'All the princes in Rome (and even cardinals) present.... The Princess Ruspoli (a Buonaparte) appeared in the tricolor. She is most beautiful.'[24] Nathaniel Hawthorne observed the success of Browning the talker at dinners and parties, the assertive wit and force of argument which amused and intimidated his hearers at the same time. The amusement was, said Hawthorne, 'of very genuine and excellent quality, the true babble and effervescence of a bright and powerful mind'.[25]

At the other extreme he allowed himself to be led by Val Prinsep into the artistic underworld of Rome, where the banned 'Hymn to Garibaldi' was sung in literary taverns and where the papal guards who arrived to investigate the outrage were bought off with drink while Browning and Prinsep watched.

Far off, almost in another world of experience, the quiet invalid voice of Elizabeth described Browning's 'dissipations', as she called them, with a mingled forbearance and apprehension. 'He is plunged into gaieties of all sorts, caught from one hand to another like a ball, has gone out every night for a fortnight together, and sometimes two or three times deep in a one night's engagements. So plenty of distraction, and no Men and Women.'[26] 'No Men and Women' was a phrase which betrayed an unease more openly expressed to Sarianna Browning in the last year of Elizabeth's life. Browning, to judge by appearances at least, had written nothing for some time. Lacking any apparent will to do so, he had continued modelling in clay. He had no wish to follow Tennyson's example of working regularly at his poetry for a set number of hours each day. 'I have struggled a little with him on this point,' Elizabeth confessed, 'for I don't think him right.' As a result, 'Robert waits for an inclination – works by fits and starts'. Moreover, he seemed to prefer clay modelling even to reading. 'The consequence of which is that he wants occupation and that an active occupation is salvation to him with his irritable nerves.... He has an enormous superfluity of vital energy, and if it isn't employed, it strikes its fangs into him.'[27]

One or two pieces that were to appear in *Dramatis Personae* had been written in 1859-60, probably including 'Confessions' and 'Youth and Art'. Since then, as Elizabeth suggested, it seemed that Browning at the age of forty-nine had lost the inspiration which he claimed was necessary to his work. He could not, like Tennyson, labour in the hope of generating such a spark. Elizabeth described the consequence of this to Sarianna.

I wanted his poems done this winter very much – and here was a bright room with three windows consecrated to use. But he had a room all last summer, and did nothing. Then, he worked himself out by riding for three or four hours together – there has been little poetry done since last winter, when he did much. He was not inclined to write this winter. The modelling combines body-work and soul-work, and the more tired he has been, and the more his back ached, poor fellow, the more he has exulted and been happy – '*no, nothing ever made him so happy before*' – also the better he has looked and the stouter grown.[28]

It was in the last Roman winters that the change which overcame Browning in middle life seemed most evident. There was no doubt among those who saw Elizabeth in these years that she was dying; her appearance and her movements betrayed it equally. Browning, it seemed, was building his strength against the calamity to come. The disease was so common, demonstrated in his own experience by the deaths of the Flower sisters, that he could scarcely have been in great doubt. Indeed, his reaction when the time came suggested that he was well prepared.

In these years there was a sense in which he seemed to separate himself by some distance from the two things which were themselves inseparable from one another: Elizabeth and poetry. 'I'm not a literary man' was the phrase he later used.

In place of the dedicated poet there now appeared the apprentice sculptor, the horseman, swimmer, and bon viveur. As Elizabeth's health declined further, his own vigour seemed to increase. While she remained housebound during the Roman winter, he went his round of dinners and parties, returning home at two or three o'clock in the morning. In the very shadow of Elizabeth's approaching death he signed himself to George Barrett, 'Ever yours heartily'.[29] All this was less a gesture of insensitivity than a means of self-protection.

The headaches from which he had suffered in his youth had diminished in strength and frequency after his marriage. In March 1858 they returned with such violence that he believed he was suffering from congestion of the brain. It was almost the only indication that the 'prosperity' and 'high spirits' which were most often to distinguish him in the eyes of others might not convey the whole truth.

The image of Browning in 1861, the year of her death, was caught by Elizabeth in her description of him for Sarianna. The beardless and aspiring young romantic of 1845 had now matured into the firm self-confident poet of the resonant voice and the proprietory manner.

Robert is looking remarkably well and young – in spite of all lunar lights in his hair.... He is not thin or worn, as I am – no indeed – and the women adore him everywhere far too much for decency. In my own opinion he is infinitely handsomer and more attractive than when I saw him first, sixteen years ago.[30]

Almost two years earlier, in the summer of 1859, the Brownings and the Storys had spent the hottest months of the year close to one another in Siena. Even at that time, William Wetmore Story had few illusions as to Elizabeth's prospects. As they sat together on the lawn under the ilexes and cypresses, watching the moon rise, he observed the contrast between husband and wife. 'He is well and full of life as ever,' Story wrote to Charles Eliot Norton, 'but poor Mrs Browning is sadly weak and ill.' She caught cold easily and was prostrated by every item of bad news, whether it concerned the fate of Italy or the well-being of a friend. He warned Norton that 'she is terribly weak, so that she cannot walk across the room, and is afflicted by a racking cough which often robs her of sleep by night'. Speech itself was an effort to her. 'When she came up she was carried in arms to the carriage and thence to the house, and looked like a dark shadow.'[31]

In the eighteen months which followed there was tragedy and disappointment enough to lower her spirits. Her unease over Browning's poetic inactivity had been met by his remark that the writing of poetry was not to him what it seemed to her or to Tennyson. She hoped that his conversion to homoeopathy in 1859 presaged a possible conversion to spiritualism and even a sympathetic understanding of Napoleon III. In both cases she was misled. It is probable that Browning's major poem written at this time, though not shown to her, was 'Mr Sludge, "The Medium"', a contemptuous likeness of D. D. Home and his dupes. Napoleon III, whom Elizabeth called 'the only man who has it in his heart and head to do anything for Italy', had acted at last.[32] But to what effect? The declaration of war on Austria in May 1859 had been followed by French victories at Magenta and Solferino in June. Yet the Treaty of Villafranca in July left Austria in possession of Venice, while Lombardy and Parma were ceded in the first place to France. Though these were transferred to the kingdom of Sardinia, the territories of Nice and Savoy passed to France under the Treaty of Turin in March 1860. Italy's salvation lay in military action by Garibaldi in Sicily and Cavour in the Papal States.

The intensity of Elizabeth's feeling over Italian politics was hard to understand even for those closest to her. As she protested to Henrietta, 'you from your point of view, can't judge what I see and feel from mine'. She made Pen take off the Napoleon medal which he wore on his blouse and concluded sadly, 'Napoleon had done so much, risked so much –

his dynasty, his life – that one was not prepared for his retreating before the risk of a general war. One was not prepared.'[33] She believed even then that the fault was not Napoleon's. It was that of England and Germany who had refused to support him against Russian threats.

There was worse to come. Henrietta, the closest of all her family to Elizabeth, was gravely ill by the summer of 1860. An internal growth had been diagnosed as cancer and Henrietta was in great pain, perhaps as much from the medicinal use of caustic as from the disease. Browning opened all the letters from George Barrett and tried as far as possible to prepare Elizabeth for their contents before reading them to her. In the autumn, as the news grew worse, he arranged an abrupt departure from Florence for Rome so that for six days they would be beyond reach of any news. Weak and thin as she was, the long road journey was an agony for Elizabeth who wrote to Arabel soon afterwards that the stones along the way must be stained with the blood of her heart.[34] There was a delay in the post and it was not until 3 December that they received news. Henrietta had died ten days earlier.

It was not the only bereavement of that year, since Mrs Jameson, 'Aunt Nina', had died in March, but the tormented love and solicitude for Henrietta which Elizabeth's letters to George Barrett had shown were evidence enough of its impact upon her. To Isa Blagden and Mrs Martin she confessed that she was unwell and weak, more so perhaps than even those around her realized. Story had noticed that Browning remained optimistic about Elizabeth's prognosis, as much to keep up his own spirits as to rally hers. Yet in the progress of her tuberculosis the declines were sharper and the temporary recoveries more difficult to sustain.

Even so, there was no expectation at the end of May 1861, as they left Rome for Florence, that Elizabeth might be setting out on her last journey. For well over twenty years she had been suffering from what was vaguely termed an 'affection of the lungs'. There had been periods at Wimpole Street when she was scarcely able to move from the sofa in her room. She had revived from such a condition many times before and might be expected to do so again. Her disease was incurable but apparently not rapid in its progress.

Indeed, Florence was intended only as a temporary resting-place upon a longer summer journey in 1861. 'Our intention is to go to Florence for a week or two on our way to the neighbourhood of Paris,' she wrote to Eliza Ogilvy on 12 May, 'where we shall spend three months with Robert's family & my sister Arabel who will meet us there.' At the same time she added, 'I am very little "up" to this effort, either in my body or my soul, & am most averse to it'.[35] It was the knowledge that Browning's father might be ailing and that previous meetings between father and son had been postponed because of her health which led Elizabeth to face the arduous 'duty', as she termed it.

The Brownings left Rome on the six-day journey to Terni, Foligno, Siena and Florence. They arrived on 5 June, Elizabeth bruised and exhausted by the jolts of the carriage, as she had been on her first arrival in Italy. They had scarcely arrived at Casa Guidi when news reached them of the death of Cavour. To him Elizabeth had transferred her hopes for Italy upon the withdrawal of Napoleon III from the struggle. It was suggested that this shock was fatal to her. While she was greatly distressed by it, her death had a more specific cause.

She was much weakened by the travelling and Browning realized, as he wrote to Story, that any attempt to visit Paris would be absurd. Yet she appeared to regain strength. None of those friends, like Isa Blagden, who saw her had reason to suppose that she would never leave Casa Guidi alive. Alternative plans for the summer were discussed with a view to escaping from Florence before the heat of August was upon them. Browning discovered that the Storys were at Leghorn, not having set out on their projected visit to Switzerland. He suggested that the two families might pass the summer together at Viareggio, Siena, or Lucca. There were also items of Florentine gossip to hand on for their amusement, including the appearance of Landor without his 'King Lear' beard and speculation as to whether he had shaved it off to look younger or cleaner.

To encourage Elizabeth in preparing for the summer journey to Viareggio or Siena, Browning suggested that she should try walking the length of the Casa Guidi verandah. 'We used, you know, to walk on this verandah so often,' he said; 'come and walk up and down once. Just once.' She managed to reach the window and take two steps. Then she made her way slowly back to the sofa from which she had risen.[36]

On 20 June the summer heat began. In the early evening, while Browning had gone out to scan the newspapers in a reading-room, Isa Blagden was sitting with Elizabeth. The windows had been closed all day to exclude the hot air and were now opened to admit the cooler evening currents. Elizabeth put her chair in the doorway to feel the cross-draughts. When Isa Blagden warned her of the danger, she replied that the cushion at the back of the chair was protection enough.

By the time that Browning returned Elizabeth was complaining of a sore throat. On the next day she had developed a bad cold and an accompanying cough. It was during the evening of 22 June that she showed restlessness and difficulty in breathing. At ten o'clock Browning ran to a chemist's and then applied the so-called 'blister' himself to draw the fluid from her lungs. By one o'clock she was worse, lacking even the strength to cough and so clear the congestion in her lungs. Leaving her with the maid Annunziata – Lily Wilson's successor – Browning was able with difficulty to knock up Dr Wilson, an English practitioner in Florence.

Elizabeth was now breathing in such a manner that 'it really seemed as if she would be strangled on the spot, and that for six hours together'.[37] Dr Wilson sent Browning and the Casa Guidi porter for two further prescriptions. He applied mustard plasters to Elizabeth's breast and back, and hot water with mustard to her feet. By five in the morning her breathing was easier and Dr Wilson left. His diagnosis was clear. There was 'consolidation' of the right lung and probably an abscess.

For the time being there could be no summer journey. 'Such a fright this attack has been,' Browning wrote to Story on the following day. 'Suppose we had been pleasantly travelling!'[38] Yet all hope of their vacation together was not abandoned. In the six days that followed, Elizabeth grew no worse. Indeed, she assured Isa Blagden that she felt better. Siena and Viareggio were talked of. There were also plans for leaving Casa Guidi altogether. They would take a villa in Florence for spring and autumn residence. In the winter they would have an apartment in Rome, close to the Storys' home in the Barberini Palace. For the summer there were villas to be had in the cool Tuscan hills.

Each day Browning carried Elizabeth into the cooler and more airy drawing-room where she sat in her own chair. She read the newspapers, refused solid food in favour of clear broth, and returned to bed early. Despite Dr Wilson's warnings she had no doubt of her recovery this time. The attack two years earlier had been worse, she maintained, and she had rallied from that.

On the evening of 28 June she told both Lily Wilson – now Signora Romagnoli – and Pen that she felt truly better. With Isa Blagden she discussed Cavour's successor, Baron Ricasoli. Browning spent the night in the room watching over her, as he had done since the attack began. She seemed to wander a little in her thoughts, which was perhaps the effect of the morphine she was still taking; or possibly she was delirious.

By three o'clock in the morning Browning was sufficiently concerned over her dozing or semi-consciousness, and the extreme cold of her feet, to send the porter for Dr Wilson. Meantime he bathed her hands and feet with warm water. 'Well, you do make an exaggerated case of it,' she said, smiling at him. Perhaps it seemed that he did. Only a few hours before, though she had not been in the drawing-room that day, she raised herself easily to wash her face, clean her teeth and comb her hair without the least assistance. The restless sleep and wandering speech might have been accounted for by the increased dose of morphine which Dr Wilson had prescribed.

Uncertain of her state of mind by this time, Browning asked her if she knew him. She put her arms about him and said, 'My Robert – my heavens, my beloved'. She kissed him and said, 'Our lives are held by God'. Then he persuaded her to eat a little chicken jelly for his sake, since it was a food she disliked. With her arms about him and kissing him, she repeated, 'God bless you', still kissing the air as he laid her down. At four o'clock she drank a glass of lemonade. When he asked if she was comfortable, Elizabeth replied with a single word: 'Beautiful.' At about half-past four Browning thought that she needed to be raised to assist her breathing. He took her in his arms and, doing so, felt a movement in her chest like a struggle to cough. This time there was no cough. Instead, her head fell against him and he thought she had fainted. The truth came in a cry from the maid Annunziata, who had seen a movement in Elizabeth's face, a knitting of the brows.

'Quest' anima benedetta è passata! – The blessed soul has passed away!'

Later that morning Isa Blagden came and took Pen away to the Villa Brichieri. Browning too was to sleep there every night, returning to Casa Guidi during the day. Until the funeral he spent much of the time sitting beside Elizabeth's body. 'How she looks now,' he wrote to Sarianna, 'how perfectly beautiful!'[39] More prosaically, he reported that death had been caused by the bursting of the abscess which had punctured the trachea. In the view of Dr Wilson, Elizabeth could never have recovered, only survived in a state of decline which would have robbed her of travel, movement, and in the end even the visits of friends.

The strength and independence which Browning had cultivated over the past few years stood him in good stead. To him, Elizabeth's death represented both the end of his former life and the beginning of his new one. There was even a sense of relief in his words to Sarianna on the day after Elizabeth died. 'My life is fixed and sure now.'[40] His love for

Elizabeth was undimmed, but devotion to her memory was quite different from a life of devotion to a living person. The care of Pen and the pursuit of writing were to be his objects. Indeed, the latter was an activity so far removed from the sight of the world that it had ultimately excluded Elizabeth, 'the only thing I have always been used to do absolutely by myself'.[41]

Perhaps it was the knowledge that no misfortune, not even the death of the woman he loved, could destroy that private domain which gave Browning such strength at this time. 'Don't be in any concern for me,' he told Sarianna as he wrote beside Elizabeth's body.[42] A fortnight later he assured her, 'I am very much better than I could have supposed possible'.[43] 'Do not believe I am "prostrated" ', he replied to the Ogilvys in July when they wrote to condole with him in his grief.[44]

William Wetmore Story, hurrying from Leghorn to his bereaved friend, found Browning in the same philosophical mood, putting on a display of robust independence. He stood with Story in the sitting-room of Casa Guidi. Elizabeth's chair and table were in their usual place, the table holding her books and letters, one of which was left unfinished. 'The cycle is complete,' Browning repeated, referring to the fact that Casa Guidi had been almost the beginning of their married life and that Elizabeth had died as they were proposing to leave it.[45]

As the two men stood together in the room, Browning talked of the deliberate transition which he proposed to make. 'Looking back at these past years I see that we have been all the time walking over a torrent on a straw. Life must now be begun anew – all the old cast off and the new one put on.'[46]

Elizabeth was buried in the Protestant cemetery of Florence on 1 July. Browning had chosen the Church of England burial service in order, as he said, that it might open with the words, 'I am the Resurrection and the Life'. He was moved by the sympathy of Elizabeth's friends and the respect shown by the Italian population who closed their shops for the funeral in that area of the city and wrote admiring notices of her work in the Florentine newspapers. Story was less impressed by the proceedings. The English parson, he wrote, blundered through the service 'in a brutally careless way, and she was consigned by him to the earth as if her clay were no better than any other clay'.[47] It was left to Story to lay upon her coffin two wreaths, one of white roses and the other of laurel.

Later on, Browning was to transcribe a passage of Dante into Elizabeth's Bible, as if to set the seal upon his life with her. 'Thus I believe, thus I affirm, thus I am certain it is, that from this life I shall pass to another better, there, where that lady lives of whom my soul was enamoured.'

While these words partook of the sublime nobility of stoicism, they shared also its finality.

12

'How Much One Misses in this Bustling London!'

In the first weeks after Elizabeth's death a single theme dominated Browning's letters and conversation. The break with the past must be as complete as possible. That it could not be absolute was the consequence of two sacred trusts which were to be safeguarded. Pen must be raised to manhood, however little Browning might ordinarily care for the world of children and child-rearing. Moreover, the pursuit of writing now became not only a necessary occupation to him but a duty owed to the dead as, in respect of his father and mother, he once owed it to the living.

During the days of desolation at the beginning of July he had turned to Isa Blagden with his terrible cries: 'I want her! I want her!' By her natural kindliness of nature, Isa had proved the best comforter. Until her death in 1873 she was to be his most consistently sympathetic female friend, if not always the closest.

It took him until the middle of July to hide his grief behind a rebuilt barrier of self-reliance and control. For the future, when his feelings about Elizabeth were revealed, they were more likely to be anger at some indignity to her memory on the part of others than his own gentler veneration of that memory. 'Don't fancy I am "prostrated",' he wrote to Frederic Leighton on 19 July, in much the same terms as he had described his state to the Ogilvys. 'I don't mean to live with anybody, even my own family.'[1]

The same defiant independence coloured the letter which he wrote to Story on 20 August. 'I shall have no ties, no housekeeping, nothing to prevent me from wandering about if circumstances permit. I want my new life to resemble the last fifteen years as little as possible.'[2]

On 1 August, accompanied by Pen and Isa, he left Casa Guidi and Florence for ever. Unlike Elizabeth who had told Eliza Ogilvy in May that she wished, 'never to set foot out of Italy again', Browning's inclinations drew him to the metropolitan society of Paris and London.[3]

Between 1851 and 1858 the French capital had been the scene of his most agreeable 'dissipations', as Elizabeth chose to term them. Now the two cities contained those whom he regarded as his immediate family – his father and Sarianna in Paris, Elizabeth's unmarried sister Arabel in London.

After his decision never to live with his family, it might seem odd that his first instinct was to return like a wandering son. Chronologically, at least, the oddity was deceptive. Despite the romance of Wimpole Street and Italy, and though he was close to his fiftieth birthday, more than two-thirds of his life so far had been spent under his parents' roof. Of the twenty-eight years which remained to him, all but five were to be passed keeping house with his sister Sarianna.

The journey to Paris and the city itself reanimated his grief by leading him to those places which he had known so well in Elizabeth's company. The remedy for this was to part with Isa for the time being and to go with Pen, Sarianna and his father to the village of St Enogat, just beyond Dinard on the north coast of Brittany. It was a wild and remote contrast after Florence and Rome, 'a solitary sea, bays, sands and rocks, and green, pleasant country'.[4]

St Enogat was the first scene of that new life which Browning had promised himself, the first of a succession of small towns in northern and western France in which he was to spend so many summer months. Robert Browning senior proved as delightful a friend to Pen as he had done to his own son. The boy was soon swimming and riding, laughing at his grandfather's stories, as if his recovery from grief was complete. By the end of August Browning himself was pining for an occupation. 'I feel impatient at doing nothing,' he wrote to Story, 'and long to begin with Pen.'[5]

The problem of Pen was to exercise Browning for the rest of his life. It was not made easier by what Sarianna described to Mrs Sutherland Orr as the poet's weak parental instinct.[6]

Until the year of her death, Elizabeth had undertaken by far the greater responsibility for Pen's formal education and appearance. They had shared the same room at night, the boy wishing her 'Good night, darling' as he blew out his light. The exotic clothes and the long golden curls in which she kept him were widely commented upon. The Hawthornes described him as a Ganymede. 'His face is very pretty and most intelligent. . . . He is nine years old, and seems at once less childlike and less manly than would befit his age.'[7]

In 1861 he was twelve years old and the curls had been cropped after Elizabeth's death. He dressed and acted like a healthy and even athletic boy of his age. The lack of a brother or sister, about which he had complained as a small child, had accustomed him to adult society. To his elders he was an agreeable if somewhat precocious companion. Browning's ambition was that his son should enter an English university without passing through an English public school. Therefore, as he told Story, a private tutor must be engaged as soon as they reached London. Pen had reached a critical age, in the light of his long residence in Italy, when the stamp of Englishness would be 'taken or missed'. That it should be missed was unthinkable to his father. 'I distrust all hybrid and ambiguous natures and nationalities and want to make something decided of him.' To this Browning added a comment which reinforces the impression of the extreme privacy and consistency of his inner world, showing how easy it was for him to be in society without being of society. 'I find, by myself, that one leans out the more widely over one's neighbour's field for being effectually rooted in one's own garden.'[8] The emergence of Browning into London society, upon which the successful hostesses congratulated themselves, was indeed little more than the foray of the entomologist in search of specimens for analysis and study.

With the waning of the summer, Browning and Pen made their way to England, whither Isa had preceded them. At Amiens they saw Tennyson and his wife coming back from a European journey. But Browning could not bear a meeting just then. At Boulogne the Tennysons boarded the Folkestone boat. Unknown to them, Browning kept them under scrutiny for a full quarter of an hour, his hat pulled down over his face, the spy from another sphere of existence.[9]

London brought him to lodgings in Chichester Road, Westbourne Terrace, where the more genteel terraces and crescents were enclaves amid shabbier streets. He was close to Arabel Barrett, however, and endeavoured to persuade Isa to return to London from her visits to Clifton and Kent. A tutor, G. K. Gillespie, was found for Pen. 'Dear old Gillespie', as Browning continued to call him eight years later, remained to teach and advise during the boy's adolescence and the disappointments of his time at Oxford. Each day when he arrived at the cramped lodgings, Browning would go out and walk the dull November streets around the Edgware Road. To the Storys he wrote, 'my life is as grey (or yellow) as this sky'.[10]

Chichester Road ran through an area of substantial, if unfashionable, early Victorian property, divided by the Paddington canal. To Browning its appeal lay in the proximity of Arabel, who had made her home at 7 Delamere Terrace, facing the canal, a few minutes walk from Browning's lodgings. In the spring of 1862 he moved to a more spacious house close by, 19 Warwick Crescent, near the junction of the Harrow Road and Warwick Avenue. Here the books and furniture from Casa Guidi were assembled. It was to be his home for all but the last two years of his life.

To the world at large, the progress of Browning's recovery from his bereavement seemed slow. When he was recognized by those like Anne Thackeray, whom he carefully avoided, he was still the solitary figure walking in black through Kensington Gardens or the roads which lay just to the north of the park. In March 1862, when Thackeray himself resigned the editorship of the *Cornhill* because of his declining health, Browning was invited to succeed him. Though he did not dismiss the offer at once, the work held no appeal for him. 'What do I want with more money?' It was a question he could afford to ask as the recipient of Elizabeth's royalties and Kenyon's legacy. Even the sales of his own poetry were improving.

Under the mourning cloak of the widower, the robust Browning of the new life was ready to emerge. Those who subsequently encountered him as a public figure were to find him more self-confident, louder, coarser and more readily cantankerous than the dark-haired romantic who had left England for Italy in 1846. There were, of course, the compensating virtues of honesty and forthrightness, as well as a strength belonging to one who had suffered the worst that fate could do and was therefore largely indifferent to its threats.

In the privacy of his correspondence, notably in his letters to Isa, he regained his spirits quickly after Elizabeth's death, more vigorously even than report suggested. During the next few years he took an obvious relish in assailing her with stories and experiences which would generally have been regarded as indelicate or indecent between a man and a woman in the 1860s. Two months after Elizabeth's death Browning was already entertaining Isa with a story of the attempted rape of a mutual female acquaintance at the Carmelite monastery of Camaldoli. Because the victim was a Catholic, the monks assumed she would make no scandal about it. Browning had the details from Lytton who was one of her rescuers.[11]

Though he was sympathetic to Dante Gabriel Rossetti, there was an unmistakable relish in his report to Isa and the Storys of the death of Lizzie Rossetti in February 1862 from an overdose of laudanum. The account he gave spared no detail of the dying woman's stertorous breathing and the application of a stomach-pump. The same enthusiasm for the morbid and the lewd recurs in his later correspondence with Isa. There was an almost prurient excitement at Pornic in 1862 over the thought of sleeping behind a thin partition on the other side of which a woman was dying of pleurisy. At Pornic again, three years later, he found further material for Isa's amusement. The mayor, in whose house he lodged, slept in a single room with his three daughters, the eldest fifteen, his son, and a maidservant of nineteen or twenty. Lest Isa should overlook any of the implications, he added that the servant was 'somewhat less ugly than usual' and that the beds in the room were arranged conveniently in a row. Soon after, he urged Isa to picture the servant girl for herself. 'Shall I be cruel enough to bid you? ... yes, I will.' He describes for Isa's benefit the sight of the girl, dressed only in a short kilted gown, the view revealed to him as she stooped down to gather linen for the clothes-line.[12]

Even in the first year of his bereavement he was assuring Isa of his continued sexual interest in women and his susceptibility to them. At a dinner party in June 1862 he was both repelled and fascinated by the manner in which a pretty young bride hugged and held her husband during the meal. Browning himself was much taken by the beauty of Parsee girls, 'prettier to my corrupt & rotten cheese loving taste than any of the English fineness & loveliness'. In the matter of beautiful eyes he added, as if in compliment to Isa herself, 'give me those coal black little bitter-almonds!'[13] Story and other American friends paid Browning a compliment by suggesting that he was unlike the pattern of an English gentleman. Some of his compatriots held the same opinion but for less flattering reasons.

Before the first year of widowerhood was over, Browning had begun his return to public life. By November 1861 Isa Blagden had moved into a house near his own in Chichester Road, where she remained for three months. On the last day of the year he assured Story, 'I mean to go out and see friends as I used'.[14] In February 1862 he was elected to the Athenaeum, by the good offices of Monckton Milnes, and came to regard the club as an important element in his social life.

The dinners, supper parties, balls and recitals which filled his evenings increasingly over the next twelve months were more than a reversion to the life he had known in the early 1840s or at Rome in the late 1850s. He was no longer the hopeful young playwright living out a prolonged childhood at Hatcham. W.J. Stillman saw Browning the widower as 'a strong man armed in the completest defensive armour'.[15] The figure who graced the fashionable houses of Portman Square and Mayfair exercised an easy superiority in conversation and power of personality over hostesses and guests alike. However, as Henry James remarked, the door in the wall which enclosed the private reality of Browning's life remained securely locked. It was to be opened only by a golden key, which he alone possessed, 'carrying the same about with him even in the pocket of his dinner-waistcoat, yet even in his most splendid expansions showing it, happy man, to none'.[16]

To James the 'defensive armour', as Stillman called it, was an impenetrable wall. To others it took the form of a genial disguise. 'It may safely be alleged,' announced the *New Review*, 'that no one meeting Mr Browning for the first time, and unfurnished with a clue, would guess his vocation. He might be a diplomatist, a statesman, a discoverer, or a man of science.' He was, it was said, like the Monsignore in Disraeli's *Lothair* who could 'sparkle with anecdote and blaze with repartee'. Yet, added the *New Review*, 'the edge of his sword is mercilessly whetted against pretension and vanity. The inflection of his voice, the flash of his eye, the pose of his head, the action of his hand, all lend their special emphasis to the condemnation.'[17]

Charming, anecdotal or caustic as the occasion demanded, Browning's conversation was his defence, distancing him from friend and foe alike. The technique was faultless, as William Michael Rossetti observed: 'every touch told, every nail was hit on the head'.[18] Yet no one was deceived. It was generally noticed that Tennyson 'hides himself behind his laurels, Browning behind the man of the world'.[19]

More important to Browning himself than the meetings of fashionable society were the more celebrated dinners where he sat with men of intellectual power and influence the equal of his own. There was an auspicious dinner on 12 February 1864, for example, held at the York Gate house of Francis Palgrave, editor of *The Golden Treasury*. Among a dozen guests were Browning, Tennyson, Gladstone, the poet Sir Francis Doyle, the sculptor Thomas Woolner, Dr John Ogle, a leading specialist in nervous diseases, and Gifford Palgrave the diplomat and Arabian traveller. To converse with such men upon equal terms, to demonstrate the capacity of his mind and the force of his utterance, won him a congenial place close to the heart of intellectual and political influence in mid-Victorian England.

Among the London dinner tables, friendship prospered with men like Tennyson and Carlyle, acquaintanceship thrived with such other and more recent luminaries as Anthony Trollope, George Eliot and G. H. Lewes. To his old admirer Dante Gabriel Rossetti he gave his sympathy after Lizzie's death. There were visits to the 'poor kind fellow' at the new communal dwelling in Cheyne Walk, where 'he lives after an easy fashion in a large old house ... amid carvings and queernesses of every picturesque kind'.[20] As with Rossetti, so with Swinburne. Browning liked the man but had reservations over the poetry. Swinburne, fiery prophet of a new generation, was to shock the literary world by a mixture of scandalous subject matter and technical brilliance in *Poems and Ballads* (1866). Browning had a foretaste of this in 1863 when he heard the young man recite some of the pieces. 'I know next to nothing of Swinburne, and like him much', he told Monckton Milnes, though qualifying this in his reaction to the poems. 'I thought them moral mistakes, redeemed by much intellectual ability.'[21]

Ten months after Elizabeth's death Browning had forced himself to dine out every night 'in a cold-blooded way'. The habit became easy, sometimes agreeable when in the company of men whom he respected. Behind the defensive wall he judged the mere glitter of fashion and gossip for what it was worth. 'London mud', he described it to Story, by contrast with the porphyry and marble of Rome.[22]

To the society in which he moved Browning appeared as a man of strong masculine virtues. The Russian novelist Turgenev described him as having a handshake like an electric shock. What more natural than that he should cast around for a woman as a companion in marriage? The physical needs of a man turning fifty were well understood if little discussed. Sometimes to his amusement and sometimes to his annoyance, Browning's name was linked with those of a number of unmarried women in the 1860s. Among these, it seems, were Mary Ann Virginia Gabriel, a composer, Miss Bonham Carter, a sculptress, the poetess Jean Ingelow, Julia Wedgwood, and Amelia Otter, the daughter of the Bishop of Chichester. Much of this, Browning told Story, came from a dinner-table joke of Lady Westmorland's, with Monckton Milnes grinning 'monkey-fashion' on the same occasion about Browning's attentions to the ladies who were present.[23] As he later assured Isa Blagden, the 'cackle' about his remarriage was no more than cackle. Most of the women named were virtually unknown to him. Jean Ingelow he had seen once and had exchanged half a dozen words with.[24]

This denial, made in 1867, came very close to the truth but it was not quite the whole truth. One woman, Julia Wedgwood, had been known to him intimately between 1863 and 1865.

When they first met, Browning was fifty-one and Julia Wedgwood thirty. She was the daughter of a family distinguished in the literary and social life of England, her great-grandfather being Josiah Wedgwood the potter and pattern of a self-made man. A spinster and a victim of deafness, she nourished literary pretensions and evangelical convictions. Hers was a secluded, even solitary life in Cumberland Place, among the magnificent Nash terraces of Regent's Park.

It was probably through her brother, James Mackintosh Wedgwood, that Browning and Julia Wedgwood met. Certainly the death of James in the following year allowed an emotional deepening of their friendship through profound expressions of sympathy and attempts at spiritual consolation.

In retrospect the parallel between the situations of Julia Wedgwood in 1863 and Elizabeth Barrett in 1845 seems clear. Both were separated by their afflictions from general society, both were under the shadow of recent bereavement, and both offered admiration and intellectual companionship. Yet throughout two years of correspondence and meetings the attitude on both the part of Browning and Julia Wedgwood was ambivalent. They talked about the fact that they were intimate and that the world might take them for a suitor and the woman he loved, but they never addressed themselves squarely to the question of whether the world was right in its assumption. Miss Wedgwood admitted at the first that she had 'taken the initiative' in their friendship, and insisted that Browning need not end the association if his only purpose was to spare her pain. In reply he promised vaguely that she would find how much he valued her 'if you will but wait'.[25]

Miss Wedgwood widened the range of their relationship to include the memory if not the spirit of Elizabeth. 'Oh, I hope your wife hears my thoughts as I write to you!' This was in July 1864 when letters were going back and forth several times in a week. Five days after the reference to Elizabeth, Browning assured her of 'the pure truth that you are most dear to me, and will ever be so'.[26]

As was Browning's wont in such exchanges, he passed from this stage to a more vigorous and jocular style, teasing her as a coquette or cajoling a letter from her with smoking-room heartiness in the manner of his correspondence with Isa Blagden.[27]

By the spring of 1865, after two years of friendship, Julia Wedgwood had broken her first self-imposed rule. Her feelings for Browning had grown beyond the bounds of friendship. Though, as she said, she had taken the initiative in 1863, she was too scrupulous or too fearful to take the lead in what lay ahead. Browning had made no move. On 1 March Miss Wedgwood tried three times to write to him. After discarding the first two attempts she completed the third and posted it. She did not break off their relationship in her letter as coldly as it was to be interrupted in practice, saying only 'that it would be better that we did not meet again just now'. His visits to her were the subject of talk, a possibility which they had foreseen from the first but which now offered a pretext for the ending of their friendship. The letter was, in her words, 'this last goodbye'.[28]

In all probability it was too late for Browning to retrieve the situation by protestations of affection, even had he chosen to do so. As it happened he was content to reply to her, 'I thought from the beginning it was too good to last', and for good measure he described Julia Wedgwood not as one whom he had loved but as 'entirely fit' to have been a friend to Elizabeth.[29]

Two years later the correspondence was to resume in a tone of cool and distant courtesy. For the time being there was silence whose cause was referred to in letters between Miss Wedgwood and her friend Julia M. Sterling. The latter was permitted to read the correspondence on both sides. Miss Sterling congratulated her friend on concealing the truth from Browning – 'that your heart had betrayed you' into loving a man who was, by agreement, to be only a friend. 'If he guesses the truth, he certainly most honourably ignores it.'[30]

'If he guesses the truth. . . .' It would be hard to imagine that Browning failed in this. If in the end he could not respond, it may have been because Miss Wedgwood was perceived as a dowdier Elizabeth, lacking the creative gifts, the vivacity and the wit of her predecessor. What might at first have seemed a resemblance between them became, perhaps, as time went on a nagging contrast which scarcely favoured Julia Wedgwood.

There was, of course, a further consideration. To offer Miss Wedgwood or any other woman a limited share in Elizabeth's memory was one thing. To embark on marriage was to risk sharing, by consent or stealth, the golden key which opened the door in the defensive wall of privacy.

Whatever other treasures lay within that wall, Browning never left his contemporaries in any doubt that the memory of Elizabeth was among them. How great its value was another matter. The degree of possessiveness and irritability which he showed in respect of this might even have suggested that his belligerence often did duty in default of any more admirable feelings. Elizabeth, the light of his world, was ironically the fuse which detonated his anger and expletives.

When, for example, the ridiculous and pathetic figure of Sophie Eckley surfaced again in 1863 Browning denounced her as 'a familiar blotch on a picture of the past' for the manner in which she had striven to retain Elizabeth's friendship by inventing spiritualist 'experiences' to please her. These inventions, Browning announced as he heard of her again, 'were not at all more prodigious than the daily-sprouting toad-stools of that dunghill of a soul'. In his denunciations he could rival the brutal language of some of his seventeenth-century Puritan forebears. In other respects his vindictiveness had more in common with seventeenth-century witchcraft. He found two photographs of Sophie Eckley, presumably among Elizabeth's effects, and assembled them in a ludicrous collage with a 'delicious' nude given to him by Leighton. Vengeance required this effigy.[31]

By now there were also those who saw themselves as Elizabeth's biographers and who sometimes naïvely hoped that Browning might aid them. To such creatures he was implacable. In 1863 an otherwise unknown George Stampe of Grimsby was discovered by Browning to be working at a 'life and letters' of Elizabeth, having already acquired her correspondence with H. S. Boyd. 'Think of this beast working away at this,' raged the widower, 'not deeming my feelings or those of her family worthy of notice.' He was fully prepared to obtain an injunction restraining the culprit from publication.[32] To Isa he offered his complaint on the subject with self-dramatized anguish. 'But what I suffer in feeling the hands of these blackguards (for I forgot to say another man has been making similar applications to friends), what I undergo with their paws in my very bowels, you can guess, and God knows!'[33] With characteristic pugnacity Browning was prepared to resist 'at whatever cost ... if I can stop the scamp's knavery along with his breath'. From this battle he retired to Warwick Crescent where he had hung all the portraits of Elizabeth from her childhood at Hope End to the last years in Italy. His homage, like his hatred, had acquired the finality of a cult.[34]

When the London season ended in July Browning's custom in the 1860s was to seek a means of complete withdrawal by spending two months or so in France. Though he was accompanied by Pen, and on most occasions by his father and Sarianna, these long summer visits represented more clearly than any other period his retirement behind the defensive wall.

His most frequent choices were the seaside villages of Sainte Marie, just to the north-west of Pornic, where the Atlantic coast of France curved south from the Loire, and Le Croisic, to the north of the river, enclosed among flat fenland and salt marsh. Beyond reach of London and Paris, he found himself here at what seemed, in the 1860s, the world's end. In these primitive coastal villages where, as he remarked, the phallic stones seemed more influential than the emblems of the Church, civilization, let alone Christianity, enjoyed an uncertain tenure.

Pornic to Browning was 'a wild little place ... the little church, a field, a few houses, and the sea'.[35] To Frederic Leighton he wrote, 'I live upon milk and fruit, bathe daily, do a good morning's work, read a little with Pen and somewhat more by myself, go to bed early, and get up earlyish – rather liking it all'.[36]

To those who knew only the Browning of public life, who were never permitted a glimpse, much a less a visit, behind the private wall, his enthusiasm for such places and their culture was baffling. Yet as surely as the denizens of York Gate or Cumberland Place, the unsophisticated natives of Pornic and Le Croisic offered the material for his art. Here one could eavesdrop on a woman dying behind a thin partition. (Had anyone dared to do so in Elizabeth's case, Browning would scarcely have stopped short of physical violence.) Here the elemental sexual passions were displayed, no less than the bodies of those in whom they thrived. Here was human society in its most basic form, devoid of the crinolines and silk hats which clothed the metropolitan bourgeoisie, often devoid of decency in its more simple forms. Here, then, was humanity displayed to the scalpel of poetic analysis and contemplation. Its value to Browning was clear from his poetry. Whatever the vices and imperfections, or the gentler virtues, of these people, they deviated scarcely a hairbreadth from those of London society or for that matter from the men and women of the Renaissance.

A good deal of his poetry, notably in *Dramatis Personae* (1864) was to exhibit the influence of Pornic and Le Croisic upon its subject matter. The sequence 'James Lee's Wife', with its Atlantic coastal setting, or such poems as 'Gold Hair' and even '*Dîs Aliter Visum; or, Le Byron de nos Jours*' are evidence of it: but nowhere was Browning's experience of this remote and elemental life reflected more clearly than in *Fifine at the Fair*. The poem, a meditation upon the legend and motives of Don Juan, was not published until 1872. Yet its perception of the remote coastal hamlets, the fleeting gaudiness and sexuality of summer, remains the fullest record of his annual isolation from 1861 until 1868.

The character of Fifine, according to Sarianna, was based upon a gypsy girl whom Browning had seen under such circumstances. The backdrop of the fair is that of the Loire Maritime.

> Since, what lolls full in front, a furlong from the booth,
> But ocean-idleness, sky-blue and millpond-smooth?

Far from the facile gentility of the London society whose dining and dancing and recitals he patronized in the winter months, Browning was able to annotate the prostitution of wives and daughters by the master of the fair on a remote summer coast of France. The implications of the poem reflected this conduct everywhere, whether the women were dressed in the fashions of Cumberland Place or the fleshings of the trapeze girl, or even in very little at all.

> Go boldly, enter booth, disburse the coin at bar
> Of doorway where presides the master of the troop,
> And forthwith you survey his Graces in a group,
> Live Picture, picturesque no doubt and close to life:
> His sisters, right and left; the Grace in front, his wife.
> Next, who is this performs the feat of the Trapeze?
> Lo, she is launched, look – fie, the fairy! – how she flees
> O'er all those heads thrust back, – mouths, eyes, one gape and stare, –
> No scrap of skirt impedes free passage through the air,
> Till, plumb on the other side, she lights and laughs again,
> That fairy-form, whereof each muscle, nay, each vein
> The curious may inspect, – his daughter that he sells
> Each rustic for five sous.

Like the Don Juan of his poem, Browning's interest was divided between the type of Elvire, 'chaste, temperate, severe', the heroines of public life, and the stranger beauty and viciousness of Fifine the fairground performer in his private thoughts. To that private domain, 'the dangerous edge of things' as Blougram had called it, the experience of these remote primitive summers belonged. Like the Parsee girls and like Isa Blagden herself, Fifine attracted Browning by her dark suggestive beauty and the ambivalence of her sexual role. He catalogues the woolly trace in her hair, 'the Greek-nymph nose', the Hebrew eyes 'o'er arched by velvet of the mole', the cut of the ears, 'Thin as a dark-leaved rose carved from a cocoa-nut'. In her acrobat costume with the tumbling-troop on their trestle stage it is she, not Elvire, who is distinctively Browning's creation, as much a moral oddity as Johannes Agricola or Caliban upon Setebos. At the necklace of mock-turquoise,

> ... girlhood terminates ... with breasts'–birth commence
> The boy, and page-costume, till pink and impudence
> End admirably all: complete the creature trips
> Our way now, brings sunshine upon her spangled hips,
> And here she fronts us full, with pose half-frank, half-fierce!

His interest in feminine beauty is more Renaissance than Victorian in such instances, a curiosity which applied also to the girl's fate.

> ... there was no worst
> Of degradation spared Fifine: ordained from first
> To last, in body and soul, for one life-long debauch.

With an evident relish Browning turned immediately from this comment to the refined creatures of bourgeois society, mocking their amazement in anticipation.

> You comment 'Fancy us
> So operated on, maltreated, mangled thus!
> Such torture in our case, had we survived an hour?'

There was, perhaps, a sardonic satisfaction in obliging Julia Wedgwood and his other female admirers to cast themselves for a moment in that role.

From London and Parisian society, as well as from these summer retreats, Browning brought back the material for his poetry. If Pornic and Le Croisic featured more obviously in his writing during the 1860s and early 1870s it was because he did a good deal of composition in those places. There was, however, one summer in the period 1861–8 when he forsook his usual destinations for Cambo, a little town in the French foothills of the Pyrenees, some twenty miles inland from St Jean-de-Luz. From there, in August 1864, and from Biarritz on his way home he wrote two letters to Isa Blagden, his 'proud puss', as he affectionately called her. In the first letter, on 19 August, he wrote of female beauty rather as he was to do in *Fifine at the Fair*, finding Englishwomen insipid by contrast with the darker and more volatile goddesses of Isa's type. It was not merely the reiteration of a prejudice. During the stay at Cambo he had at last drawn up a plan for a poem greater in scope and more terrifying in its analysis of human evil and sexual cruelty than any other work of its century. By contrast with the sunlit meditations of the Atlantic coast, this was a drama of darkness and flame. To Isa Blagden, in September, he wrote that he now had in his head the plan of his 'Roman murder story'. Four years later this was to fascinate or repel its readers, according to taste, as *The Ring and the Book*. It was to consist of over 21,000 lines in twelve books. Its writing was to occupy most of his time from the return to London in October 1864 until the proofs of the final volumes had been completed by the beginning of 1869.[37]

The Ring and the Book and *Men and Women* were the two works upon which Browning's fame ultimately rested, although in the early 1860s, even before the publication of *Dramatis Personae* in 1864, his popularity had begun to grow. This was not in itself the consequence of any development on his own part. He published nothing new in the nine years between *Men and Women* and *Dramatis Personae*. Yet in 1863 there was another edition of his collected poems, the first having appeared in 1849, and two selections from his work. Browning viewed this rise in his reputation with a vindictive irony, as he expressed it to Story:

> There's printing a book of 'Selections from R.B.' (SCULPTOR and poet) which is to popularise my old things; and So-and-so means to review it, and Somebody-or-other always was looking out for such an occasion, and What's-his-name always said he admired me, only he didn't say it, though he said something else every week of his life in some journal. The breath of man![38]

The first selection of his poems was the work of John Forster and Bryan Proctor ('Barry Cornwall'), his old friends of the 1830s, who bluntly announced Browning in their preface as 'among the few great poets of the century'. As Browning himself remarked, the increase in his stature was evident from the rising sales. 'Chapman says, "the new orders come from Oxford and Cambridge," and all my new cultivators are young men – more than that, I observe that some of my old friends don't like at all the irruption of outsiders who rescue me from their sober and private approval, and take those words out of their mouths "which they always meant to say" and never did.'[39]

To one of the 'young men' of the 1860s, Edmund Gosse, the reasons for this change in taste were quite clear. The 'tyranny of Tennyson', as the new generation saw it, had begun to wane with the poetic failure of *Enoch Arden* in 1864. Though Browning was of the same generation as Tennyson, only three years younger, he had never been identified with that first age of Victorian literary success to which Dickens and Carlyle, and even Elizabeth, had belonged. His admirers had been younger men like Rossetti, now themselves achieving fame with the flowering and extension of Pre-Raphaelite influence.[40]

There was, before the decade ended, a mood of literary revolution among the younger readers of the 1860s. As early as 1857 the undergraduate Swinburne boldly announced that the work of another undergraduate – *The Defence of Guenevere* by William Morris – was superior to anything in Tennyson. Swinburne's Balliol contemporary, John Nichol, was dismayed to hear that Benjamin Jowett thought Thomas Moore a greater poet than Browning.[41]

'There was an idea abroad,' wrote Gosse, 'and it was not ill-founded, that in matters of taste the age in England had for some time been stationary, if not stagnant. It was necessary to wake people up.'[42] For the new movement, Swinburne among its own members seemed a natural leader, the fierceness of his temper and appearance matching that of his verses. He was, in Gosse's view, 'not merely a poet, but a flag; and not merely a flag, but the Red Flag incarnate'.[43] The same young men at Oxford and Cambridge who were increasing Browning's sales linked arms on the pavement and chanted the sado-masochistic verses of Swinburne's 'Dolores' into the scandalized ears of their elders. To this new generation the time was gone when poetry was to be merely the decorative or improving pastime of the drawing-room and the deanery.

Browning's sympathy with this rebellion was less than wholehearted. Yet he was to shock a good many people by the morbid and indecorous subject matter of such poems as *The Ring and the Book* or *Red Cotton Night-Cap Country* in 1873. That he incurred so little adverse criticism was in part the result of Swinburne's *Poems and Ballads* in 1866. Whatever the defects of the poems, their subject matter signalled a new territory which it was permissible to explore in published verse. The collection dwelt with relish upon sexual oddities and perversions. Lesbianism, bisexuality and sado-masochism were among the topics not so much displayed as flaunted by the young rebel. The reviewers responded with consternation and indignation; there were rumours of a prosecution for obscene libel. The book survived, however, and by this helped to create a climate where much that was not tolerable in Browning's work in the 1830s appeared largely acceptable in the later 1860s and 1870s.

As Ruskin became the father-figure of the Pre-Raphaelites so Browning now stood revealed as that of English poetry and its younger readers. When *Dramatis Personae* appeared in 1864 it soon went into a second edition, a success without precedent in his experience, even in the case of *Men and Women*.

As a collection, *Dramatis Personae* has the air of concluding a good deal of unfinished business in Browning's earlier poetic life. It contains several of his most accomplished love poems which, despite their settings, are much in the vein of his earlier work. The longer poems of the collection deal with issues of faith and doubt, in a different manner but to the same purpose as his writing about religion since *Christmas-Eve and Easter-Day*. Elsewhere the volume indulges rather more in *vers de société* which parallel, if they do not reflect, his forays into the world of dinners, recitals and supper parties which had begun several years before Elizabeth's death. Of the major poems in the collection only 'A Death in the Desert' is a formal historical piece. A more noticeable characteristic is the extent to which the poems employ not merely modern themes and settings but the fashions and idioms of the society in which Browning moved.

Dramatis Personae is dominated by the length and theme of three poems: 'A Death in the Desert', 'Caliban upon Setebos' and 'Mr Sludge, "The Medium"'. The last of these, though a dramatic monologue in scope, has the length of a major poem. In each of these cases the size of the poem is sustained by a theme common to them all: religious faith and doubt. Though in the case of Sludge, alias D. D. Home, the faith is distorted by charlatanism, the poems reflect aspects of a common search for spiritual truth.

In the last two verses of a quite different poem of the collection, 'Gold Hair: A Story of Pornic', Browning chose to describe the occasion of his return to the religious debate and his own views in the matter.

> The candid incline to surmise of late
>   That the Christian faith proves false, I find:
> For our Essays-and-Reviews' debate
>   Begins to tell on the public mind,
> And Colenso's words have weight.
>
> I still to suppose it true, for my part,
>   See reasons and reasons; this, to begin:
> 'Tis the faith that launched point-blank her dart
>   At the head of a lie – taught Original Sin.
> The Corruption of Man's Heart.

As a matter of chronology, *Essays and Reviews* had been published in 1860 and among its most eminent contributors were Benjamin Jowett, Mark Pattison and Frederick Temple. An attempt was made to prosecute Jowett before the Vice-Chancellor's Court at Oxford for heretical views in his essay 'On the Interpretation of Scripture' with its subjection of the Bible to stricter textual criticism. H. B. Wilson and Rowland Williams underwent a successful prosecution before the Court of Arches, the former for advocating a national Church with a broadly interpreted creed, the latter for reducing the Bible to the status of an historical document. Both convictions were reversed on appeal. J. W. Colenso, Bishop of Natal, was condemned for his work on the Pentateuch, published in 1862, which attacked the historical authenticity and usefulness of the Books of Moses.

Browning dealt first with the historical arguments in 'A Death in the Desert'. St John the beloved disciple, also for Browning the author of the Gospel, seer of Patmos and author, too, of the Revelations, lies dying in a desert cave, tended by his converts. The drama of the poem, sixty-four years after the Crucifixion, consists of the final words and the death of the last man who saw and knew Christ on earth. 'How will it be when none more saith "I saw"?' The witness of St John's dying discourse passes on his account of it while himself about to die in a Roman arena.

> So, lest the memory of this go quite,
> Seeing that I to-morrow fight the beasts,
> I tell the same to Phoebas, whom believe!

By such means the account comes to be a written text in a parchment of Pamphylax the Antiochene. Hidden from his pursuers in the desert cave, Browning's St John had already foreseen the methods by which his testimony must be preserved and the arguments which historical criticism would level against it. After sixty-four years the passage of time has already bred doubts. One day the existence of St John himself will be doubted by

> ... unborn people in strange lands,
> Who say – I hear said or conceive they say –
> 'Was John at all, and did he say he saw?
> 'Assure us, ere we ask what he might see!'

Browning makes St John answer directly, as if specifically countering the contributors to *Essays and Reviews* as well as Strauss and Renan. With the passing of contemporary witnesses, the 'absolute blaze' of historical truth is dead. The texts which remain will yield it only if read with the love which is the essence of Christian faith. In this argument Browning echoes *Christmas-Eve*, his rejection of the Göttingen professor and his loveless academic criticism.

'A Death in the Desert' stands as a sombre counterpart to the theological acrobatics of Bishop Blougram, the irony of Cleon and the misled scepticism of Karshish. The enlivening touches of scene and incident are now largely subordinated to the requirements of abstract argument. None the less, to the general reader Browning offered a commentary on the problems of belief which was sympathetic, moving in its simplicity, and shrewdly devised.

'Caliban upon Setebos; or, Natural Theology in the Island' deals with one of Browning's growing preoccupations in matters of religion, the attempt to reconcile a benevolent Christian God with the suffering and evil which afflicts humanity. It may be that the publication of Darwin's *Origin of Species* in 1859 influenced the choice of Shakespeare's Caliban, a pre-human form of life still wallowing in the mud, as the speaker of the poem. In 1881 Browning denied that he had ever opposed Darwin's hypothesis, 'a conception familiar to me from the beginning', and that as early as *Paracelsus* he had anticipated its general theme.[44]

The main purport of 'Caliban upon Setebos' is to attack the interpretation of Christianity as if it were a human science. Caliban comprehends only Setebos, a minor divinity who torments his creatures and whom Caliban conceives as his own likeness. Of the Quiet, which created all things, he knows nothing. In Browning's view this is the limitation of natural theology, devoid of all divine revelation. Setebos is to Caliban as Caliban is to the crabs upon the beach.

> 'Am strong myself compared to yonder crabs
> That march now from the mountain to the sea;
> 'Let twenty pass, and stone the twenty-first,
> Loving not, hating not, just choosing so.

Caliban is a less amiable Fra Lippo Lippi, the underdog who exploits where he can and cringes when he cannot.

> Fool to gibe at Him!
> Lo! 'Lieth flat and loveth Setebos!

This characterization and the quirky childish babble of his words endow the speaker with an individuality which matches the best of *Men and Women* with an anticipation of Samuel Beckett.

The same alternation between truculence and obsequiousness marks 'Mr Sludge, "The Medium"', Browning's lampoon on D. D. Home, probably written at the end of the 1850s. Perhaps it was a personal loathing for Home which focused Browning's power with such brilliance and energy into the image of the dishonest medium caught out by his client. The result is that rarest of Victorian poetic achievements, a verse satire which seems more akin to Dryden's *MacFlecknoe* or passages in Pope's *Dunciad* than to the poetry of the 1860s.

> Now, don't, sir! Don't expose me! Just this once!
> This was the first and only time, I'll swear, –
> Look at me, – see, I kneel.

With equal directness, Sludge, the cornered beast, rounds on his attacker when exposure seems inevitable and then cringes again in earnest.

> You'll tell?
>   Go tell, then! Who the devil cares
> What such a rowdy chooses to . . .
>   Aie-aie-aie!
> Please, sir! your thumbs are through my windpipe, sir!

All too easily such a poem might have degenerated into farce, a mere recitation-piece of broad comedy. In the best tradition of Dryden or Pope, Browning is careful to show that Sludge is not only hateful but capable of hatred. Like any prostituted creature he claims that his clients are no better than he. Only his poverty obliged him to be lifted from gorging 'on offal in the gutter' so that he might find himself

> Sweet and clean, dining daintily, dizened smart,
> Set on a stool buttressed by ladies' knees,
> Every soft smiler calling me her pet.

Even this rouses his secret anger, for Sludge is treated by his hosts and hostesses as an emasculated, sexless creature, safe to be left alone with women. Yet his fictions are superior, as he insists, to Hawthorne or Longfellow. If his work takes a less honest form than theirs that is only because his patrons have corrupted him by their demands and then, worst of all, expected his gratitude. Sludge has no illusions as to his role in this.

> Gratitude to these?
> The gratitude, forsooth, of a prostitute
> To the greenhorn and the bully-friends of hers.

Browning's achievement in the poem is not merely to present a caricature of Sludge or Home, an impersonation so ludicrous as to be incredible. Sludge is a realistic and credible presentation of a man who happens also to be a heartless cheat. As in the most effective satire, the object of it provokes a shudder as well as a smile. There is a chill of spiritual death in the simple self-revelations, the moral prospectus of the psychopath.

> Because, however sad the truth may seem,
> Sludge is of all-importance to himself.

The strength of *Dramatis Personae* lay in these major poems. At the same time the rigours of intellectual argument were softened by such laments for love lost or frustrated as 'James Lee's Wife', 'The Worst of It', '*Dîs Aliter Visum*' and 'Too Late'. For those who found the arguments of St John or Caliban too recondite, there was the brisk thumping optimism of 'Rabbi Ben Ezra', whose ease of quotation brought Browning general popularity at the expense of literary esteem.

> Grow old along with me!
> The best is yet to be,
> The last of life, for which the first was made.

No less an appeal to popularity were such poems as 'A Likeness', in which Browning entertained his readers with allusions to fashions and pleasures of the day, as if sharing his experience of high society with them. Far from the theological arguments of the major poems, he dealt here in contemporary boxing heroes, Sayers and the Tipton Slasher, a cigar case made out of a girl's satin shoe, playing-cards from which a young sportsman had shot the ace-marks with his pistol. The Browning of clubs and dinners, the connoisseur of high life and low life, made his appearance in such *vers de société* which echoed the poems of Praed in his own youth and which were to mark much of his work for the future.

The honours and rewards, withheld for so many years, came to him at last. As he remarked, his young admirers ensured the success of his collected poems of 1863 and of *Dramatis Personae*, thereby forcing his claims upon the attention of their elders who had consistently ignored him in the 1840s and 1850s. By 1867 it was urged that he should succeed Matthew Arnold as Professor of Poetry at Oxford.

He was ineligible. Because that university had been closed to Nonconformists in his youth, Browning had not been able to take the Master of Arts degree which would have made him a senior member of it. Without this he could not be a candidate. As it happened, he was never to be Professor of Poetry. Yet the disqualification had an important consequence. Benjamin Jowett, though not yet Master of Balliol, was Professor of Greek and a powerful influence in the college. In June 1867 Browning received an honorary MA. This dignity, the Keeper of Records told him, had been 'hardly given since Dr Johnson's time except to kings and royal personages'.[45] In October he was elected to an Honorary Fellowship at Balliol.

He had already set his sights on Balliol as a suitable college for Pen, 'a reading college' as he approvingly termed it. This brought him into contact and friendship with Jowett who became Browning's frequent host and adviser upon Pen's future. At their meeting in 1865 Jowett was deeply impressed by Browning. 'It is impossible to speak without enthusiasm of his open, generous nature and his great ability and knowledge.' Believing himself too old to make new friendships, Jowett found that he had made one after all.[46] Judging Browning's poetry as if for examination honours, Jowett awarded it 'a shady First', though hoping for greater things to come. 'Browning has more knowledge, wit, and force of mind than Tennyson, and I can imagine him at any moment rising to the first rank in poetry. At present he is hardly a poet.'[47]

Poetry apart, the two men had much in common, sharing a strong belief in self-reliance and the virtues of sound scholarship. Both had achieved eminence through considerable endeavour and knew the frustration and humiliation of finding their merit unrewarded. Such was Jowett's experience when he had been passed over for the Mastership in 1854.

In another sphere, Browning's poetry became the subject of a full-scale work in 1868, John T. Nettleship's *Essays on Robert Browning's Poetry*, published by Macmillan. The book was less an attempt at literary criticism than a misty sermon on the value of *Sordello* or 'Childe Roland' as guides to life and eternity. As such, the warmth of its praise left nothing to be desired. Of Browning's achievement Nettleship wrote: 'wide and ripe as is his learning, his highest glory is the unflinching zeal with which he has mastered and given to the world the results of human strife, toil, and achievement.'[48]

That part of the world which was in a position to do so showed its appreciation. 'He is in all the grand houses in London,' Arnould wrote to Alfred Domett in August 1868, 'and made a god of.'[49]

The dangers of recognition were as clear in their way as those of rejection. Nettleship's book heralded the transformation in the public mind of Browning the poet into Browning the moralist and religious teacher. The easy prestige of honorary fellowships and degrees, the dinners and admiration of London society, bore perils of their own. Browning's reaction was never in doubt. There was in his response a self-knowledge which preserved him from the worst effects of fame. When he was receiving an honorary LLD from the University of Edinburgh in 1884, his hostess was unwise enough to ask him whether he did not object to all the adulation. 'Object to it!' said Browning incredulously. 'No; I have waited forty years for it, and now – I like it!'[50]

Against this background of recognition in public life, the pattern of his domestic existence underwent the changes of time and mortality. His father died in Paris in the spring of 1866 at the age of eighty-four. He was remembered as a kindly old man pottering among the bookstalls of the Seine and bearing home more treasures to join his accumulated hoard. Sarianna, now left on her own, came to Warwick Crescent. Brother and sister kept house together for the rest of Browning's life. In this matter, too, it seemed that the pattern of his future was more clearly defined than it had been even at the time of Elizabeth's death.

In June 1868 Elizabeth's younger sister Arabel was seriously ill with heart disease. Browning, assured that there was no cause for alarm, went as arranged to a party at which Rubinstein was playing. Early the next morning a servant arrived at Warwick Crescent and asked him to come to Delamere Terrace. Arabel was dying. Browning stayed with her and, like Elizabeth, she died in his arms as he raised her to ease her breathing. Five years earlier Arabel had had a strange dream, of which she told Browning at the time and which he had written down on that day, 21 July 1863. In the dream she had seen her dead sister Elizabeth and asked, 'When shall I be with you?' The reply was: 'In five years.' Arabel died five years to the month, though not to the day, from the date of that dream. 'Only a coincidence, but noticeable,' Browning remarked.[51]

Life had its griefs, no less than death. Pen had not fulfilled his father's hopes. There were rumours that he had two children by Breton girls during the visits to Pornic and Le Croisic. Despite Jowett's friendly interest and advice on the classical authors to be read, he failed to get his place at Balliol. Christ Church received him instead, in 1869. Pen evinced an enthusiasm for art and even broke into what Browning called 'violent poetry'.[52] That apart, his aptitudes proved to be for music and billiards, riding and shooting, even for coxing the Christ Church boat, rather than for passing examinations.

The problem of Pen was to remain with Browning for the rest of his life. Yet the avenue of escape was always there, through the secret door in the mysterious wall. Within that, as the public acclaim and the private disappointments of the 1860s were excluded from his mind, he worked upon his Roman murder story. Not only was it, for Browning in his fifties, the greatest single work of his life. Its story was quite as remarkable as that of the ill-fated *Sordello* thirty years before.

13
Morbid Anatomy

Quite apart from its merits as a poem, *The Ring and the Book* had a simple and direct appeal to the liberal-minded reader of the 1860s. Browning tapped a rich vein of middle-class culture in this case, a fascination for 'trial literature', which had attained a popularity unknown before or since. The so-called 'rogue histories' of famous criminals had enjoyed popularity since Elizabethan times, but nineteenth-century taste was more sober. It lay in the pathos, as well as the thrill, of reading the very words in which men fought for freedom of the press, political liberty, even their own lives, not knowing as they spoke what the outcome might be.

The vogue had begun with *A Complete Collection of State Trials*, edited first by William Cobbett, then by T. B. Howell, and issued in thirty-three volumes from 1809 until 1826. This was followed by such collections as William Townshend's *Modern State Trials* in 1850, G. Lathom Browne's *Narratives of State Trials in the Nineteenth Century* in 1882, and the volumes of *State Trials: New Series* which ran for ten years from 1888.

The human appeal, rather than the legal interest, of such transcripts was acknowledged in the view of Leslie Stephen. His essay on *State Trials* was accorded a place in *Hours in a Library* (1892) alongside the criticism of more orthodox literature: the novels of Fielding and George Eliot, the poetry of Crabbe and Shelley. The merit of trial literature, wrote Stephen, is in 'the harsh, crude, substantial fact, the actual utterance of men struggling in the dire grasp of unmitigated realities'.[1]

To such a taste *The Ring and the Book* made an appeal in its dramatic dimension. The poem was not, of course, a direct transcript even of the legal arguments. Yet Browning maintains, both in the first and last books, that art may offer the truth of what Stephen called 'unmitigated realities'.

> Art may tell a truth
> Obliquely, do the thing shall breed the thought,
> Nor wrong the thought, missing the mediate word.

For eight years and under the most varying circumstances of his public life, the writing of *The Ring and the Book* offered Browning a stronghold and a retreat. Its inner forms of psychological analysis, still more its personal recollections, were hinted at only to a handful of close friends. The doors of this artistic refuge stood open to none.

For Browning the attraction of attempting so ambitious a work was twofold. At one level it was the story of the Roman murder case of 1698 whose examination laid bare the best and worst of human compassion and viciousness, the highest wisdom and the shabbiest criminality. Secondly, however uncharacteristic such revelation might seem, it was the story of Browning's own past, describing how the poem came to be written. Yet here he indulged his own nostalgia rather than his readers' curiosity.

To dwell within this double theme, in which the image of Elizabeth lay reflected, was a sustaining experience of Browning's interior life in the decade of bereavement. 'The remembrance of that past must have accompanied him through every stage of the great work', wrote his friend Alexandra Orr: 'Its subject had come to him in the last days of his greatest happiness. It had lived with him, though in the background of consciousness, through those of his keenest sorrow. It was his refuge in that aftertime, in which a subsiding grief often leaves a deeper sense of isolation.'[2]

The very title – *The Ring and the Book* – linked the two dimensions of the poem. The ring, of Etruscan design, which bore the Greek inscription AEI – 'Evermore' – had belonged to Elizabeth and was worn by Browning on his watch-chain after her death. The book was the so-called Old Yellow Book containing a contemporary account of the proceedings in the murder case of 1698. An English translation indicates the nature of the crime and punishment:

> A Setting-Forth of the entire Criminal Cause against *Guido Franceschini*, Nobleman of Arezzo, and his Bravoes, who were put to death in Rome, 22 February 1698, the first by beheading, the other four by the gallows. Roman Murder-Case. In which it is disputed whether and when a Husband may kill his Adulterous Wife without incurring the ordinary Penalty.

In June 1860 Browning had been walking through the busy open-air market of the Piazza San Lorenzo in the centre of Florence and had discovered the old vellum-covered volume on a stall. It was a compendium of legal pleadings in the case against Franceschini together with letters and manuscripts relating to his execution. The whole of these papers had been bound as one volume for the original owner. Several years after this discovery, in the first book of his poem, Browning recaptured the excitement of the purchase in the busy Florentine market on a hot summer day.

> I found this book,
> Gave a *lira* for it, eightpence English just,
> (Mark the predestination!) when a Hand,
> Always above my shoulder, pushed me once,
> One day still fierce 'mid many a day struck calm,
> Across a Square in Florence, crammed with booths,
> Buzzing and blaze, noontide and market-time.

The place of the discovery was among the debris of a stall selling the typical second-hand bric-à-brac of the San Lorenzo market.

> 'Mongst odds and ends of ravage, picture-frames
> White through the worn gilt, mirror-sconces chipped,
> Bronze angel-heads once knobs attached to chests,
> (Handled when ancient dames chose forth brocade)
> Modern chalk drawings, studies from the nude....
> And 'Stall!' cried I: a *lira* made it mine.

His own story appears as important to Browning, in this respect, as that of the book. Drawn at once to the contents of the volume, he describes himself leaning by the fountain-railing in the square and reading,

> While clinked the cans of copper, as stooped and rose
> Thick-ankled girls who brimmed them, and made place
> For marketmen glad to pitch basket down,
> Dip a broad melon-leaf that holds the wet,
> And whisk their faded fresh.

Compelled by the macabre details of the murder case, his eyes followed the printed page as he walked home.

> Still read I on, from written title-page
> To written index, on, through street and street,
> At the Strozzi, at the Pillar, at the Bridge;
> Till, by the time I stood at home again
> In Casa Guidi by Felice Church,
> Under the doorway where the black begins
> With the first stone-slab of the staircase cold,
> I had mastered the contents, knew the whole truth.

This whole truth was to prove rather more elusive, even for Browning. Yet the facts of the case alone made it one of the most bizarre ever to come before a court of law.

In 1693 a decayed nobleman of Arezzo, Guido Franceschini, married Pompilia, the twelve-year-old daughter of Pietro and Violante Comparini. Violante later revealed to Pietro that the girl was not his own child but the daughter of a Roman whore. Violante had secretly adopted her in order to gain a legacy. Pietro thereupon sued Guido for the return of Pompilia's legacy. Under her husband's roof in Arezzo, Pompilia had suffered increasing persecution and cruelty. In April 1697 she at last managed to escape with the aid of a young priest, Canon Giuseppe Caponsacchi. The couple were overtaken at Castelnuovo, arrested, and tried for adultery. Pompilia was duly sent under penance to a nunnery, where she proved to be pregnant and was allowed to return to her parents. The child born in December 1697 might, chronologically, have been fathered by either Guido or Caponsacchi. Guido, cheated and outraged, came to Rome with his four 'bravoes'. On the night of 2 January 1698 he murdered Pietro and Violante who had deceived him about Pompilia, while the girl herself was so badly injured that she died four days later. At his trial he was condemned to death. Only after this did the more interesting proceedings begin, when Guido moved in arrest of judgement on the grounds that a husband who killed his adulterous wife ought not to be punished as a murderer. The issue at stake was of sufficient importance for the case to be passed to the highest authority, that of Pope Innocent xii. The Pope decided against Guido who died, with his four accomplices, on 22 February 1698.

Such was the material with which Browning was to occupy himself over the next eight years. In 1862 he was still searching for more sources, and wrote to Isa Blagden with a request. She was to ask Georgina Baker if a manuscript in that lady's possession, describing the trial of Count Francesco Guidi for the murder of his wife was that of 'my Count Francesco Guidi of Arezzo'.[3] It proved to be so and Mrs Baker forwarded her account for Browning's use. In 1863-4 Browning was visited at Warwick Crescent by W. C. Cartwright, whom he had first met in Siena. Cartwright reported that the poet was fully engaged on his Roman murder case.[4]

Cartwright's remarks may refer to the autumn of 1864, after Browning's journey through western France to St Jean-de-Luz and the little spa of Cambo at the foot of the Pyrenees. It was there, as he told Isa Blagden and others, that the final shape of The Ring and the Book was settled in his mind. After his return to London in October he began work systematically. On 17 October he wrote to Frederic Leighton in Rome, asking him for details of the interior of the church of San Lorenzo where the bodies of the murdered Comparini were to be displayed in the second book of his poem.[5] By July 1865 he was able to tell Edith Story that 8,400 lines of the poem were completed, which represented the first five books.[6] These contained the account by Browning of how the poem came to be written, the reactions of various sections and opinions in Roman society to the murders of the Comparini, and Guido's self-justification.

That summer was spent in Pornic, from where he returned in the autumn to further systematic writing in Warwick Crescent. Now in his middle fifties, he followed a routine of rising early and beginning work at once on *The Ring and the Book*. Then there was 'other work' to be done, as well as supplementary coaching of Pen in Latin and Greek. All these tasks, he confessed in May 1866 when 16,000 lines of the poem were finished, 'take the strength out of one'.[7] Though he described the poem on this occasion as 'nearly done', the last three of the twelve books still remained to be written. These included the magnificent monologue of Pope Innocent XII which filled the tenth book. Not until March 1868 did William Michael Rossetti report after a visit to Browning that the poem, of more than 20,000 lines, was to be published in July or soon afterwards.[8]

Apart from Browning's own account of the poem at its opening and conclusion, the voices are those of participants and observers, each revealing the story of the murder and the trial from a fresh point of view. Hence it is foremost an analysis of motive and character, prejudice and compassion. Both in this and in the direct self-revelation of the participants to the reader, as if through genuine documentary reporting, *The Ring and the Book* achieved a realism and a depth of psychological perception which English literature had not seen since Samuel Richardson's *Clarissa* in 1747–8. It had, in addition, the vivacity and pace which characterized the monologues of *Men and Women* at their best. Though the murders and the first trial are not the immediate subject of the poem, it exercises a fascination which parallels G. M. Young's famous comment that 'the central theme of History is not what happened, but what people felt about it when it was happening'.[9]

From one aspect, Browning's triumph in *The Ring and the Book* might seem to have been a simple piece of good fortune. The requirements of his subject brought together everything that he did best, uniting this in a poem whose stature had been unrivalled since Byron's *Don Juan*. The art of dramatic monologue, its creation of character or caricature, the evocation of scene and the pursuit of argument represented the excellences of his earlier writing. The speed of the poem seems to reflect the rapidity of Browning's composition and recalls Coleridge's remarks on the poetry of Dryden that it 'catches fire by its own motion; his chariot wheels get hot by driving fast'.[10]

The three voices of Books II to IV define the conflicting views in Roman society over Guido's conduct as well as contrasting the lurid and pathetic scenes of the drama. Half-Rome in Book II is Guido's supporter, pushing his way into the crowded church of San Lorenzo where the bodies of Pietro and Violante are laid out for display on the chancel steps. The Roman mob presses forward eagerly for a view of the corpses, the organ loft crammed with spectators, women fainting, woodwork broken, 'no few fights ensued'.

Among the crowd is Luca Cini, for seventy years an eager voyeur of such exhibitions. The old man's enthusiasm that Pompilia 'can't outlive the night' and will be similarly exposed reaches a pitch of almost sexual excitement. He is expert on stab-wounds and commends those which have killed Pompilia and her parents, made by a Genoese dagger,

> Armed with those little hook-teeth on the edge
> To open in the flesh nor shut again.

Half-Rome is in no doubt that the Comparini tricked Guido into marriage, that Pompilia was persuaded to drug Guido, rob him and then escape with her lover Caponsacchi, 'the courtly Christian'. Even though Pompilia was convicted of adultery and sent under penance to a nunnery, she was thereby consigned to men of Caponsacchi's cloth and kind. Half-Rome describes the waggery of the world by which Guido was tormented.

> 'What, back, – you?
> 'And no wife? Left her with the Penitents?
> 'Ah, being young and pretty, 'twere a shame
> 'To have her whipped in public: leave the job
> 'To the priests who understand! Such priests as yours –
> '(Pontifex Maximus whipped Vestals once)
> 'Our madcap Caponsacchi: think of him!'

To those who still doubt him, Half-Rome puts the question: 'Ask yourself, had you borne a baiting thus?'

Taking up the theme in respect of his own wife and those who would court her, Half-Rome lays down the pre-eminence of the male sex as a law of life and physical retribution as the lot of a faithless woman and her seducer. Guido's misfortune is to have resorted to law rather than the remedy of physical vengeance. 'No: take the old way trod when men were men!' Thinking of the forthcoming carnival and his wife's flirtatious disposition, the speaker recommends his own method of dealing with womankind.

> The thing is put right, in the old place, – ay,
> The rod hangs on its nail behind the door,
> Fresh from the brine: a matter I commend
> To the notice, during Carnival that's near,
> Of a certain what's-his-name and jackanapes
> Somewhat too civil of eves with lute and song
> About a house here, where I keep a wife.
> (You, being his cousin, may go tell him so.)

In Book III, the Other Half-Rome answers for the Comparini family. By contrast with the harsh vindictive voices in the mob of San Lorenzo, Browning conveys the sober assessment of events in the tranquillity of 'the long white lazar-house' of Saint Anna's. Here Pompilia lies dying of her wounds, her last hours disturbed only by the chink of the bell, the turn of the hinge, as doctors, priest and lawyers are admitted.

A new interpretation is put upon events by the quiet, thoughtful voice of the Other Half-Rome. Violante rescued Pompilia from a life of vice and misery by taking her from her mother as 'The illicit offspring of a common trull'. It was the fifty-year-old Guido who coveted the twelve-year-old girl as his wife and urged the marriage by misrepresenting his status and wealth. Despite Pietro's opposition, Violante arranged a clandestine wedding. Guido took the girl and her parents to Arezzo, where he treated the old couple so cruelly that they fled back to Rome, leaving him with Pompilia, 'Guido lord o' the prey, as the lion is'.

As to the affair between Pompilia and Caponsacchi, Guido was proved a liar in the view of the Other Half-Rome. The love-letters from Pompilia to Caponsacchi were Guido's forgeries, the girl herself 'Being incompetent to write and read'. She accepted Caponsacchi as her deliverer only because her confessor and the archbishop refused to listen to her complaints of cruelty against Guido. Her conduct with Caponsacchi – appearances to the contrary – was not necessarily adulterous. Guido, despite his claim that he did not intend to kill the Comparini when he went to their home at Christmas 1697, arrived there with murder in his heart and four bravoes to carry out his intentions.

Less partisan than the coarse voices of San Lorenzo, the Other Half-Rome allows that the case is by no means clear. Anticipating the predicament of the court in its judgement, the speaker considers the proclaimed innocence of Pompilia and Caponsacchi in their flight,

> ... a tale
> Hard to believe, but not impossible:
> Who can be absolute for either side?

Tertium Quid in Book IV is the voice of fashionable society and patrician disdain, discussion of life and death punctuated by satorial admiration.

> 'Faith, this was no frank setting hand to throat
> And robbing a man, but.... Excellency, by your leave,
> How did you get that marvel of a gem,
> The sapphire with the Graces grand and Greek?

To Tertium Quid, the Comparini and their kind represent only 'the middle rank' of Roman social hierarchy; the scandal and the murder are 'an episode/In burgess-life'. The motives of an adulterous woman of rank and reputation interest Tertium Quid and his companions more than the actual murder of Pompilia. One such woman, in the previous week, 'Was caught in converse with a negro page'. She frankly admitted that her husband's saintly demeanour was the cause. As a woman she would have loved him more had he

> ... once never so little tweaked my nose
> For peeping through my fan at Carnival.

The tone, if not the setting, of Tertium Quid balances the two preceding books with a studied languor which might almost have been that of after-dinner conversation at a Victorian house party, an occasion with which Browning had become increasingly familiar.

Between the first four and the last books of the poem lie the splendid characterizations of Guido, Caponsacchi, Pompilia and the pope, as well as those of the two trial lawyers. Two books are occupied by Guido, his appeal against sentence in Book V and his last desperate hours preceding execution in Book XI.

To the Victorian reader Guido's self-revelation before his judges in Book V was a *tour de force* in the exposure of sexual evil. In terms of Browning's poetry he is descended from the plausibility of Fra Lippo Lippi or Blougram, the cold possessive cruelty of the speaker in 'My Last Duchess', and Mr Sludge's repellent and exclusive love of self. The decaying nobleman, four times the age of his child bride, is a portrait of physical and moral horror. He comes before the court fresh from interrogation under torture, obsequiously and hopefully forgiving his arbiters of life and death, excusing the clumsiness of his movements in a dog-like appeal for sympathy.

> I have been put to the rack: all's over now,
> And neither wrist – what men style, out of joint:
> If any harm be, 'tis the shoulder-blade,
> The left one, that seems wrong i' the socket, – Sirs,
> Much could not happen, I was quick to faint,
> Being past my prime of life, and out of health.

He does not even presume to quarrel with the decision to torture him. At the end of his appeal he promises that if spared and surviving to have a son who starts in dismay at the deformed hand,

> I engage to smile 'That was an accident
> 'I' the necessary process, – just a trip
> 'O' the torture-irons in their search for truth, –
> 'Hardly misfortune, and no fault at all.'

From hopeful pathos Guido turns to a cold and logical self-justification, as redolent of righteous psychopathic cruelty as 'My Last Duchess'. For the dying Pompilia he feels nothing but vindictiveness. Neither law nor justice can be indifferent to his fate.

> That I, having married the mongrel of a drab,
> Am bound to grant that mongrel-brat, my wife,
> Her mother's birthright-license as is just, –
> Let her sleep undisturbed, i' the family style,
> Her sleep out in the embraces of a priest,
> Nor disallow their bastard as my heir!

The law entitled him to buy a twelve-year-old girl as his wife – as it would have done in England at the time when *The Ring and the Book* was published.

> I'll say – the law's the law:
> With a wife, I look to find all wifeliness,
> As when I buy, timber and twig, a tree –
> I buy the song o' the nightingale inside.

Yet Guido gives way on the matter of the murders. He regrets willingly that he had not taken measures to prevent adultery and revenge by means for which the law could scarcely reprove him. With a lunatic reasonableness which recalls Porphyria's lover, he describes the atrocities by which their marriage and their lives might have been preserved.

> If I, – instead of threatening, talking big ....
> Had, with the vulgarest household implement,
> Calmly and quietly cut off, clean thro' bone,

But one joint of one finger of my wife,
Saying 'For listening to the serenade,
'Here's your ring-finger shorter a full third:
'Be certain I will slice away next joint,
'Next time that anybody underneath
'Seems somehow to be sauntering as he hoped
'A flower would eddy out of your hand to his
'While you please fidget with the branch above
'O' the rose-tree in the terrace!' – had I done so,
Why, there had followed a quick sharp scream, some pain,
Much calling for plaister, damage to the dress,
A somewhat sulky countenance next day,
Perhaps reproaches, – but reflections too!

Seeing too late this error of omission, Guido none the less reflects upon the happier and more contented state which such trivial severity might have produced.

So, by this time, my true and obedient wife
Might have been telling beads with a gloved hand;
Awkward a little at pricking hearts and darts
On sampler possibly, but well otherwise:
Not where Rome shudders now to see her lie.

To this, in Book XI, is added the ghastliness of Guido's monologue in the dungeon where he awaits beheading. To those who watch over him, Cardinal Acciaiuoli and Abate Panciatichi, he exhibits terror, defiance, demands for intercession with the pope, and finally the abject hysterical disintegration of manhood at the approach of those who come to lead him out to death.

Sirs, my first true word, all truth and no lie,
Is – save me notwithstanding! Life is all!
I was just stark mad, – let the madman live
Pressed by as many chains as you please pile!
Don't open! Hold me from them! I am yours,
I am the Granduke's – no, I am the Pope's!
Abate, – Cardinal, – Christ, – Maria, – God, . . .
Pompilia, will you let them murder me?

The character of Guido might appear as an exercise in rather superior Victorian melodrama were it not for the skill with which Browning exhibits the facets of behaviour, defiant or self-abasing, mean and vindictive, hopeful and conciliatory.

Nor are the other characters cut to the pattern of nineteenth-century

melodrama. Caponsacchi is the intelligent young priest, critical of outmoded ideas respecting the celibacy enjoined upon him. He is of Fra
Lippo Lippi's opinion in such matters, though more articulate and
informed in argument than Browning's earlier hero had been. Caponsacchi was drawn into the Church, as a gifted young man, by his bishop.
As the bishop explained, renouncing the world was an outmoded fetish.
The saints and martyrs of the early Church had done all the suffering
that was necessary. Indeed, it was Caponsacchi's talent for madrigals
and poetry which recommended him to his superiors in the first place.

That he loved and pitied Pompilia is clear. Yet Caponsacchi still
denies, despite the verdict against him, that he was guilty of adultery
with her. As he speaks, she lies dying, and the anger of the young priest,
her soldier-saint, is turned against all those who by design or neglect
have contributed to the real martyrdom of an innocent victim. For
Guido he evinces hatred, for his judges a cold scorn. The law, which
they represent, did nothing to save her. Six months earlier, when
Caponsacchi appeared before them charged with adultery, the trial
was no more than an amusement to them, moving their judicial, ill-
concealed mirth.

> There was the blameless shrug, permissible smirk,
> The pen's pretence at play with the pressed mouth,
> The titter stifled in the hollow palm
> Which rubbed the eyebrow and caressed the nose,
> When I first told my tale: they meant, you know,
> 'The sly one, all this we are bound believe!
> 'Well, he can say no other than what he says.
> 'We have been young, too, – come, there's greater guilt!'

Caponsacchi's moral anger on behalf of the dying Pompilia, no less
than the monologues of the two lawyers in Books VIII and IX, reveal
Browning's aversion to the corruption of law. The poem was redeemed
for many of its readers only by the purity and pathos of the dying
Pompilia in Book VII and the wisdom and humanity of Pope Innocent
XII in Book X.

Though the themes of Pompilia's monologue are piety and forgiveness, the brutality of the past five years is never far removed from her
thoughts. To the twelve-year-old girl, the sexual duties of the proposed
marriage were a subject for vague imaginings.

> – Well, I no more saw sense in what she said
> Than a lamb does in people clipping wool;
> Only lay down and let myself be clipped.

Guido Franceschini, the cavalier promised to her, was no youthful figure of chivalry from a childhood tapesty. He was, to her,

> ... old
> And nothing like so tall as I myself,
> Hook-nosed and yellow in a bush of beard.

The marriage was a matter of buying and selling, not of love and chivalry. Once the child understood this, all else was plain to her. Whether Guido was ugly or beautiful, a clean or dirty coin, was of no consequence in a matter of commerce.

> Here, marriage was the coin, a dirty piece
> Would purchase me the praise of those I loved:
> About what else should I concern myself?

As for the experience of sexual intercourse, Pompilia equates it with the memory of undergoing an examination and treatment at the hands of a doctor. What matter, then, if the doctor be ugly or handsome? Without once crossing the line of mid-Victorian decorum, Browning uses his heroine's words to develop the dark drama of Pompilia's loveless submission to Guido and the ordeal which it precipitates. Nor is it forgotten, in the pathos and deepening horror, that when Guido came to see her first, Pompilia had still been playing with her toys.

Despite the historical nature of the subject, the psychological realism of the dying Pompilia contrasts markedly with the euphemistic accounts of child deaths in *Bleak House* or *The Old Curiosity Shop*. While it is true that Pompilia is seventeen by the time of the stabbing, to turn from her to the last moments of Little Nell or Little Jo is, in every sense, to step from the adult world into the nursery. There is no room in Browning's dark universe of *The Ring and the Book* for a Little Pompilia. The same contrast can be remarked between the quality of his realism and the approach to sexual infidelity in Tennyson. The elegiac lamentations of the betrayed lover in *Locksley Hall* or *Maud*, even the voluptuous suggestiveness of 'Vivien' in *Idylls of the King*, whatever their more obvious merits, are a schoolroom study beside the adult analysis of character and conduct in Browning's poetry. Tennyson's finest achievements in poems such as these – including in another dimension *In Memoriam* – derive from the lovelorn male of song and ballad. Browning's best poetry, apart from *The Ring and the Book*, is more apt to show the woman as victim.

Guido's execution, even the horror of his last hours, is an anti-climax in *The Ring and the Book*. If the poem has a true champion of Pompilia's innocence it is the pope himself in Book x. As Pompilia's is the voice of persecuted and forgiving virtue, so the pope stands for humanity and justice. The force of his monologue lies in the shock of mere law measured against such humanity and Christian rectitude.

> First of the first,
> Such I pronounce Pompilia, then as now
> Perfect in whiteness: stoop thou down, my child,
> Give one good moment to the poor old Pope
> Heart-sick at having all his world to blame....
> ... Everywhere
> I see in the world the intellect of man,
> The sword, the energy his subtle spear.
> The knowledge which defends him like a shield –
> Everywhere; but they make not up, I think,
> The marvel of a soul like thine, earth's flower
> She holds up to the softened gaze of God!

Wisdom, compassion and justice are the guiding qualities of the elderly pope as he meditates alone in his study upon the verdict in the case and Guido's appeal against it. All about him the corruption of the world is evident. To look for legal precedents in the past is vain, showing only the divisions and hatred between men who in turn occupied the throne of St Peter. In a grisly descriptive passage, a match for Browning's childhood reading in Nathaniel Wanley, Innocent xii recalls the conduct of Pope Stephen who untombed Pope Formosus eight months after burial.

> They set it, that dead body of a Pope,
> Clothed in pontific vesture now again,
> Upright on Peter's chair as if alive.

The corpse stood trial for ecclesiastical crimes at the insistence of its successor, was condemned, ceremonially mutilated and its remains thrown in the Tiber. After Pope Stephen himself had been strangled by the mob a few months later, fragments of the corpse of Formosus were retrieved and given honourable reburial. Looking back at such divisions, Innocent xii may well ponder:

> Which of the judgments was infallible?
> Which of my predecessors spoke for God?

In a mood that corresponds more closely to Browning's own than to that of the pope himself, Innocent takes up the theme of *Easter-Day*: 'How very hard it is to be / A Christian!' How much easier in the days of the early Church when faith and martyrdom brought out the best in men.

> Who is faithful now?
> Who untwists heaven's white from the yellow flare
> O' the world's gross torch, without night's foil that helped
> Produce the Christian act so possible
> When in the way stood Nero's cross and stake, –
> So hard now when the world smiles 'Right and wise!'

Browning's achievement in his portrayal of the pope is the triumph of the man over the figurehead, by which Innocent does away with law, precedent and authority, judging the cause instead by the light of Christian humanity. Caponsacchi is condemned for his hypocrisy and vanity but commended for his 'healthy rage' at Pompilia's suffering. Pompilia is a figure of 'purity and patience . . . faith held fast'.

What of Guido? There are strong incentives to quash the conviction against him. To condemn him is to destroy the 'main prop' of social order, 'Supremacy of husband over wife'. Count Guido Franceschini is, moreover, the emperor's man. His execution can do no good to the reputation of Innocent XII, an old and dying pontiff. The pope imagines the voices of the world which will be heard if Guido goes to the scaffold, the slanders directed at the Church and its head.

> 'His last act was to sacrifice a Count
> And thereby screen a scandal of the Church!
> Guido condemned, the Canon justified
> Of course, – delinquents of his cloth go free!'
> And so the Luthers chuckle, Calvins scowl.

Yet expediency and reputation weigh nothing against the main argument in the pope's mind: 'Who is upon the Lord's side?' The thought of this is enough to move his pen in confirming the sentences of death, and in concluding the monologue with an abrupt, dramatic aside: 'Carry this forthwith to the Governor!'

Throughout the poem Browning remained aware of its likely effect upon his reputation. In the first and last books he turned aside to address his Victorian readership in terms which varied slightly but significantly at the beginning and ending of the work. In Book I there was still a tolerant condescension.

> Well, British Public, ye who like me not,
> (God love you!) and will have your proper laugh
> At the dark question, laugh it! I laugh first.

By the end of *The Ring and the Book* the tone is one of confidence and expectation, as if he had already divined the extent of his forthcoming success.

> So, British Public, who may like me yet.

Thus it proved to be, though the liking was not universal. He had resumed his correspondence with Julia Wedgwood, who not only expressed her own moral disapproval of *The Ring and the Book* but elicited from Browning that its theme had never been favoured by Elizabeth either. 'By the way,' he wrote to her on 21 January 1869, 'my wife would have subscribed to every one of your bad opinions of the book; she never took the least interest in the story, so much as to wish to inspect the papers.'[11]

Miss Wedgwood had taken the occasion of their polite and restrained resumption of correspondence to remind Browning how abhorrent *The Ring and the Book* seemed in its moral aspect both to her and, by implication, to the shade of Elizabeth. He had been unwise enough earlier on to confess to her than Elizabeth had lacked his own 'scientific interest in evil', the consuming curiosity about 'the physiology of wrong'.[12] On the basis of this, and with Elizabeth as her spiritual ally, Julia Wedgwood continued for eighteen months to castigate Browning's relish for 'morbid anatomy'. Why could he not write about the pure and the beautiful – Pompilia and the pope – without the evil against which they were cast? Why did Guido and his kind merit such 'impartiality of attention'?[13] The final rebuke came in July 1870. Miss Wedgwood taxed Browning with a betrayal of his own life with Elizabeth by returning from such an 'Eden' only to cast all his emphasis on the 'undesirable truth' that 'Human beings are devilish'.[14]

Such comments as these lie in the context of a relationship whose wounds were not healed by the formal renewal of their correspondence. Moreover, Julia Wedgwood's isolation and piety sought the poetry of love and reassurance, rather as she had sought Browning's deeper affection. In both matters he had disappointed her.

To the world at large the moral ambiguity of *The Ring and the Book* was wholly fascinating. Whatever Miss Wedgwood – or even Innocent XII – might think, even Pompilia's own purity was not absolute. If the feelings which she voiced for Caponsacchi at the end bore any resemblance to her state of mind at the beginning, there was some reason for scandal. Similarly, Guido is a villain in many of his dealings, but had he not been wronged? By the code of his contemporaries, was he not the victim of injustice? The result of Browning's 'anatomizing' is not simply to leave the reader in a state of speculation about the characters. The same speculative doubts are shown within the minds of the characters themselves.

Long before the poem's appearance Browning was assured that he had at last established his poetry, and himself, as a commercial success. 'Booksellers are making me pretty offers for it,' he told Isa Blagden on 23 April 1867. 'One sent to propose, last week, to publish it at his risk, giving me *all* the profits, and pay me the whole in advance – "for the incidental advantages of my name" – the R.B. who for six months once did not sell one copy of the poems! I ask £200 for the sheets to America, and shall get it.'[15]

As it happened he had changed publishers, leaving Chapman and Hall for Smith, Elder. George Murray Smith, who became both publisher and friend, celebrated this acquisition by publishing a six-volume edition of Browning's collected poems, including both *Sordello* and, for the first time, the despised *Pauline* which had not been reprinted since 1833. The appearance of these volumes at the same time as the first parts of *The Ring and the Book* set the seal upon Browning's contemporary fame. If he was still less read than Tennyson, his appeal confined to a rarer and more sophisticated audience, the strength of his new reputation was no longer in question. The reviews of *The Ring and the Book* brought him that recognition for which he had struggled so long and with increasing bitterness. On 20 March 1869 his old antagonist the *Athenaeum* capitulated at last. Its review described *The Ring and the Book* as 'the supreme poetical achievement of our time'. In words that could scarcely have been anticipated by the struggling author of *Paracelsus* or even *Men and Women*, the *Athenaeum* delivered its decisive verdict, describing Browning's Roman murder case as 'the most precious and profound spiritual treasure that England has produced since the days of Shakespeare'.

14
'The Horse Goes Round the Mill'

With his place assured at the banquet of fame, Browning discovered an appetite for more than literary recognition alone. High on the list of rewards greatly to his taste were weeks in the country houses of the wealthy or the noble, the patrician artistic society of Little Holland House or the Royal Academy dinners. If, as he received the congenial admiration of the titled and the powerful, he complained of himself that 'The horse goes round the mill', he none the less gave to his contemporaries the impression of an extremely willing horse.[1]

In March 1869, while maintaining his refusal to be presented to the Queen at court, Browning had been a member of an intimate tea party arranged by Lady Augusta Stanley at the Deanery, Westminster. There, with the geologist Sir Charles Lyell, George Grote the historian of Greece, and Carlyle, he was introduced to Queen Victoria at her request. Whatever the royal feelings about his poetry, Browning's physical appearance remained clear enough in her memory for Victoria to comment on the inaccuracies which she detected in Rudolf Lehman's Royal Academy portrait six years later.[2]

For those who would never enter the portals of the Royal Academy, Browning beamed full-faced from shop windows. By the early 1870s the more famous photographs of him were displayed in this manner, as was the custom with victorious generals or celebrities of the day.[3] For this purpose Browning had once been a 'terrified victim' of the famous Indian-born photographer, Julia Margaret Cameron. From her home at Freshwater on the Isle of Wight, close to Tennyson and the painter G.F. Watts, the redoubtable Mrs Cameron was wont to abduct ferry passengers to act as her models. Meditating a photograph whose subject was to be 'Despair', she seized an unfortunate girl, locked her in a dark cupboard for two hours, and then photographed her, looking suitably abject, upon release.[4] Browning was abandoned 'in a position of extreme discomfort' before the Gorgon-eye of the camera with fierce injunctions against moving. Mrs Cameron went off to look for a piece of equipment and forgot him. He was 'remembered and rescued, more dead than alive', some two hours later.[5]

For more than ten years he had been at home in the well-heeled bohemia of Rossetti's ménage at Cheyne Walk or that of Sara Prinsep at Little Holland House, the dower house of Holland House, a few miles from central London and yet still embowered by woodland. Little Holland House was the resort of Tennyson and Rossetti, Burne-Jones and Watts, Carlyle and Browning. 'Throughout the sunny summer afternoons,' wrote one of Sara Prinsep's guests, 'under the shade of the fine old trees, were placed big sofas and seats, picturesque in their gay coverings, and the desultory talk around the tea table was varied by games of bowls and croquet on the lawn beyond.'[6]

It was here that the forty-seven-year-old painter Watts brought his sixteen-year-old bride Ellen Terry during their brief and bitter marriage. Ellen Terry summed up Browning in phrases that had the clear-sightedness of youth and the shrewdness of maturity. She noticed 'his carefully brushed hat, smart coat, and fine society manners', but found Browning the man far more incomprehensible than his poetry.[7]

Why did the willing horse plod so assiduously round the social mill? In the first place it was a demonstration of success, the life of a man who has risen above the range of such arrows as the penny-a-line critics might fire. In 1871 Browning referred to his standing feud with the poet and critic Alfred Austin in these terms. 'The town is full & I can't keep half the engagements I have. . . . I stimulate myself by the reflection that it stings such vermin as little Austin to the quick that I "haunt gilded saloons".'[8]

In society at large, Browning made the acquaintance of Disraeli, maintained the friendship of Gladstone for the time being, and was the guest of Sir John Duke Coleridge (Gladstone's Attorney-General) at the case of Arthur Orton, the famous Tichborne claimant later convicted of perjury. To be seen rubbing shoulders with men of the greatest power and influence pleased him. In part, he claimed, it was his duty to win favour for Pen. At the same time he demonstrated a public material triumph over those who had withheld their literary approbation for so long.

At this level, one measurement of his fame after *The Ring and the Book* was the extent to which Browning of the dinner tables of London hostesses became instead Browning the house guest of England's great families. '*I* nourish "animosity to country houses"?' he wrote to Monckton Milnes in December 1870, '– who spent all last autumn in some dozen, one after one!'[9] The letters he wrote in the next few years came often from his temporary retreats, Alton Towers as the guest of Lord Shrewsbury, Highclere Castle and a house party of Lord Carnarvon's, Wrest Park, the home of Earl Cowper, or Blickling Hall, where he was staying with Lord Lothian. Browning's love of animals and his anti-vivisectionist beliefs did not preclude a healthy relish in reporting the massacre of local wildlife, as in a résumé to Sarianna of the shooting-party from Highclere Castle in 1873. '5 o'clock / Day's sport (5 guns) – 218 pheasants, 40 hares, 20 rabbits, 1 partridge.'[10]

In the summer of 1871, as in the autumns of the two previous years, he set out on a grand tour of country houses in Scotland, an alternative to his French holidays and a respite from the strain of life in London. His hosts included Ernest Benzon near Loch Tummel and Lady Louisa Ashburton at Loch Luichart. This second visit was to have profound consequences for the rest of his life, but the visit to the Benzons brought him agreeably close to Benjamin Jowett and an Oxford reading-party. Swinburne, whose family and friends were by now seriously concerned about his drinking – 'bilious influenza', as he preferred to term its effects – had also been entrusted to Jowett. To his summer tour Browning added a call upon Jowett, Swinburne and the young men who were his own most constant admirers.

Even the honours bestowed upon him through Jowett's interest seemed to partake of country house living. He wrote to Isa in the autumn of 1869 about the two 'capital rooms' provided for his use in Balliol, next to Jowett's own. Browning had already begun to furnish them with a view to being a regular guest. Though he added that he might find the travelling to Oxford too irksome after all, that would have been uncharacteristic. Jowett, as Master, was able to attract company and provide hospitality of a kind that Browning found irre-sistible. After one Balliol dinner he wrote rhapsodically of the prestige and brilliance of those who had been fellow guests and speakers. They included the Archbishop of Canterbury, the Bishop of London, Lords Coleridge, Lansdowne and Cardwell, T. H. Green, and Stanley, the Dean of Westminster. The speeches were full of studied praise for the College poets: Matthew Arnold, Clough, Swinburne and Browning himself.[11]

That Browning had become a social and intellectual snob by the early 1870s is a plausible but untenable charge. The praise withheld for so long was all the sweeter when it came, and sweetest of all when bestowed by men who represented all that seemed best in the society and culture of his time. To such plaudits he returned congeniality, acknowledging a world of which he was no more a part than he had been a member of the fairground troop at Pornic which gave him the material for *Fifine*. He lived with the shade of Elizabeth, a private life whose structure was best defined by the poems he wrote. Within that world of imagination and in the personalized vision of his past he could endure forever.

Not even the closest friends were a part of this. Few were even admitted the type of glimpse given to Isa from time to time. Ten years after Elizabeth's death he passed what was a final judgement. 'The simple truth is that *she* was the poet, and I the clever person by comparison ... my uninterrupted health and strength and practice with the world have helped me.'[12] The round of clubs and dinners, house parties or the roll call of success at Jowett's gatherings was, as Browning termed it bluntly, his 'practice with the world'. Rarely was the inner vision revealed, perhaps to Isa alone. 'Oh, me! to find myself some late sunshiny Sunday afternoon, with my face turned to Florence – "ten minutes to the gate, ten minutes *home*!" I think I should fairly end it all on the spot.'[13]

Next moment, even Isa was no more than the smoking-room companion to whom indelicate stories might be told. So, for example, the robuster Browning passed on to her the tale of the wife who admitted to her husband having committed adultery with the parson. She could not remember how often, only recalling that as Bible reading turned to sexual intercourse the clergyman would turn down the corner of the page. The husband found, as Browning assured Isa, every page dogs' eared, 'from Genesis to Revelation!'.[14]

Isa's death in 1873, at the age of fifty-five, deprived him of his closest female friend, one to whom he constantly expressed his love. Browning, now sixty-one, was never to find a relationship of such intensity again.

Other friendships were retained and restored. Alfred Domett returned from his long exile in 1871 and the youthful companionship with Browning matured easily and quickly into the more sedate but enduring affection of men in their sixties. Joseph Milsand, who had acclaimed Browning's poetry in the *Revue des Deux Mondes* in 1851, had become another lifelong friend and was actually staying at Warwick Crescent when Domett and Browning met again after so many years in March 1872. When, in the summers of the early 1870s, Browning and Sarianna went abroad, it was to the Normandy coast, St Aubin or Villiers-sur-Mer, where Milsand was a frequent companion.

Above all, there remained the benevolent but faintly sardonic voice of friendship in Thomas Carlyle. In what might have seemed like a moment of irresponsibility he informed Browning that the poet's true *métier* should be as a translator of Greek drama. *The Ring and the Book* he described with a weary tolerance as 'a wonderful book, one of the most wonderful poems ever written ... all made out of an Old Bailey story that might have been told in ten lines, and only wants forgetting'.[15]

There were newer friends and acquaintances as well. Edmund Gosse, among the young men of the 1870s, grew close enough to Browning to be entrusted with the poet's personal reminiscences for publication. In Gosse, moreover, Browning politely but erroneously acknowledged one of the great poetic luminaries of the new generation. The error was common enough to be excusable. By 1881 Browning confided to his young admirer that he was 'tired of this tangle of facts and fancies' which represented his life to the world at large. He thereupon gave Gosse his own account, to be published in the *Century Magazine* in December that year.[16]

Among the hosts and hostesses of the London season, a few were admitted to a closer friendship. Charles Skirrow, Master in Chancery, and his wife were among these from 1870 onwards. Mrs Skirrow was described as a hunter of social lions with a collection of 'some remarkably good specimens'. Browning's was 'the finest head of the collection'.[17] His amiability towards her was at the least a return for the birthday gifts of stationary or books as well as the solicitude with which she looked after him at dinner. He shared Tennyson's preference for drinking port rather than dinner wine. Unlike Tennyson, who drank his daily pint of strong port with his dessert, Browning consumed it throughout the meal. It was Mrs Skirrow's pleasure to keep him well supplied.

As the decade following Elizabeth's death drew to its close, the stories of Browning's friendships were eclipsed by a half-revealed scandal. There had been, as he told Isa, rumours of his impending marriage to various women, most of whom he scarcely knew. Yet by 1871 he had made his choice and, in an apparent act of sacrilege to the memory of Elizabeth, he proposed to Lady Louisa Ashburton, a widow of wealth and beauty fifteen years his junior.

It was no sudden inclination or temporary aberration which provoked Browning to this action. As early as 1862 he had met both Lady Ashburton and her husband, who were also friends of the Storys. In 1869 he and the Storys were summer guests at her home, Loch Luichart, where Browning read passages from *The Ring and the Book* to the party. A further association was through Hatty Hosmer, the American sculptress, to whom Lady Ashburton was attached in Rome during 1857.

The third daughter of James Stewart Mackenzie, Louisa Ashburton was an heiress who at her death in 1903 left more than a quarter of a million pounds. In 1859 she married a sixty-year-old widower, William Baring, the second Baron Ashburton, a member of the famous banking family. At the time of his death, five years later, the young widow was described as having a classic beauty, softened by dark eyes, a ready smile and a voice of rich appeal. By others she was less favourably regarded. They saw in her a woman of inconstant tastes who was easily persuaded by the latest shallow pretensions of the world of art.

Whatever courtship existed between Browning and Louisa Ashburton was apparently undocumented. Yet their close relationship prospered sufficiently for a proposal of marriage to be made in 1871, probably in October. The young Mary Gladstone, recalling a visit to Belton where Lady Ashburton and Browning were present, remarked sardonically, 'we all supposed he was proposing to Lady Ashburton . . . at least she let it be thought so'. Browning indicated that he proposed under pressure, never leaving Louisa in any doubt that 'my heart was buried in Florence, and the attractiveness of a marriage with her lay in its advantage to Pen'.[18] Whether he proposed in terms of such unprepossessing bluntness, or whether her refusal obliged him to save his pride by pretending a lack of interest from the start, is uncertain. The only certainty is that Browning turned bitterly against her and, indeed, against Hatty Hosmer, for the way in which he understood they were later reviling him in public. Before the end of 1871 he was already prepared to cut Louisa Ashburton when their paths crossed at dinners or recitals. 'I see every now and then that contemptible Lady Ashburton,' he told Story in 1874, 'and mind her no more than any other black beetle – so long as it don't crawl up my sleeve.'[19]

Browning's experience of his closest female friends after Elizabeth's death was one in which intimate exchanges stopped short of a final and exclusive commitment. His gentleness with Isa was balanced by a bawdy robustness, his attachment to Arabel was an extension of family obligation. For the future, those women to whom he seemed closest were shared in his affections either with their husbands or with Sarianna. Louisa Ashburton stood in a different relationship to him. Browning had committed himself further, perhaps, than he envisaged. At the point where a proposal of marriage seemed called for, his inclinations were – if he is to be believed – to draw back. Louisa Ashburton asked for nothing less than the right of admission to his private world. If that were the case, it is entirely in keeping that he should have made a proposal in terms so unflattering that it was bound to be refused.

Whatever Browning's conduct towards Louisa Ashburton, his preoccupation with family affairs during the two years of their closest friendship was real enough. Pen, after continued failure in university examinations, had been removed from Christ Church in 1870. He lived for a while in imitation of his father, making the round of shooting-parties and the hospitality of great houses as the guest of Monckton Milnes and others. By 1874 it seemed clear that his only serious talent was for painting and sculpture. In Browning's view, the profession of an artist was the most admirable. It had, moreover, the virtue of removing Pen from a life of wasted possibilities. The fatuous pleasure-seeking of many of his young contemporaries was more disturbingly seen, in Pen's case, through the rumours of children being fathered on Breton girls during the family's visits to Pornic and Le Croisic. At length, in 1874 when he was twenty-five years old, Pen was dispatched to Belgium to study painting as a pupil of Jean-Arnould Heyermans.

After the visit to Scotland in the summer of 1869, Browning's own thoughts turned again to Europe. In 1870 and then from 1872 until 1875 his summer journeys took him to the coast of Normandy, in the first place to St Aubin and the flat land with its sandy beaches between the Cherbourg peninsula and the mouth of the Seine. The first visit in 1870 was prompted by the hope of spending the season there with his friend Milsand, whose 'dear and perfect kindness' had never failed Browning in the twenty years of their acquaintanceship. 'I never knew or shall know his like among men,' the poet told Isa.[20]

The visit began auspiciously enough. 'Milsand lives in a cottage with a nice bit of garden, two steps off, and we occupy another of the most primitive kind on the sea-shore – which shore is a good sandy stretch for miles and miles on either side.' As in Brittany, so in Normandy Browning was invigorated by the sea. 'I don't think we were ever quite so thoroughly washed by the sea-air from all quarters as here – the weather is fine, and we do well enough.'[21] At night the beam of the lighthouse shining across the water from Le Havre brought back to him memories of having been there with Elizabeth in 1858.

The primitive tranquillity of St Aubin ended abruptly with the rapid advance of Prussian armies into France. Milsand went to Paris to remove the valuables from his house to a place of greater safety. The ferries from Calais and Boulogne to England had stopped running, the railways were in chaos and horses everywhere were being requisitioned.

When they reached the railroad, Browning and Sarianna were assured that the Prussians would be at the other end of it before nightfall. Their escape to England was made hastily and with minimal dignity in a cattle-boat which put out from Honfleur for Southampton at midnight.

The later visits to Normandy, to Villiers and Le Treport in 1874 and 1875, were chiefly the inspiration of Annie Egerton Smith who accompanied the Brownings there as she did to the Isle of Arran and to La Saisiaz near Geneva in the two following years. Browning and Elizabeth had first met Miss Egerton Smith in Italy, the friendship being renewed with Browning and begun with Sarianna after his return to England.

Annie Egerton Smith was a woman of considerable wealth and artistic interests. She was part owner of the *Liverpool Mercury* and a devotee of the London concert and recital season. She it was, rather than Sarianna, who was Browning's chosen companion to hear the performances of Rubinstein or Joachim, the violinist, for which he was prepared to sacrifice almost any other engagement. To him, as he said, the grandeur of Beethoven's thirty-second piano sonata represented the opening of the gates of heaven.

With the visit to Le Treport in 1874 the friendship with Annie Egerton Smith acquired a new intimacy. Though she was 'dearest Annie' in Browning's letters to her, Miss Egerton Smith remained as much Sarianna's friend as his own – perhaps more so despite the recital visits. His manner towards her was restrained, however, having none of the robust indelicacy or the yearning nostalgia which he indulged with Isa. It certainly had nothing of the sentiments which had so bitterly compromised him with Louisa Ashburton. That last entanglement had made him doubly cautious for the future. Yet within such limits his affection for Annie Egerton Smith and her successors appears whole-hearted and profound. If it seemed less impetuous than in earlier days, perhaps this merely reflected the truth that Browning, if not wiser, was growing older. In the summer of the first holiday at Le Treport he was already sixty-two, however vigorous for his years. At such an age he might reasonably regard the difficulties of sexual involvement as more evident than its compensations.

After the visit to Milsand at St Aubin, the sudden drama of war and escape to England, two more years passed before Browning saw the same Normandy coast again. Its fertile countryside, the ancient churches and ornate retreats of the Parisian bourgeoisie proved powerfully interesting to him. There, in 1872, he found among this landscape and its inhabitants the material for the strangest poem which he – or any of his Victorian contemporaries – ever wrote. He called it by the innocent-sounding title of *Red Cotton Night-Cap Country*. Behind this description, suggestive of a story for children at bedtime, lurked a monster who might well have made Guido Franceschini shudder. The contrast was characteristic of a darker side of Browning's humour.

While Browning was at St Aubin in 1872, a court at Caen upheld the will of Antoine Mellerio, who had died in 1870. Mellerio was the profligate son of an international jeweller with shops in Paris and Madrid. He took as his mistress a married woman, Anna de Beaupré. Reproached by his family, he attempted suicide by jumping in the Seine. Torn between his love of religion and the Church on the one hand and that of his mistress on the other, he continued to live with her on his estate at Tailleville, a few miles inland from St Aubin.

The crisis of the drama was precipitated by his return to Paris where he found his mother dead. Mellerio decided to take a ferocious revenge upon himself for his libertinage. He held his hands in an open fire, with almost superhuman fortitude, until the flesh was burnt away and there remained only carbonized stumps. In the ecstasy of penance he seemed not to feel the pain. Yet Mellerio's reformation was only temporary. He recovered from the atrocious injuries sufficiently to have artificial hands fitted to the stumps of his wrists, and in this state he returned to Anna de Beaupré at Tailleville. There, in 1870, he attempted suicide for the third time by throwing himself from the belvedere of the house on to the lawn. He was killed at once.

By his will, Mellerio bequeathed the bulk of his estate to the Church and the remainder to his mistress, the two irreconcilable loves of his last years. His family, not surprisingly, contested the will on the grounds of his insanity in the case at Caen.

Mellerio's story made the same kind of immediate appeal to Browning as *The Ring and the Book* had done. He collected reports of the hearing and evidence from local people, even meeting Anna de Beaupré. By the autumn of 1872 he was working with daunting energy, at Warwick Crescent, upon his new novel in verse.

The court upheld the will and Mellerio's sanity. To Browning such an obsession as the victim's, even if not technically madness, was a gift from Fortune. He added to the facts his own interpretation of the last suicide attempt. From the belvedere of Tailleville it was possible to see the statue of the Virgin on the church tower of the old village of La Délivrande. Browning makes Mellerio trust in his own redemption through an act of faith, a miracle of the nineteenth century to restore an age of belief. Throwing himself from the belvedere, he will not fall.

Divine power shall keep him aloft. By crediting Mellerio with this delusion, Browning returns to madness as divorce from reality, the sealed world of lunacy.

With considerable naïveté, Browning completed the poem and sent it to Smith, Elder in January 1873, retaining in the text the names of real people – living and dead – and of the actual locations of the events. Only when the book was in proof did he or George Smith consider the possibility that they might be sued for libel, if it were printed in its present form. At this date it had yet to be finally decided that the dead could not be libelled except in criminal libel: but there were survivors of the scandal who might take exception to Browning's treatment. His first refuge was to hope that he would be protected by having taken most of the facts from published reports of the case at Caen. Failing that, he had the even slimmer hope that a French subject could not sue successfully for libel in a British court.

On 8 March 1873, Browning drew up a disclaimer for George Smith's benefit, describing the poem as 'a mere account treated poetically' of facts elsewhere available in law reports and newspapers. It would not do. A week later he sought the advice of his friend Sir John Coleridge, the Attorney-General. Coleridge was tactful but firm. Not only was it necessary to use fictitious names for the real ones; the work should be altered 'rather more' than that, if compatible with its status as a poem. Coleridge conceded that the risk was not great, and any damages awarded might be small. Far worse would be the inconvenience. As his fee, the Attorney-General asked for a copy of the book when it was published.

The names in the poem were duly altered. Mellerio became Miranda and the fashionable jeweller's shop in the Place Vendôme went by the same name. Anna de Beaupré was changed to Clara de Millefleurs, and La Délivrande to La Ravissante. With such minimal precautions as these the poem was published.

As a fiction, the poem had less in common with English verse of the 1870s than with the novels of Maupassant or Zola. Though Maupassant as a novelist belonged to the next decade chronologically, his peculiar combination of *haut-monde* and *demi-monde* is anticipated by Browning in the poem. Zola's Rougon-Macquart series of novels had already begun to appear in 1871, involving a dissection of the moral cancer in French society so harrowing that his English publisher, Henry Vizetelly, was tried and sent to prison in 1889 when Zola's fiction was judged obscene.

With ease and precision Browning captured the air of Paris under the Second Empire, the casual morality which turned women into

'Boulevard game', ensnared by the compliments and shallow generosity of their followers.

> 'Repaid alike for present pain and past,
> 'If Mademoiselle permit the contre-danse,
> 'Sing "Gay in garret youth at twenty lives,"
> 'And afterward accept a lemonade!'
> Such sweet facilities of intercourse
> Afford the Winter-Garden and Mabille!

Browning's Miranda played the 'Boulevard game' in the manner approved by his male sympathizers.

> He understood the worth of womankind, –
> To furnish man – provisionally – sport:
> Sport transitive – such earth's amusements are:
> But, seeing that amusements pall by use,
> Variety therein is requisite.

By this philosophy, woman is not like the royal stag to be hunted with respect or chivalry, but rather like the bat who may be caught at roost, since 'The lantern and the clapnet suit the hedge'. The poet, of course, is putting a case in which he does not wholly believe. Thirteen years later, in Browning's own lifetime, a younger but equally famous contemporary author was to use the same image to state a thesis of psychopathology. The Baron Richard von Krafft-Ebing won his reputation as Professor of Psychology at the University of Strasbourg, then at those of Graz and Vienna. In the third chapter of his *Psychopathia Sexualis* (1886), on 'General Pathology', he remarked: 'In the intercourse of the sexes, the active or aggressive *rôle* belongs to man; woman remains passive, defensive.' To this he added a footnote on general animal behaviour. 'Among animals it is always the male who pursues the female with proffers of love. Playful or actual flight of the female is not infrequently observed; and then the relation is like that between the beast of prey and the victim.'[22]

The attitude was by no means unique to the later nineteenth century. What characterizes it, both in Browning's fiction and in Krafft-Ebing's thesis, is the cold, analytical manner of its statement. Despite the consistency of Browning's own preoccupations during a long lifetime of writing, it also serves to remind his readers of the cultural distance between the disciple of Shelley and the contemporary in tone and subject of Zola, Maupassant and Krafft-Ebing. Like the admirers of Zola's Nana, Miranda frequents the Varieties to fall slave to a girl's beauty. Like Laroche-Mathieu, Minister of State for Foreign Affairs, and Madeleine Du Roy, in Maupassant's *Bel-Ami*, Miranda and Clara are found committing adultery by the commissary and his assistant. The two officials break in upon the lovers in bed in the rue du Colisée.

> One glance sufficed them. 'A marital pair:
> We certify, and bid good morning, sir!
> Madame, a thousand pardons!'

As if to make plain to his English readers the nature of the Parisian society in which Miranda moves, Browning lists those who remain his friends after Clara's divorce and her recognition as his mistress. Chief among these is 'Duke Hertford', an accurate and possibly libellous evocation. The third Marquis of Hertford, the most dissolute of all the Regency rakes, was safely dead. Indeed, he had already been portrayed as the Earl of Monmouth in Disraeli's *Coningsby* and the Marquis of Steyne in *Vanity Fair*. His name endured as a cipher for cynical viciousness. There was, however, a more recent Hertford, the fourth Marquis, who inherited much of his predecessor's weakness. If Browning was as avid an amateur of dinner table and smoking-room gossip as he led his friends to believe, he had no doubt heard the story of the younger Hertford and Catherine Walters, 'Skittles', the famous courtesan. In the 1860s she sold herself to him for a single night at a price of some thousands of pounds. He exercised his prerogatives as her customer 'so violently, so frequently and with such perversity that she was ill for three days afterwards'.[23]

Such was the world of *Red Cotton Night-Cap Country*, and yet as a background it was misleading. Parisian scandal or the perverse love of woman as a beautiful animal to be hunted was too wearisome a subject to be the centre of Browning's poem. In itself it was too hackneyed to represent that 'dangerous edge of things' where, as Blougram remarked, a man's true interest must lie. To Browning, the sight of Miranda, withdrawn to his Normandy estate, struggling between the demands of love and remorse, Clara and the Church, offered the true drama.

Miranda's madness, if that is what it is, progresses by stages during the poem. After his mother's death he separates himself from Clara and returns to the family business until the dreadful day when his family break in upon him at the rue du Colisée where he has been burning Clara's letters. Then comes 'a cry, a host of cries/Screams hubbub and confusion thrilled the room'. Taking the casket of letters between his hands, Miranda has held both casket and hands in the fire. His flesh has been consumed by flame. His rescuers stand in horror:

> he had no hands to hurt –
> Two horrible remains of right and left,
> 'Whereof the bones, phalanges formerly,
> 'Carbonized, were still crackling with the flame.'

Between life and death, Miranda lives in the contentment of religious faith, only kicking and licking to keep the visions of Clara away from himself. Like a religious ecstatic, he feels no pain. The medical diagnosis of such a state, in terms of Victorian psychiatry, could scarcely be in doubt. More surely than Porphyria's lover or Johannes Agricola, Miranda has locked himself into the madhouse cell of delusion where even the most elemental message of physical agony will never reach him.

> 'Mad, or why thus insensible to pain?
> 'Body and soul are one thing, with two names
> 'For more or less elaborated stuff.'

Browning allows his hero to recover, as Mellerio had done in reality, to have artificial hands fitted to the burnt stumps of bone, and to live again on his estate with Clara. Yet now, for both of them, religious devotion is the prime emotional impulse. The Church, while unable to condone their living in sin, gratefully accepts Miranda's gifts of some £40,000 in the next two years.

With total plausibility, Browning traces the fatal advance of insanity. Miranda stands upon the belvedere of his estate, surveying the Norman countryside.

> Yon white streak – Havre lighthouse....
> To steeple, church, and shrine, The Ravissante!

In his final moments, religious ecstasy drives him from Clara to the figure of the Virgin upon the tower of La Ravissante. He begs her to do the one thing that will save the Church, France and himself from an age of unbelief. 'Only suspend the law of gravity.' His last act, comic and macabre, is accompanied by a vision of the new world that must follow the triumph of his miracle.

> The news will run
> Like wild-fire. 'Thousands saw Miranda's flight!'
> 'Tis telegraphed to Paris in a trice.
> The Boulevard is one buzz.

The divine revelation, of which Miranda seeks only to be the grateful instrument, must restore an age of law and belief. Napoleon III will abdicate at once in favour of a legitimate monarch, 'And Henry, the Desired One, reigns o'er France'! The names of sceptics like Rousseau will be removed from Paris streets and Renan, before becoming editor of a Catholic paper, will burn his *Vie de Jésus* on the quay of the Seine. Best of all, by this act of faith Miranda will bring the blessing of the Virgin of La Ravissante upon both Clara and himself. 'And may I worship you, and yet love her?' he cries to the distant figure. Confident of the answer, he throws himself from the tower and lies, in an instant, dead on the turf below.

With a casualness that has the modernity of such poems of W. H. Auden's as 'Embassy' or 'Musée des Beaux Arts', the death of Miranda is observed by a witness, briefly distracted from a more relevant task.

> A gardener who watched, at work the while
> Dibbling a flower-bed for geranium-shoots,
> Saw the catastrophe, and, straightening back,
> Stood up and shook his brows.

Sixty years before his time, Browning captured that precise, if traditionally unpoetic, casualness in the presence of catastrophe which Auden records as the diplomats negotiate for war:

> Two gardeners watched them pass and priced their shoes:
> A chauffeur waited, reading in the drive:

or as Icarus falls from the sky in Brueghel's painting:

> and the expensive delicate ship that must have seen
> Something amazing, a boy falling out of the sky,
> Had somewhere to get to and sailed calmly on.

If it did nothing else, *Red Cotton Night-Cap Country* showed that Browning's imagination, invention and energy remained as vigorous in his early sixties as at any time in his life. However, the poem's reception was poor and its popularity has remained relatively low. Reviewers and readers were deterred by its title and its subject. Browning had wanted to call it *White Cotton Night-Cap Country*, a reference to the headwear of the French peasants in the 1870s. When the possibility of libel arose, he changed the colour to red. Red or white, the title remains the least satisfactory aspect of the poem. Its interest in 'morbid anatomy' was certainly more pronounced than ever. It was, of course, no defence to the implausibility of the story to say that it was true in its external details. Yet through his analysis of Miranda's delusions, Browning adds that interior dimension of his character which endowed the mere historical events with a poetic conviction.

As truly as in *Pippa Passes*, thirty-two years before, Browning's art reveals character and motive in a corrupt society. As surely as in 1841 he is the poet of post-romantic modernism. That modernism had taken a form, by the 1870s, which was unpalatable to a good many people. Maupassant as well as Zola was judged obscene by the English law in 1889.[24] Perhaps it was the removal of Elizabeth's restraining influence which allowed Browning to enter newer and more dangerous territory. However laudable his spirit of adventure in this journey to the lower depths, he took few of his readers and fewer still of his critics with him.

When in 1875 he published *The Inn Album*, the basis of the poem was once again open to similar moral objections – and similar justifications. Based on the conduct of the notorious Lord de Ros, as recorded in the memoirs of Charles Greville, the poem describes the attempt of an elderly roué to prostitute his seduced and discarded mistress to his young companion in exchange for the cancellation of a gambling debt. In this case, if Greville is to be believed in his entry, Browning toned down the profligacy and cynicism of his central character. He also sets the poem in the 1870s with its references to Gladstone and Disraeli, the Tichborne case, and polo at Hurlingham.

Browning's reputation ensured a respectable sale for the poem, but critical opinion remained at odds on the direction his work appeared to be taking. The analysis of the criminal or vicious personality seemed at times to be an apology for the conduct of such men and women. As the reading public was deeply divided over the moral fervour or obscenity of Zola and Maupassant, so it was divided over Browning. The young Henry James was unimpressed by *The Inn Album*, though he was to be Zola's defender. Another advocate of French realism – though not of Zola – was Swinburne, who saw in Browning's verse novels 'a fine study in the later manner of Balzac'. 'I always think,' Swinburne added, 'the great English analyst greatest as he comes nearest in matter and procedure to the still greater Frenchman.' [25]

Red Cotton Night-Cap Country and *The Inn Album* were Browning's two most striking poems of the earlier 1870s by virtue of their size and their sensational subject-matter: yet they were only two of several major poems written during these years, which testified to Browning's undiminished productive power in his sixties. After Elizabeth's death he had assured his friends that he intended to keep on working 'whether I like it or not'. It was in part a tribute to her memory, but also the acknowledgement of a world into which he could withdraw from the desolation of life.

To one so active in mind (if less in body) as Browning the simple gospel of work offered a means of salvation in the face of his own dissolution. It was a gospel whose believers included some of his most distinguished contemporaries, his new friend Jowett being among them. To Walter Morrison, who had trifled away his time as an undergraduate, the Master said sternly: 'You are a fool. You must be sick of idling. It is too late for you to do much. But the class matters nothing. What does matter is the sense of power which comes from steady working.'[26]

That sense of power, or more specifically of self-confidence in the face of declining vitality, drove Browning into unremitting literary activity for two more decades as no sense of bereavement alone would have done. Some of the poems of the early 1870s, most of them written at considerable length, were to convey an impression of work for work's sake rather than work for the sake of art. In several of these he turned to his childhood reading in the literature of Greece and Rome. The poems which stemmed from this were not, as some critics supposed, mere transcriptions from Jowett's table-talk of Euripides or Aristophanes; however, there was a sense in *Balaustion's Adventure* in 1871, or *Aristophanes' Apology* four years later, of Browning as a poet in search of occupation.[27]

Between 1871 and 1875 he published well over 20,000 lines of new poetry, the majority of which was devoted to subjects of the contemporary world rather than to praise of Euripides and his rivals. Even in the case of Greek drama there was a certain new relevance. Swinburne's neo-Hellenic verse-drama of 1865, *Atalanta in Calydon*, had stimulated a general mid-Victorian interest in the form and subject matter of the Athenian stage. In the wake of this, Browning's two poems were no dry-as-dust academic exercises. However, *Balaustion's Adventure* is largely taken up by a loose translation and paraphrase – 'transcript' was Browning's term – of the *Alcestis* of Euripides. A considerable part of *Aristophanes' Apology* is occupied by a direct translation of the *Herakles* of Euripides. Like the *Alcestis*, the *Herakles* is the story of a return from death. Moreover, its subject of temporary insanity, even the presence of Madness as a character in the drama, was precisely of the kind that appealed to Browning's interest in morbid psychology.

While such poems as this were received with respect rather than enthusiasm, and admired for their scholarship rather than their poetry, the versatility of Browning's achievement in his sixties was undeniable. There was to be a translation of the *Agamemnon* in 1877 continuing the style of the two earlier poems. Yet the decade had begun with a poem which was far more a companion-piece to 'Mr Sludge, "The Medium"' on one hand and *Red Cotton Night-Cap Country* on the other.

Prince Hohenstiel-Schwangau, Saviour of Society, appeared in 1871. It is a monologue by a deposed European autocrat, easily recognizable in that year as the exiled Napoleon III. The speaker reveals himself to a girl whom he has picked up in the neighbourhood of the Haymarket, the accepted promenade in London's West End for genteel 'courtesans', as Henry Mayhew chose to call them. With the laconic contemporaneity of Blougram and the frank indifference to others of Mr Sludge, the prince opens his heart to the young woman among the shabby decorations of a London tea-room.

> You have seen better days, dear? So have I –
> And worse too, for they brought me no such bud-mouth
> As yours to lisp 'You wish you knew me!'. . . .
> Suppose my Oedipus should lurk at last
> Under a pork-pie hat and crinoline,
> And, lateish, pounce on Sphynx in Leicester Square?

As surely as Mayhew in *London Labour and the London Poor*, the prince categorizes the girl as

> . . . you, good young lady that you are,
> Despite a natural naughtiness or two,
> Turn eyes up like a Pradier Magdalen.

At his ease in her presence – 'I don't drink tea: permit me the cigar! – this incarnation of the defeated Napoleon III speaks for himself. Browning assured Isa Blagden that he had allowed the prince to speak as he might have done in reality, without authorial intervention.[28] It was, after all, the proven technique that had given life to so many other and more notable villains in his earlier monologues. In this case he allowed the speaker such latitude that the poem was mistaken by some reviewers for what the *Edinburgh Review* called a 'eulogium on the Second Empire'.

Browning permits the prince to describe himself as an intelligent conservative, prepared to tolerate change provided that the essential pattern of society is not altered.

> Let us not risk the whiff of my cigar
> For Fourier, Comte, and all that ends in smoke.

In other matters, apart from politics, the ex-monarch stands for modern thought, casting a sidelong glance at the debate on Darwinian evolution, which had taken another turn in the year of Browning's poem with the intervention of Charles Kingsley. Does it matter, the prince asks, whether life is a metal bar forged at one instant or a series of separate links making up a chain? In either case, the evidence of a design and a presiding intelligence is clear to see. The inspiration for this part of the poem, other than Browning's own belief, is presumably Kingsley's lecture on 'The Natural Theology of the Future', given at Sion College on 10 January 1871 with its single crucial sentence: 'We knew of old that God was so wise that He could make all things; but behold, He is so much wiser than even that, that He can make all things make themselves.'[29]

In more vivid terms Browning's poem encapsulates the world of the Second Empire, its grandeur and folly, the growing public appetite for war,

> tired of the illimitable line on line
> Of boulevard-building, tired o' the theatre
> With the tuneful thousand in their thrones above,
> For glory of the male intelligence,
> And Nakedness in her due niche below,
> For illustration of the female use.

Then, in a single line, the speaker sums up the public revulsion from party politics which brought the emperor to power: ' "The trusty one! No tricksters any more!" ' The poem was never to be one of Browning's most popular. None the less, it is a well-etched cameo of one adventurer addressing another, and a fine analysis of a nation's frame of mind which made the Second Empire a possibility in an age of democratic revolution.

The other major poem of the earlier 1870s was *Fifine at the Fair*, which appeared in June 1872. Its discussion belongs to Browning's life at Pornic and Le Croisic; yet in 1872 there was a further significance in the rival attractions for Don Juan of Fifine, the half-naked trapeze girl, a harlot by implication, and Elvire, the goddess-wife. One does not need to suppose that Fifine is a burlesque of Louisa Ashburton in order to guess that the poem reflects Browning's own experience. With the exception of poems written specifically to Elizabeth, he preferred to devise fictions for the analysis of sexual love at its creation or destruction. If *Fifine at the Fair* reflects his own life, it is as a portrayal of his situation as a widower, a man still wedded to an ideal yet always aware of the seductive power of womankind.

The consequence of such poems as *The Inn Album* and *Red Cotton Night-Cap Country* was that Browning, with his fame secure, was none the less the subject of critical shrugs and reproaches. Nor was it merely that he was an elderly poet whose waning powers, as in the case of Tennyson, might be made the topic of gentle regret. Browning's poetry was morally and aesthetically repulsive to some of those who were now called upon to pass public comment.

He responded in characteristic manner, laying about him with a will. Alfred Austin, who disliked the morbid analysis of the poetry and announced that Browning, like Molière's M. Jourdain, had been writing prose all his life without knowing it, was summarily dealt with. Austin's own poetry enabled Browning to denounce him as 'Banjo Byron', and his critical opinion as that of 'a filthy little snob' and 'a literary "cad"' who was rabid with envy over the dinners to which Browning was invited and he was not.[30] For good measure he told the story of how Austin had taken his literary efforts, whining and cringing, to Thackeray, editor of the *Cornhill*, and how Thackeray had mistaken him for a beggar and sent him away with half a crown.

At times he pretended a lofty indifference to all criticism, though even in doing so the violence of resentment showed plainly. 'I have had too long an experience of the inability of the human goose to do other than cackle when benevolent, and hiss when malicious; and no amount of goose criticism shall make me lift a heel at what waddles behind it.'[31] This was true in the sense that he did not actually call at the offices of *Temple Bar* with a view to horsewhipping Alfred Austin. Short of physical violence, his resentment knew very few limits.

A favourite theme, and one that had some justification in fact, was the manner in which critics who had scorned him during the previous quarter of a century pretended to have had good opinions in secret all that time once his fame and popularity were clear. 'I always intended, for the benefit of my successors, to leave on record some memorial of my feeling for the authorities which have sate in judgment on me this long while,' he told Mrs Thomas Fitzgerald in 1876, 'especially the "poets" who, dropping out of the ranks, condescended to hide behind a wall, throw a handful of mud at their so-called "rival": and then slink out and stand by his side as a "fellow-poet" just as if nothing had happened.'[32]

A combination of circumstances made Browning unfit to raise insult to the level of art as Dryden had done in *MacFlecknoe* or Pope in the *Dunciad*. As a matter of private vindictiveness it was perfectly appropriate for him to apply excremental images to his enemies, to dismiss D. D. Home as a 'dung-ball' or to depict his critics as men who gathered the sewage of London in order to empty it by cartloads upon their readers. No one could reasonably object to his private sneers at Alfred Austin's slight build, or the fact that the future Poet Laureate wore cork heels to increase his height and had been known, when teetering upon them, to fall backwards into the fireplace.

A century and a half before, such matters might have been made the subject of personal satire in the manner of Dryden or Pope, but a gentler age was apt to regard violence of language or the public mockery of a man's physical appearance as lacking in literary decorum. The type of outburst which Browning meditated would scarcely be fatal to his growing reputation but it would, at the least, be ill judged.

Mournful though the admission might be, those who knew him intimately were obliged to concede that Browning was guilty of much the same breach of literary comradeship with which he charged others. The splendid indignation of his forties and fifties was apt to flare again as the mere cantankerousness of old age. By 1870 he had turned against his young admirers, privately at least. Swinburne's poems were 'florid impotence', Rossetti's merely '*scented* with poetry'. He attacked the 'effeminacy' of their admirers, 'the men that dress up like women', the affected pronunciation which spoke of lil*y* and lil*ies*.[33]

Not even Tennyson was to be spared. When *The Holy Grail and other poems* appeared in 1869, Browning pronounced it as monotonous as the books that had preceded it. 'Tennyson thinks he should describe the castle, and effect of the moon on its towers, and anything *but* the soul.'[34] After one of these denunciations he confessed to Isa Blagden: 'I am getting ill-natured.'[35] That opinion was increasingly widespread.

It was not to be expected that Browning's private views, so forcibly expressed, should remain private for the rest of his life. Stories began to circulate which developed his opinions into fantasies of actual encounters and scenes that had never taken place. His relationship with Swinburne, for example, was one of mutual admiration at first, cooled by Browning's increasing dislike of the younger man's poetry, then a reconciliation in which he found Swinburne 'a noble heart', and finally a break between them caused by Browning's association with Swinburne's arch enemy, F.J. Furnivall.

Apart from the publicity which it was to receive, the progress of the relationship illustrates one cause of Browning's unfitness for public polemic – the ease with which his opinion might increasingly be turned by flattery. At the same time there were fewer secrets than ever which could be safeguarded from the journalism of newspapers and magazines. One day, in the reading room of the Athenaeum, he picked up a copy of *Truth*. The mutual admiration and the later rift between Swinburne and himself were described in terms of pure fiction and in a manner calculated to bring laughter upon both men. Swinburne, it was said, had taken a camp-stool to 19 Warwick Crescent in order to sit at the feet of his idol and worship him. As the influence of the superior mind failed to take effect, Browning confronted Swinburne one day at a railway station, shook his umbrella at him, and cried: 'Ah, you foolish boy, why will you so degrade such splendid talent?' The writer added that Browning's language had been far stronger than this, much too indelicate to be printed verbatim.[36]

Whether he liked it or not – and on the whole he did not mind it as much as might have been expected – Browning in the later 1870s and the 1880s was a public figure. To that extent he was even public property. Those who had ignored him in the past but wished now to share his reflected glory were not his main concern. The chief irritant consisted of small-minded critics and impertinent journalists by whom he was increasingly liable to be 'flea-bitten', to use his own term. Towards such creatures he now strove to be what Edmund Gosse called the 'tiger' of public life rather than the 'domestic cat' of private friend-ship.[37]

15
How He Worked in Distemper

In the last fifteen years of his life, Browning the public figure was a match for the national and imperial self-confidence which characterized Victorian England in the late 1870s and the 1880s. 'I don't think you know who I am,' he said firmly to Disraeli after a Royal Academy dinner at which the Prime Minister had been guest of honour. 'Oh yes, I do, very well,' said Disraeli quickly. Browning then proceeded to make the statesman retract all his praise for the exhibits, uttered in his dinner speech, and admit that the collection was one of the worst he had ever seen. 'A noisy, conceited poet,' said Disraeli privately. He also went out of his way to snub Browning, when the two men were present at Lady Airlie's dinner with Matthew Arnold, by congratulating Arnold on being the only living Englishman to become a classic in his lifetime.[1]

Despite his friendship with Gladstone, Browning parted company with the Liberal leader over the question of Irish Home Rule. It was one thing to support the independence of Italy, occupied by foreign powers, quite another to attack the integrity of a single, united sovereign state. His attitude in this was matched by the far more radical figure of Swinburne. That *enfant terrible* of the 1860s, whose support for Italy and Mazzini reached near hysteria, threatened to kick downstairs a Fenian who came looking for support at 2 The Pines, Putney.

Browning's true Liberalism, as he saw it, remained unaltered despite the Gladstonian apostasy. He went so far as to write his famous sonnet, 'Why I am a Liberal'. It was in part a tribute to his public fame in 1885 that the world should care whether he was a Liberal or not. The creed which the sonnet describes is a belief in fundamental individual freedom rather than in the dismemberment of nation states.

> Who then dares hold – emancipated thus –
>   His fellow shall continue bound? Not I
> Who live, love, labour freely, nor discuss
>   A brother's right to freedom. That is 'Why.'

To causes, rather than to men, he devoted his allegiance as time went on. Political demonstrations he dismissed as 'mob meetings'.[2] As early as 1870 he warned Isa Blagden; 'put not your trust in princes neither in the sons of men'. Among those who had betrayed such confidence he listed Garibaldi and Mazzini.[3] Even the god of poetry in his youth, Shelley, was scarcely untainted. The publication of letters describing Shelley's treatment of his first wife put a strain upon Browning's loyalty. He suggested that Shelley was deranged, though culpable, and that he was also in bodily pain. When offered the presidency of the Shelley Society in 1885, Browning declined it.

To the new world of the middle-class magazines, as well as to the more exclusive society among which he dined and talked, Browning became a figure so easily recognized as to be worth the pains of carica-ture. By 1881 the weekly journalism of the *World* commented less on his poetry than on his 'compact little figure, the urbane and genial bearing, the well-made clothes ... as far a dandy as a sensible man can be'.[4] Browning's tailor, reading this, assured him; 'Well-dressed you *are*, sir, – but "almost a dandy" – no!'[5] On 22 July 1882 he was to achieve the ultimate eminence of this sort by appearing in caricature as one of *Punch's* 'Fancy Portraits'.

Browning in the years of his triumph was intimidating to some of those who met him and repulsive to others. Released from that private world of his own poetry and meditation, he showed a hunger for society. And yet it was not society as human company which appealed to him but rather society as an arena in which he could perform more publicly than in his study or library. He behaved like a frustrated actor. The novelist W. H. Mallock was disconcerted on first meeting Browning to be grasped by both hands and surveyed by the man of fashion with his sparkling eyes and trim beard as if he were an old friend. Any hope of conversation – in the sense of an exchange between two or more people – was shattered at once. Mallock and Jowett were soon reduced 'to something like complete silence by a constant flow of anecdotes and social allusions'.[6] The energy with which Browning pounced from be-hind his wall of privacy, seizing upon his companions as if they were conversational prey, is far more suggestive of the neurotic than of the sociable companion. Charles Hallé, for example, recalled a dinner party at which Browning talked without interruption throughout the meal and ate nothing. When at last he paused, another guest two places away attempted to say something. Browning leant across his neighbour, laid his hand on the interrupter's arm, and himself began another un-stoppable monologue.[7]

To some of those who witnessed these performances in his sixties, Browning was not merely an agreeable eccentric. There were sneers at his dazzlingly white waistcoat and pomaded hair, which was cared for more tenderly as it receded further. Hallam Tennyson predicted Browning's death, expiring in a white choker at a fashionable dinner party. Gladstone's daughter Mary disliked being too near to him. He edged too close to her, brushed her face with his beard, and blew and spat as he ate.[8]

Though it was said that he rarely talked about literature or anything much beyond trivia upon these occasions, it was men of letters who found him most sympathetic even then. Henry James, recalling the Browning of 1878-9, deprecated his eagerness to monopolize the conversation at those functions he attended. Writing to Alice James, her brother described the poet's 'shrill interruptingness' and 'a kind of vulgarity'. To which James added: 'Besides which, strange to say, his talk doesn't strike me as very good. It is altogether gossip and personality and is not very beautifully worded.' But James had sufficient perception to intimate what others lacked either the wit or the patience to observe. There were, he remarked, 'two Brownings – an esoteric and an exoteric. The former never peeps out in society, and the latter has not a ray of suggestion of *Men and Women*.'[9]

The public and private characters were reconcilable in one personality, nevertheless. Yet Browning's performances, not least in reading his own poetry, strengthened the doubt as to whether the reader could possibly be endowed with a sensibility capable of writing the poems. He read them, said James, with a suggestion that 'at least, if you don't understand them, he himself apparently understands them even less. He read them as if he hated them and would like to bite them to pieces.'[10]

Henry James guessed at the private personality of the poet, not displayed on such occasions. Edmund Gosse was privileged to observe it. Gosse was well acquainted with the Browning of public life, the loud 'trumpet-note' of welcome and 'the talk already in full flood at a distance of twenty feet'.[11] There were those who were offended by the manner in which the poet 'took his acquaintances easily – it might almost be said superficially'.[12] Then, as the strengthening of friendship won the young man admission to the study at Warwick Crescent, crammed with the libraries of Robert Browning senior and of Casa Guidi, a transformation began. The voice was still loud and imperious, the visitor trapped in a low armchair while the great man strode about, talking and gesticulating. But now the subject matter of the compulsive flow of talk had changed. Gone were the dinner table anecdotes. In their place came a 'turmoil of thoughts, fancies, and reminiscences'. The visitor carried away 'an image of intellectual vigor, armed at every point, but overflowing, none the less, with the geniality of strength'.[13]

Gosse was one of the few men, towards the end of Browning's life, who was permitted to penetrate to the very wall and its secret door, as James described it. Appropriately, the moment was to come on a cloudless summer afternoon in the Fellows' Garden at Trinity during Browning's visit to Cambridge in 1889. There, among a 'green mist' of summer foliage and 'a pink mountain of a double-may in blossom', the booming voice grew quiet and the subdued confession began. It was no less than an outline of Browning's intellectual life and it hinged upon one obsession. From earliest manhood he might have enjoyed 'unfettered leisure', but always he had been subject to an overriding phobia. He was, quite simply, 'afraid to do nothing'.[14]

On that summer afternoon, Browning also described with considerable frankness the 'long-drawn desolation' of his early and middle life as a writer. No more was he the neglected genius savaging the numbskull critics who had condemned him to this long obscurity and whose pettiness touched him not the slightest. The scars of that neglect were exhibited at last.

Perhaps it was the security of his fame, to which his visits to the two universities bore witness, which made such a revelation possible. Cambridge conferred its honorary LLD on him in 1879 and Oxford its DCL three years later. The latter occasion was the one on which a wag in the gallery of the Sheldonian Theatre lowered a red cotton night-cap dextrously on to the head of the distinguished visitor during the ceremony. He was offered the Rectorships of the Universities of Glasgow and St Andrews, a tribute to the continued and vigorous exercise of his poetic talent which continued until the end of his life. He was grateful for the tribute but declined the honours.

He might have been advised to decline the presidency of the New Shakespere Society, founded by the scholar F.J. Furnivall in 1873. Furnivall was a Christian Socialist, a pioneer of adult education, the originator of the Early English Text Society, the Chaucer Society, and the Browning Society of the 1880s. He represented the best tradition of Victorian educational zeal. Unfortunately, he was also a party to the bitter feuds with Swinburne and with Browning's acquaintance, J. O. Halliwell-Phillips. Browning's fate was to be caught in the crossfire of an unpleasant little squabble. It remains cautionary and yet instructive to see two middle-aged men like Furnivall and Swinburne slanging one another like schoolboys as 'Pigsbrook' and 'Brothelsbank Flunkivall' respectively. Unhappily, Browning was soon involved. Swinburne remarked privately that Browning's association with Furnivall proved that 'he has not the feelings of a gentleman', that his name was tarnished by association with 'this "brothel lackey," the bastard of Thersites'.[15] The quarrel culminated in Browning declining to take sides and in Swinburne dashing off a rebuke to Warwick Crescent, sputtering with indignation. To attack his own character, Swinburne insisted, as Furnivall had done, revealed the attacker as 'an infamous and impudent liar'. Browning was 'the figure-head of a ship of which the captain is such a person as I have just defined ... it is obvious that in addressing the President of the "New Shakespere" Society I could no longer without degradation subscribe myself as yours very sincerely, A. C. Swinburne'.[16]

The brandy-inspired young rebel of the 1860s, now living under the tutelage of Watts-Dunton at Putney, rationed to a daily bottle of Bass, was clearly spoiling for a fight. So, for that matter, was the older but no less flamboyant tenant of Warwick Crescent. It was not Swinburne, however, but Alfred Austin again who was the principal target of *Pacchiarotto and How He worked in Distemper; With Other Poems*, which was published in July 1876.

Not since *Dramatis Personae* in 1864 had Browning published a volume of personal poetry as opposed to dramatic verse or tales of considerable length. Significantly, the title poem of the present collection took a new theme, the dim-witted malevolence of his critics and of Austin in particular. The poem is written in doggerel stanzas, the critics made to compare themselves to chimney-sweeps penetrating the vapours of Browning's obscurity.

> 'We critics as sweeps out your chimbly!
> Much soot to remove from your flue, sir!
> Who spares coal in kitchen an't you, sir!
> And neighbours complain it's no joke, sir,
> – You ought to consume your own smoke, sir!'

Browning's answer is to have the sweep-critics caught by his housemaid 'In bringing more filth into my house/Than ever you found there!'. The attack moves to individual reviewers of his work and once again to Austin, alias Banjo-Byron.

> While as for Quilp-Hop-o'-my-thumb there,
> Banjo-Byron that twangs the strum-strum there –

> He'll think, as the pickle he curses,
> I've discharged on his pate his own verses!

Harping on Austin's slight build, Browning even addresses himself in a verse footnote.

> No, please! For
>   'Who would be satirical
>   On a thing so very small?'

One does not need to sympathize much with Alfred Austin in order to see the major poem of this collection as a poetical and tactical mistake on Browning's part, its doggerel no better than the 'Pigsbrook' and 'Brothelsbank Flunkivall' insults which Swinburne and Furnivall were exchanging. It would have been far better for Browning to be content with his prose dismissal of Austin as a man who had been 'flea-biting me for many years in whatever rag of a newspaper he could hop into'.[17] The doggerel poem was precisely the kind of production which Mary Gladstone and others might have associated with the dinner table Browning of the loud voice and the heavy breath.

Nor were these obsessive literary hostilities confined to one poem of the collection. 'At the "Mermaid"', the second poem in the book, was ostensibly the voice of Shakespeare. In fact, it is a dismissal of Austin's claim to be 'next poet' after Tennyson, whom he was to succeed as Laureate. Austin's verse, in the words of the poem, is fit only to enter the belly and to be expelled from it by the usual route.

> Such song 'enters in the belly
>   And is cast out in the draught.'

It may seem surprising or significant that Browning in his fame was not merely content to ignore Alfred Austin. Of Austin's appointment as Poet Laureate, the Prime Minister, Lord Salisbury, could only remark: 'I don't think anybody else applied for the post.' The unfortunate poet was destined to live in popular legend as the author of lines on the illness of the Prince of Wales in 1870:

> Across the wires the electric message came,
> He is no better, he is much the same.

or, a quarter of a century later, on the Jameson Raid:

> They went across the veldt,
> As hard as they could pelt.

In the light of his own achievements, he scarcely needed Browning to delineate his weaknesses.[18]

Elsewhere in the collection there were other aspects of Browning in his sixties, reflected more or less clearly. 'St Martin's Summer', a poem of quiet intimacy in his best manner, may be read as a calmer reflection upon his attachment to Lady Ashburton. The poet warns his mistress that he can build only a bower for her, not a mansion. To him it is the past love which remains real and the present which glimmers like a ghost at twilight.

> Ay, dead loves are the potent!
> Like any cloud they used you,
> Mere semblance you, but substance they!

At one level the volume is a statement by Browning in his fame of the terms upon which he was prepared to live with the world. That world may be variously represented by Austin and his other critics, by Louisa Ashburton, or merely by the public which read his poetry and was intrigued by the strange romance of Browning and his dead wife. The limits of decorum in such curiosity were set by his poem 'House', with its famous warning to the world to keep its distance.

> A peep through my window, if folk prefer;
> But, please you, no foot over threshold of mine!

Twenty-one years earlier, in 'Love in a Life', Browning had used the same image of a house to open his love for Elizabeth to the world, describing the recent presence of a woman among the sofas and curtains of its rooms. Now the matter was very different, and he imagined only the gaping crowd who speculated upon the ruin of a house torn open by an earthquake.

> 'I doubt if he bathed before he dressed.
> A brazier? – the pagan, he burned perfumes!
> You see it is proved, what the neighbours guessed:
> His wife and himself had separate rooms.'

Was it possible that Browning in Warwick Crescent might be pestered as Tennyson had been at Farringford by the Isle of Wight's summer trippers? Unlike Tennyson, he was prepared to issue a warning to trespassers, delivering an absolute and memorable rebuff to readers and critics by means of denying Wordsworth's well-known lines on Shakespeare's sonnets.

> 'Hoity toity! A street to explore,
> Your home the exception! "*With this same key
> Shakespeare unlocked his heart*," once more!'
> Did Shakespeare? If so, the less Shakespeare he!

As time went by and public enthusiasm for his own poetry increased, Browning's attitude in the matter of his individual privacy underwent a certain change in that most sensitive area of all, the writing of Elizabeth's biography. Even in 1880 he still told John Ingram, who proposed to write such a book, that he would give no assistance whatever. In Browning's view, it was impossible that the work could be done properly, and if it were possible then it would be improper.[19] Yet within a few weeks of this he was compelled to acknowledge the continued popularity of her poetry and the increasing – and sympathetic – interest in her life.[20]

In 1877 he had agreed to the publication of Elizabeth's letters to Richard Hengist Horne on the grounds that the correspondence was on literary topics only and therefore as proper for publication as a volume of essays.[21] In all other matters concerning her papers his views were unaltered. However, by 1882 he was obliged to lend some assistance, if only to correct the inaccuracies that were appearing in print about Elizabeth and himself. He checked Richmond Ritchie's entry for Elizabeth in the *Dictionary of National Biography* while continuing to tell the unfortunate John Ingram to mind his own business.[22] It was three years later, when Browning was seventy-three and knew that all too soon the matter might be beyond his control, that he wrote to one of his greatest admirers, the founder of the Browning Society, F. J. Furnivall, 'by all means biographize about both of us'.[23] This time he offered, however vaguely, whatever assistance it might be in his power to render. Even so, he stopped short of making available to Furnivall any private correspondence.

Browning's attitude in these matters was not merely one of hypersensitivity over Elizabeth's memory or excessive self-protection. Frauds and opportunists thrived as easily in the 1870s and 1880s as at any other period. He may have heard the story of Charles Augustus Howell, known to Gosse by 1879. Howell, an Anglo-Portuguese adventurer, secretary to Ruskin and exhumer of Lizzie Rossetti, had prompted some sexually embarrassing correspondence from Swinburne. As a blackmailer, Howell began to give semi-public readings of these gems and then ensured that the Swinburne family had to buy back the letters for a considerable sum.

Browning's enemy in these matters was Thomas Powell, whom he learnt too late was both a forger and a thief. Powell had long since tried to elicit copies of the childhood poems from Browning's father. He then called on Browning, borrowed his rare first edition of *Adonais*, published at Pisa, and sold it. According to Browning it was only his employers' refusal to prosecute which saved Powell from prison for forging their authority. He was given to signing letters with the names of Dickens and Thackeray, as well as Browning, and had published falsehoods about Elizabeth. With the example of Swinburne before him, Browning could guess easily enough what might happen if he ever surrendered his own private correspondence with Elizabeth and if a rogue like Powell should lay hands upon it.

After his own time the fate of the letters would matter less, and there were signs that such time might be growing short. To Domett and others Browning boasted that he had not suffered from one of his crippling headaches for years. Until his late sixties his health remained vigorous and there was no sign of the weakness that would sooner or later kill him. Only the London winters towards the end of the 1870s began to take their toll. Coughs and colds and bronchitis of increasing severity plagued him. It would of course have been possible to escape the fogs and cold by travelling to southern Europe. Yet that would have deprived him of the London season, its dinners, recitals and exhibitions, as well as the only arena in which he could release his pent-up energy. There was, moreover, the problem of Pen, or rather of Pen's paintings. It was Browning who acted almost as his son's agent, cajoling the London art galleries, sweetening influential friends, and rebuking insensitive critics.

The consequence of this was seen, for example, in the mid-winter of 1880–81. On 29 December 1880 he attended George Eliot's funeral, the long procession to Highgate Cemetery, where, as he told Mrs Fitzgerald, he stood bareheaded in wind and rain and caught a heavy cold.[24] In similar conditions he went to a wedding next day and thereafter dragged himself to the dinners where he was engaged, talking and sneezing alternately. By the middle of January he was cancelling dinner appointments, despite the deprivation, unable to face the shortest journey in such winter weather.[25] It was reminiscent of the condition in which Elizabeth had been during the 1850s.

If he seemed to have grown old in his mind, it was only because he showed a determined self-centredness and a genially absent-minded attitude. This quality of vagueness was noticed in his private prose, to the extent that he could make an appointment by telegram 'from which it was absolutely impossible to gather where the appointment was, or when it was, or what was its object'.[26] In 1879 Alfred Domett was present at one of Pen's exhibitions in Queen's Gardens, where Browning was handing in 'a rather finely dressed lady', treating her with more flattery and consideration than the other guests as a stranger who had honoured his son's work. She was recognized, though not for some time by Browning, as his own cook.[27]

His life in London assumed the regularity of an old man's, though it was diversified by the summer and autumn visits to friends in England and abroad. William Grove, his servant, described the daily and weekly routine soon after Browning's death. He would get up at seven, read for an hour in his room, bath at eight and take breakfast at nine. After reading *The Times* and the *Daily News*, he worked in his study from ten until a light lunch at one. The afternoons were spent in visiting friends or art galleries. He returned home by six to dress for dinner. Frequently he dined out and would return in time to go to bed by about half-past twelve. Certain days were customarily set apart for specific visits. On Tuesday and Friday afternoons he would call upon Alexandra Orr – Mrs Sutherland Orr, his future biographer. On Sundays he visited Mrs Thomas Fitzgerald, an accomplished linguist and one of his correspondents, who lived in Portland Place. On Monday evenings he generally dined with A. P. Stanley, the Dean of Westminster. Saturdays were devoted to his visit to the Athenaeum Club, where he read the weekly papers.[28]

In his private life, so far as it involved others, his greatest continuing concern was for the future of Pen. This would have been natural enough in any event. As it happened, Browning had more reason for it than most parents.

Soon after Pen's removal from Oxford in 1870, Browning had summed the matter up by telling Isa Blagden that, though his son was not cold-bloodedly selfish and though he had ability, his failure to apply that ability had become a source of despair.[29] After 1874, when Pen had been dispatched to study under Heyermans, the despair began to lift. If the young Browning had a talent for anything, apart from billiards and shooting, it was for art. His paintings and sculptures began to appear in the more modest galleries of Brussels and Paris. There was nothing very novel about them. They were pleasing, rather bland portrayals of figures and scenes, precisely the type of art against which the great rebellion was gathering.

In London, Browning organized annual exhibitions of his son's work, borrowing the premises and services of his publisher, George Smith, for the purpose. By the end of the 1870s the paintings were being exhibited more widely in London and in Paris, where Pen was by now able to describe himself as a pupil of Rodin. In the winter of 1880–81 Pen's work was shown at the Hanover Gallery in New Bond Street, and later still at the Grosvenor Gallery whose reputation stood high in the world of Victorian painting. The critics were not greatly impressed. Of Pen's Inquisition painting *Delivery to the Secular Arm*, *The Times* of 20 November 1880 remarked that 'we discover no merit of any kind in the picture except a somewhat careful and level execution of the technical portion of the painting'. It was, in brief, uninspired by anything much greater than a father's determination to make the best of his son.

Being who he was, Pen found it rather easier to sell his paintings than to please his critics. A good many of them were bought by an American widow, Mrs Bloomfield-Moore, as a gesture of gratitude for the poetry of Elizabeth Barrett Browning and as a gesture of hope towards Browning himself. 'Don't be a fool – take it,' said Browning as Pen hesitated over payment for an early work.[30]

In the prolonged absences of Pen, who pursued his studies in Europe, Browning was consoled in part by his succession of pets. To the wounded owl and other companions of his working hours he had, at length, added geese which lived in the back garden of Warwick Crescent. Alfred Domett, visiting the house one day, was alarmed by the raucous screeching which came from the garden but was at once reassured by his host with the indulgence of one who saw nothing odd in his attachment to this brood. 'They are such affectionate creatures,' said Browning mildly, fondly viewing the four screeching birds, 'and I am sure it is not for what one gives them.'[31]

Such glimpses of Browning were misleading because they gave him the appearance and reputation of a 'character', that exhausted cliché of the English eccentric rivalling the no less tired image of the poetic eccentric. The truth was that even in his attitude towards animals Browning's apparent oddity concealed firm logic and clear-headed morality. He had taken up a cause which, to most people then and since, appears too disturbing to be admitted to prolonged consideration. That respect for the natural world which he had learnt from his mother's example and his repugnance to cruelty in fact – as opposed to fantasy – made the cause of anti-vivisection irresistible to him. He lobbied the members of parliament for St Marylebone on the subject and became vice-president of the Victoria Street Society for the Protection of Animals, an office he held until the end of his life. In 1875 he had already given his support to a memorial to the Royal Society for the Prevention of Cruelty to Animals seeking the banning of vivisection. 'I would rather submit to the worst of deaths,' he wrote, 'so far as pain goes, than have a single dog or cat tortured on the pretence of sparing me a twinge or two.'[32]

Because Browning can so easily be seen as a public figure of noisy and comic vanity in his later years, the self-important 'tiger' of the dinner table with pomaded hair and dazzling waistcoat, the simple nobility which characterized his private conduct is too easily missed. In his poetry too he attacked the vivisectionists, the despoilers of the animal kingdom. During the months before his death he delivered a final retort to contemporary self-righteousness in 'The Lady and the Painter'. Lady Blanche accuses the painter of degrading and exploiting womanhood by his use of nude models. The painter, ignoring this, asks Lady Blanche to describe the fashionable hat she wears.

> Ah, do they please you? Wild-bird-wings
> Next season, – Paris-prints assert, –
> We must go feathered to the skirt:
> My modiste keeps on the alert.
> Owls, hawks, jays – swallows most approve.

The way is open for the painter to point out that Lady Blanche would degrade herself less by going naked, gratefully admired in the beauty which God gave her. In her present garb it is she, not the nude model, who presents the greater obscenity of exploitation:

> You – clothed with murder of His best
> Of harmless beings.

However important to Browning his support for anti-vivisectionism, it was merely one portent of an attitude and belief which had been constant and consistent in his character since childhood.

As the *Pacchiarotto* volume of 1876 had been largely the poetry of public controversy, so in 1878 the poetry of private friendship and conviction appeared in *La Saisiaz and The Two Poets of Croisic*. Between these two books Browning had published only his translation of the *Agamemnon* of Aeschylus in 1877.

The occasion of 'La Saisiaz', the major poem of the later volume, was the sudden death of Annie Egerton Smith, the companion of Browning and Sarianna during their holidays in Normandy and the partner in Browning's love of music who accompanied him during the London season to hear Liszt, Joachim, Rubinstein and Clara Schumann.

In September 1877 the Brownings and Miss Egerton Smith chose a new venue for their holiday, the villa of La Saisiaz at the foot of Mt Salève, a few miles from Geneva. From this villa on 14 September Browning went out early to bathe in a nearby pool. He returned towards the villa in the perfect stillness of a beautiful morning, looking for Annie

Egerton Smith on the terrace and seeing Switzerland through the eyes of a Victorian traveller.

> No, the terrace showed no figure, tall, white, leaning through
>   the wreathes,
> Tangle-twine of leaf and bloom that intercept the air one breathes,
> Interpose between one's love and Nature's loving, hill and dale
> Down to where the blue lake's wrinkle marks the river's inrush pale
> – Mazy Arve: whereon no vessel but goes sliding white and plain,
> Not a steamboat pants from harbour but one hears pulsate amain.

It was Sarianna who, as the curtains of Miss Egerton Smith's room remained closed, went in and found their friend lying face down on the floor. As Browning came to her assistance, Sarianna put her arm around Miss Egerton Smith and said anxiously, 'Are you ill, dear?' She saw that her friend was already unconscious. A doctor arrived from Geneva three hours later. By then, Annie Egerton Smith was dead.

The shock of Miss Egerton Smith's death, his own ordeal of trying in vain to revive her during the terrible hours before the doctor's arrival, surely woke echoes in Browning's mind of those other deaths at which he had been the principal witness, Elizabeth's and her sister Arabel's. A few days later he went alone up Mt Salève, following the path which he and his friend would have taken. From that experience he developed a major poem, 'La Saisiaz', written during the next two months. Addressed to Annie Egerton Smith, its theme was the last full-scale discussion of religion and immortality by Browning, summed up in a single line: 'Does the soul survive the body? Is there God's self, no or yes?' It was a debate which began in his poems with *Christmas-Eve and Easter-Day* twenty-seven years earlier, and which had been continued by voices as varied as those of Cleon and Karshish, Bishop Blougram and Mr Sludge, Caliban and the admirer of Galuppi.

Browning's poem certainly followed in the wake of articles by Frederic Harrison and a symposium among eminent believers and doubters, which appeared in the *Nineteenth Century* between June and September 1877 on the subject of *The Soul and Future Life*. He and Miss Egerton Smith had both read these contributions. 'La Saisiaz' itself is a symposium to the extent that the possibilities of the soul's extinction and of God's non-existence are considered. The problem of suffering is presented, the thought 'Of the serpent pains which herald, swarming in, the dragon death'. Human love too must be measured against the doubt of immortality. 'Can we love but on condition, that the thing we love must die?'

To Browning, though he puts the opposing arguments, such questions are only answerable by the presumption of a future life. Rallying to the standard of belief, he embodies in his poem that sublime quotation from Dante which he had written in Elizabeth's Testament after her death.

> Is it fact to which I cleave,
> Is it fancy I but cherish, when I take upon my lips
> Phrase the solemn Tuscan fashioned, and declare the soul's eclipse
> Not the soul's extinction? take his 'I believe and I declare –
> Certain am I – from this life I pass into a better, there
> Where that lady lives of whom enamoured was my soul' – where this
> Other lady, my companion clear and true, she also is?

In its lament for a lost friend, its balancing of faith and doubt, 'La Saisiaz' has an obvious parallel in Browning's work with *In Memoriam* in Tennyson's. While it is not the equal of *In Memoriam*, it shows as clearly as any comparison could the distinction between the two most celebrated poets of their age. 'This haunting wail of fear and loneliness', in Harold Nicolson's memorable description of *In Memoriam*, is not reflected in the poetry of Browning.[33] The emotional climax of *In Memoriam* is the prayer to God and Arthur Hallam, 'crying in agony across the grave', as Nicolson describes it, in Section 50: 'Be near me when my light is low.'[34] The climax of 'La Saisiaz' is one of assertion and nobility, the clarion call of Dante issued through Browning's breath. So ringing, indeed, is the nobility of the tone that the reader may feel he would rather be wrong with Browning than right with his antagonists.

'La Saisiaz' concludes, of course, that immortality and the nature of God are beyond human comprehension. Human reason, historical analysis of biblical texts prove nothing, one way or the other. How, then, does Browning believe? The answer in 1877 was the same as it had been half a century before. In the tradition of Nonconformist experience, God was not revealed by dogma or rationality but by revelation to the individual soul. By that divine illumination were the biblical narratives to be read and the arts of reason exercised. So, like a figure of Faithful or Great-Heart from the Bunyan of his childhood, Browning bears witness before the industrial society of the later nineteenth century, where 'Mid the millions stands the unit'. The argument ends with a description of Browning, lightly cloaked as Voltaire for purposes of modesty.

> He there with the brand flamboyant, broad o'er night's forlorn abyss,
> Crowned by prose and verse; and wielding, with Wit's bauble,
>   Learning's rod . . .
> Well? Why, he at least believed in Soul, was very sure of God.

Ever since his departure from Florence in 1861, the image of Italy had haunted Browning's thoughts. At first, in the 1860s, he wrote to Isa Blagden and the Storys of his longing to return, as if only the problem of Pen's education prevented him from doing so. During the long composition of *The Ring and the Book* he travelled far enough south in Europe to have gone by an equivalent distance to the splendid towns of northern Italy. At La Saisiaz in 1877 he was close enough to have made the journey, but the holiday was cut short by the death of Annie Egerton Smith.

There was, of course, a perpetual ambivalence in Browning's attitude towards the past, most of all towards his life with Elizabeth. To Isa Blagden in May 1867 he had written that he remembered the pain of it, and would not choose to live a day of it again. Yet, like the Greeks of Homer's poetry whose entire lives had been at Troy, it was the years with Elizabeth which still seemed to him his whole existence.[35]

Nowhere was such ambivalence more evident than in the recurring dream which Browning reported to William Allingham. In this he would see himself travelling, accompanied by a friend. They would pass a town on a hillside and Browning would recognize it as Asolo, the symbol of his youthful experience of Italy and the inspiration behind *Pippa Passes* and the final version of *Sordello*. Browning would beg the friend to stop so that he might once again visit the scene of so much remembered happiness. Always the friend refused. It would not require a great feat of interpretation to see the friend as Browning's *alter ego* and the town as symbolizing both Asolo and Florence.

In the summer of 1878, however, Browning and Sarianna set out for Italy, which he had not seen for seventeen years and which she had never seen at all. The truth was that he had become bored with summer visits to 'some more or less uninteresting northern spot'.[36] Indeed, it was only when he saw Italy and Venice again that he fully realized just how bored he had been. With Sarianna, he paused on the Splügen, looking down into Italy and waiting for the heat of August to subside. Browning passed the time by working on his new collection of poems, *Dramatic Idylls*. Then at last they came down to Lake Como and Lombardy. Asolo, after so much anticipation, proved a disappointment. It was Venice which stood in all the desolate splendour of Browning's memory and imagination of it.

In all but three of the remaining years of his life he made the journey to Italy, and in all but one of those years his destination was Venice. There was no attempt to go as far as Florence or to visit again the scenes of his life with Elizabeth. Whatever hope he shared with Dante of heavenly reunion, he showed no inclination to revive such memories on earth.

From the first, Venice was agreeable. The Brownings were accommodated in the Albergo Dell' Universo on the Grand Canal, near the Accademia. It was less a hotel than an exclusive *pensione* kept by a lady of noble birth in reduced circumstances. Browning could remain shielded from those admirers whom he had no wish to see while enjoying the society of those whom he found agreeable.

As the mellow Venetian autumns passed, the chief among these new worshippers was Katherine de Kay Bronson, a natural American aristocrat who lived with a beautiful daughter, Edith, at Casa Alvisi opposite Santa Maria della Salute on the mouth of the Grand Canal. She held court there on the splendid balcony, with its crimson cushions and cigarettes, above the lamplit Venetian waters. It was natural, even inevitable, that Browning should become one of her courtiers. Among the others was the young Henry James, who left in print his affectionate recollections of her and sketched her portrait lightly as Mrs Prest in *The Aspern Papers*.

Mrs Arthur Bronson, as she was known, and her daughter became Browning's 'two beloveds', as he termed them, the collective successors to Isa Blagden and Louisa Ashburton. Katherine Bronson had exchanged the well-bred waterside calm of Newport, Rhode Island, in her youth for the more flamboyant and exciting society of waterside Venice in her maturity. It seemed her blue eyes and chestnut hair betrayed a soft, mild kindliness. She was certainly generous, to the extent of providing a home for the Brownings in the Palazzo Giustiniani-Recanati adjoining the Casa Alvisi.

Browning was used to gifts from women by this time. Mrs Bronson offered him a grand piano, Mrs Skirrow sent him stationery, Mrs Benzon presented him with railway stock worth £1,860. He was well trained in the matter of accepting such tokens of esteem graciously. The Venetian palazzo was another matter, however, and suggested possibilities of a quite different kind. He accepted the offer readily and for specific purposes. The time would come when Pen must need a home and a studio. Where more agreeable than among the glories of Venice? Browning himself was increasingly troubled by the bronchial ordeal which London winters represented. Moreover, the lease of 19 Warwick Crescent would soon have run its twenty-five years. Why not a refuge in the warmer climate of southern Europe where a part of the year, at least, might be spent?

If Italy was in any sense his home, Browning in 1879 had not come home to die, appearances to the contrary. The plans which he made were for himself as much as for his family. He was yet to publish six more volumes of poetry, one of which showed an intellectual vigour and originality which suggested a man in the ascent of his powers rather than a poet approaching the end of his seventies. The greatest celebration of fame in his lifetime still lay before him. In every respect, it seemed, he had come back to Italy with his gaze firmly upon life rather than death.

16
'Never Say of Me That I Am Dead!'

Whatever pathos attached itself to Browning's marked physical decline in the 1880s was enlivened, however incongruously, by the tones of farce so apt to creep into the loud celebration of public fame.

Among Browning's admirers in 1881 was a lady in early middle age, Miss Emily Hickey, a friend of the learned and pugnacious F. J. Furnivall. During that summer she expressed to Furnivall such admiration for Browning's works – greater to her than Shakespeare's – that he asked if she would assist in founding a Browning Society in the poet's honour. Not only was Miss Hickey willing to collaborate, she claimed to have had the idea first and to have suggested it in a letter to Furnivall, which she then forgot to post.

On 3 July 1881 the two enthusiasts went to see Browning. Perhaps surprisingly, he offered little opposition. There was, of course, a 'Shakespere' Society of which he was president and the Wordsworth Society of which he was a member, even a Shelley Society. Yet for a living poet to be honoured in this manner was likely to promote sceptical questioning and a good deal of open amusement. He remained ambivalent, allowing the project to proceed while remaining dissociated from it. To Furnivall he even refused the names and addresses of friends who might assist in promoting the Society.[1]

Furnivall, with the experience of the Early English Text Society, the Chaucer Society and the Shakespere Society to build upon, was undaunted. To those who complained that it was '300 years too early for a Browning Society' he replied with total conviction: 'Browning is the manliest, the strongest, the life-fullest, the deepest, the thoughtfulest living poet, the one most needing earnest study, and the one most worthy of it.'[2] Such estimates, emphasizing the manly strength and 'life-fullest' qualities, were of a kind to do Browning's poetry a true disservice, opening the way to ripostes – equally limited – like that by

F. R. Leavis: 'Browning would have been less robust if he had been more sensitive and intelligent.'[3]

While Browning waited in the wings, his supporters came upon the public stage. They were a gratifyingly large number. Three hundred attended an inaugural meeting in the Botanic Theatre of University College, London, on 28 October 1881. Furnivall became chairman of the committee and Miss Hickey the honorary secretary. The enthusiasm for Browning Societies spread until by 1884 there were twenty-two of them across the world, dedicated to the reading, discussion and elucidation of his poetry.

The scope for hilarity among those who, whatever their admiration for Browning, found the societies ridiculous appeared infinite. Comic verse attributed a satisfied conceit to Browning himself – 'There's a ME Society at Cambridge....' – and Max Beerbohm's cartoon, 'Browning taking tea with the Browning Society', showed him seated smugly among earnest young men and intense maiden ladies. Augustine Birrell remarked that 'a company has been recently floated, or a society established, having Mr Browning for its principal object. It has a president, two secretaries, male and female, and a treasurer. You pay a guinea, and you become a member. A suitable reduction is, I believe, made in the unlikely event of all the members of one family flocking to be enrolled.'[4]

Browning did not attend the Society's meetings. He refused to have any direct part in it, though acknowledging the good it had done him. For the rest he was content to leave its conduct to Furnivall and his associates. These included the young bibliophile and forger T. J. Wise, the yet unheralded Bernard Shaw – and the laconic Augustine Birrell. Among his own friends Domett and Milsand were members but Jowett refused.

Within a year of the Society's foundation, Browning's first reservations gave way to feelings of gratitude for the manner in which his supporters had taken up his cause against the hostility of professional critics. To Mrs Fitzgerald he wrote in July 1882 of the Society's members: 'They give their time for nothing, offer their little entertainment for nothing, and certainly get next to nothing in the way of thanks – unless from myself who feel grateful to the faces I shall never see, the voices I shall never hear. The kindest notices I have had, at all events those that have given me most pleasure, have been educed by this Society.'[5]

The Browning Society was not content merely to print and circulate its discussions of the poetry. With the accession of T. J. Wise to membership in 1882 the question was raised of reprinting some of Browning's neglected work in the manner in which the Shelley Society, under the aegis of Wise and Buxton Forman, printed facsimiles of the poet's rarest editions. Only half a century later was it proved that access to the materials for skilful facsimile reproduction also constituted access to the means of forgery.

In addition, the Society put on 'entertainments' in which such dramatic poems as 'In a Balcony' were performed, and productions of Browning's plays. In 1885 *Colombe's Birthday* was staged at the St George's Hall with Alma Murray in the title role. In the following year there was a revival of *Strafford* at the Strand Theatre on 21 December, and it seemed that the Society had established the appeal of Browning's drama for a small, poetically enthusiastic public. *A Blot in the 'Scutcheon* was revived in 1888 with Alma Murray playing Mildred, and she was also proposed for a production of Browning's least successful drama, *The Return of the Druses*. Plans were made to produce this in 1889 but the play was not staged.

Browning's death in 1889, the lack of dramatic power in the play, and the sheer expense of the production might have led to the Society abandoning its plan. There was, however, a further difficulty which stemmed from the character of Furnivall. To his scholarly enthusiasms for other men's work, his belief in exercise and cold showers which accompanied a missionary confidence in the education of the working man by literary excellence, he added a degree of cantankerousness which was rarely justified by its effect upon his adversaries. Far from being awed by it, they retorted with a vindictiveness to equal his own.

When *Strafford* was produced in 1886, the title role was played by L. S. Outram, while Alma Murray was engaged to play the female lead as Lady Carlisle. Admission to the performance was free but Outram was to be paid £60 by the Society and was to receive any further sums raised by subscription. He thereupon appealed to the members of the Society to subscribe to this fund from which he was to benefit. Furnivall's name, without his sanction, was used to support this appeal. Furious at this, Furnivall wrote to members of the Society, warning them of Outram's 'scandalous attempt to get money' by this duplicity. Alma Murray was persuaded by Furnivall not to act for Outram's benefit.

The consequence was that Outram sued Furnivall for libel and in February 1888 the affairs of the Browning Society were duly paraded in court, to the mortification of its members and the amusement of those who had always regarded the Society as self-parodying. Furnivall, under cross-examination, maintained that Outram was morally if not legally guilty of an 'attempt to hoodwink the members of the Society'. This intransigence won favour neither with judge nor jurors. The jury found for Outram and judgement of £100 damages with costs was given against the chairman of the Browning Society's committee.[6]

Though this particular storm blew over, other similar clouds of scandal had gathered about Furnivall's head. There was the Pigsbrook-Brothelsbank slanging match with Swinburne, the expulsion of recalcitrant members from the New Shakespere Society, and such parting shots as Furnivall's to the Duke of Devonshire: 'I am glad to be rid of you.' Apart from all this, the Browning Society and its offshoots were a vogue which had prospered too easily. Soon after the poet's death it was to become clear that such enthusiasm was not to be sustained. In 1891 it was agreed to make the forthcoming year the last of the Society's activity and it was duly wound up. Yet, as Browning himself had believed, it had served its purpose. The manifest enthusiasm of so many men and women for his work answered the prejudice and spite of reviewers, as he saw it. In the 1860s and 1870s his admission to 'gilded saloons' and fashionable society had rebuffed the cavillers. Now, in the more democratic 1880s, the ordinary reading public of England were to give the critics their answer.

The great public honours of the kind received by Tennyson were not given to Browning. In any case, the Laureateship was not vacant in his lifetime, and he was not to be raised to the peerage as Tennyson was in 1884. Perhaps the price of such favours was too high, since he had sworn never to wear livery or take wages as Tennyson had done. In 1886 he accepted an appointment as foreign correspondent of the Royal Academy on the death of his friend Monckton Milnes, now Baron Houghton. It was an agreeable compliment by men with whom he had long associated and in whose company he felt at home.

Fame brought him disagreeable chores. Writing letters became such a burden that he complained of being exhausted by daily correspondence before he had even started upon his poetry. In his celebrity, the letters and the manuscripts of the past became a burden of another kind. After his death there could be little doubt that his early unpublished verses would be sought out and published. Letters written by him and to him would be hunted out and printed likewise. One day in 1884 T. J. Wise and Furnivall called upon him in Warwick Crescent. Browning was busy at the fire in the front room. He had brought down from the attic an old leather trunk of his father's which was crammed with letters and manuscripts. These were being thrown by handfuls into the flames. Wise, the great collector, watched in horror and fascination as he glimpsed some of the material which was being delivered to destruction. The correspondence between Browning and Carlyle – the greater part of it – was burnt while he watched, and the last pages of Browning's childhood manuscript 'Incondita'. One collection was spared, the letters in the inlaid box, exchanged between Browning and Elizabeth in 1845–6. 'There they are,' said Browning to his son, according to Pen's prefatory note to the first edition of 1899. 'Do with them as you please when I am gone.'

It was easy enough to regard the Browning Society as a ludicrous vanity on the part of worshippers and idol alike. In the great romantic tradition it was the poet unacknowledged during his life who won the immortal laurels, while the bard fêted by his contemporaries went the way of such gods of the 1830s as James Montgomery and 'L.E.L.'

Yet this was a false judgement, in part at least. The existence of the Society was evidence of the continued power and innovation which his readers found in Browning during his seventies. He was not again to reach the heights of *Men and Women* or *The Ring and the Book*. Yet in each of the six books published in his final decade there was something to show that the old fire of his poetry might still flare again. Tennyson too worked until the end, but there was nothing in Tennyson's final years to match the unpredictability and novelty of his great rival. True, a good deal of Browning's later poetry consisted of verse tales – many of them macabre in subject. Nevertheless, when he was seventy-one he published a love poem in *Jocoseria* which was as haunting in its simplicity as anything in his earlier work of this sort:

> Never the time and the place
>   And the loved one all together!
> This path – how soft to pace!
>   This May – what magic weather!
> Where is the loved one's face?

At seventy-five he published *Parleyings with Certain People of Importance in Their Day*. It was a poem in nine sections, longer than any of his major works of the 1860s and 1870s except for *The Ring and the Book*. In intellectual scope it had more in common with the longer poems of T.S. Eliot or W.H. Auden than with his own contemporaries. Even in *Asolando*, upon which he was still working in the autumn of his death, poems like the series 'Bad Dreams' or the childhood recollections of 'Development' were memorable revelations of a private world.

With the air of one who was indeed not a literary man – at least not any longer – he either drew a veil across his later literary activity or pretended that he had turned his back upon it. His letters were full of daily trivia, and his friend Domett found that Browning was more interested in questioning him upon poetry which he might be writing than discussing any plans of his own. At that time he was working upon *Parleyings*.

Much of what Browning published in his last decade looked to the past, perhaps most profitably to his distant past. The very titles of his two series of *Dramatic Idylls* in 1879 and 1880 suggested a resumption of a style and form not fully displayed since *Dramatis Personae* in 1864. This was not the case. The two collections relied heavily on his versifying of stories from history and from his own reading. Sudden death, murder, judicial execution made their appearance with some predictability in such pieces.

Drawing on his own memories of Russia in 'Iàn Iànovitch', Browning tells a gruesome story of the woman who threw her three children, one by one, to the pursuing wolves in order to save herself. 'Ned Bratts', which Browning confessed was based upon the story of Old Tod in Bunyan's *Life and Death of Mr Badman* (1680), told a story that was bizarre rather than melodramatic. Ned Bratts, a publican fresh from a religious conversion, comes into court during Bedford Assizes and begs to be executed for his sins.

The poem depicts the scene with precision and economy, the hot market town during a 'broiling blasting June', the fun of seeing malefactors condemned and punished, 'things at jolly high-tide, amusement steeped in fire'. The Puritans are brought to judgement:

> And ten were prescribed the whip, and ten a brand on the cheek,
> And five a slit of the nose – just leaving enough to tweak.

Upon this assembly bursts Ned Bratts, full of the terror of divine revelation from reading *Pilgrim's Progress*, and urging his hearers to ''scape the wrath in time', as destruction descends upon Bedford Town. Only if he is hanged before Satan can convince him of his folly will there be salvation for Ned Bratts and his woman, Tab.

> Sentence our guilty selves: so, hang us out of hand!
> Make haste for pity's sake! A single moment's loss
> Means – Satan's lord once more: his whisper shoots across
> All singing in my heart, all praying in my brain,
> 'It comes of heat and beer!'

He is seconded by the woman, 'While Tab, alongside, wheezed a hoarse "Do hang us, please!" '

The poem's fascination lies partly in Browning's skill in presenting the ecstasy of martyrdom through the figures of a loutish publican and his drab. More chillingly it suggests by anticipation the psychology of the willing confession to be heard from political opponents in the totalitarian courts of the twentieth century.

At the other extreme, in the second volume of *Dramatic Idylls*, 'Pan and Luna' is an erotic meditation on the first eclipse of the moon, as suggested by Virgil. Luna, the naked moon goddess, takes refuge in a cloud at the top of a pine tree. There she becomes a girl, a 'naked Moon, full-orbed', who is caught and possessed 'By rough red Pan, the god of all that tract'.

Jocoseria, published in 1883, is interesting chiefly for its love poetry in 'Never the Time and the Place', whose lines seem obviously addressed to the spirit of Elizabeth. It is not simply a young man's plea of sexual passion written by an old man. The lines are a dimly lit evocation.

> In a dream that loved one's face meets mine,
>   But the house is narrow, the place is bleak.

By the end of the poem, indeed, the beloved is surely separated from the speaker by death rather than by distance.

> Thro' the magic of May to herself indeed!
> Or narrow if needs the house must be,
> Outside are the storms and strangers: we –
> O, close, safe, warm sleep I and she,
> – I and she!

The images suggest a more sombre seclusion than the erotic games of the two snowbound lovers almost thirty years earlier in 'A Lover's Quarrel'. While the poem may be read as a pledge of faith in his ultimate reunion with Elizabeth, there is an acceptance that they may only lie together in the grave, the narrow and dark house where neither storms nor strangers will disturb them.

Ferishtah's Fancies, published in 1884, was the least successful of the later volumes, Browning the philosopher in Eastern guise. There were good grounds for Norman MacColl's judgement in the *Athenaeum* on 6 December 1884: 'If the pessimism of the present day is to be confronted and answered, it is not by such optimism as this.' The contents might well have suggested the final decline of Browning's genius. Certainly there was little in it to prepare his readers for the weight and argument which appeared, after a silence of more then two years, with the publication of *Parleyings with Certain People of Importance in Their Day* in January 1887.

After a prologue, 'Apollo and the Fates', which reads as if it were part poem and part choreography, Browning chose to parley with seven men of the past: Bernard de Mandeville, author of *The Fable of the Bees: or, Private Vices, Public Benefits* (1714); Daniel Bartoli, a seventeenth-century Jesuit historian; the poet Christopher Smart; George Bubb Doddington, the Whig politician; Francis Furini, a seventeenth-century Florentine painter opposed to the nude in art; Gerard de Lairesse, the blind author of *The Art of Painting*; and Charles Avison, a composer of the eighteenth century. The epilogue, 'Fust and his Friends', is an account of Johann Fust, the partner of Gutenberg, whose contribution to the 'magic' of printing led the monks who visited him to suppose that he had made a compact with the devil, that Fust was really Faust and that Helen of Troy was his mistress.

The parleying 'With Bernard de Mandeville' is less about Mandeville's own philosophy – 'Private Vices, Public Benefits' – than an account of Browning's own conception of the roles of good and evil in the universe. He first read *The Fable of the Bees* when he was twenty, a copy given him by his father. Mandeville's argument that vices are necessary to the economic well-being of society, that evil is as necessary in the world as good, left Browning undismayed. Whether evil was necessary or not, his own poetry suggested the difficulty that the world had in managing without it. To Mandeville's claim that God was nowhere to be seen in human affairs, Browning opposes his argument from 'La Saisiaz', the impossibility of finite comprehension of the infinite. Life is a balance of good and evil as warmth is a compromise between the extremes of heat and cold. To that extent, Browning's poem stands Mandeville's theory on its head and comes to Pope's optimistic conclusion: 'All partial evil, universal good.'

The parleying 'With Daniel Bartoli' is no more than a verse tale, but in the case of Christopher Smart the subject held a double fascination: Smart's ecstatic, rhetorical religious poetry and his madness. To Browning, Smart's poetry appears as a house, some of its rooms decently ordered, its chapel splendid with the beauty of the *Song to David*, then chaos and dereliction. That dereliction was presumably represented by *Jubilate Agno*, so obviously the work of a lunatic that its magnificent prophetic cadences remained unpublished until 1939, more than a century and a half after Smart's death.

279

The nature of Smart's madness intrigued Browning. Was it the ebullience of some poetic force, long suppressed, which broke out in this way, a divine possession as Apollo had possessed the Sibyls of the ancient world? Or were the doctors to be believed in diagnosing the poetic outbursts as merely a physical disorder of the brain?

> No matter if the marvel came to pass
> The way folk judged – if power too long suppressed
> Broke loose and maddened, as the vulgar guessed,
> Or simply brain-disorder (doctors said),
> A turmoil of the particles disturbed
> Brain's workaday performance in your head,
> Spurred spirit to wild action health had curbed.

Only in divine madness, Browning concluded, was Smart's genius set free. What followed?

> Why, what Smart did write – never afterward
> One line to show that he, who paced the sward,
> Had reached the zenith from his madhouse cell.

It was more than half a century earlier that Browning's first 'Madhouse Cells' had appeared in the *Monthly Repository*, and fifty-two years since he had first referred to the enigma of Christopher Smart in *Paracelsus*. Like his preoccupation with crime and cruelty, his interest in the world of lunacy was still not exhausted. As a rule he allowed the voices and sympathies of the criminal or the madman to come directly to the reader. The only difference in *Parleyings* was that he spoke on Smart's behalf in his own voice.

Bubb Doddington, the fourth of his 'people', seemed an unlikely partner for Browning. He clearly regarded Doddington, for all his wit and flair, as both a fool and a knave. Doddington, as depicted by Browning, even despises himself. The truth was, as Browning told Alexandra Orr, that he merely used the mask of Doddington in order to portray his contempt for the cynical opportunism of Disraeli, the true subject of the poem.

The choice of Francis Furini for the fifth parleying was dictated by a controversy over the nude in painting which was a match for Furini's own time. Furini had been a skilful and famous painter of the nude who, on his death-bed, expressed a wish that all such examples of his painting should be destroyed. By the 1880s it was Pen Browning who was having problems in the same sphere. Opposition to the nude, including Pen's paintings, had been voiced by John Horsley, treasurer of the Royal Academy, and the criticism gathered strength. Even Browning's admirer Edward Berdoe, who produced *The Browning Cyclopaedia* in 1891, took issue with him over his celebration of the female nude.

> Mr Browning deals very severely with those who think that pictures of the nude have a deleterious influence on the public character, and who endeavour to prevent their exhibition. It is instructive, however, to notice the fact that the Paris police are adopting even severer measures than our own against shopkeepers and others who exhibit pictures of the nude. Where the governing bodies of the two greatest cities of the world take the same view of this serious moral question, we must take leave to hold that if 'the gospel of art' has no better means whereby to elevate the race than those of familiarising our youth of both sexes with –
>
> 'The dear
> Fleshly perfection of the human shape,'
>
> we can very well afford to dispense with it. 'Omnia non omnibus,' concludes the poet. What is perfectly innocent for the artist is not expedient for the general public, just as the dissecting room, though an excellent school for doctors, is not a suitable place for the people in the street below.[7]

The commentary is instructive if only to show the width of the gulf between Browning's true Puritanism – its absolute faith, political liberalism, reverence for knowledge and beauty – and the mere prudery which regarded nudity as comparable to pathology. Browning's own view is summarized in the poem when he hopes that the dying Furini – reports to the contrary – actually gave thanks to God for

> That marvel which we dream the firmament
> Copies in star-device when fancies stray
> Outlining, orb by orb, Andromeda –
> God's best of beauteous and magnificent
> Revealed to earth – the naked female form.

Towards the end of the poem Furini is allowed to address a word to the Darwinians of the Victorian period. He recognized, long before them, that nature was in flux and therefore sought to capture beauty in his paintings. The value of the Darwinian hypothesis, as Browning makes Furini describe it, is to direct men's eyes towards higher things, the absolute values of art and religion.

> Only by looking low, ere looking high,
> Comes penetration of the mystery.

In his parleying 'With Gerard de Lairesse' Browning indulges an old affection for the *Treatise on the Art of Painting* which had transformed the woods and fields of childhood into landscapes of Ovidian romance and legend:

> 'twas a boy that budged
> No foot's breadth from your visioned steps away
> The while that memorable 'Walk' he trudged
> In your companionship.

This world of fantasy imposed upon reality was invested also with images from paintings attributed to Lairesse which hung in Dulwich Gallery. These landscapes were dreams which

> showed our sky
> Traversed by flying shapes, earth stocked with brood
> Of monsters, – centaurs bestial, satyrs lewd, –
> Not without much Olympian glory, shapes
> Of god and goddess in their gay escapes
> From the severe serene: or haply paced
> The antique ways, god-counselled, nymph-embraced,
> Some early human kingly personage.

In his parleying Browning enters the dream country of Lairesse, where the passing of the storm in such Arcadian settings seems a parallel to the Pastoral Symphony of Beethoven. Then the poem returns to reality with rhythms and images which again have less in common with the 1880s than with Edward Thomas's quiet ruralism thirty years later in, say, 'The Mountain Chapel'.

> There's sunshine; scarcely a wind at all
> Disturbs starved grass and daisies small
> On a certain mound by a churchyard wall.

Parleying 'With Charles Avison' is Browning's recognition that music remained for him, potentially, the greatest of the arts, but music is transient and cannot be given permanence in the manner of painting or poetry. Like all the parleyings, that with Avison shows the astonishing range of Browning's knowledge, in this case of the minor keyboard composers and executants of the eighteenth century.

That hard-worked term a *tour de force* is undoubtedly the aptest description of *Parleyings* as a whole. If the purer inspiration of earlier years was lacking, there was none the less a gusto and enthusiasm behind the intellectual debates which went some considerable way to make up for it. Indeed, the pictorialism which had lent much decorative charm to Browning's poetry in his twenties proved no less effective fifty years later in such passages as his description of private landscapes which he shared with Lairesse.

The last volume of poetry, *Asolando*, completed when he was seventy-seven and published on the day of his death, shows his curiosity and enthusiasm unabated. His interest in human psychology penetrates a step further and deeper in the four 'Bad Dreams' poems into the subconscious imagery of sleep. The obvious line of comparison for Browning runs through the underworld dream-devices of Virgil or Dante – even of Edgar Allan Poe – rather than in any anticipation of Freud. It was not until 1895 that Freud and Josef Breuer published *Studies in Hysteria* and five years more before *The Interpretation of Dreams*, though the first Freudian treatments took place during Browning's life.

In the second of the 'Bad Dreams' there is a vision of the underworld where the damned are dancing at a ball. Strange rituals are being practised in an adjoining chapel to which the poet's mistress comes to confess a secret sin. By hindsight, it is hard to escape the comparison with Freud rather than Virgil in the account of the mind's subconscious freedom.

> Sleep leaves a door on hinge
>   Whence soul, ere our flesh suspect,
> Is off and away: detect
>
> Her vagaries when loose, who can?
>   Be she pranksome, be she prude,
> Disguise with the day began:
>   With the night – ah, what ensued
> From the draughts of a drink hell-brewed?

The image of the door left ajar, of the waking mask discarded in sleep, have much in common with new mythology rather than old. As a whole, the poem offers an astute insight into the way in which a dream may reveal to a man his subconscious feelings about the woman whom he loves.

In the third of the 'Bad Dreams' the scene is a marble dream city set in a primeval forest. Once again, the image reflects the past. The city

> Of architectural device
> Every way perfect,

recalls the ideal city of Renaissance perspective, seen in the design at Urbino attributed to Piero della Francesca, or even the Holy City of St John's vision. Yet in its surreal strangeness it might almost be an anticipation of the cold night-cities and their ghostly female nudes of the 1930s and 1940s in the paintings of Paul Delvaux.

For the rest, the tone of *Asolando* was principally one of clear, defiant optimism all too easily calculated to reinforce the 'robust' and 'manly' reputation of his poetry at the expense of some of its finer qualities. 'Development' was both an evocation of childhood and, in its denunciation of Wolf's scepticism as to Homeric truth, became an implicit trouncing of all those who presumed to doubt the pagan or Christian past.

The epilogue to *Asolando* was to prove Browning's farewell to the world. Its tone was that of the conclusion to 'La Saisiaz', if anything more succinct and trenchant as the poet bluntly described himself and his beliefs.

> One who never turned his back but marched breast forward,
>   Never doubted clouds would break,
> Never dreamed, though right were worsted, wrong would triumph,
> Held we fall to rise, are baffled to fight better,
>   Sleep to wake.

One evening in the last days of his life, Browning read these lines to Sarianna and to Fannie Coddington, by then his daughter-in-law. He knew his death would not be long delayed and remarked simply of the verse: 'It almost looks like bragging to say this, and as if I ought to cancel it; but it's the simple truth; and as it's true, it shall stand.'[8]

However much the optimism of such poems may have grated upon other readers after Browning's death, his attitude was certainly borne out in his own life. When he was seventy he acknowledged Mrs Skirrow's birthday greetings with a hearty assurance. 'Well, – let who may find "Life not worth living." *I* have had reason enough to enjoy it!'[9] Unlike other men of his age who lamented their present state of health and future prospects, Browning appeared to take his own ill health and bereavements with easy acceptance.

From 1886 he was 'rudely shaken' in health, as Gosse termed it, by what Browning and his doctor chose to call 'spasmodic asthma', colds and coughs which confined him to his house for weeks at a time during the winter months.[10] This imprisonment at home while the dinners, receptions and recitals of the London season continued all about him seemed as difficult to endure as the illness itself. He promised not to complain at having to take his turn in the ranks of the disabled, and yet the weakness of his chest puzzled him. 'I used to boast foolishly that my lungs would outlast my legs and arms – and it is just these lungs that teaze me.' By 1886 he was almost convinced that he must spend the winters abroad.[11]

For the rest, he relished his life as much as ever. Indeed, his own approaching death did not the least diminish his appetite for the macabre. He wrote to his correspondents, from Venice, of strange murders and interesting suicides. The Skirrows were regaled with the gruesome details of an avalanche whose remains Browning had visited. Apart from the slaughter of the victims, the long burials alive, the appalling frost-bite, there was the intriguing incident of a man badly bitten by his delirious, dying daughter while they were entombed together under the debris.[12] Nathaniel Wanley could scarcely have improved upon such a prodigy.

The same vigour appeared in Browning's political sympathies, with his growing contempt for Gladstone after the abortive attempt at legislation for Irish Home Rule in 1886, and his delight at the political success of Joseph Chamberlain. He continued to meet Gladstone at other men's dinner tables, without enthusiasm, but found Chamberlain a charming companion as well as the great hope of the Liberal Unionists who had defected over Gladstone's Irish policy.

For all his vital enthusiasm, the evidence of mortality was plain in the case of those who were close to him. Sarianna was ill in 1886, as she had been two years earlier. It was out of the question to take her to Venice and, on the second occasion, she and Browning retired quietly to the Hand Hotel, Llangollen.

There were also the deaths of friends whom he had known for most of his life. Carlyle had died in 1881, though Browning had been separated from his company to a greater extent in recent years by virtue of Carlyle's long-standing friendship with the Ashburton family. Browning would only say that he rarely saw Carlyle, 'for a reason'. That reason was presumably the disagreeable possibility of being confronted at Cheyne Row by Lady Louisa Ashburton.

Three successive years brought the deaths of two of Browning's most amiable companions and one of his closest friends. Monckton Milnes, who had been a friend to Pen as well as Browning, died in 1885, followed by Joseph Milsand in 1886 and Alfred Domett in 1887. Two of these losses he bore with comparative equanimity. Milnes had been sympathetic, amiable, hospitable, but scarcely the most intimate of acquaintances. It was perhaps gratitude rather than love which Browning felt for him. The friendship with Domett had been resumed upon the latter's return from New Zealand but it appeared more sedate and perhaps rather more distant than the relationship of their youth. It was Milsand's death which removed the man who was regarded as Browning's most intimate male friend. From Milsand's first appreciation of the poetry in 1851, their first meeting in Paris soon afterwards, the relationship had grown. After Elizabeth's death it was Milsand who was Browning's only male comforter, to whose memory he dedicated *Parleyings with Certain People of Importance*, and who was remembered in the summer of 1870 at St Aubin.

> There he stands, reads an English newspaper,
> Stock-still, and now, again upon the move,
> Paces the beach to taste the spring.

There was no privacy required in the case of the poet's feeling for so great a heart as Milsand.

> He knows more and loves better, than the world
> That never heard his name, and never may.
> What hinders that my heart relieve itself,
> Milsand, who makest warm my wintry world,
> And wise my heaven, if there we consort too?

Of Milsand's death, as opposed to their friendship during his life, Browning said little. Perhaps the most eloquent tribute was in the dedication of *Parleyings with Certain People of Importance in Their Day*, published in the following year: 'In Memoriam J. Milsand, Obiit IV Sept. MDCCCLXXXVI', and in the epigraph to the poem, 'Absens absentem auditque videtque'.

The most obvious convulsions of old age were of a more trivial kind. Life at Warwick Crescent was coming to an end, though its style altered little. The pet geese, two of them named Quarterly and Edinburgh as a comment on literary critics, were still in residence. Indeed, Browning's affection for them far exceeded his feeling for the reviewers, since he was found nursing a sick goose in his arms. Yet in 1887, twenty-five years of tenure at the Georgian villa were over. The new Regent's Park Canal Bill, with its extension of that waterway, had doomed the area to dereliction and eventual demolition. It was this, rather than any symbolism of success, which decided Browning on a move to De Vere Gardens in South Kensington. The new house was certainly grander, the location south of the park was considered both smarter and healthier, and for good measure he acquired Henry James as a neighbour.

Precisely because he made his way so easily in society, social prestige was something he did not require. It was his friends, not Browning, who discovered a pedigree for him and got a coat-of-arms from the College of Heralds. It was not Browning but his son who seized upon this and dressed the family gondoliers in appropriate livery.[13]

The pleasures of congenial company still meant much to him in his final years as he struggled to dinners and receptions through the London winter between bouts of his 'spasmodic asthma'. Among those who had been friends to Pen as well as to himself he enjoyed the company of painters like Leighton and Alma-Tadema. Much of his leisure was spent in visiting galleries and in promoting Pen's professional interests. There were agreeable companions from other walks of life, including judges and men of law, Coleridge and Fitzjames Stephen – brother of the critic Leslie Stephen. By membership of the Cosmopolitan Club he won a prestigious friend in Lord Wolseley, the future commander-in-chief who had been raised to the peerage after the ill-fated relief expedition to Khartoum in 1884. It was a comfortable circle of friends who had at least one accomplishment in common, the publicly recognized achievement of personal success.

There were times in the 1880s when Browning assured his friends that his most enjoyable evenings were spent in dining alone at home – 'blessings on it – I dine at home' – yet the pleasures of society, its art galleries and recitals as much as its dinners, had yet to pall.[14] He dined with the violinist Joachim and attended the soirées for Liszt on the composer's last visit to London. While such poems as 'Abt Vogler' or 'Master Hugues of Saxe-Gotha' testified to Browning's admiration for the music of the seventeenth and eighteenth centuries, 'The Founder of the Feast', published in the *World* on 14 April 1884 was an enthusiastic tribute to the virtuosi of the Victorian concert hall and recital room.

> My cup was filled with rapture to the brim
> When, night by night, – Ah, memory – how it haunts! –
> Music was poured by pefect ministrants
> By Hallé, Schumann, Piatti, Joachim!

For the first time, in the 1880s, his travels abroad began to represent an alternative social amusement – even the possibility of an alternative home – rather than a mere retreat for a month or two of the summer. It was, in any case, the autumns rather than the summers which took him to Venice, an attempt to shorten the London winter by a few months. The cornerstone of his social life in Venice was, of course, Katherine de Kay Bronson, to whom he had been introduced first by Story's wife Emelyn. After their meeting in 1880 she had put at his disposal the Palazzo Giustiniani-Recanati. Her salon, to which he had such easy access, included younger writers like Henry James as well as European nobility and minor royalty – the Prince and Princess Metternich, and Don Carlos, the Spanish Pretender. Nor was Venice devoid of artistic spectacle. At the Rossini Theatre Browning attended a performance of the first *Barbiere di Sevilla* – that by Paisiello – in the presence of Wagner.

If Venice seemed to replace Florence – to which he never returned – in Browning's affections, that was in part the result of Pen's enthusiasm. In August 1885 he told Mrs Skirrow that Pen was going to Venice to paint, 'good boy that he is'.[15] It was the first time that Pen had been to Italy since the death of Elizabeth twenty-four years earlier, though he appeared by temperament and upbringing more Italian than English. By November 1885 it seemed clear that Browning's own devotion to the city was shared by his son, and he entered into negotiations to buy the Palazzo Manzoni on the Grand Canal from its absentee Austrian owner. It was to Mrs Skirrow once again that he explained his reasons.

> I did this purely for Pen – who became at once simply infatuated with the city which won my whole heart long before he was born or thought of. I secure him a perfect domicile, every facility for his painting and sculpture, and a property fairly worth, even here and now, double what I gave for it – such is the virtue in these parts of ready money! I myself shall stick to London – which has been so eminently good and gracious to me – so long as God permits; only, when the inevitable outrage of Time gets the better of my body – (I shall not believe in his reaching my soul and proper self) – there will be a capital retreat provided: and meantime I shall be able to 'take mine ease in mine own inn' whenever so minded.[16]

Unfortunately, the negotiations came to nothing, the vendors making no attempt to proceed with the transaction, and Browning had acquired nothing but the expenses of law. It was left to Pen, in 1888, to accomplish what his father had failed in and to buy the Palazzo Rezzonico, described by Henry James as a stately temple of rococo.

From the period of his first residence in the Palazzo Giustiniani-Recanati, Browning devised a routine for his life in Venice, watched over by Mrs Bronson. It was a mere variation of his London itinerary. After breakfast he and Sarianna went to the Public Gardens, she in her distinctive gowns of 'rich and sombre tints', a neat French cap and 'quaint antique jewels'. There they fed the animals, the elephant, baboon, kangaroo, ostrich, pelicans and marmosets. The morning's visits over, there was lunch at noon followed by the gondola to the Lido at three. 'You don't know how absolutely well I am after my walking, not on the mountains merely, but on the beloved Lido. Go there, if only to stand and be blown about by the sea-wind.'[17] On other afternoons, in the company of Mrs Bronson's beautiful daughter Edith, he walked the little streets beyond the wider canals, surveying the contents of antique shops, carrying off brass church lamps and Jewish sabbath lamps to embellish the house in De Vere Gardens. At five he returned for tea, dressing later for one of those dinner parties which were as frequent a conclusion to his day's proceedings in Venice as they were in London.

In England he was conscious of his delining health. In Italy, as he said, he felt as if he were 'good for ten years yet'.[18] It was in November 1883, when Browning was already in his seventies, that he and Sarianna contemplated their first visit to Greece, by ship from Venice. But there would have been time only to see Athens and so the journey was postponed with a view to making an extended tour of Greece the next autumn.[19]

Even in the last weeks of his life he planned busily for the future. On a visit to Asolo, despite his shortness of breath in climbing its hills, he found a piece of land and proposed to buy it. Standing upon it, overlooking a ravine of vine and olive, was an unfinished building. Browning was seized by the idea of completing the structure with a tower 'whence I can see Venice at every hour of the day'.[20] He would call it Pippa's Tower. The municipality approved his plan on 12 December 1889, the day of his death.

The attraction of Venice was all the stronger in his last years by virtue of Pen's residence there. For, it appeared, the problem of Pen which had caused Browning more worry than any other in the past quarter of a century was about to be solved by marriage. In 1887, with his father's ready approval, he married Fannie Coddington, five years his junior. It was said that he had first proposed to her fourteen years earlier and had renewed that proposal on meeting her unexpectedly at a house party. She was American by parentage and English by upbringing, 'a fine handsome generous creature', as Browning called her, the object of his own devotion as well as Pen's.

He lived to be reassured by the semblance of married love, when Fannie was still the slightly plump bride with the red hair of a Titian beauty and fine blue eyes. There were, indeed, disappointments. Already thirty-three at her marriage, Fannie suffered miscarriages and bore no children. As time went by her behaviour hovered between the highly strung and the hysterical. Natural jealousy, as much as the fundamentalist religion of childhood, provoked her shrill disapproval of Pen's nude models and, indeed, the nude paintings and statuary in which they were immortalized. The marriage was to founder a few years later in a mass of rumour about Pen's philandering and the illegitimate children whom he was said to have fathered before and during his life with Fannie. Their servant Ginerva was variously supposed to have been Pen's mistress at the Palazzo Rezzonico and his daughter by a youthful liaison in the late 1860s.

Browning saw only the early stages of the marriage when there was still every hope for Pen of a settled and productive future. The young man was eccentric, certainly. During his time in Belgium he had allegedly wanted to marry an innkeeper's daughter. His father had put a stop to that. Pen later owned a ten-foot python from Senegal and draped it about one of his nudes while working on a statute. He was obliged to shoot the python, said the rumours, as it tightened its embrace upon the helpless young woman.

Had Browning indeed been 'good for ten years yet', his presence might have held the couple together. Equally, his old age might have been a period of the greatest disillusionment of all. However, he was to go to the grave with his optimism over Pen undimmed and with the feeling that in this matter at least all had proved for the best.

The animosity between himself and individual critics or acquaintances continued until the end of Browning's life and, indeed, some of the literary scandals associated with his name and work were to have a posthumous fame of their own. 'Robert Browning: Chief Poet of the Age' was the title of W. G. Kingsland's lecture in 1887 and, it seemed, those who denied such acclaim to Browning himself or to Elizabeth did so at their peril.

His friend Alexandra Orr found his 'intellectual egotism' a chief characteristic of his last years. Flattery or sympathy would work their charm upon him, argument and demonstration would not. 'But his dominant individuality also barred the recognition of any judgement or impression, any thought or feeling, which did not justify itself from his own point of view. The barrier would melt under the influence of a sympathetic mood, as it would stiffen in the atmosphere of disagreement.... He appeared, for this reason, more widely sympathetic in his works than in his life.'[21]

Towards those who had crossed him, Browning showed a characteristic and undiminished vituperation. Louisa Ashburton was never forgiven for her refusal to be a second subordinate wife under the magisterial shade of Elizabeth. Fifteen years after the break between them, Browning still fumed over the 'calumnies which Lady A. exploded in all the madness of her wounded vanity'.[22] Hatty Hosmer, who had been the 'pet' of the Brownings' Roman winters and then disgraced herself by taking Lady Ashburton's side, endeavoured to patch up her quarrel with the poet by writing an affectionate and conciliatory letter in 1887. But sixteen years had not softened his resentment. 'Impudence,' he said, discarding her hopeful entreaty.[23]

By far his most vigorous outburst concerned the publication of Edward Fitzgerald's letters in 1889. Fitzgerald, the friend of Tennyson and famous for his translation of the *Rubáiyát of Omar Khayyám*, had died in 1883. What he had said about Elizabeth in his letters, published six years later, was popularly supposed to have been a mortal blow to Browning himself.

> Mrs Browning's death is rather a relief to me I must say. No more Aurora Leighs thank God! A woman of real Genius I know but what is the upshot of it all? She and her Sex had better mind the Kitchen and their Children; and perhaps the Poor. Except in such things as little Novels, they only devote themselves to what Men do much better, leaving that which Men do worse or not at all.[24]

Browning's response was immediate. He wrote a savage twelve-line poem on Fitzgerald and his opinion, sending it to Norman MacColl for publication in the *Athenaeum*.

TO EDWARD FITZGERALD

I chanced upon a new book yesterday:
I opened it, and where my finger lay
   'Twixt page and uncut page, these words I read
– Some six or seven at most – and learned thereby
That you, Fitzgerald, whom by ear and eye
   She never knew, 'thanked God my wife was dead.'

Ay dead! and were yourself alive, good Fitz,
How to return you thanks would task my wits;
   Kicking you seems the common lot of curs –
While more appropriate greeting lends you grace:
Surely to spit there glorifies your face –
   Spitting – from lips once sanctified by Hers.

Sarianna declared to Pen that Browning had been made ill by the pain of the insult to Elizabeth's memory. Certainly he raged against Fitzgerald in private as a brute and a blackguard, no less than as Tennyson's 'adulatory lick-spittle'. Before the poem appeared he wrote to MacColl in a half-hearted manner, indicating that if its tone were inconsistent with that of the *Athenaeum* he would be prepared to take it back. There was nothing in his words to suggest that he truly regretted having vented his indignation upon Fitzgerald in such terms. The lines were duly published above Browning's name on 13 July 1889.

Aldis Wright, the editor of Fitzgerald's letters, apologized publicly for the oversight in allowing such a tasteless extract to appear. Privately he complained of the disgraceful insults which Browning offered in his poem. The whole incident had the makings of a vicious little literary squabble by which the readers of the *Athenaeum* might have been diverted during the ensuing months. That this did not occur was the consequence of Browning's departure for Italy a few weeks later and his death there in December 1889.

A posthumous exploitation of quite a different kind lay in the future, though the seeds from which it was to germinate were presumably already planted in the mind of Thomas James Wise. During their acquaintanceship in the 1880s, Wise brought to Browning's attention 'rare editions' of Elizabeth's poetry. *The Battle of Marathon* was an early work, written and published before Browning met her. There was room for uncertainty on that. But 'The Runaway Slave at Pilgrim's Point' had appeared in the *Poems* of 1850, having previously been printed in the *Liberty Bell* at Boston in 1848. It belonged to the years of their marriage, and Browning felt sure that the poem had never been published separately. Wise produced a copy of this 'first edition' complete with names of publisher and printer. Browning was reluctantly convinced.

It may have crossed his mind that Wise had access to the means of facsimile production for the Shelley and Browning Societies and that these might easily become the tools of forgery. Wise also had a useful dupe – more probably a collaborator – in the distinguished editor of Shelley and Keats, Henry Buxton Forman. Why was T.J. Wise not suspect? In the first place he was wealthy enough not to commit forgery for mere profit. More important, he was a prominent member of the Browning Society, therefore a worshipper rather than a calumniator.

It was five years after Browning's death when Edmund Gosse first spoke of the rare private edition of *Sonnets from the Portuguese* printed privately at Reading in 1847, three years prior to the generally acknowledged first edition of 1850 in the collected *Poems*. Presumably inspired or prompted by Wise, Gosse added that Browning himself had mentioned to 'a friend' that he had first seen the sonnets at Pisa in 1847, not at Bagni di Lucca two years later. The poems had certainly been written in 1846 which, by however narrow a margin, made the private edition of 1847 plausible. It was then left to Wise to 'discover' a copy of it.

The results of a scientific investigation of these claims forty years later by John Carter and Graham Pollard are too well known to need more than a summary. *Sonnets from the Portuguese* (1847) was printed on paper not available until about 1860 and with type not available until later still. In the wake of this, a host of other Victorian 'first editions' by the most eminent authors of the age were traced to the fertile genius of T. J. Wise. Perhaps the insult would have been more evident to Browning than the comedy. For all his powers of scorn and disparagement he lacked a keen sense of humour. It would, all the same, be agreeable to suppose that the unmasking of the forger and the discomfiture of so much literary snobbery occasioned a gust of Homeric laughter in the Elysian Fields.

Despite the belief that Browning might be crushed by such insults as those offered by Fitzgerald to Elizabeth, the evidence is that he rather relished conflict on the whole. The kicking and the spitting in his retaliatory poem suggest that the enthusiasm had not altogether left him. It was not the shrill clamour of literary invective – Browning raving like a street walker, as Julian Hawthorne judged – but rather the 'spasmodic asthma' which would destroy him in the end.

Even in the summer of 1888 he was so unwell that the journey to Venice was almost abandoned. Yet Italy worked its old magic upon him and he was temporarily restored. The London winter undid all the good of Venice and he was housebound in De Vere Gardens by early January. The next summer brought him less comfort than before and by the end of June 1889 he confessed to Mrs Fitzgerald that he felt 'washed out'.[25] None the less, his last weeks in England were occupied by a round of congenial dinners and celebrations. There was the visit to Cambridge and the tête-à-tête with Edmund Gosse in the Fellows' Garden at Trinity. He was Jowett's guest at the Balliol Commemoration in June and stayed on for the Gaudy which the College gave to the Provost and Fellows of Eton. In London he attended a reception on Waterloo Day, 18 June, at Lord Albemarle's, the last survivor of the famous battle seventy-four years earlier. There was an invitation from Millais to meet the queen's daughter, Princess Louise, and her husband, the Marquis of Lorne. He attended the dinner given by Lord Rosebery, the future Liberal prime minister, to meet the Shah of Persia. Whatever the future held, Browning as a public figure still seemed equal to doing his duty.

Here and there the echoes and premonitions of fate seem clearer. His confession to Gosse in the gardens of Trinity has something of the air of a last testament. On leaving Jowett for the last time, Browning paused to shake hands with Evelyn Abbott, a Fellow of Balliol and Jowett's future biographer. 'Jowett knows how I love him,' Browning said.[26] Then he left his Oxford friends forever. On 5 August he exchanged greetings with Tennyson, whose eightieth birthday fell on the following day. In all this there was a sense of finality.

By now the London season was over, the great houses empty. On 16 August Browning reported that he had not had a dinner away from home for three weeks. Sarianna confided to Pen that her brother's health had improved somewhat and that it was important to start for Italy without delay before he fell ill again.[27] Soon afterwards they set out on the journey, their first destination being not Venice but Asolo where Browning meditated his plans for Pippa's Tower. In the mellow October of an Italian autumn he wrote to Mrs Skirrow and Mrs Fitzgerald of the beauty of the old town at the fall of the year.

> Autumn is now painting all the abundance of verdure, – figs, pomegranates, chestnuts, and vines, and I don't know what else, – all in a wonderful confusion, – and now glowing with all the colours of the rainbow. . . . In fine, we shall stay here probably for a week or more, – and then proceed to Pen, at the Rezzonico; a month there, and then homewards![28]

At the beginning of November he and Sarianna reached Venice, taking up their usual quarters in the Palazzo Rezzonico. To Pen and to his friends Browning boasted of health and energy. One evening at dinner he stretched out his wrist to Dr Bird who was also a guest and invited him to feel the steady rhythm of his pulse. The doctor accepted the invitation but felt a beat that was ominously irregular.

The milder autumns of Venice gave way on this occasion to fog and an early onset of winter. Returning from his customary walk on the Lido, Browning developed a bronchial cold. He maintained firmly that it was merely a slight disorder of the liver, contrary to the symptoms, and he abstained from food and wine in order to put it right. By the end of November he conceded that it was his chronic 'asthma'. The truth was that he had bronchitis aggravated by a failing heart.

He still proposed to start for England during the first week of December and began to speak of his illness as one of the 'scrapes of this kind' which he got into and then out of again. By now, however, there were nurses in residence at the Palazzo Rezzonico and Browning had withdrawn to his room. Yet even at this late stage, according to Pen, he walked up the three flights of stairs easily and without any assistance.

He was to die within two weeks. During the first days of his illness he complained that he would be better out of bed and walking about. On 12 December *Asolando* was published and the news of its favourable reception and excellent sales was telegraphed to Venice. Browning was already suffering periods of delirium. The regime of the sick-room, the regular poulticing and the night watches kept by Pen, Fannie and the nurse, had become well established. Yet he read the telegram from England and said simply, 'How gratifying!'

By five o'clock on the afternoon of 12 December whatever temporary exhilaration he may have felt over the success of *Asolando* gave way before the increasing weight of mortality. To his nurse, Margherita Fiori, he said, 'I feel much worse. I know now that I must die.' And to Pen, 'I am dying. My dear Boy, my dear Boy.' At eight o'clock he slipped into unconsciousness, the last stage of a life which he seemed to sense was coming to its end when he took leave of Jowett and those other friends who were to survive him. As he turned from autumnal Asolo to the Venetian winter, his parting words to William Wetmore Story carried the same tone of a life completed. 'We have been friends for forty years,' he said, as they took their final leave of one another.

There were perhaps only three ghosts to whom his expectations might have turned in the shadow world of approaching death. The longest absent was his mother with her musical gifts, her tenderness towards humanity and the animal kingdom. She was a memory of the sunlit hills and woods of Camberwell, the enclosed garden with its white phlox and gravel walks, its roses and its rockery. At her side was the shade of his father, sometimes absurd in his lack of practicality but always beloved. He was the presiding genius of book-laden shelves and old folios, of walks which became mythological adventures under the spell of Gerard de Lairesse.

In the third ghost, Elizabeth, lay the promise of the future as well as the memory of the past. Had she ever been absent from him? Not long before his own death, he spoke of her and then said, 'I felt as if she had died yesterday'. It was she, most of all, who transformed death into the living hope of that better world 'where that lady lives of whom my soul was enamoured'. The quality of his love for her shown in such faith as this was his greatest nobility.

It was at about ten o'clock on that evening of 12 December that those who were watching by his bed, where he lay with scarcely a movement, saw a sudden 'violent heaving of his big chest' and then the final immobility of death.[29]

Browning had assumed that he would be buried with Elizabeth. Yet since the middle of the century municipal authorities had been increasingly aware of the hazard to health which emanated from overcrowded graveyards in heavily populated districts. Accordingly, the little cemetery in Florence had been closed for further burials. Browning had once speculated on the comparative advantages, for the Englishman who died abroad, of being buried on the spot as opposed to being sent home pickled. It was the price of fame, however, that a grave was prepared for him in Westminster Abbey.

In the first place a preliminary funeral service of pomp and rich colour was staged by the city of Venice. It was held in the great hall of the Palazzo Rezzonico, where the coffin lay under a purple pall and with a single wreath of laurel which Pen had placed upon it. There followed an impressive spectacle, a cortège of ornate funeral gondolas with the city dignitaries in their liveries, down the Grand Canal in the December afternoon and out to Browning's temporary resting-place on the burial island of San Michele. 'As we passed under the Rialto Bridge,' wrote one of the mourners, Constanza Hulton, 'the setting sun burst out of the clouds which had covered the sky all that day and shone with fantastic lights upon the funeral barge and the gilded ornaments.'[30]

Soon afterwards, the coffin was moved less ceremoniously by night to the railway station and put in charge of a courier to be taken by train to England. There, on the last day of the year, in the presence of six hundred distinguished ticket-holders, the celebration of his life and death was concluded in the Abbey. It was, appropriately, a social occasion to match any which he had known in the twenty-eight years since his return from Florence.

It proved a good deal easier to find an appropriate place for his mortal remains than to lay his reputation decently to rest. The double enigma of his poetry and personality invited speculation and analysis. Tennyson had decorously taken his place behind the romantics in the procession of literary history. Browning, it seemed, had jumped several places further on, springing from the accepted romanticism at the beginning of the nineteenth century straight to a style of realism and psychological analysis which was not generally characteristic until that century was almost over. His readers had been left to catch up as best they could and, not surprisingly, they had generally felt more comfortable in the elegiac Victorian landscapes of the Poet Laureate. Browning had not, of course, made matters easier by the demands which he made upon his readers' knowledge of the by-ways of history or literature. Yet that was perhaps the lesser of the two difficulties.

Notoriously, there was also the question of 'morbid anatomy' in his poetry from first to last. The apparent celebration of crime, sexual violence and insanity, as his critics saw it, was tolerable only by selecting judiciously from the great mass of his work. At the most banal level, therefore, he became the poet of 'God's in his heaven – All's right with the world!' or 'O to be in England/Now that April's there'.

At a more exalted level the Browning of mottoes for needlework cases – 'Ah, but a man's reach should exceed his grasp/Or what's a heaven for?' – became an object for philosophical investigation. In vain had Matthew Arnold warned the world not to follow a path so narrow, castigating Leslie Stephen for his endeavour to show that Wordsworth was possessed of an ethical system 'as distinctive and capable of exposition as Bishop Butler's'.[31] What Wordsworth had once been to Stephen, Browning seemed now about to become to some of his admirers.

The tendency to regard him as a preacher or a teacher was, of course, established before his death, and he himself had laid a foundation for it by his discussion of religious faith – and doubt – over a period of almost forty years, from *Christmas-Eve and Easter-Day* in 1850 until *Asolando* in 1889. By 1871 he was already the subject of two articles on 'Browning as Preacher', written by Edward Dowden's future wife, Miss E. Dickinson West, and published in *The Dark Blue* for October and November. In the year before his death he was gratified by a favourable account of his poetry in Frank Wakely Gunsaulus' *The Higher Ministries of Recent English Poetry*.

The greater danger, of course, lay in the books published after his death. In 1890 there appeared a second edition of *Browning as a Philosophical and Religious Teacher* by Henry Jones, Professor of Logic, Metaphysics and Rhetoric in the University of St Andrews. Like Jowett and so many of his intellectual contemporaries, Henry Jones had been influenced by the idealism of Hegel. His book first of all demonstrates that Browning's poetry showed him 'as the exponent of a system of ideas on moral and religious subjects, which may fairly be called a philosophy'.[32] Predictably, Professor Jones then found in Browning's poetry no consistent philosophical framework, Hegelian or otherwise. 'The idea that truth is unattainable was represented by Browning as a bulwark of the faith. . . . The evidence of the heart, to which he appealed, was the evidence of an emotion severed from intelligence, and, therefore, without any content whatsoever.'[33]

That Browning's writing, particularly in the latter part of his life, should be examined as philosophy rather than poetry was regarded with favour by all too many critics of the 1890s. A. C. Bradley discussed the poet's 'theory of knowledge' in the *International Journal of Ethics* for January 1892. The *New York Nation* had already announced, on 30 July 1891, that 'The sifting of Browning's doctrines by a philosophical scholar has long been a desideratum, for the estimate of these later works did not belong to poetic criticism'. For good measure the *Modern Church* on 18 June 1891 deplored the discussion of the poetry in 'the criticism of the mere *litterateur*'.

The plight of Browning's poetry in the years and decades which followed was plain enough. To the philosophers he was, after all, merely the purveyor of a lusty irrational optimism which scarcely went beyond the assertion that God was in his heaven and all was right with the world. To readers at the other intellectual extreme he was the writer of a few popular poems and of a mass of other material which clearly belonged to the darker ways of idealist philosophy. He had, in this reputation, a talent for the impenetrably obscure and the blindingly self-evident but not for very much in between.

So the two words 'obscurity' and 'optimism' attached themselves to Browning's poetry and proved almost fatally self-perpetuating. As Augustine Birrell remarked, no intelligent reader could pretend to find much obscurity in a vast body of Browning's work. The plays, the collections of shorter poems before and after *Men and Women*, certainly *The Ring and the Book*, were not above criticism but they were scarcely works of a baffling obscurity. Nor for that matter were *Pippa Passes* or *A Soul's Tragedy*. As Birrell saw it, the problem was largely one of reputation. A man who objected that Shakespeare's minor plays were unreadable was always in danger of being contradicted by someone who had read them. Yet the time came when a man who had not read Browning's plays, for example, could talk about their obscurity, secure in the knowledge that there would be no one else who had read them either.[34]

To more discriminating readers it was the reputation for optimism and robustness which proved the greater deterrent. As it happened, Browning's optimism rested upon two things, neither of which prevented him from writing poetry that reached the depths of evil in its portrayal of human conduct. In the first place he showed an enthusiasm for life, even in his greatest trials. It was an appetite which was evident in much that he wrote. Secondly, he had the traditional Puritan certainty of belief in God and hence that ultimate assurance. At the level of human affairs, his poetry remained upon that familiar and dangerous edge of things where the evidence of original sin would have defeated every hope of mere humanism. The proper study of the speculative and poetic intelligence was never in doubt.

Original Sin.
The Corruption of Man's Heart.

The private world where such investigations were pursued housed its share of criminals and madmen, but in a wider sense it was the domain of uneasy minds. Love blossomed there with unnatural power and died with undramatic ease. Humanity fashioned the implements of murder or torture with a consummate artistry, embellishing the death or agony for which they were designed. 'Horror coquetting with voluptuousness', as he termed it in 'A Forgiveness' in 1876, was closer to the truth of his poetic world than the buoyant snatches of verse which went so glibly into pokerwork mottoes and embroidery.

A century after his death this aspect of his poetry is not confined to a mere indulgence of 'morbid anatomy' to which Julia Wedgwood objected. Within it, Browning's sense of tradition and modernity coexist most clearly. He echoes the curiosities of the ancient world, of the Renaissance and of Wanley's anthropological monstrosities. Yet the direction of his interest is to the future. There are lines or passages which in attitude and cadence anticipate Rilke or Auden. There is a frame of mind, as early as *Pippa Passes* in 1841, which observes the world with the objective detailing of the cinema. By the 1870s and 1880s the developing realism of his verse fiction parallels that of Balzac, Zola or Maupassant. Coincidentally, certain threads in his work were being woven at the same time into the theories of Krafft-Ebing and Freud. If he now seems the most modern of the major Victorians, it is because he was also the most uncompromisingly adult in his microscopy of 'The Corruption of the Human Heart'. To turn from Browning to the poetry of his peers often carries the impression of stepping from the life of men and women into a child's garden.

The private refuge behind the wall, as James called it, was in essence the poetic structure. That it should house so many horrors did not invalidate this. It was Browning's kingdom, of which he was master. Its inhabitants, however mad or villainous, were subject to his laws. On these terms he needed Mr Sludge or Guido Franceschini as much as he needed Elizabeth Barrett. After her death he sustained himself during his heaviest grief or his neglect in the literary world by turning upon his subjects with the avidity of a Frankenstein. In the poetic laboratory of Browning's mind there was perhaps an apter parallel with Mary Shelley than with his boyhood idol. Secure in this industrious solitude he seemed proof against almost the worst that time and chance could do, his natural appetite for such pursuits reinforced by the self-assurance of his Puritan heritage. Within this privacy, to use Alfred Adler's terminology again, Browning might live as absolutely by his own rule and intellectual compulsions as the less fortunate who denied the external laws of the world in their pursuit of crime or in the labyrinth of neurosis. Because he was criminal or mad only by proxy, Browning enjoyed a periodic release into the outer sphere of companionship and affability, seizing the chance with an enthusiasm redoubled by the isolation of his occupational confinement.

The evidence of his own words and the observations of his close contemporaries point to this as the pattern of Browning's personality. Yet the evidence which counts for most, as Burne-Jones remarked, is not in letters or reminiscences but in the poems themselves. He was the noisy anecdotalist of the dinner party, the public Liberal and man of faith who went home, as it were, to the underworld of Porphyria's lover and Guido Franceschini, to an anatomy theatre where sexual love and human virtue were meticulously vivisected.

Such truth as this ought not to belittle Browning as a friend or a public figure. He was noisy and at times spiteful and conceited. He also radiated strength, constancy and nobility. 'He was one of the noblest men I ever knew,' Jowett wrote to Pen on hearing of Browning's death, '& one of the kindest to me – I value his friendship more than I can express, it was so strong, so unchanging.'[35]

The experience of biography suggests that it is often the extremes of character which are truer than a grey compromise that denies them. Browning was certainly spiteful and noble, vain and yet constant. In that respect one does not need to accept Henry James's hypothesis of there being 'two Brownings' in order to appreciate that James wrote the best and the most fitting literary epitaph after the funeral service in Westminster Abbey. If there had ever been a golden key to the door in the mysterious wall, it had now been returned to its place for the last time. The secret door was shut for ever, leaving James to contemplate the blankness and draw his last conclusion. 'A good many oddities and a good many great writers have been entombed in the Abbey,' James wrote, 'but none of the odd ones have been so great and none of the great ones so odd.'[36]

Notes

Abbreviations:

American Friends   *Browning to His American Friends: Letters between the Brownings, the Storys, and James Russell Lowell, 1841-1890*, ed. Gertrude Reese Hudson (London 1965)

Dearest Isa   *Dearest Isa: Robert Browning's Letters to Isabella Blagden*, ed. Edward C. McAleer (Austin and Edinburgh 1951)

Domett   *The Diary of Alfred Domett*, ed. E. A. Horsman (London 1953)

EBB   *The Letters of Elizabeth Barrett Browning*, ed. Frederic G. Kenyon, 2 vols. (London 1897)

EBB/Horne   *Letters of Elizabeth Barrett Browning addressed to Richard Hengist Horne*, ed. S. R. Townshend Mayer, 2 vols. (London 1877)

George Barrett   *Letters of the Brownings to George Barrett*, ed. Paul Landis and Ronald E. Freeman (Urbana, Illinois 1958)

Gosse   Edmund Gosse, *Robert Browning, Personalia* (London 1890)

Hood   *Letters of Robert Browning, Collected by Thomas J. Wise*, ed. Thurman L. Hood (London 1933)

Huxley   *Elizabeth Barrett Browning: Letters to her Sister, 1846-1859*, ed. Leonard Huxley (London 1929)

Learned Lady   *Learned Lady: Letters from Robert Browning to Mrs Thomas Fitzgerald, 1876-1889*, ed. Edward C. McAleer (Cambridge, Massachusetts 1966)

Macready   *The Diaries of William Charles Macready, 1833-1851*, ed. William Toynbee, 2 vols. (London 1912)

New Letters   *New Letters of Robert Browning*, ed. William Clyde DeVane and Kenneth Leslie Knickerbocker (London 1951)

Ogilvy   *Elizabeth Barrett Browning's Letters to Mrs David Ogilvy, 1849-1861*, ed. Peter N. Heydon and Philip Kelley (London 1974)

Orr   Mrs Sutherland Orr, *Life and Letters of Robert Browning*, ed.
                        Frederic G. Kenyon (London 1908)

RB/EBB   *The Letters of Robert Browning and Elizabeth Barrett Browning, 1845–
                        1846*, 2 vols. (New York and London 1902)

Robert Browning   *Robert Browning and Alfred Domett*, ed. Frederic G. Kenyon (Lon-
and Alfred Domett   don 1906)

Story   Henry James, *William Wetmore Story and His Friends, From Letters,
                        Diaries, and Recollections*, 2 vols. (London 1903)

Wedgwood   *Robert Browning and Julia Wedgwood: A Broken Friendship as Re-
                        vealed in Their Letters*, ed. Richard Curle (London 1937)

1 'Poor Old Camberwell!'

1 J. A. Froude, *Thomas Carlyle, A History of His Life in London* (London 1897), I, p. 19
2 *New Letters*, p. 263
3 *Correspondence of Emerson and Carlyle*, ed. J. Slater (New York 1964), p. 329
4 *Robert Browning and Alfred Domett*, p. 30
5 Domett, p. 124
6 RB/EBB, II, p. 480
7 ibid., II, p. 480
8 32 *State Trials*, pp. 673–756
9 RB/EBB, II, pp. 495–6
10 ibid., II, p. 474
11 ibid., II, p. 474
12 ibid., II, p. 474
13 ibid., II, p. 474
14 *Letters of D. G. Rossetti*, ed. O. Doughty and J. R. Wahl (Oxford 1965), I, p. 281
15 W. J. Stillman, *Autobiography of a Journalist* (London 1901), I, p. 277
16 Orr, p. 14
17 *The Works of John Ruskin*, ed. E. T. Cook and A. Wedderburn (London 1908), XXXV,
     p. 47
18 Douglas Allport, *Collections Illustrative of the Geology, History, Antiquities, and Associations
     of Camberwell* (Camberwell 1841), p. 81
19 ibid., p. 94
20 G. K. Chesterton, *Robert Browning* (London 1903), p. 186
21 ibid., p. 186
22 ibid., p. 19
23 Orr, p. 22
24 RB/EBB, II, p. 424
25 ibid., II, p. 226
26 Orr, p. 43
27 Domett, pp. 212–13
28 C. G. Duffy, *Conversations and Correspondence with Carlyle* (New York 1892), p. 58
29 RB/EBB, II, p. 544
30 Stillman, *Autobiography of a Journalist*, I, p. 278
31 Public Record Office MS. K.B. 28/478/52

32 Edmund Gosse, *Father and Son: A Study of Two Temperaments* (London 1907), p. 291
33 *Learned Lady*, p. 193
34 Gosse, *Father and Son*, p. 366; *Dearest Isa*, p. 88
35 Gosse, p. 20
36 Nathaniel Wanley, *Wonders of the Little World* (London 1678), p. 6
37 ibid., p. 6
38 ibid., p. 7
39 ibid., p. 53
40 ibid., p. 54
41 ibid., p. 55
42 Gerard de Lairesse, *The Art of Painting in All Its Branches* (London 1738), p. 332
43 ibid., p, 335
44 RB/EBB, I, p. 77
45 ibid., I, p. 523
46 *Letters of D.G. Rossetti*, ed. Doughty and Wahl, I, p. 280
47 John Ruskin, *Modern Painters* (London 1856), IV, p. 379
48 Chesterton, *Robert Browning*, p. 41
49 W. M. Rossetti, *Preraphaelite Diaries and Letters* (London 1900), pp. 262-3
50 Orr, p. 24
51 RB/EBB, I, p. 443
52 Orr, p. 28
53 Domett, p. 74
54 BL. Add. MS., 45, 563, ff. 186-94
55 MS. D. M. S. Watson Library, University College, London
56 *The Times*, 14 December 1889
57 *British Weekly*, 20 December 1889
58 ibid.
59 Domett, p. 132
60 *The Works of John Ruskin*, xxxv, p. 386
61 RB/EBB, I, p. 524
62 Orr, p. 46
63 RB/EBB, I, p. 161
64 Orr, p. 35
65 ibid., p. 33
66 M.D. Conway, *Centenary History of the South Place Society* (London 1894), p. 46
67 Public Record Office MSS. K.B. 28/477/76, 77; K.B. 28/484/56
68 *Poetical Works of P.B. Shelley* (London 1839), I, p. ix
69 Shelley, Preface to *Alastor*
70 RB/EBB, I, p. 78
71 *Browning Society Papers* (London 1881-91), I (1881), p. 12
72 EBB, I, 466
73 Gosse, p. 27

2 A Fragment of a Confession

1 *Robert Browning and Alfred Domett*, p. 141
2 RB/EBB, I, p. 347
3 *Argosy*, February 1890

4 *Catalogue of the Papers of Lieutenant-Colonel Harry Peyton Moulton-Barrett*, Lot 6, Sotheby (London 1937)
5 The manuscript note is in the copy of *Pauline* in the Forster and Dyce Collection of the Victoria and Albert Museum
6 Gosse, p. 27
7 ibid., p. 26
8 EBB, I, p. 387
9 *New York Evening Post*, 17 December 1889
10 Cf. Victor Hugo, *Oeuvres Complètes*, ed. J. Massin (Paris 1967-9), III, p. 57
11 *Essays, Letters from Abroad, Translations and Fragments* (London 1840), I, p. 25
12 RB/EBB, I, p. 200
13 ibid., I, p. 205
14 ibid., I, p. 400
15 *Athenaeum*, 6 April 1833
16 Hood, p. 172
17 MS note in the Victoria and Albert copy of *Pauline*
18 *Pauline*, op. cit.
19 *Lippincott's Magazine*, XLV (1890), p. 691
20 *Letters of D. G. Rossetti*, ed. Doughty and Wahl, I, pp. 32-3
21 RB/EBB, I, p. 199
22 Gosse, p. 33
23 Orr, p. 60
24 Fyodor Dostoevsky, *A Gentle Creature and other stories*, tr. David Magarshack (London 1950), p. 25
25 RB/EBB, I, p. 154
26 ibid., I, p. 207
27 EBB, I, p. 387
28 W. Hall Griffin, 'Early Friends of Robert Browning', *Contemporary Review*, LXXXVII (1905), p. 440
29 *Robert Browning and Alfred Domett*, p. 104
30 Orr, p. 67
31 *New Monthly Magazine*, XLVI (1836), pp. 289-308
32 Macready, I, p. 267
33 ibid., I, p. 265
34 Gosse, pp. 38-9
35 ibid., pp. 41-2
36 ibid., p. 42
37 ibid., pp. 42-3
38 ibid., p. 43

3 The Madhouse and the Shrine

1 Wedgwood, p. 162
2 *William Allingham: A Diary*, ed. H. Allingham and D. Radford (London 1907), p. 248
3 *Diaries of Lewis Carroll*, ed. Roger Lancelyn Green (London 1953), p. 76
4 RB/EBB, I, p. 28
5 ibid., I, p. 113

6 Cf. Hugo, *Oeuvres Complètes*, III, p. 56
7 Mary Gladstone (Mrs Drew), *Diaries and Letters*, ed. Lucy Masterman (London 1930), pp. 116–17
8 ibid., p. 94
9 Domett, pp. 181–2
10 Alfred Adler, *Individual Psychology* (London 1940), p. 8
11 EBB, II, p. 435
12 Mary Gladstone, *Diaries and Letters*, p. 135; Hood, pp. 78, 311–12
13 *William Allingham: A Diary*, p. 36. Cf. *Robert Browning and Alfred Domett*, pp. 28, 38–9, 45–6, 55, 58
14 RB/EBB, I, pp. 200, 205
15 EBB, II, p. 131
16 Wedgwood, p. 168
17 Mary Gladstone, *Diaries and Letters*, pp. 94, 454; Gosse, pp. 82–7

4 Macready

1 Macready, I, p. 321
2 ibid., I, p. 302
3 *Morning Chronicle*, 7 August 1840
4 Macready, I, p. 340
5 *Ivanhoe: A Romance*, ed. Andrew Lang (London 1900), p. xlvii
6 *Past and Present*, Book II, Chapter 2, 'St Edmundsbury'
7 Macready, I, p. 361
8 ibid., I, p. 362
9 ibid., I, p. 368
10 ibid., I, p. 380
11 ibid., I, pp. 382–3
12 ibid., I, p. 389
13 Orr, p. 84
14 *Poems of Thomas Lovell Beddoes*, ed. R. Colles (London n.d.), p. x
15 ibid., p. xvii
16 Orr, pp. 96–7
17 ibid., p. 97
18 Macready, II, p. 23
19 ibid., II, p. 72
20 ibid., II, p. 76
21 Hood, p. 5
22 ibid., p. 5
23 John Forster, *Life of Dickens* (London 1873), II, p. 25
24 ibid., II, p. 25
25 Gosse, p. 62
26 Orr, p. 114
27 Macready, II, p. 194
28 ibid., II, p. 194
29 ibid., II, p. 196
30 *Argosy*, February 1890
31 *Robert Browning and Alfred Domett*, p. 65

32 *Robert Browning and Alfred Domett*, p. 66
33 ibid., p. 66
34 Hood, p. 235
35 *New Letters*, pp. 11–12
36 ibid., p. 12
37 Cf. Chesterton, *Robert Browning*, p. 166, on Browning's indelicacy
38 Gosse, *Father and Son*, p. 267
39 Domett, p. 301
40 *Robert Browning and Alfred Domett*, p. 67

5 *Sordello:* The Scapegoat

1 RB/EBB, II, p. 131–2
2 *The Cantos of Ezra Pound* (London 1964), p. 10 ('Hang it all, Robert Browning,/there can be but one "Sordello".' Canto 2, lines 1–2)
3 Orr, p. 66
4 *New Letters*, p. 12
5 Gosse, pp. 46–7
6 *Autobiography*, ed. Chapman (Boston 1877), II, p. 325
7 Orr, p. 91
8 ibid., p. 91
9 ibid., p. 92
10 ibid., p. 94
11 ibid., p. 93
12 ibid., p. 94
13 E. P. Hood, 'The Poetry of Robert Browning', *Eclectic and Congregational Review*, IV (1863), pp. 436–64
14 Gosse, p. 48
15 *On Poetry and Poets* (London 1957), p. 140
16 T. R. Lounsbury, *The Early Literary Career of Robert Browning* (New York 1911), p. 92
17 *The Works of T. H. Green*, ed. H. L. Nettleship (London 1888), III, p. 36

6 *Bells and Pomegranates*

1 Hood, p. 4
2 ibid., p. 1
3 ibid., p. 5
4 RB/EBB, I, p. 107
5 ibid., I, p. 457
6 ibid., II, pp. 78, 525, 528
7 'The Psychic Treatment of Trigeminal Neuralgia', *The Practice and Theory of Individual Psychology*, pp. 78–99 *passim.*
8 RB/EBB, II, p. 76
9 ibid., II, p. 75
10 ibid., I, p. 28
11 ibid., I, p. 28
12 Hood, p. 8
13 *Poetical Works of Laman Blanchard* (London 1876), p. 7

14 *Robert Browning and Alfred Domett*, p. 58
15 C. G. Duffy, *Conversations with Carlyle*, pp. 56–7
16 Hood, p. 7
17 *Robert Browning and Alfred Domett*, pp. 51–2
18 ibid., p. 52
19 ibid., p. 52
20 H. Buxton Forman, *The Vicissitudes of Shelley's Queen Mab*, Shelley Society Papers, Pt. I (1888), p. 21
21 Public Record Office MS. K.B. 28/555/ 9,10,12,13
22 *Modern State Trials*, ed. W. C. Townsend (London 1850), II, pp. 356–91
23 *Athenaeum*, 11 December 1841
24 *The Times*, 31 May 1889
25 For the problem encountered by Dickens, see Kathleen Tillotson, *Novels of the Eighteen-Forties* (London 1962), pp. 66–7
26 EBB/Horne, I, p. 91
27 *Robert Browning and Alfred Domett*, p. 33
28 ibid., pp. 45–6
29 ibid., p. 55
30 ibid., p. 92
31 ibid., pp. 95, 96
32 Orr, p. 126
33 *Robert Browning and Alfred Domett*, p. 122
34 ibid., p. 86
35 ibid., p. 101
36 ibid., pp. 41–2
37 ibid., p. 36
38 ibid., pp. 42–3
39 ibid., pp. 111, 114
40 ibid., p. 56
41 ibid., p. 45
42 ibid., p. 45
43 W. G. Kingsland, *Robert Browning: Chief Poet of the Age* (London 1890), p. 131
44 *Robert Browning and Alfred Domett*, p. 30
45 ibid., p. 35
46 RB/EBB, I, p. 78
47 EBB, I, p. 288
48 RB/EBB, I, p. 1
49 ibid., I, p. 2

7 'The Sleeping Palace'

1 EBB, I, p. 158
2 RB/EBB, II, p. 210
3 ibid., I, p. 403
4 ibid., I, p. 404
5 Rosalie Mander, *Mrs Browning: The Story of Elizabeth Barrett* (London 1980), p. 13
6 EBB, I, p. 84
7 ibid., I, p. 88

8 EBB., I, p. 93
9 ibid., I, p. 86
10 ibid., I, p. 87
11 ibid., I, p. 93
12 ibid., I, p. 100
13 ibid., I, p. 112
14 ibid., I, p. 274
15 ibid., I, p. 275
16 RB/EBB, I, p. 280
17 Orr, p. 129
18 RB/EBB, I, pp. 2-3
19 ibid., I, p. 4
20 ibid., I, p. 12
21 ibid., I, p. 19
22 ibid., I, p. 26
23 ibid., I, p. 42
24 ibid., I, p. 33
25 ibid., I, p. 49
26 Rosalie Mander, *Mrs Browning*, p. 29
27 EBB, I, p. 289
28 ibid., I, p. 289
29 RB/EBB, I, pp. 74-5
30 EBB, I, p. 289
31 Wilfrid Blunt, *England's Michelangelo: A Biography of George Frederic Watts* (London 1975), p. 53
32 EBB, I, p. 289
33 RB/EBB, I, p. 374
34 ibid., I, p. 433
35 ibid., I, p. 144
36 ibid., I, p. 122
37 ibid., I, p. 203
38 ibid., I, p. 225
39 EBB, II, pp. 14, 18
40 RB/EBB, I, p. 241
41 ibid., I, p. 242
42 ibid., II, p. 231
43 ibid., I, p. 405
44 ibid., II, pp. 382-3
45 ibid., I, p. 223
46 ibid., I, p. 224
47 ibid., II, p. 227
48 ibid., II, p. 246
49 ibid., II, p. 230
50 ibid., I, p. 26
51 ibid., I, p. 161
52 ibid., I, p. 198
53 ibid., II, p. 9
54 ibid., I, p. 511
55 ibid., II, pp. 404, 487

56 ibid., I, p. 406
57 ibid., II, p. 415
58 ibid., II, p. 169
59 ibid., II, p. 484
60 ibid., II, p. 525
61 ibid., II, p. 532
62 ibid., II, p. 533
63 ibid., II, p. 537
64 ibid., II, p. 539
65 ibid., II, p. 546
66 EBB, I, p. 306

8 Casa Guidi

1 Sophia Hawthorne, *Notes in England and Italy* (London 1869), p. 342
2 EBB, II, p. 169
3 Huxley, p. 15
4 MSS. Yale University Library, Letters of Miss Mitford to Miss Partridge, 27
   October 1847, 18 October 1847, 2 January 1849
5 T. Wemyss Reid, *The Life, Letters, and Friendships of Richard Monckton Milnes, First
   Lord Houghton* (London 1890), I, pp. 384-5
6 Orr, pp. 149, 150
7 EBB, I, pp. 312, 376
8 ibid., I, p. 355
9 Huxley, p. 15; EBB, II, p. 224
10 Huxley, p. 65
11 Maisie Ward, *The Tragi-Comedy of Pen Browning* (New York and London 1972),
   p. 1
12 EBB, I, p. 399
13 ibid., I, p. 404
14 ibid., I, p. 410
15 Hood, p. 23
16 EBB, I, p. 415
17 ibid., I, p. 421
18 RB/EBB, II, p. 353
19 Wedgwood, pp. 114-15
20 *New Letters*, p. 77
21 Gibbon, *Decline and Fall of the Roman Empire*, ed. Oliphant Smeaton (London 1950),
   I, p. 452
22 G. S. Hillard, *Six Months in Italy* (London 1853), I, pp. 177-8
23 Hood, p. 27; EBB, II, p. 132
24 EBB, II, p. 111
25 Story, II, pp. 68-9
26 EBB, I, p. 448
27 ibid., I, p. 458
28 ibid., I, p. 466

9 Boulevard Life

1 G. K. Chesterton, *Robert Browning*, p. 101
2 EBB, II, p. 20
3 ibid., II, p. 27
4 *Robert Browning and Alfred Domett*, p. 142
5 EBB, II, p. 23
6 ibid., II, pp. 59–60
7 ibid., II, p. 63
8 ibid., II, p. 33
9 George Barrett, pp. 154–7
10 EBB, II, p. 37
11 Huxley, p. 146
12 *New Letters*, p. 55
13 Orr, p. 183
14 ibid., p. 183
15 Domett, p. 164
16 Huxley, p. 168
17 *New Letters*, p. 54
18 Hood, pp. 37–40
19 Th. Bentzon, 'A French Friend of Browning – Joseph Milsand', *Scribner's Magazine*, xx (1896), p. 115
20 Huxley, p. 173
21 ibid., p. 190
22 ibid., pp. 208–9
23 ibid., pp. 212–13
24 ibid., p. 181; EBB, II, pp. 93, 96, 108
25 Story, I, p. 266
26 ibid., I, p. 267
27 EBB, II, p. 131
28 Hood, p. 40
29 EBB, II, p. 135
30 Huxley, p. 175
31 ibid., p. 189
32 EBB, II, p. 142
33 ibid., II, p. 168
34 ibid., II, p. 160
35 ibid., II, pp. 159–60
36 ibid., II, p. 168
37 ibid., II, pp. 203–4
38 Story, I, p. 288
39 Gosse, p. 33
40 Story, I, p. 288

10 'My Fifty Men and Women'

1 Huxley, p. 216
2 ibid., p. 210

3 EBB, II, p. 202
4 Huxley, p. 218
5 Robert-Houdin, *The Secrets of Stage Conjuring* (London n.d.), p. 70n
6 *The Times Literary Supplement*, 5 December 1902
7 D. D. Home, *Incidents in My Life: Second Series* (London 1872), pp. 105–8
8 *The Times Literary Supplement*, 28 November 1902
9 ibid.
10 Huxley, p. 249; Gardner B. Taplin, *The Life of Elizabeth Barrett Browning* (London 1957), p. 296
11 EBB, II, p. 213; W. M. Rossetti, *Some Reminiscences* (London 1906), I, pp. 235–6
12 G. K. Chesterton, *Robert Browning*, p. 116
13 Public Record Office MS. K.B. 28/484/56; *The Industry of All Nations: The Art Journal Illustrated Catalogue* (London 1851), pp. 73, 225
14 EBB, II, pp. 106, 151, 304; Érastène Ramiro, *Félicien Rops* (Paris 1905), p. 129
15 Cf. Brian Fothergill, *Nicholas Wiseman* (London 1963), pp. 222–3
16 *Oxford Book of Light Verse*, ed. W. H. Auden (Oxford 1938), p. xviii
17 Lilian Whiting, *The Brownings: Their Life and Art* (London 1911), p. 261
18 W. G. Collingwood, *Life and Works of John Ruskin* (London 1893), pp. 232–5
19 *New Letters*, p. 97
20 Huxley, p. 232
21 Domett, p. 52
22 EBB, II, p. 238
23 *Letters of D. G. Rossetti*, ed. Doughty and Wahl, I, p. 309

11 Choosing the World

1 *Saturday Review*, 27 December 1856
2 *New Letters*, p. 99
3 ibid., p. 392
4 Taplin, *Elizabeth Barrett Browning*, p. 350
5 George Barrett, p. 253
6 *Agnes Tremorne* (London 1861), II, p. 37
7 *Life of Frances Power Cobbe* (London 1894), II, pp. 14–15
8 *Dearest Isa*, p. 75
9 ibid., p. 72
10 ibid., p. 73
11 ibid., p. 85
12 Orr, pp. 212–14; *Spectator*, 30 January 1869
13 EBB, II, p. 253
14 John Forster, *Life of Walter Savage Landor* (London 1869), II, p. 561
15 Malcolm Elwin, *Landor: A Replevin* (London 1958), p. 435
16 Forster, *Landor*, II, p. 562
17 Story, II, pp. 18–19
18 Taplin, *Elizabeth Barrett Browning*, pp. 355–6
19 *Dearest Isa*, p. 314
20 Huxley, pp. 276–7
21 Orr, p. 208
22 *William Allingham: A Diary*, ed. H. Allingham and D. Radford, p. 76

23 EBB, II, p. 303
24 ibid., II, p. 418
25 *Works of Nathaniel Hawthorne: Centenary Edition* (Ohio 1980), XIV, p. 339
26 EBB, II, p. 303
27 ibid., II, pp. 434-5
28 ibid., II, p. 435
29 George Barrett, p. 263
30 EBB, II, p. 434
31 Story, II, p. 16
32 EBB, II, p. 308
33 Huxley, pp. 318-19
34 Taplin, *Elizabeth Barrett Browning*, p. 392
35 Ogilvy, p. 171
36 Story, II, p. 65
37 ibid., II, p. 57
38 ibid., II, pp. 57-8
39 Hood, p. 63
40 ibid., p. 62
41 *New Letters*, p. 135
42 Hood, p. 63
43 *New Letters*, p. 134
44 Ogilvy, p. 173
45 Story, II, pp. 64-5
46 ibid., II, p. 66
47 ibid., II, p. 66

12 'How Much One Misses in this Bustling London!'

1 Orr, p. 239
2 Story, II, p. 91
3 Ogilvy, p. 171
4 Story, II, p. 90
5 ibid., II, p. 97
6 Orr, p. 271
7 *Works of Nathaniel Hawthorne: Centenary Edition*, XIV, p. 300
8 Story, II, p. 91
9 ibid., II, p. 100
10 ibid., II, p. 111
11 *Dearest Isa*, p. 85
12 ibid., pp. 98, 125, 223, 227-8; Story, II, p. 115
13 *Dearest Isa*, p. 106
14 Story, II, p. 109
15 Stillman, *Autobiography of a Journalist*, II, p. 210
16 Story, II, p. 89
17 Edward Dowden, *The Life of Robert Browning* (London 1904), pp. 330-31
18 W. M. Rossetti, 'Portraits of Robert Browning', *The Magazine of Art* (1890), p. 182
19 Mary L. Bruce, *Anna Swanwick* (London 1903), pp. 130-31
20 Story, II, pp. 115, 139

21 *New Letters*, p. 150
22 *American Friends*, pp. 106, 114
23 ibid., p. 142
24 *Dearest Isa*, pp. 280-81
25 Wedgwood, pp. 27, 30
26 ibid., pp. 40, 53
27 ibid., pp. 64, 73
28 ibid., pp. 132, 134
29 ibid., p. 135
30 ibid., p. 14
31 Story, II, pp. 136-8
32 Orr, p. 252
33 ibid., pp. 252-3
34 ibid., p. 253
35 ibid., p. 256
36 ibid., p. 255
37 *Dearest Isa*, p. 193
38 Story, II, p. 117
39 Orr, p. 259
40 Edmund Gosse, *Life of Algernon Charles Swinburne* (London 1917), p. 108
41 W. A. Knight, *Memoir of John Nichol* (London 1896), p. 127
42 Edmund Gosse, *Portraits and Sketches* (London 1912), p. 4
43 ibid., p. 4
44 Hood, p. 199
45 Orr, p. 265n
46 Evelyn Abbott and Lewis Campbell, *The Life and Letters of Benjamin Jowett* (London 1897), I, p. 400
47 ibid., I, p. 402
48 John T. Nettleship, *Essays on Robert Browning's Poetry* (London 1868), p. vi
49 *Robert Browning and Alfred Domett*, p. 143
50 W. H. Griffin and H. C. Minchin, *The Life of Robert Browning* (London 1938), p. 276
51 Orr, p. 267
52 *Dearest Isa*, p. 331

13 Morbid Anatomy

1 Leslie Stephen, *Hours in a Library* (London 1892), III, p. 307
2 Orr, p. 270
3 *Dearest Isa*, p. 124
4 Griffin and Minchin, *Robert Browning*, p. 235
5 Orr, p. 273
6 *American Friends*, p. 154
7 *Dearest Isa*, p. 239
8 W. M. Rossetti, *The Rossetti Papers* (London 1903), p. 302
9 *Victorian England: Portrait of an Age* (London 1953), p. vi
10 *Table Talk*, 1 November 1833
11 Wedgwood, p. 168
12 ibid., p. 153

13 Wedgwood, p. 171
14 ibid., p. 208
15 Orr, p. 269

14 'The Horse Goes Round the Mill'

1 *Dearest Isa*, p. 380
2 Domett, p. 146
3 ibid., pp. 79–80
4 Blunt, *England's Michelangelo*, p. 126
5 ibid., p. 129
6 ibid., p. 77
7 Ellen Terry, *Memoirs*, ed. Edith Craig and Christopher St John (London 1933), p. 44
8 *Dearest Isa*, p. 359
9 *New Letters*, p. 197
10 ibid., p. 224
11 *Dearest Isa*, p. 326; Orr, pp. 295–7
12 Orr, p. 278
13 ibid., p. 276
14 *Dearest Isa*, p. 333
15 *Letters of D. G. Rossetti to W. Allingham* (London 1897), p. 284
16 Gosse, pp. 5–6
17 W. B. Maxwell, *Time Gathered* (London 1937), p. 113
18 Mary Gladstone, *Diaries and Letters*, p. 454; Hood, p. 326
19 *American Friends*, p. 175
20 Orr, p. 277
21 ibid., p. 276
22 *Psychopathia Sexualis: With Special Reference to Contrary Sexual Instinct*, tr. C. G. Chaddock (Philadelphia and London 1894), p. 59 and note. The distinction of the sexes is described in a blander context by such divisions of the sexual roles as that by Tennyson in *The Princess*.

Man is the hunter; woman is his game:
The sleek and shining creatures of the chase,
We hunt them for the beauty of their skins.

23 Henry Blyth, *Skittles: The Last Victorian Courtesan* (London 1970), p. 118
24 Donald Thomas, *A Long Time Burning: The History of Literary Censorship in England* (London 1969), pp. 472–81
25 Henry James, *The Nation*, XXII (1876), pp. 49–50; *The Swinburne Letters*, ed. Cecil Y. Lang (London 1959–62), III, p. 87
26 Geoffrey Faber, *Jowett: A Portrait with Background* (London 1957), p. 359
27 *Athenaeum*, 17 April 1875
28 *Dearest Isa*, p. 372
29 Charles Kingsley, *Scientific Lectures and Essays*, new edn. (London 1880), p. 332
30 *Dearest Isa*, p. 332

314

31 Griffin and Minchin, *Robert Browning*, p. 259
32 *Learned Lady*, p. 36
33 Hood, pp. 136-8
34 *Dearest Isa*, p. 328
35 Hood, p. 138
36 *Truth*, 8 July 1880
37 Gosse, p. 81

15 How He Worked in Distemper

1 Domett, p. 162; W. F. Monypenny and G. E. Buckle, *The Life of Benjamin Disraeli, Earl of Beaconsfield* (London 1929), II, pp. 1155, 1455
2 Domett, p. 46
3 Hood, p. 139
4 *The World*, 7 December 1881
5 *Learned Lady*, p. 132
6 W. H. Mallock, *Memoirs of Life and Literature* (London 1920), p. 53
7 Charles Hallé, *Life and Letters* (London 1896), p. 9
8 Mary Gladstone, *Diaries and Letters*, pp. 90, 116-17
9 Leon Edel, *Henry James: The Conquest of London 1870-83* (London 1962), pp. 330-31
10 ibid., p. 376. The contrary view, that Browning's reading clarified the meaning of his poetry, was put by another listener, Katherine de Kay Bronson, in the *Century Magazine* (April 1900), p. 929.
11 Gosse, pp. 81-2
12 ibid., p. 90
13 ibid., p. 82
14 ibid., pp. 83-5
15 *The Swinburne Letters*, IV, p. 194
16 ibid., IV, p. 197
17 Griffin and Minchin, *Robert Browning*, p. 260
18 E. F. Benson, *As We Were* (London 1930), pp. 192-6
19 Hood, pp. 188-9
20 ibid., p. 190
21 ibid., p. 210
22 ibid., p. 210
23 ibid., p. 239
24 *Learned Lady*, p. 109
25 *New Letters*, p. 259
26 Chesterton, *Robert Browning*, p. 67
27 Domett, pp. 226-7
28 *Pall Mall Budget*, 19 December 1889
29 Hood, pp. 147-8
30 Domett, p. 169
31 ibid., p. 165
32 Edward Berdoe, *The Browning Cyclopaedia* (London 1892), p. 558
33 Harold Nicolson, *Tennyson, Aspects of his Life, Character, and Poetry* (London 1923), p. 302

34 *Tennyson, Aspects of his Life, Character, and Poetry*, p. 69
35 *Dearest Isa*, p. 267
36 Orr, p. 307

16 'Never Say of Me That I Am Dead!'

1 Orr, pp. 326-7
2 *Frederick James Furnivall: A Volume of Personal Record*, ed. J. Munro (London 1911), pp. lxiv-lxv
3 F. R. Leavis, *New Bearings in English Poetry* (London 1932), p. 20
4 Augustine Birrell, *Selected Essays, 1884-1907* (London 1908), pp. 160-61
5 Orr, p. 329
6 *The Times*, 3 February 1888
7 Berdoe, *The Browning Cyclopaedia*, p. 187
8 *Pall Mall Gazette*, 1 February 1890
9 *New Letters*, p. 274
10 Gosse, pp. 77-8
11 *Learned Lady*, p. 193
12 *New Letters*, pp. 319-20
13 Ward, *The Tragi-Comedy of Pen Browning*, p. 105
14 *Learned Lady*, p. 165
15 *New Letters*, p. 317
16 Orr, pp. 341-2
17 Katherine de Kay Bronson, 'Browning in Venice', *Cornhill Magazine* (February 1902), p. 158
18 Katherine de Kay Bronson, 'Browning in Asolo', *Century Magazine* (April 1900), p. 925
19 *Learned Lady*, p. 173
20 *Century Magazine* (April 1900), p. 925
21 Orr, pp. 351-2
22 Hood, p. 249
23 ibid., p. 264
24 *Letters and Literary Remains of Edward Fitzgerald*, ed. William Aldis Wright (London 1889), I, p. 280
25 *Learned Lady*, p. 199
26 Campbell and Abbott, *Jowett*, I, p. 401n
27 Hood, pp. 316-18
28 Orr, pp. 389-90
29 ibid., pp. 400-401; Griffin and Minchin, *Robert Browning*, p. 282; Maisie Ward, *Robert Browning and his World: Two Robert Brownings?* (London 1969), p. 293
30 Rosalie Mander, *Mrs Browning*, p. 126
31 Matthew Arnold, *Essays in Criticism: Second Series* (London 1888), p. 150
32 Henry Jones, *Browning as Philosophical and Religious Thinker* (Glasgow 1890), p. vii
33 ibid., pp. 342-3
34 Augustine Birrell, *Selected Essays 1884-1907*, p. 163
35 Balliol MS. Letter from Jowett to Pen Browning, 16 December 1889
36 Leon Edel, *Henry James: The Middle Years* (London 1963), p. 214

Select Bibliography

1 Editions of Robert Browning's Poetry

The Poetical Works of Robert Browning, ed. Augustine Birrell, 2 vols. (London 1896) (Smith, Elder)

The Complete Works of Robert Browning (Florentine Edition), ed. Charlotte Porter and Helen A. Clarke, 12 vols. (New York 1910)

The Works of Robert Browning (Centenary Edition), ed. Frederic G. Kenyon, 10 vols. (London 1912)

The Complete Works of Robert Browning, ed. Roma A. King Jr. (Athens, Ohio, in progress)

Robert Browning: Poems, ed. John Pettigrew and Thomas J. Collins, 2 vols. (London 1981) (Penguin Poets)

Browning: Poetical Works, 1833-1864, ed. Ian Jack (Oxford 1970) (Oxford Standard Authors)

Robert Browning's Poems and Plays, ed. John Bryson and Mildred M. Bozman, 5 vols. (London 1956-64) (Dent, Everyman's Library, nos. 41, 42, 502, 964, 966. These volumes contain the complete works down to and including *The Ring and the Book*, and a selection of the later poetry from 1871 onwards.)

Men And Women And Other Poems, ed. J. W. Harper (London 1975) (Everyman's Library)

The Ring and the Book, ed. R. D. Altick (London 1971) (Penguin English Poets)

2 Letters

The Letters of Robert Browning and Elizabeth Barrett Barrett, 1845-1846, 2 vols. (New York and London 1902)

The Letters of Robert Browning and Elizabeth Barrett Barrett, 1845-1846, ed. Elvan Kintner, 2 vols. (Cambridge, Massachusetts, 1969)

Robert Browning and Alfred Domett, ed. Frederic G. Kenyon (London 1906)

Letters of Robert Browning, Collected by Thomas J. Wise, ed. Thurman L. Hood (London 1933)

From Robert & Elizabeth Browning: A Further Selection of the Barrett-Browning Family Correspondence, ed. William Rose Benet (London 1936)

Robert Browning and Julia Wedgwood: A Broken Friendship as Revealed in Their Letters, ed. Richard Curle (London 1937)

New Letters of Robert Browning, ed. William Clyde DeVane and Kenneth Leslie Knickerbocker (London 1951)

Dearest Isa: Robert Browning's Letters to Isabella Blagden, ed. Edward C. McAleer (Austin and Edinburgh 1951)

Letters of the Brownings to George Barrett, ed. Paul Landis and Ronald E. Freeman (Urbana, Illinois, 1958)

Browning to His American Friends: Letters between the Brownings, the Storys, and James Russell Lowell, 1841-1890, ed. Gertrude Reese Hudson (London 1965)

Learned Lady: Letters from Robert Browning to Mrs Thomas Fitzgerald, 1876-1889, ed. Edward C. McAleer (Cambridge, Massachusetts 1966)

Letters of Elizabeth Barrett Browning to Richard Hengist Horne, ed. S. R. Townshend Mayer, 2 vols. (London 1877)

Letters of Elizabeth Barrett Browning, ed. Frederic G. Kenyon, 2 vols. (London 1897)

Elizabeth Barrett Browning: Letters to Her Sister, 1846-1859, ed. Leonard Huxley (London 1929)

Elizabeth Barrett Browning's Letters to Mrs David Ogilvy, 1849-1861, ed. Peter N. Heydon and Philip Kelley (London 1974)

3 General

Allingham, William, *William Allingham: A Diary*, ed. H. Allingham and D. Radford (London 1907)

Berdoe, Edward, *A Browning Cyclopaedia* (London 1892)

——*Browning and the Christian Faith* (London 1899)

Birrell, Augustine, *Selected Essays, 1884-1907* (London 1908)

Bronson, Katherine de Kay, 'Browning in Asolo', *Century Magazine* (April 1900), pp. 920-31

——'Browning in Venice ... With a Prefatory Note by Henry James', *Cornhill Magazine* (February 1902), pp. 145-71

Browning, Fannie Barrett, *Some Memories of Robert Browning* (London 1928)

Browning Society's Papers, 12 parts in 3 vols. (London 1881-91)

Burdett, O., *The Brownings* (London 1929)

Carlyle, Thomas, *Letters of Carlyle to John Stuart Mill, John Sterling and Robert Browning*, ed. Alexander Carlyle (London 1923)

G. K. Chesterton, *Robert Browning* (London 1903) (English Men of Letters series)

Conway, Moncure D., *Centenary History of the South Place Society* (London 1894)

DeVane, William Clyde, *A Browning Handbook* (London 1937; 2nd edn. 1955)

——*Browning's Parleyings: The Autobiography of a Mind* (New Haven 1927)

Domett, Alfred, *The Diary of Alfred Domett*, ed. E. A. Horsman (London 1953)

Dowden, Edward, *The Life of Robert Browning* (London 1904)

Drew, Philip, *The Poetry of Robert Browning: A Critical Introduction* (London 1970)

Edel, Leon, *Henry James: The Conquest of London, 1870-83* (London 1962)

——*Henry James: The Middle Years, 1884-94* (London 1963)

Gladstone, Mary (Mrs Drew), *Diaries and Letters*, ed. Lucy Masterman (London 1930)

Gosse, Edmund, *Robert Browning, Personalia* (London 1890)

——*Portraits and Sketches* (London 1912)

Griffin, W. Hall and Minchin, Harry Christopher, *The Life of Robert Browning with Notices of His Writings, His Family, and His Friends*, rev. edn. (London 1938)

Hovelaque, Henri-Léon, *La Jeunesse de Robert Browning* (Paris 1932)

Irvine, William and Honan, Park, *The Book, the Ring, and the Poet: A Biography of Robert Browning* (London 1975)

Jack, Ian, *Browning's Major Poetry* (Oxford 1973)

James, Henry, *William Wetmore Story and His Friends, From Letters, Diaries, and Recollections*, 2 vols. (London 1903)

Jones, Henry, *Browning as a Philosophical and Religious Teacher* (Glasgow 1890)

Kingsland, W. G., *Robert Browning: Chief Poet of the Age* (London 1890)

Lairesse, Gerard de, *The Art of Painting in All Its Branches*, tr. John Frederick Fritsch (London 1738)

Litzinger, Boyd and Smalley, Donald, *Browning: The Critical Heritage* (London 1970)

Lounsbury, T. R., *The Early Literary Career of Robert Browning* (New York 1911)

Macready, William Charles, *The Diaries of William Charles Macready*, ed. William Toynbee, 2 vols. (London 1912)

Mander, Rosalie, *Mrs Browning: The Story of Elizabeth Barrett* (London 1980)

Maynard, John, *Browning's Youth* (Cambridge, Massachusetts 1977)

Miller, Betty, *Robert Browning: A Portrait* (London 1952)

Nettleship, John T., *Essays on Robert Browning's Poetry* (London 1868)

Orr, Mrs Sutherland (Alexandra Orr), *Life and Letters of Robert Browning* (London 1891; rev. edn. by Frederic G. Kenyon 1908)

——*A Handbook to the Works of Robert Browning* (London 1885)

Ritchie, Anne Thackeray, *Records of Tennyson, Ruskin, and Browning* (London and New York 1892)

Sharp, William, *Life of Robert Browning* (Edinburgh and London 1890)

Taplin, Gardner B., *The Life of Elizabeth Barrett Browning* (London 1957)

Treves, Giuliana Artom, *The Golden Ring: The Anglo-Florentines; 1847-1862*, tr. Sylvia Sprigge (London 1956)

Wanley, Nathaniel, *The Wonders of the Little World: Or, A General History of Man* (London 1678)

Ward, Maisie, *Robert Browning and His World: I. The Private Face* (London 1968)

——*Robert Browning and His World: II. Two Robert Brownings?* (London 1969)

—— *The Tragi-Comedy of Pen Browning* (New York and London 1972)

Whiting, Lilian, *The Brownings: Their Life and Art* (London 1911)

Index

Strauss, David, 12, 104, 129, 133, 165,168
Sue, Eugène, 177; *Mystères de Paris*, 177
Swinburne, Algernon Charles, 2, 15, 17,
    35, 60, 76, 86, 138, 209, 258-9, 260,
    262, 275; *Poems and Ballads*, 202, 210;
    Atalanta in Calydon, 249

Talbot, William Henry Fox, 79
Talfourd, Thomas Noon, 42-3, 56, 57,
    58, 60, 87-8, 102, 147
Temple, Frederick, Archbishop, 211
Tennyson, Alfred, 1st Baron, 2, 17, 30,
    35, 36, 39, 41, 42, 51, 52, 60, 67, 76,
    78, 80, 86, 89, 101, 102, 113-14,
    134, 135, 139, 140, 147, 156, 170,
    173, 174, 187, 189, 198, 201, 215,
    216, 229, 233, 235, 238, 251, 253,
    260, 261, 268, 275, 276, 291, 296; *In
    Memoriam*, 92, 129, 140, 178, 229,
    268; *Maud*, 159-60, 161, 229;
    Locksley Hall, 161, 229; *Enoch Arden*,
    209; *Idylls of the King*, 229; *The Holy
    Grail*, 253: *Poems by Two Brothers*, 149
Tennyson, Frederick, 149, 150; *Poems by
    Two Brothers*, 149
Tennyson, Hallam, 147, 257
Terry, Ellen, 235
Thackeray, Anne Isabella (Lady
    Ritchie), 199
Thackeray, William Makepeace, 121,
    152, 199, 252
Thomas, Edward, 282
Townshend, William, 218
Trelawny, Edward John, 99
Trollope, Anthony, 121, 180, 201
Trollope, Frances, 121, 180
Turgenev, Ivan, 202

Vasari, Giorgio, 14, 70
Verdi, Giuseppe, 162; *La Traviata*, 162
Vespasian, 165
Victoria, 186, 234, 293
Vidocq, Eugène François, 48
Virgil (Publius Virgilius Maro), 77, 171-
    2, 278, 283
Vizetelly, Henry, 89, 243
Voltaire, François Marie Arouet de, 24,
    105, 268
Von Muller, Minny, 141, 143, 146

Wagner, Richard, 145, 288
Walters, Catherine, 'Skittles', 245
Wanley, Nathaniel, 12-13, 15, 48, 49,
    133, 230, 299; *Wonders of the Little
    World*, 12-13, 19
Ward, Mrs Humphrey, 129
Watteau, Jean-Antoine, 20
Watts, George Frederic, 110, 121-2, 234,
    235
Watts, Isaac, 18
Watts-Dunton, Theodore, 259
Wedgwood, James Mackintosh, 203
Wedgwood, Josiah, 202
Wedgwood, Julia, 46, 47, 54, 202-4, 208,
    232, 299
Wells, C. J., 60
West, Miss E. Dickinson, 297
Westmorland, Priscilla Anne Fane,
    Countess of, 202
Wickman, Professor, 162
William IV, 26, 40
Williams, Rowland, 211
Willmott, Mr, 63
Wilson, Dr, 192-3
Wilson, Effingham, 40
Wilson, H.B., 211
Wilson (Romagnoli), Elizabeth 'Lily',
    118, 120, 139, 144, 151, 155-6, 184,
    192
Wise, Thomas James, 273-4, 275-6, 292-
    3
Wiseman, Nicholas Patrick, Cardinal,
    167, 172
Wolf, Friedrich August, 11-12, 20, 284;
    Prolegomena in Homerum, 11-12
Wollstonecraft, Mary, 105, 107
Wolseley, Field-Marshal Garnet Joseph,
    Viscount, 287
Woolner, Thomas, 159, 201
Wordsworth, William, 7, 27, 28, 40, 41,
    42-3, 71, 77, 82, 101, 102, 106, 135,
    261, 272, 297; *The Prelude*, 27, 28,
    71, 146
Wright, William Aldis, 292

Yescombe, Hon. Mary Jane, 183
Young, G.M., 222

Zola, Émile, 89, 243, 244, 248, 299